ACPL ITEM
DISCARDED
S0-BXL-629

AUG 23 '63

A TREATISE OF COMMERCE

A TREATISE *of* COMMERCE

BY JOHN WHEELER

Secretary of the Society of Merchants Adventurers of England

1601

Edited with an Introduction and Notes by

GEORGE BURTON HOTCHKISS, M.A.

Professor of Marketing ,New York University

THE NEW YORK UNIVERSITY PRESS

WASHINGTON SQUARE EAST, NEW YORK CITY

1931

Copyright 1931 by New York University

THE NEW YORK UNIVERSITY PRESS
Arthur Huntington Nason, Ph.D., Director

PRINTED IN THE UNITED STATES OF AMERICA
THE GEORGE BANTA PUBLISHING COMPANY
MENASHA, WISCONSIN

1225624

Dedicated to
The Association of New York University
Men in Advertising
in commemoration of the
One Hundredth Anniversary
of the founding of
New York University

FOREWORD

FEW books that compare in importance with Wheeler's *Treatise of Commerce* have had to wait so long for a reprinting. The least of the lesser Elizabethan dramatists has been edited and reissued; practically every known work of that day pretending to literary or scientific significance has been made available to modern readers. Yet until this year the only complete copies of the *Treatise* have been the few remaining specimens of the original editions published in 1601; these few, of course, are in the great research libraries and accessible only to scholars.

Until recently there has been no other audience that could read it with interest or appreciation. Even the scholars, with the exception of the economic historians, have not regarded it as important. For it is a business book; furthermore, it is a piece of commercial propaganda—what would be called advertising, nowadays—on behalf of a private profit-making corporation. Such a work has been considered somewhat outside the pale of serious scholarship. That the *Treatise of Commerce* is the earliest important example of corporation publicity of the sort that is so extensively used to-day, has been but a doubtful recommendation.

The fact that the *Treatise* is a piece of commercial propaganda does depreciate its claim to a high rank as history or as literature. As history it suffers from its obvious bias. However, we should not be too strongly prejudiced against it on this account. Avowed bias can be discounted more accurately than concealed bias, and unbiassed historical documents of any sort are rare. Besides giving an authentic picture of business organizations and methods in the Elizabethan period, it reveals a few glimpses of great personages: Burghley and the younger Cecil and, most of all, the fascinating Elizabeth herself.

As literature it suffers from the fact that it was written by a business man, to whom authorship was an emergency operation. Wheeler does not shine in the company of Shakespeare and Bacon, or even of Greene and Nash. Yet we may find something illuminating in the views of a middle-class merchant, one of those substantial citizens who furnished the background and the financial support for the brilliant pageant of Elizabethan drama. The book itself, and the Company in whose interest it was written, cannot safely be ignored by those who seek a complete understanding of the literature of the period.

Thus the *Treatise of Commerce* is not without literary and historical significance. But its great claim to distinction is that it marks an important milestone in the development of marketing. In its substance, it represents the characteristically medieval theory of the trade monopoly, bolstered by monarchical authority and jealously guarded against competition. In its method, it anticipates the characteristically modern practice of winning popular support through the medium of the printed word.

Only within recent years has marketing claimed a place among the sciences. To-day its machinery and its intangible forces of selling and advertising are being carefully analyzed. The student, however, like the business man, is still preoccupied with the problems of the present and future, and gives scant attention to past history. Nevertheless, we may find some value as well as interest in "case studies" from the commercial life of centuries ago.

Unfortunately, the material for this purpose is not plentiful. With few exceptions, the economic historians have been more concerned with industry than with trade. Too often they have been content to present only the outward and visible aspects of markets and commerce, without delving very deeply into their underlying forces or the business man's philosophy. Hence the few references they make to Wheeler's *Treatise* and their citations from it reveal little of its true character and significance. It needs to be read as a whole and with full recognition of the fact that it was a tool or instrument designed to accomplish certain objects.

The objects of the *Treatise* are partly indicated in its pages. But to understand and appreciate it fully demands a more exact knowledge of the circumstances in which it appeared. Hence I have preceded it with a somewhat lengthy introduction that attempts to reconstruct from the fragmentary evidence available, a picture of the critical situation that John Wheeler and the Merchants Adventurers faced near the close of Queen Elizabeth's reign, and to trace the results of their pioneer venture into corporation publicity. With this background, I hope that the business man and the student interested in the problems of advertising and marketing will be in a position to read the *Treatise* with enjoyment as well as appreciation.

The fact that this edition was prepared primarily for business men and students of business will explain, if it does not excuse, some omissions and inclusions that may displease the historian or the literary critic. I am chiefly interested in the dynamic aspects of Wheeler's *Treatise*—what it tried to do and what it accomplished; its merits and faults as an historical document or as a work of art do not concern me deeply. I have neither the scholarly equipment nor the inclination to verify every fact, point out every error, and trace every assertion and allusion to its source. Naturally, I have done these things to some extent, but my original research is neither exhaustive nor faultless. I have relied heavily on the research of others for the facts upon which I have based my interpretations and conclusions. It may happen that these conclusions will be invalidated by the discovery of new facts; in any event, they are subject to disagreement by those who have a viewpoint different from mine.

Since one of the chief barriers to a more general appreciation of Wheeler's *Treatise* is its spelling, I have ventured to modernize this, as well as its punctuation and paragraphing. This edited text is accompanied with explanatory notes, and translations of obsolete terms and Latin phrases. For those who relish the quaintness of the original, a complete facsimile of the rare Middelburg edition is included.

The *Treatise of Commerce* has never before been completely reprinted. While the present work was in process, a reprint of the London edition was announced by the Facsimile Text Society, as one of their forthcoming publications. Besides making Wheeler's *Treatise* available at a modest price, this reprint of the London edition will permit a leisurely comparison with the Middelburg edition by those who are interested in textual collation.

The facsimile of the Middelburg edition is made possible by the courtesy of the British Museum, with the exception of the page of *errata* which is from the copy in the Henry E. Huntington Library and reproduced by their special permission. To both these libraries I extend my thanks for these and other kindnesses; also to the Bodleian Library, the New York Public Library, and the Libraries of Yale University, New York University, the University of London, and the New York Historical Society. My indebtedness to numerous authorities is specifically indicated in the footnotes, though these do not adequately show my obligations to W. E. Lingelbach, George Unwin, Sir Charles Lucas, and Astrid Friis for their valuable research in this field.

I owe a special debt of gratitude to Professor T. W. Edmondson for translations of the Latin letters and Latin quotations in the text, to Professor Edwin F. Gay for reading the proof of the Introduction, and to Professor Arthur H. Nason, Director, and Mr. Harold C. Whitford, Editorial Assistant, of the New York University Press, for help and suggestions.

George B. Hotchkiss

New York University
February 1, 1931

TABLE OF CONTENTS

INTRODUCTION

CHAPTER I

JOHN WHEELER

IN the long roll of members of the Merchants Adventurers of England are a few great names. There is Sir Thomas Gresham, Queen Elizabeth's financial advisor, whose name is familiar to all students of economics in "Gresham's Law." There, according to tradition, is Geoffrey Boleyn, an ancestor of Elizabeth. And greatest of all is William Caxton, the first English printer.

In such illustrious company, the name of John Wheeler is somewhat overshadowed. His chief claim to distinction is that he wrote *A Treatise of Commerce*, and there is little else we know with certainty about him. The brief biography of him in the *Dictionary of National Biography* (by W. A. S. Hewins) does not identify him definitely. This is not surprising; many greater men of the Elizabethan period have left few traces of their activities. And Wheeler was merely a plain business man with a plain and common name. In all probability, however, the author of *A Treatise of Commerce* was John Wheeler the Elder, of Great Yarmouth. This John Wheeler was born about 1553 and died about 1611. He rose from humble circumstances to a position of considerable wealth and influence. His career furnishes some slight evidence that the late Elizabethan romances of Deloney and others were not mere figments of the imagination, but were based on instances from real life.

That he came from a humble family is indicated by the entry of his admittance as a freeman of Great Yarmouth.[1] This was in 1577 and reads:

> J. Whelter, mariner, apprentice of J. Wakeman (A)

The (A) indicates that his father was not a freeman of the

[1] *A Calendar of the Freemen of Great Yarmouth*, Norfolk and Norwich Archeological Soc. (1910).

town and John Wheeler had to earn his right by apprenticeship. He must have been at least 24 years old, for the rules of the Merchants Adventurers required an apprenticeship of eight years (in some cities ten) beginning not younger than 16. Wheeler may have been even older. The term *mariner* would suggest some experience as a sailor. We might, if we chose, conjure up a picture of a young sailor on one of Wakeman's ships attracting the attention of his master, rising to the chief command of the vessel, then handling the sale of the cargo at Antwerp or Hamburg, and finally becoming a full-fledged merchant. But this is a field for the novelist, not the biographer. The spelling *Whelter*, in place of *Wheeler*, in the entry need not disturb us. Elizabethan spelling, especially of surnames, was notoriously variable. Identification is made probable by the later entry in 1589 of

Benjamin Wheler, apprentice to J. Wakeman (A)

John Wheeler had a younger brother Benjamin, who became his partner, and, upon his death, one of the executors of his will.

John Wheeler soon became one of the prominent citizens of the town. In 1589 he was a bailiff; in 1598 he became the senior bailiff.[2] In 1604 he was one of the nineteen wealthiest men in the community who were called on for twenty pounds each by a letter of the Privy Seal. At that time he had become a member of Parliament as a burgess of the port of Great Yarmouth. His conduct was not altogether satisfactory to all of his fellow-townsmen. In 1604 Henry Manship declared that

> Mr. Damer and Mr. Wheeler, the Burgesses in Parliament, had behaved themselves in parliament like sheep, and were both dunces.[3]

This criticism hurt Manship more than it did Wheeler, for it led to his removal from the Common Council of the town, whereas Wheeler kept his seat in Parliament to the end of his life. There is no indication that he ever said or did anything

[2] Henry Swinden, *The History of Great Yarmouth* (1722).

[3] Henry Manship, *A Booke of the Foundacion and Antiquitye of the Towne of Greate Yermouthe* (1619), edited by C. J. Palmer (1847), preface, vii.

to distinguish himself there. Indeed, he would be unlikely to do so; the respect he shows in the *Treatise* for order and discipline suggests that he would become a quiet and tractable part of the political machine.

These various duties in civic and national politics did not necessarily interfere with Wheeler's business. Most of the merchants went abroad only for brief periods. Some of them did not go at all, but entrusted the sale of their goods to apprentices. Wheeler, as Secretary, must have had to be in Middelburg, their foreign headquarters, a part of the time. But he too had apprentices to execute a part of his business. In 1610, when he wrote his will, two of his ships were out on voyages. Just how he rose to the office of Secretary of the Merchants Adventurers has not been ascertained. That he rose to it at all would argue rather unusual talents, for he was not of the London clique that dominated the organization. In all probability, he was elected when George Gilpin left that office for the important diplomatic post of Councillor to the Council of Estate in the Low Countries.

When Gilpin died in 1602, Wheeler was mentioned as a probable successor and was strongly recommended by Alderman Christopher Hoddesdon, the governor of the Company.[4] Sir Thomas Bodley was offered the post, but refused.[5] Perhaps Wheeler refused also, but probably he did not have the chance. Apparently he had been offered something by the Queen and had asked to be excused. In a letter to her, Thomas Mortimer and George Turner wrote:

> We were unable to execute the business . . . . We went to John Wheeler's house and he pleaded want of leisure.[6]

A man so busy that he could plead "want of leisure" to Queen Elizabeth certainly had little time to write books. Wheeler wrote but one, and that, as we shall see, was written under pressure of necessity. Out of his whole life of fifty-eight or sixty years, he gave two months to authorship.

[4] *Cal. State Papers Dom. Eliz.*, vol. CCLXXXV, Oct. 2, 1602. See also *Salisbury Papers*, vol. XII.

[5] *Ibid.*, Oct. 15, 1602.

[6] *Ibid.*, April (Yarmouth), 1602(?).

Masterpieces of literature are seldom produced in that way. But masterpieces of advertising and propaganda may be.

It is likely, however, that Wheeler did not regard his work as a masterpiece of any sort. He gave no signed copies to the Bodleian. Outside his own family and business, his sole passion seems to have been the Company of Merchants Adventurers. In 1608 he carefully compiled its laws and ordinances. Perhaps he also arranged for their copying in the imposing volume that is now one of the manuscript treasures of the British Museum,[7] but the copying was not completed until 1612, for the last entry is of December, 1611. This was after Wheeler's death.

The will of John Wheeler, dated March 17, 1610, but not probated until May 10, 1611, is a lengthy document full of bequests to relatives, servants, and friends. He owned many parcels of real estate and two ships. His son John, who had been admitted a freeman of Great Yarmouth in 1606 by birth, had predeceased him, leaving a minor son also named John. Whether this lad followed in his grandfather's footsteps is not recorded. Perhaps he became a "gentleman."

That, at any rate, was the course taken by his other grandson. Wheeler's son-in-law, John Dasset, had been a merchant, but his later history is graphically indicated by two entries in the *Calendar of Freemen*, as follows:

> 1608 Walter Harbeast, apprentice of John Dasset, Merchant
> 1633 John, son of John Dasset, gentleman

It would be interesting to know how soon after the settlement of the Wheeler estate the Dasset family were transformed into gentlefolk, and whether their inheritance ever rid itself entirely of the taint of "trade." John Wheeler himself would have continued as a merchant, we may be sure, but the succeeding generation was, as often happens, a decadent generation.

Future research may bring to light new facts about John Wheeler the Elder, of Great Yarmouth. They may even prove that he was not the John Wheeler who wrote the *Treatise of*

[7] Br. Mus. Addit. Ms. 18913, f. 5. (Reprinted in *The Merchant Adventurers of England; their laws and ordinances with other documents*, edited by W. E. Lingelbach, 1902.)

Commerce. But it matters little. The author was this same kind of man: the self-made business man who is firmly convinced that the system that gave him the opportunity of success is a thoroughly good system. Such men seldom express their views; unlike the professional reformers, they do not rush into print on the slightest provocation. But when sufficiently provoked they defend their position with the same energy and earnestness that has won their material success.

It does not detract from Wheeler's credit as the pioneer writer of corporation publicity to say that he was forced into authorship. Another man in his place might not have seen so clearly what was required or have had the ability to produce it. The trite axiom that the occasion makes the man has seldom been better exemplified. Circumstances called forth the *Treatise of Commerce.* To understand these circumstances we shall need to survey the situation of the Merchants Adventurers of England, not only in 1601 but in their earlier history.

CHAPTER II

THE SIGNIFICANCE OF THE TREATISE

IT should not be necessary to explain the Merchants Adventurers of England, but unfortunately it is necessary. Most business men know something about the Hanseatic League and the East India Company, but a large proportion have never heard of the Merchants Adventurers; few of the remainder have more than a hazy conception of their place in history. Yet their importance is on a par with that of the Hanseatic League and the East India Company. Between the decline of the former and the rise of the latter, they were the dominant commercial organization in the world. At the beginning of the seventeenth century, their Governor justly described them as the "most famous company of merchants in Christendom." And it may be fairly claimed for them that their contributions to the development of an English national commerce were greater than those of any other group either before or since.

Their romantic name has been a hindrance rather than a help to their enduring fame, for its associations are misleading. The word *adventurer* to most minds suggests the picture of a daring explorer or pioneer: a Magellan or Cook or Richard Byrd. When linked with *merchant,* it suggests one whose ventures by sea were highly hazardous, like Shakespeare's Antonio, who might lose all his ships and a pound of flesh besides on some unlucky voyage.

The Merchants Adventurers of England were not of so romantic a kind. In the beginning, no doubt, they answered more or less to this description. The first English merchants who became Adventurers (or "Venturers," as they were called in some cities) undertook considerable risk in sending their cargoes of goods across the channel to the ports of the Netherlands. But by the time the title "Merchants Adventurers" was used officially to designate their organization (which was about the beginning of the sixteenth century), the adventurous aspect of the business had largely disappeared. During practically the whole time in which they bore their title—from 1505 to 1564 simply "Merchants Adventurers," and from 1564 to 1689, "Merchants Adventurers of England" —their voyages were a routine matter, almost as commonplace and regular as sailings of steamship lines across the Atlantic are to-day. Scoffers held up to ridicule the term "Merchants Adventurers" as applied to those who merely shipped goods from some English port to Holland and Germany. Moreover, it was a part of the policy of the Merchants Adventurers—unromantic, perhaps, but good business—to diminish the risks of their enterprise in every possible way. Their fleets sailed at regular periods (under armed convoy, if necessary) and usually to only one or two foreign ports where they had established markets. They sought to protect themselves against outside competition, and guarded against glutting the market by a system of quotas for members. In short, they were a monopolistic trading organization, as different from the popular conception of "Adventurers" as can well be imagined.

There were also a number of minor companies, mostly offshoots of the great company, that borrowed the name and prestige of the Merchants Adventurers. Some of these companies more nearly correspond to our conception of the term. Such, for example, was Sebastian Cabot's short-lived Company of Merchants Adventurers for the Discovery of Unknown Lands[1] that failed in its effort to find the Northeast Passage but did open a northern sea-route to Russia. This company ultimately developed into the Muscovy Company, a minor trading company, but it is often confused still—even in histories and encyclopedias—with the Company of Merchants Adventurers of England. So strong is the power of words over the imagination!

[1] Full title: "The Merchants Adventurers of England for the discovery of lands, territories, isles, dominions and seignories unknown," W. R. Scott, *Joint-Stock Companies*, vol. II, p. 37.

There were fellowships of Merchants Adventurers in most of the leading ports of England. Some of these were component parts of the great company; some withdrew; some maintained their independence throughout their existence. No wonder historical references to the Merchants Adventurers[2] are often inaccurate or misleading. At best we have a very incomplete knowledge of them, and many questions are still matters of dispute.

Little as we know about the Merchants Adventurers, we should know even less if it had not been for John Wheeler. His *Treatise of Commerce*, published in 1601, was the first official public statement of their history and policies, and, amazingly enough, it still remains the most complete authoritative account of the organization. It is not absolutely reliable, of course, but many of the statements that were formerly doubted have been corroborated by modern research.[3] Together with Wheeler's codification of the laws and ordinances, it remains by far the most important source that has come down to us.

Naturally enough, Wheeler himself was in no position to make an adequate historical estimate of the Merchants Adventurers. He may have had a vague idea that they were the first exponents of what might be called a "national policy

[2] Throughout this edition I have followed Wheeler's example in referring to the members of his Company as *Merchants Adventurers*, instead of *Merchant Adventurers* which was used by some others at the time and has been adopted by most writers since. (J. A. Williamson and Clive Day are careful to use the form *Merchants* Adventurers.) Wheeler's choice may have been due merely to a desire for legal exactness, since it is the form used in their charters, or he may have had other reasons. Stow in speaking of the Company says they "grew very famous, whose rising, and increasing, was the Staplers decreasing, calling themselves the Merchaunte-adventurers, of which name they are now much ashamed." (*The Annales* . . . by John Stow . . . continued unto 1614 by Edmund Howes, edition of 1615, p. 904.) In any form their title was a misnomer, but the form *Merchant Adventurers* (with or without a hyphen) emphasized the part that was most misleading and objectionable. They were *Merchants*, first of all; *Adventurers* should be thought of as the modifying word indicating this particular company, just as *Eastland* in *Eastland Merchants* indicated membership in the Company of Merchants of Eastland. It would have been better if they could have called themselves *Adventurer Merchants* or Merchants of Adventures; later, even before their corporate title was changed, they were called *Hamburg Merchants*. However, at this time they were compelled to make the best of a bad matter, and *Merchants Adventurers* had just a shade more of dignity and exactness than *Merchant Adventurers*.

[3] George Unwin, *Studies in Economic History* (1927), p. 138; also W. E. Lingelbach, *The Merchant Adventurers of England*, p. 199.

in trade." He knew that they provided a model for the other English trading companies, such as the Russia or Muscovy Company, the Eastland Company, and the East India Company which had just been created in 1600 and which did not get beyond the stage of infancy in his lifetime. He certainly recognized the fact that the Merchants Adventurers had been instrumental in diverting England's commerce from foreign into domestic hands. He could hardly have foreseen, however, the part they were to play in political history under the Stuarts, when the Crown and the merchants were no longer allies but enemies.

Still less was Wheeler able to appreciate the significance of his *Treatise*. He regarded it merely as a piece of propaganda to meet an emergency. Propaganda for political and religious purposes was of course plentiful enough and there were some few examples of propaganda for individual private interests. Doubtless it never occurred to him that his book was an "innovation" in that it was the first example of commercial publicity in behalf of a private profit-making organization. He may have hoped that this publicity policy would help to establish the principle of English trade for and by Englishmen —the most important legacy of his Company to his own nation; he could not have dreamed that the publicity policy itself would become a legacy to all nations, to be used most extensively by a nation that was then unborn.

If the *Treatise* had no other merits to commend it, it would still warrant careful reading as the earliest extant example of what is to-day known as good-will advertising. But in addition it is the most complete summary—and one of the few authentic sources of information—concerning the marketing policies and methods that prevailed during the Tudor period. These methods and policies, it is true, seem shockingly inefficient and economically unsound to the modern critic. Nevertheless, the fact that they were used over a long period and produced results which at the time seemed satisfactory makes them historically important. Moreover, they were the outgrowth of the whole medieval attitude toward business, and thus tend to reveal other social and economic aspects of medieval civilization.

A TREATISE OF COMMERCE

The *Treatise of Commerce* was written in haste and under the pressure of an urgent need. The prefatory dedication was signed June 6, 1601, at Middelburg, Zeeland, which was then the chief foreign headquarters of the Merchants Adventurers. The first edition was printed there by Richard Schilders, a Dutchman who had lived and practiced his trade several years in England before setting up his shop in Middelburg. This first edition had 184 pages of large type, although only 178 pages are numbered. The book was then entered with the Stationers Company of London on August 14, 1601, for publication by John Harison. That a copy of the Middelburg edition was used in making the entry is indicated by the fact that the title in the entry contains the same typographical error ("Commodies" for Commodities") that is found on the Middelburg title-page. Harison's edition, printed in smaller type, occupies only 126 pages, but follows closely in other respects the format of the Middelburg edition. The small type of the London edition would indicate that 2,500 or 3,000 copies were required. The regulations of the Stationers Company limited large-type editions to 1,250 or, at most 1,500 copies; but small-type editions might run to double these amounts; if more were required the type had to be thrown in and reset.[4] It is fair to estimate, therefore, that at least 4,000 to 5,000 copies of the *Treatise* were printed. Of these only about a dozen are known to exist to-day.

Both editions are fine specimens of typography for their time, and far superior to the majority of seventeenth century pamphlets. The Middelburg edition is somewhat the better, and has been used as a basis for this edition. Both contain numerous typographical errors, presumably due to haste. There seem to be no important variations in the readings. The omission or insertion of a word here and there in the London edition may well have been the fault of the printer, rather than the intention of the author. In fact, some of the omissions and insertions obviously were not his intention; for example, the omission of a *not* in one sentence, (see page 377)

[4] E. Arber, *A Transcript of the Registers of the Company of Stationers of London*, vol. II, pp. 23, 43, and 883.

and the insertion of a superfluous *of* in another (see page 440). Some errors of spelling and diction in the Middelburg edition, other than those already corrected in the page of errata, are corrected in the London edition, but far more important errors stand uncorrected in both. Hence it is safe to conclude that Wheeler did not avail himself of the opportunity of revising his work for the London edition, and did not see this edition through the press.

Aside from the *Treatise* itself, our chief first-hand sources of information regarding the Merchants Adventurers are state papers and government records, private letters and diaries, and a few contemporary books and manuscripts. The records of the Merchants Adventurers themselves have disappeared; possibly they were destroyed in the great fire of 1666. Nevertheless, from the information available it is possible to construct a fairly complete picture of the situation that prompted Wheeler to write his *Treatise* and of the results which it produced.

CHAPTER III

THE HANSEATIC LEAGUE

FROM a superficial examination of the situation of the Merchants Adventurers in 1601, it might appear that they were at the peak of their prosperity. For the first time in their three centuries of existence as an organized body, they held the upper hand over their commercial rivals, the Hanseatic League and the Merchants of the Staple. In their earlier days, from the thirteenth to the fifteenth century, they had been obliged again and again to bend the knee to either or both of these organizations. They had been forced to take only the crumbs and scraps of England's foreign trade. Now they had the greater part of it, and the Hanseatic League—exiled from England in 1598—had none at all. The Merchants Adventurers were in command.

Upon the face of it, Wheeler's *Treatise* may seem to have the purpose of celebrating their victory and insuring its permanence, and it has been so interpreted. This, as we shall see later, is an inadequate interpretation. The plea of English trade for Englishmen was stressed for strategic reasons. However, it was more or less justified by the long struggle between the Merchants Adventurers and the Hanses, and by the part each had played in the commercial history of England.

Before the rise of the Merchants Adventurers, Englishmen had played an insignificant rôle in international commerce. Under the sceptre of the Normans, England had been mainly an agricultural country, far behind the continent in industrial and commercial development. Historical documents contain a few vague references that have been taken to indicate the presence of English merchants in continental ports before the Norman conquest, but no evidence that they were ever numerous or powerful. For a long time after the Norman conquest, their share in international commerce was small. They received little help or encouragement from their rulers; more often they were handicapped by special favors shown to the French subjects of the kings of England or, still worse, by preferential treatment of German merchants.

It may fairly be said that during this medieval period no nation was engaged in commerce as a nation. The cities were the great powers in trade, especially the cities on the Mediterranean and the North Sea. The Italian cities of Venice, Florence, and Genoa strove with one another for dominance, and each enjoyed supremacy for a time. The bitterness of their rivalry was not mitigated by their bonds of race and language. Although England had to look to them for spices and other products of the Orient, no one of these cities seems to have established itself on a firm and permanent basis in England.

With the northern cities the situation was somewhat different. For a variety of reasons, they organized themselves into a league for mutual protection and advancement. The description of this organization given by Wheeler[1] is substantially correct, although the plausible derivation of their name which he offers has been discredited. Modern scholars trace the *Hanse* to "Hansa" (O.H.G.), a group of men. This league under the leadership of Lübeck, Hamburg, Cologne, and Danzig gradually extended its membership until at one time it was reputed to contain 72 cities.[2] The list of member-towns varied from time to time, and was a carefully guarded secret—a fact that weakened their legal status in England—but during the period of their dominance the great majority of the cities were in what was then the Holy Empire (territories comprising roughly the lands later included in Germany and Austria). The Emperor, however, was not the powerful monarch that his name implies, and the Hanseatic

[1] *Treatise of Commerce*, p.86, *infra*, pp. 384-5.

[2] Anderson, examining this question, cites statements from Thuanus which indicate that there must have been eighty Hanse towns prior to 1518; over against this he places the declaration of their own historiographer, Werdenhagen, that there were only 64 who ever paid annual contributions to the expenses of the Confederacy. Adam Anderson, *Origin of Commerce*, 1801 edition, vol. II, pp. 35-36.

League did not depend upon him for support. Instead, they developed their own fighting fleets and relied upon these for protection against pirates and other enemies. Although the League was originally and ostensibly for mutual protection, it naturally happened that they sometimes used their power for aggression as well. They were in a position to dictate—and did dictate—to Scandinavian princes, and they aimed to exercise a monopoly of trading along the northern coasts.

The government of the Hanseatic League was democratic, in form at least. Important decisions were made at a diet or council composed of representatives of all the cities. Messages bearing the seal of the League with its double eagle and "Signum Civitatum Maritimarum" were respected, if not dreaded, by the most powerful princes in Christendom.

In England the Hanseatic League had an exceptionally strong position from the thirteenth to the fifteenth century. German merchants had traded in London as early as Saxon times, but these were from a single city or two, notably Cologne. Later, when the League had become powerful, the Hanseatic League established a residence or "Kontor" in London. Their commercial influence may be judged from the fact that they occupied the Steelyard, where the great standard weighing-balance of London, the "steelyard" or "stillyard," was kept. Some authorities assert that the residence derived its name from the balance and others that the balance derived its name from the residence.[3] In any event, the Steelyard was a place of commanding importance in the commerce of the City. The Hanseatic merchants, or Easterlings as they were sometimes called,[4] also had colonies in other parts of the realm. They held themselves aloof from the English population except in business transactions and had a strict rule against intermarriage with English natives.

[3] Wheeler and his contemporaries generally accepted the simple and obvious derivation of the word as a place where steel was kept and sold, for steel was one of the most important Hanseatic commodities in early days. Although this was not the true derivation, it was probably the reason why the name gained currency in English. The word probably comes from Stälhof, a sample-yard. See also the explanation of J. M. Lappenburg, *Urkundliche Geschichte des Hansischen Stahlhofes zu London*, pp. 70–71.

[4] Other names used by Wheeler or his contemporaries are *Hanses* and *Steelyard Merchants;* many modern writers refer to them as *Hansards.*

In the early part of their history in England, the Hanses had merely the modest and innocuous trading privileges which merchants from foreign cities commonly obtained from the rulers of countries where they traded; namely, the right to trade unmolested, to be free from discriminatory taxes, and to hold their own courts of law. Later, by making loans and gifts to needy English kings, they obtained special privileges. The most important was the privilege of exporting and importing at a very low flat rate which was less than other merchants, even English merchants, had to pay. With this privilege the Hanseatic merchants naturally acquired an increasing proportion of England's commerce.

Although the material advantage of the privileges of the Hanse has probably been exaggerated,[5] it was great enough to constitute a sore grievance to the mercantile class in London. The resentment of the citizens sometimes culminated in fights, with considerable bloodshed, and more than once the Steelyard was compelled to invoke the protection of the king. This protection he could hardly refuse, not only for legal reasons, but because he depended upon the Germans for loans. From Richard II to Henry VIII, there probably was not a single king of England who was not at some time in debt to the Hanseatics. More than once the crown jewels of Edward III were in pawn with German merchants, and yet he was compelled to ask for fresh loans from them because there was no one in England from whom he could borrow money. It was obvious that there was no chance to free commerce from the dominance of German merchants so long as they were financing the King. On the other hand, there was little chance that any merchants in England could be wealthy enough to finance him until commerce in England had been freed from the Hanseatic dominance. There was no escape from this dilemma except by building up the Merchants Adventurers, and we may be sure that this fact was fully realized by their shrewder members long before it was apparent to the Crown.

[5] N. S. B. Gras, *The Early English Customs System*, p. 112.

CHAPTER IV

THE MERCHANTS OF THE STAPLE

THE Merchants Adventurers had a powerful rival nearer home in the "Merchants of the Staple."[1] These "Staplers" seem to have had a common origin with the Merchants Adventurers in a guild of merchants called the "Brotherhood of St. Thomas Becket." In the thirteenth century this brotherhood received recognition and trading privileges from John, Duke of Brabant, one of the domains in the Low Countries. Wheeler gives the date as 1248, but 1296 seems to be the date of the earliest authentic charter. Bruges was then the trading metropolis of Western Europe, and the English merchants used it as their headquarters.

At this period, England had very little to export in the way of manufactured products. The bulk of outward trade was in raw materials, chiefly wool. In order to facilitate the collection of the customs, a single city was designated as the staple or market through which all exports of the commodity had to be sold, and a royally favored group, called Merchants of the Staple, were entrusted with its sale. The staple was held at various French and Flemish towns at different times, but ultimately was fixed at Calais, which for a long period remained the staple-town. At various times the project was advanced of holding the staple in some English city, such as Southampton or Ipswich, and compelling the foreign buyers to come there. The experiment was tried once or twice; at other times certain English ports were designated as export staples for shipments to the foreign staple across the water.[2]

These Merchants of the Staple had what appeared to be an

[1] The word "staple" originally meant the market officially designated or customarily used for the purchase and sale of certain standard commodities; its application to the commodities themselves was a later development.

[2] E. Lipson, *Economic History of England*, p. 476.

assured position, with an absolute monopoly of the trade in England's most important export commodities. Those who were not members of this favored body had no sure market for their cargoes, and traded at their own risk; hence the term Adventurers was early attached to them to distinguish them from the Staplers. The largest number of these Adventurers operated in Brabant, Zeeland, and other parts of the Netherlands, and the term "Merchants Adventurers" gradually became associated particularly with this group, although it was not officially their designation until much later.[3] They must have been looked upon by the Staplers with something of the same condescension with which a curb-broker is often regarded by a member of the New York Stock Exchange. They were restricted to the trade in cloth, which was inconsiderable, and to such other minor manufactured products as might be available; and they led a precarious existence with an uncertain income. Naturally they would have liked to see their cloth trade on the same solid footing as the wool trade of the Staplers.

One slight indication of the position of the Merchants Adventurers in the fifteenth century may be gleaned from the life of William Caxton. Caxton was a member of their company in Bruges and in fact was their governor from about 1463 to 1470. Trade in Bruges was dull; it seems that many of the Adventurers had transferred their trading activities to Antwerp, twenty years earlier. In 1464, Philip the Good, Duke of Burgundy, prohibited the importation of English woolens; so Caxton and his group had to transfer their marts to Utrecht for two years. Back in Bruges in 1469, Caxton, having (as he tells us) "no grete charge of occupacion," began his translation of the *History of Troy*. This activity led him to learn the art of printing.[4] If the business of the Adventurers had been highly prosperous and profitable at this period, it is possible that Caxton might not have become England's first printer.

[3] W. E. Lingelbach, *The Merchant Adventurers of England* (1902), p. xxiii.

[4] W. J. B. Crotch, "Caxton on the Continent," *The Library*, 4th ser., vol. 7 (1927), pp. 387–401.

Toward the close of the fifteenth century, however, the situation began to change. The cloth industry was being built up in England. Exports of raw wool were gradually declining. They had averaged about 30,000 bags annually during the reign of Edward III; now they averaged only about a fifth or sixth of that amount.[5] Since wool was the chief commodity handled by the Staplers, they suffered greatly during this period of decline. As early as 1527 they were petitioning for relief. They asserted their right to export cloth as well as wool, but it was too late. The cloth trade they had neglected had fallen into the hands of the Merchants Adventurers, who were no more willing to share it than the Staplers had been to share the wool trade.

The natural evolution of English industry was therefore the chief force in building up the Merchants Adventurers at the expense of the Staplers. But they also gained the advantage of political influence. Unlike the Hanseatic merchants and most other merchants engaged in foreign trade, they were not content to secure charters of privileges from the rulers of the countries where they traded; they secured recognition from their own rulers. Wheeler asserts that they did this as early as the time of Edward III,[6] but his assertion has not been corroborated. They certainly had a charter from Henry IV in 1406 (old style) and from all his successors. These early charters were of no great value, as compared with the royal patronage of the Merchants of the Staple, but they gave the organization an official status, and paved the way for larger privileges. Another astute move gave them grounds for preference: they limited their membership to native-born Englishmen, who were not permitted to marry foreign wives. The Staplers, on the other hand, included both English and foreign members; in fact, the foreign members were in the majority.

This difference in policy doubtless weighed heavily with Henry VII, and led him to protect them in the cloth trade. In 1505 he granted them a substantial charter of privileges,

[5] Lipson, E., *Economic History of England*, p. 403.

[6] See *infra*, p. 321.

which virtually assured them the same sort of monopoly in the cloth trade that the Merchants of the Staple enjoyed in the wool trade. It was in this charter that they were first officially titled, "Merchants Adventurers." Previously they seem to have been called simply "Merchants of the English Nation."

Their period of prosperity began with this charter in 1505. From this time it was a foregone conclusion that they, and not the Staplers, would be the dominant English power in foreign trade. The only task that remained was to oust the Hanseatic League from their entrenched position in the Northern markets and secure the lion's share for themselves. For this task they were poorly equipped in wealth and in armament, but admirably organized. They had the immense advantage of support from their own ruler and, although they represented many different cities—York, Newcastle, Yarmouth, Norwich, and others, as well as London—yet they were bound together by more common interests than were the 72 cities of the Hanseatic League. Moreover, London was so much greater than any other English city that it was in a position to exercise leadership over the group, whereas with the Hanseatic cities the leadership of Lübeck was not altogether acceptable, and the loose organization gave opportunities for dissension and divided opinions.

It would be unsafe to assume that at the beginning of the sixteenth century the Merchants Adventurers had the definite ambition to overthrow the Hanseatic League. Doubtless they felt more keenly than most Englishmen the general animosity toward the foreign merchants. Certainly the lower export duties which were a part of the Hanseatic privileges annoyed them and handicapped them financially. But at the same time, the Hanseatic merchants were so strongly rooted in England that it would have been presumptuous to dream of driving them out. Up to the middle of the sixteenth century, the Merchants Adventurers undoubtedly would have been richly content with an equality of trading privileges at home and reciprocal privileges abroad. Again and again during the fourteenth and fifteenth centuries, attempts had been made in behalf of English merchants to obtain for them reciprocal trading privileges in Hanseatic territory. Treaties were negotiated, but the Hanseatic cities calmly disregarded them. Their policy was the typical medieval trading-policy of getting as much as possible in the way of special privileges for themselves and giving as little as possible in return. The Merchants Adventurers could not justly complain against this, for they subscribed to the same doctrine. Their policies and methods, indeed, were largely patterned after those of the Hanseatic League. Moreover, these were also the policies and methods of the guilds[7] that controlled domestic industry and trade throughout the Middle Ages.

[7] Although the majority of economic historians have preferred the spelling *gild*, I have chosen to retain the more popularly familiar *guild*—partly because *guild* was the form used by Wheeler.

CHAPTER V

TRADE-POLICIES DURING THE MIDDLE AGES

TO understand the organization, policies, and methods of the Merchants Adventurers—or of the Hanseatic League—it is necessary to bear in mind the fact that all trade during the Middle Ages, domestic as well as foreign, was a matter of special privilege. To-day we are so accustomed to thinking of the right to trade as a natural right that we forget how short is the period during which this idea has had any general acceptance. Throughout the Middle Ages and later, the privilege of selling goods had to be won by purchase or force, and was jealously guarded. This in spite of Magna Carta. As Gross says, "More than six centuries elapsed before the enactment of Magna Carta that all merchants 'may go through England by land and water to buy and sell free from all unjust imposts' became a realized fact throughout the realm."[1]

The doctrine that the right to trade is the natural right of every free-born Englishman was not wholly unknown in Elizabeth's day. From time to time agitators argued in favor of opening certain kinds of trade (particularly the cloth trade in foreign markets) to all who wished to engage in them. A few of these agitators doubtless were sincere; others were actuated by the selfish desire to get admitted to the favored group, after which they would gladly see the doors closed again. But whatever the motive inspiring the freedom-of-trade theory, it was regarded as an innovation. To Wheeler and his brother merchants it appeared a peculiarly dangerous innovation that needed to be vigorously suppressed. But in truth, there could be little support for it in a commercial world that was almost completely made up of specially privileged groups such as the guilds were.

[1] Gross, C., *The Gild Merchant*, p. 165.

From their first appearance in English commercial and industrial life, the guilds aimed to exercise a monopolistic control over trade in the town markets. Yet this system represented a step toward freedom of trade from what had preceded it, in the sense that oligarchic control is slightly more democratic than autocratic control. We have no evidence that men were ever free to buy and sell at their own will and discretion, even in Saxon times. On the contrary, the earliest English markets of which we have certain knowledge, were markets designated by the king and established by law. Buying and selling elsewhere was prohibited, in order to prevent traffic in stolen goods. Traders in the market were required to pay tolls to the king—a reasonable requirement, since they enjoyed his protection.[2] These original features of markets—that they were held only in designated places at stated times, that trading outside them was prohibited, and that traders in them must pay tolls—persisted long after some of the reasons for them had disappeared. Naturally the tolls assumed increasing importance. The lords, spiritual and temporal, who obtained from the king the rights to various town markets, enjoyed a rich revenue from them. In a few instances, at least, this revenue has continued down to very recent times, for the status of some markets remained substantially unchanged to the latter part of the nineteenth century.[3]

During the eleventh and twelfth centuries, however, a large number of towns purchased their freedom from the king or lord for a fixed annual rent. Some of them had little difficulty in doing this; others, particularly those in manors belonging to lords of the church, were less fortunate. The abbots and priors were reluctant to allow any powers to pass from their hands, and even when they yielded, they sometimes retained certain specific tolls such as the market-tolls or milling-tolls.[4] More than a hundred towns, however, were free before the end of the thirteenth century.

[2] F. W. Maitland, *Domesday Book and Beyond*, pp. 193–4.

[3] In 1878 the Town Corporation of Sheffield tried to acquire the market rights, which were held by the Duke of Norfolk. He offered to sell them for £247,450. See the *Report of the Royal Commission on Market Rights and Tolls*, 1889, vol. I.

[4] That a similar condition prevailed on the continent is suggested by Wheeler's comment that the Bishop of Bremen had a toll at Stade. See *infra*, p. 367.

An almost universal phenomenon in these was the organization (or recognition) of a Guild Merchant. Usually the *Gilda Mercatoria* was expressly permitted by a clause in the charter. This type of guild (presumably borrowed from Normandy and Flanders) was the first to exercise any important influence in the commercial development of England. There were English guilds for social and religious purposes earlier, and perhaps a few guilds of craftsmen (such as those of the weavers in Oxford and the bakers in London), but the Merchant Guilds were the first large-scale application of guild principles to business. Directly or indirectly, they controlled a large proportion of the town markets during the twelfth and thirteenth centuries. The term *Guild Merchant* is a somewhat misleading translation of *Gilda Mercatoria*. "Trader's Guild" would perhaps picture it more accurately. Few of the members were merchants in any modern sense of the word. They included butchers, bakers, brewers, and all sorts of craftsmen who produced articles for sale. Direct marketing from producer to consumer was considered the ideal, and the growth of a distinct class of middlemen was viewed with distaste. "Regrating" (speculative buying for resale in the same market) was a serious offense as was "forestalling" (buying outside the market). The fact that the markets were held only at periodic intervals (usually once a week) made it possible for those engaged in production to do their own selling. Nevertheless, as towns grew and a greater quantity and variety of commodities became available, a class of middlemen gradually came into being; but they never became numerous enough to constitute the entire membership of a Guild Merchant.

The preferential position of the members of a Guild Merchant in a town market is faintly paralleled by that of the members of a Produce or Cotton Exchange to-day. But the Guild Merchant was a more closely knit organization. The members were bound in bonds of brotherhood, and each one was pledged to share his bargains with his fellows. Those who were not members, the outsiders or *forinseci*, could not sell in the town market except on stated terms which discriminated against them severely, and, in fact, were sometimes virtually prohibitive. Only in the annual fairs, which remained among the king's prerogatives (though often conferred by him on some religious or charitable establishment), was there any approach to equality among the traders. This partly explains why the fairs became so popular, and why they were viewed with jealousy by many towns. In fact, London tried for a time to boycott Stourbridge Fair, but without success.

It may therefore be seen that, in its earliest wide-spread manifestation, the guild principle in English commerce meant control of the town market by an oligarchy of traders. The market regulations were no less strictly enforced than they had been under the king or lord; indeed they were probably more strictly enforced, for there were more persons to watch for violations, and unwilling for economic reasons to wink at them. The market monopoly of the Guild Merchant was of a relatively innocuous kind, so long as practically all the substantial citizens were members. Nevertheless, this selfish exclusion of outside blood would scarcely commend itself to a modern Chamber of Commerce as a means of increasing the growth or prosperity of a town.

During the fourteenth century the Guild Merchant almost everywhere ceased to be the dominant power in the town markets. This does not appear to have been due to any dissatisfaction with their policy, but rather due to the fact that their membership had grown too unwieldy and too diverse in interests for effective administration. Craft Guilds were formed in the more important trades, subsidiary to the Guild Merchant and under its regulation. Little vitality remained in the Guild Merchant, though it seems to have continued its existence. As late as 1817, a druggist in York was prosecuted (unsuccessfully) for selling imported goods without a license from the Merchant Guild of the town.[5] Perhaps in a few towns the old Guild Merchant developed into a guild of merchants proper, the Mercers Guild, or even into a fellowship of Merchants Adventurers, later to become a com-

[5] Maud Sellers, ed., *The York Mercers and Merchant Adventurers*, pp. 316–321.

ponent element of the great company of Merchants Adventurers of England. The fact that the Company of Merchants Adventurers of Newcastle had in their possession charters granted to the Guild Merchant of that town has been cited as proof of such a connection.[6] Newcastle, however, was a leading seaport, and her Guild Merchant may have contained a group of merchants even at its beginning in the reign of King John.

In most cities the Guild Merchant disappeared, without leaving any living organization that could claim to be its sole heir. Instead appeared a group of craft guilds, which became the chief forces controlling the markets and trade of the towns. In York in 1415, fifty-seven crafts were recognized. Other cities also had a large number. In London, naturally, the craft-guild system had its most extensive and elaborate development. London seems never to have had the transition stage of the Guild Merchant, possibly because the number of persons eligible was so great that this would have been unwieldly at the start; but practically every important trade, craft, and commercial occupation was organized into a guild.

Perhaps because of their name, perhaps because of the attractive theory on which they are based, the craft guilds have acquired a romantic and idealistic halo which they do not altogether deserve. It is true that they aimed at a high standard of workmanship and prescribed a lengthy apprenticeship to secure it. At bottom, however, the Craft Guild, like the Merchant Guild, embodied the medieval idea of combination and acquisition of special privilege. In short, it was a form of trade monopoly. Some of the most powerful of the London guilds, such as the Fishmongers and Grocers (the "victualling guilds") were not composed of craftsmen in the true sense of the word, as was scornfully pointed out to them by the Drapers.[7] Their apprenticeship system was less concerned with insuring quality of their personnel than with limiting its quantity. One indication of this is the fact that a

[6] J. R. Boyle and F. W. Dendy, *Extracts from the records of the Merchant Adventurers of Newcastle-upon-Tyne*, vol. II, p. xi.

[7] For a full account of the disputes of the craft guilds, see A. H. Johnson, *History of the Worshipful Company of the Drapers of London.*

man who had served his apprenticeship in one craft or "mystery" was sometimes permitted to engage in another.

The craft guilds were usually organized under the name of some patron saint and made some pretensions to religious activities, but this was well understood to be mainly a pretext.[8] They bickered with one another regarding their industrial jurisdiction and their precedence at feasts and celebrations. They fought with one another for political power and spoils. The history of the Fishmongers Company in London politics is at least as unsavory as that of Tammany Hall in New York. Even those guilds which had a genuine ideal of craftsmanship were frequently concerned largely in protecting themselves against competition. Their Committees of Standards found it possible to condemn and destroy competing merchandise brought in from outside. By this and other methods they erected a Chinese Wall of protection around their city. Not always did it have the result they intended. Occasionally it happened that industries cramped by the supervision of the guilds emigrated to the country districts. The great cloth-industry, for example, became largely a country industry, in spite of desperate efforts by various towns to retain it.

One instance of craft-guild policy which illustrates the method is of special interest because it involves Richard Schilders, printer of the first edition of Wheeler's *Treatise of Commerce*. Schilders was admitted to the Stationers Company of London as a foreign brother. In 1578 he was brought before the court of the Company on the charge that he was printing a pamphlet, contrary to the rules governing foreign members. He was ordered to turn the partly completed job over to another member and to work for him as a journeyman at weekly wages.[9] Evidently this did not satisfy Schilders'

[8] Maud Sellers, ed., *The York Mercers and Merchant Adventurers*, pp. iii–iv.

[9] E. Arber, *A Transcript of the Registers of the Company of Stationers of London, 1554–1640*, vol. II, p. 882. (It is interesting to note that the book Schilders was printing was for the "Hanse Stelle"—presumably the Steelyard. Schilders was ordered to turn it over to Thomas Dawson, but the only book recorded as licensed to Dawson about this time was entitled, "A handfull of honnie succles gyven for a new years gift unto the ladies and gentlewomen of the privie chamber." If this was indeed the publication of the Hanseatic merchants, it may have been some sort of propaganda.)

ambition, for a few years later he bobbed up as a printer in Middelburg, where he became famous as a printer of some of the most beautiful and most important English books of the period. Obviously, the restrictions upon his liberties in England deprived the Stationers Company of a member who would have added considerable lustre to their history. The Stationers Company could furnish us many other evidences of the imperfections of the guild system. They parceled out the profitable jobs to favored members. They limited the size of editions so as to insure furnishing more labor in typesetting and printing. Their philosophy and that of most other guilds seemed to be that demand was inelastic and therefore the road to profits was through rigid control and limitation of supply.

With this basic tenet of medieval economics in mind, we are in better position to appreciate the methods of the Merchants Adventurers which Wheeler so stoutly defended in his *Treatise*. The Merchants Adventurers were indeed a form of guild. As already mentioned, they were originally called "The Brotherhood of St. Thomas Becket of Canterbury." This title, like that of other guilds, does not necessarily signify any important religious purpose in their associations, though it appears that their membership fee was nominally devoted to services in honor of the saint. That this explanation was not universally believed is evident by certain petitions against the company which accused them of extorting heavy fees "under color of feigned holiness." These early merchants may all have been members of the Mercers Company of London. The Mercers, merchants dealing in small wares, were among the strongest organizations in the city. There was certainly a close relationship between them and the Merchants Adventurers. They used the same building as a meeting-place and the records of the two companies are said to have been kept in the same book.

Not all the Mercers, however, were members of the Merchants Adventurers and merchants of other cities besides London were admitted to membership. Up to 1496, however, they had difficulty in gaining admittance. In that year a petition to Parliament showed that the membership fee had been raised from the original 3 shillings 4 pence to 100 shillings, and finally to 20 pounds—an enormous sum for those days. This was in line with the usual guild policy of limiting membership and narrowing the monopoly of trade. Parliament in 1497 declared that English merchants were free to trade in the Netherlands and Low Countries upon payment of a fee of 10 marks (a little more than six and a half pounds). Although this for the moment appeared to be a blow at the Merchants Adventurers, it really turned out to be helpful rather than otherwise, because it gave official sanction to their right to control the trade in their territory. Moreover, they evaded the intention of the act by dividing their membership into the Old Hanse and the New Hanse. (They borrowed words as well as policies from the Hanseatic League.) The New Hanse members who were admitted under the act of Parliament were somewhat restricted in their trade-rights, and their sons could not acquire membership by birth, as in the case of members of the Old Hanse, but had to purchase membership anew. The internal administration took care to maintain the dominance of the favored few within the organization. This was characteristic of the operation of many of the guilds, if not all.

The incorporation of the Merchants Adventurers in 1505 also finds a close parallel in the history of the craft guilds of London. Up to the time of Henry VII, these were under the control of the mayor of the city, but Henry transferred the authority to the Chancellor, Lord Treasurer, and Chief Justice. As A. H. Johnson says, "This measure may be said to sound the passing bell of the system of 'town economy' and of the craft system which was its outcome, and to herald the rise of the new National economy which was henceforth to prevail."[10] Before the end of the fifteenth century, nearly all the powerful guilds, including the Mercers and the others ranked in the Twelve Great Livery Companies, had obtained royal charters of incorporation. These charters were essen-

[10] A. H. Johnson, *History of the Worshipful Company of the Drapers of London*, vol. I., p. 53.

tially like that which the Merchants Adventurers obtained from Henry VII in 1505.

In effect, then, the Merchants Adventurers became a national craft guild engaged in foreign trade. The seat of their government was at the scene of their operations, in the more important of the two mart-towns where they concentrated their trade. This for a long time was Antwerp, and it was here that they became great and powerful. In this city they maintained their own colony like that of the Hanseatic League in the London Steelyard. Here they sold their cloth in the seasonal markets and here they bought goods for import into England. On the average, they probably bought goods of higher valuation than those they sold, the difference being made up by the proceeds from the sale of wool and other staples at Calais.

All their business operations and their personal life as well were strictly regulated. The rules were formulated by their governor and his court of twenty-four assistants, who were elected "of the most sad, discreet, and honest persons of divers fellowships of the said Merchant Adventurers."[11] The fellowships mentioned here probably refer to the groups from the several English cities. It is unnecessary to go into detail regarding the regulations. Their general character and philosophy may be inferred from the examples cited in the *Treatise.* Obviously they were changed and added to from time to time, and the codification of 1608 by Wheeler[12] represents the accumulations of many decades of experience with violations and evasions. However, the section on "Shipping, shewing, selling," etc., is of sufficient interest from a marketing standpoint to deserve a brief summary of its more important restrictions.

With a few specified exceptions, all merchandise from England was to be shipped only to the mart-towns, and all purchases and sales were to be made there. Exceptions were

[11] *State Papers Dom. Charles II*, 27. This volume (XXVII) contains the last charter they received—that from Charles II in 1661—and recites or mentions their previous charters. The quotation is from the charter of 1505.

[12] Reprinted in W. E. Lingelbach, *The Merchant Adventurers of England, their Laws and Ordinances*, 1902.

made in the case of war munitions, certain foodstuffs, and the like. Exceptions were also made in favor of Emden and Calais, and purchases at Frankfort Fair, provided these were brought to the mart-town to be shipped to England. Shipments were to be made only in appointed vessels. Penalties for violations were severe, frequently twenty-five per cent of the value for a first offence. Interlopers were penalized more heavily for trade in cloth than for trade in other commodities; they were fined if caught with the goods, and imprisoned if caught without them.

The merchants usually had warehouses and showrooms. They were permitted to show goods for sale only on show-days—Monday, Wednesday, and Friday—but might conclude bargains on other days, and even sell "by the mark unsight and unseen." The Court usually appointed a "set shew day" upon the arrival of the cloth-fleet, sometimes on other occasions, and members were forbidden to do any business, make any offers, or name prices and deliveries before the appointed day. Business was forbidden at certain times, for example "in time of the sermon or divine exercises." Members were not allowed to have scouts stationed at street-corners, or near the lodging-houses of cloth-merchants and drapers to entice buyers to the warehouses. They were permitted to employ brokers approved by the Court (the Governor and his Assistants) but these brokers were not to interfere in the bargains of others. Strict secrecy regarding transactions was enjoined upon the members. No retailer or other non-member was to be allowed access to letters or accounts or to have information about purchases and prices. No foreigner was to have charge of a member's warehouse, or "be privy to" his sales and buyings. Price-maintenance is not mentioned in the regulations, with the exception of a few relatively unimportant commodities, but there appears to be an indication of the attitude toward price-cutting in the fact that credit terms longer than six months were forbidden.

From these examples it is readily apparent that individual initiative in the pursuit of business was not encouraged, but instead the operations of the members were to be conducted in a rigidly prescribed routine. Like all the medieval guilds, their strength was the strength of organization. Control of supply rather than increase of demand was their method, and trade-monopoly was their ideal. As this was also the ideal of the Hanseatic League, a conflict between them was inevitable.

CHAPTER VI

THE STRUGGLE WITH THE HANSEATIC LEAGUE

THE commercial war between the Merchants Adventurers and the Hanses lasted throughout the sixteenth century and furnished the chief drama in their history. It was preceded, however, by a minor skirmish with the Flemish merchants in the fifteenth century. Little Flanders had once been the center of the cloth industry, but England, by importing Flemish methods and Flemish weavers, had supplanted her. Flanders tried to protect her industry by keeping out English cloth. It was largely because of this embargo on cloth (and not the vague reasons mentioned by Wheeler) that the Merchants Adventurers left Bruges and settled at Middelburg in Zeeland. The embargo was still nominally in force when they returned to the Flemish city of Antwerp, but Antwerp was farther from the manufacturing cities and its commercial aspirations outweighed its political sympathies.

When Henry VII took the throne, trade relations between England and Flanders were reasonably friendly and Flemish merchants were enjoying trade privileges in England. The rulers of Flanders, however, were indiscreet enough to support the pretender Perkin Warbeck; so in 1493 Henry drove the Flemings from England "as well their persons as their wares."[1] Commercial relations with Flanders were suspended. The Merchants Adventurers moved their headquarters to Calais, where the wool-staple was situated. Calais was a poor market for their purposes and the cloth industry suffered. Sir Francis Bacon in his *History* gives the Merchants Adventurers credit for mitigating the depression by "taking off the commodities of the Kingdom, though they lay dead upon their hands for want of vent."

[1] Francis Bacon, *History of the Reign of King Henry the Seventh*, edition of 1790, p. 70.

The rupture was ended by a commercial treaty in 1496, whereupon the Merchants Adventurers returned to Antwerp on a firmer basis than ever before. There was no longer even a pretense at keeping out English cloth. The Flemish merchants were permitted to trade in England, but except for a few brief periods they seem to have cut only a small figure. So far as the all-important cloth export-trade was concerned, the field had narrowed down to the two great organizations, the Hanseatic League and the Merchants Adventurers. And the fate of the Flemings in their little contest with England might have been taken as an omen of what was to happen to the Hanseatics.

Looking back over the century-long struggle, we are tempted to regard it as the steady working out of a consistent policy, in which the English Crown was hand-in-glove with English merchants to win commercial dominance. This is, in effect, the view of many historians. How far it is from the truth has been clearly shown by George Unwin in his lectures on the Merchants Adventurers. As he says:

> Policy, as actually found in history, is a set of devices into which a Government drifts under the pressure of practical problems, and which gradually acquire the conscious uniformity of a type, and begin, at last, to defend themselves as such.[2]

It is possible, nevertheless, that Henry VII, the first of the Tudors, really had a vision of an English national commerce, and that his acts in laying its foundation were dictated by deeper motives than temporary expediency. Wheeler certainly thought so. To him "the peaceable, politike and Riche Prince King Henrie the seventh" was the ideal monarch. Others might consider him colorless; Shakespeare could not find in him the stuff for a drama. We never hear of him as Hal or Harry. His were the homely virtues of thrift and industry rather than the spectacular vices of war and lovemaking. Such a king was needed after the exhausting Wars of the Roses, but he could hardly hope to be a popular hero.

In some respects, at least, he had a consistent policy. He wanted no "Kingmakers" within his realm. National unity

[2] George Unwin, *Studies in Economic History*, p. 184.

 1225624

demanded the weakening of the powerful barons. By the same token, he was well pleased to see the growth of a substantial bourgeois class, and among these the merchants naturally had first place. Whether he hoped for the ultimate exclusion of aliens from English trade or not, he certainly took important steps toward this end. First he dealt harshly with the Flemings; then he struck boldly at the powerful Hanseatics. They had shipped cloth to the Low Countries, the trading territory of the Merchants Adventurers; Henry placed them under a bond of 20,000 marks to refrain from selling cloth in Antwerp.

That they submitted to this restriction that seemed to be contrary to their contract privileges, may have been due to the fact that he had another way of controlling their operations. The export of undyed and undressed cloth (white cloth), except the cheapest kinds, had been prohibited by statute at least as early as 1487. The prohibition, like many others, did not really prohibit—perhaps it was not intended to do so. It simply meant that exportations of this kind could only be made under royal licenses; these gave the king a source of revenue and also a strong weapon for political purposes. After 1504, licenses seem to have been issued to all applicants, aliens as well as natives, without much discrimination, and some cloth was exported without the formality of a license. But the Hanseatics had always to reckon with the possibility that licenses might be refused them. Even if Henry's order to the Hanseatic merchants to refrain from selling English cloth in Antwerp was strictly enforced (which is by no means certain), they may not have regarded it as a serious blow. At this time they could not have had much fear of dangerous competition from the young upstart Company of Merchants Adventurers. And in their long history they had occasionally experienced setbacks, only to regain their position with an even stronger hold. Possibly the successor of Henry VII would be a ruler of a different type.

Henry VIII was of another type altogether, as the world well knows. Probably more has been written about him than about any other English king, but his name rarely appears in Wheeler's *Treatise*. This silence is proof enough that the Merchants Adventurers owed little or nothing to him. It is true that he renewed the charters granted by his father. He also reaffirmed the statute prohibiting the export of white cloth in 1512, and fined the Hanseatic Merchants who shipped without licenses.[3] However, he seems to have been on friendly terms with the Germans. During his reign, they had plenty of opportunities for the showy pageants that were their favorite form of advertising. On some great occasions they set up fountains running with Rhine wine, which they dispensed freely to the populace—an ingenious method of sampling.

The Merchants Adventurers used similar methods on the continent. Wheeler boasts that they spent great sums for triumphal arches and pageants at coronations and other festivals. He paints a colorful picture of their splendor at the reception to King Philip of Spain at Antwerp in 1549. Liveries of purple and green and gold, threescore lackeys in white velvet, and other pages and attendants on horse or on foot made them "nothing inferior to the merchants of other nations." London was familiar with this sort of advertising by its own great livery companies, or guilds, who strove to outdo one another in showy and costly pageants; but as the Merchants Adventurers were in foreign trade, they probably never paraded their full splendor in England.

It is said that the Hanseatic merchants were strongly opposed to the marriage with Anne Boleyn and that their display at the time of her coronation contained a subtle insult to the new Queen. If she noticed it and resented it (as contemporary gossip says she did), Henry apparently chose to ignore it, and her period of influence was too short for her to take revenge even if she had so desired. That was left to her daughter. Some commentators profess to see in Elizabeth's later conduct toward the Germans a disposition to punish them for their attitude toward her mother.[4] That any such sentimental motive actuated her is exceedingly doubtful.

[3] Astrid Friis, *Alderman Cockayne's Project and the Cloth Trade*, p. 43.

[4] Ian Colvin, *The Germans in England*, pp. 151–2, 196.

Henry's extravagance forced him to seek money constantly, and he was not too particular how he got it. One method that proved a great handicap to England's trade was that of debasing the coinage. In this connection it may be mentioned to the credit of the Hanseatic League that they maintained the standard of their currency. Hence we find throughout the medieval period that sums of money in England are often stated in foreign coinage. Thus the Parliament in 1497 specified the entrance fee of the Merchants Adventurers as ten marks. For a long time it was believed that "sterling" came from "Easterling." *A Treatise Concerning the Staple,*[5] written about 1519, says that the Old Easterlings from the North used to come over and buy cloth for which they paid money of fine quality—hence the word *sterling*. Though this derivation dates back as far as the thirteenth century, the *Oxford English Dictionary* rejects it. However, it was sufficiently plausible to be accepted by many merchants, though not by Wheeler, for he emphatically states, "pounds sterling, or English money." The Hanseatics may have been adroit enough to foster the misconception that "sterling" money was due to them. The use of new and bright money as a form of good-will advertising has been practiced occasionally by modern companies operating in a hostile territory; there are certainly grounds for believing that this method is of very ancient origin.

Although Henry's policies hampered English commerce, he did make some changes that later proved of benefit. By centralizing the power of the Church in his own hands, he brought England a step farther on the road toward national unity and independence. By weakening the power of the clergy, he helped the merchants, for the clergy were generally unfriendly to business. For example, they asserted that interest (usury) was unchristian and unethical long after it had been demonstrated to be essential in the conduct of trade.[6] They opposed with equal violence many other busi-

[5] Attributed to Clement Armstrong. Reprinted in Tawney and Power, *Tudor Economic Documents*, vol. III, p. 90 ff.

[6] R. H. Tawney, ed., *A Discourse Upon Usury*, by Thomas Wilson, pp. 106–121.

ness practices that are now universally accepted as legitimate and innocent as well as economically necessary. Wheeler's opinion of the clergy may be inferred from such references as the following: "*Ordinatam Charitatem incipere a seipso, etia Theologia admittunt*" (freely translated "even the Theologians admit that charity begins at home").

It is impossible to say with certainty whether the Merchants Adventurers or the Hanseatic League gained most in trade during the reign of Henry VIII. Both certainly flourished. Both were exporting a large volume of cloth and continued to do so after Edward VI, the boy king, became the nominal ruler. Rapin in his *History of England* (1733) declared that in 1551 the Men of the Steelyard exported 44,000 cloths, and that all the English merchants together did not export 1,100 cloths. This absurd and annoying misstatement has been quoted again and again ever since.[7] The statement probably should read that all other *foreign merchants* did not

[7] Among others, by Lappenberg and Anderson; also C. P. Lucas, *The Beginnings of English Overseas Enterprise*, p. 90; H. W. Gidden, ed., *The Book of Remembrance of Southampton;* E. G. Nash, *The Hansa*, p. 216. This error is pointed out by Colvin, who traces it to a misquotation of statements by the Merchants Adventurers to the Privy Council in the trial of the Hanse in 1551–52. They declared that in the 3rd year of the reign of Edward VI the Easterlings shipped 42,897 cloths from London "in strange bottoms," whereas all the other strangers shipped only 1080 [under similar conditions?]. (See Colvin, *The Germans in England*, pp. 240–41.) But these figures still give a misleading picture of the proportions of trade done by the Hanseatics and the other foreign merchants, for they take no account of the shipments in English vessels. A few years earlier the Flemish merchants had shipped considerable quantities of cloth, practically all in English vessels, by virtue of a discriminatory custom favoring such shipments, and although their trade had dropped heavily as a result of the withdrawal of this privilege, it could hardly have sunk so low as 1080 cloths, even from London alone. The balance was doubtless still in English ships, and hence was not a dead loss to the nation, as the export trade of the Hanse was. Colvin estimates that the amount shipped by the Steelyard was at least as great as that shipped by the Merchants Adventurers, but his evidence for this is unconvincing. Unfortunately, the customs figures for this year have not been completely compiled. Schanz's valuable compilation ends with the reign of Henry VIII. But it is incredible that a cloth trade averaging about 120,000 cloths should have shrunk in three years to a trade of about 90,000 cloths without plunging the country into the deepest industrial depression. Assuming that the total still stood in the neighborhood of 120,000 cloths, the 43,000 of the Steelyard would be a much larger proportion than the 23% which Schanz estimates as their average under Henry VIII. But the gain had probably been mainly from the other foreign merchants, rather than from the Merchants Adventurers, and the chief loss to England had been to her shipping. As for the Flemish, they must have retained at least enough business to have something to lose by the Cloth Customs act of 1557–58. (See Schanz, *Englische Handelspolitik*, vol. II, p. 18; also Friis, *Alderman Cockayne's Project and the Cloth Trade*, p. 40.)

export more than 1,100 cloths *in foreign ships*. According to the figures of Schanz for the period 1509–1547,[8] the English merchants exported more than the Hanseatics and all other foreigners together, in nearly every one of these years. There were some exceptional years, but on the average the Merchants Adventurers exported twice as much cloth as the Hanseatics under Henry VIII, and doubtless continued to do so under Edward VI.

Whatever may have been the exact proportion that these two great organizations exported, Sir Thomas Gresham, financial agent of the Crown at Antwerp, considered the share of the Hanseatics too great and that of the Merchants Adventurers too small. Gresham had reason for sympathizing with the ambitions of the Merchants Adventurers. He had served his apprenticeship and had been a member of the Company. Moreover, he saw in them the only possible solution for the financial problems of the royal treasury.

Henry VIII had left his son a neat legacy of debts at Antwerp. Gresham wanted to liquidate these without recourse to foreign bankers. If the Merchants Adventurers were to become strong enough to assume the burden, it was necessary that the Hanseatic privileges in England be terminated. This was done in proper legal form by a court of the King's Privy Council in 1552. The court listened solemnly to complaints by the English merchants that the Hanse privileges were an unjust discrimination against them and furthermore that the Hanseatics had violated the terms of their contract by "coloring" (selling as their own) the goods of non-members. On this and other technical grounds, the court pronounced the contract void and placed the merchants of the Hanseatic cities on the same footing with merchants from other foreign cities. The decision may have been legally unjust. Certainly the Hanseatic League never admitted its validity. However, it righted an injustice that had been done to native English merchants for some centuries and that, as Gresham clearly saw, would continue to hamstring English commerce and prevent

[8] G. von Schanz, *Englische Handelspolitik gegen Ende des Mittelalters*, vol. II, pp. 18, 86, and 102–3.

restoration of their "obsolete" privileges and preferential export duties.

The ten-year sojourn in Hamburg seems to have been highly profitable to the Merchants Adventurers. At the end of it, however, Hamburg yielded to the pressure of her sister cities and refused to renew the contract. In reprisal, Elizabeth cancelled the export-licenses of the Steelyard and still further curtailed their privileges. The Merchants Adventurers were inconvenienced by leaving Hamburg, but the loose organization of the League enabled them to continue their operations in German territory. Wheeler gives a detailed account of their wandering in search of a better mart-town, and as this occurred in his lifetime, the account may be accepted as substantially accurate. For a time they used Emden. Emden was not one of the Hanse towns, and therefore was not moved by the pleas or threats of the League. Nor was the intercession of the Emperor more successful. A mandate exiling the Merchants Adventurers from the territory of the Empire, on the ground of monopolistic practices, was then agreed upon in 1582. This mandate, however, was not published at the time; indeed, it was held in abeyance for fifteen more years. The Merchants Adventurers and the diplomatic agents of the English Crown perceived that it was to be used as a club to frighten England into a more favorable attitude toward the Hanseatic League, and went ahead with their trading as usual.

For other reasons, which are only vaguely indicated by Wheeler, they removed their mart from Emden to Stade in 1587. This was the year when English commerce was threatened by the Spanish Armada. Industry, particularly the cloth industry, was at a low ebb, from a combination of causes. Emden was at best an inferior market for the Merchants Adventurers. They would have been glad to return to Hamburg, but Hamburg was not yet ready to defy the authority of the League. The hope of a restoration of Hanseatic privileges in England was nourished by the trouble and distress which that country was experiencing. If ever the Hanses were to regain their position this was the time to stand firm. Perhaps if Stade had not received them at this time, there might have been a different story to tell. But Stade did receive them, and liked the profits from their presence there too well to give them up. After 1588, the time for making any effective use of the Mandate had passed. England became stronger each year. The Spanish Armada had failed. Elizabeth had become vainer and more arrogant, and less inclined to fear any foreign threats. She showed no signs of extending any additional favors to the Hanseatic League. On the contrary, she gave them fresh grievances by interfering with their trade with Spain. Her men-of-war captured a number of their ships, without regard to what the League considered their rights as neutrals. Still the Emperor Rudolph temporized.

At last, in 1597, the Emperor issued his Mandate of exile, but not until one further attempt had been made to obtain restoration of Hanseatic privileges in England by intimidating Elizabeth. This final attempt provides one of the highlights of Elizabeth's reign and has been made famous by many writers, including Lytton Strachey in *Elizabeth and Essex*. His picture of the interview with the Ambassador from Poland is brilliant and amusing. Wheeler's account is more laconic—and possibly more accurate. After summarizing the Ambassador's speech, he says:

> This was in brief the effect of the said Ambassador's speech, which with a very loud voice he delivered in the Latin tongue. Whereunto it pleased her Majesty to make him a short answer, and quick for that time. . . .[10]

In short, she referred him to her ministers. They requested the Ambassador to put the matter in writing, so that they could give it their proper consideration. In due time they returned an answer which the pamphlet quotes in full.[11] As the Merchants Adventurers were not specifically mentioned, this extended treatment might seem unnecessary; but Wheeler contends that this protest is all of a piece with the Mandate

[10] See *infra*, p. 391.

[11] Stow's *Annales* contain what purports to be a literal transcript of the Queen's extemporaneous Latin speech and a brief summary of it in English. Stow does not quote the complete reply of the Queen's councillors, but refers his readers to Wheeler's *Treatise* for this. See John Stow, "The Annales . . . continued unto 1614 by Edmund Howes," London, 1615, pp. 783 and 814.

of the Holy Roman Empire that was issued at the same time and was aimed directly at them.

The long threatened Mandate of the Emperor Rudolph was finally published in 1597, and was equally ineffective with Elizabeth. Instead of yielding in her position, she countered vigorously by exiling all the Hanseatic merchants from England early in 1598. This marked the beginning of the end of the long struggle between the great organizations. The Merchants Adventurers now had an undisputed control of the English cloth exports to the richest territories of northern Europe. The only difficulty was that they were not permitted to operate as an organization within the Empire. They still had their mart in Middelburg and through this their wares could flow into Holland, and eventually into Germany, but the total volume of business suffered a great decrease. The Merchants Adventurers had every reason to expect that this decline of trade would be only temporary; that sooner or later one of the Hanseatic cities would defy the the power of the organization as well as the Emperor and welcome them back. They could afford to play a waiting game. The only question was whether the rest of England, and particularly the cloth industry, would be content to wait along with them.

CHAPTER VII

PUBLIC FEELING AGAINST THE MERCHANTS ADVENTURERS

THE exclusion of the Hanseatic merchants from England was a victory for the Merchants Adventurers, but a costly victory. Although it removed their most powerful competitors from their immediate path, and at the same time weakened the power of those competitors, it very nearly caused the disintegration of their own organization also. Possibly this might actually have been the result, if it had not been for John Wheeler. At any rate, they were brought into a highly critical situation, partly because of public feeling against them, and partly because of other more tangible factors.

The interruption of trade with Germany obviously could not prove a benefit to English industry. On the contrary, it aggravated the depression from which the business of the country was already suffering as a result of the long war with Spain. Not only was the Spanish market cut off, but the Mediterranean trade-routes were still dangerous for English shipping. Capital had been withdrawn from legitimate trade to be invested in privateering expeditions, gold-seeking explorations, and other speculative enterprises. Some of the raids on the Spanish bullion fleets had resulted in rich hauls but these were more than offset by costly failures, to say nothing of the losses to England's solid industries.

It may truly be argued that this bold and brilliant period of English history not only produced great heroes and great literature, but incubated great schemes that were later to enrich the nation. Out of it came the great East India Company, first launched in 1600, and the companies formed to colonize America. But these enterprises brought no dividends for a long time to come. Whatever credit the future might give to the closing years of Elizabeth's reign, they were lean years for most of the people who lived through them. Prices were high and many workers were unemployed. The triumph of the principle of English trade by Englishmen was a fine thing for English patriotism, but it brought no immediate gains to English purses.

As the months went by and the seventeenth century dawned without any appreciable recovery of trade, public feeling turned strongly against the Merchants Adventurers. They were not solely—or even chiefly—responsible for the depression, but they received a large share of the blame, as the party in power always does. No longer was it possible to point to the merchants of the Steelyard or other foreign merchants as the culprits. Such foreign trade as England still retained was almost entirely controlled by the Merchants Adventurers and chartered companies like them. They themselves had the richest market for cloth, including all the territory between the Somme in France and the Scawe in Germany. To the north the Eastland Company had the shores of the Baltic, and the Muscovy Company had Russia. Southward the Levant Company operated in the Mediterranean. It was said that the ports of France were practically the only ones to which a merchant could ship goods unless he was a member of one of the chartered companies. After the elimination of their most important foreign rival, the methods of these companies naturally received more careful scrutiny.

It was obvious that the trading companies bore heavily upon the people, both as producers and consumers. Through their control of the supply of imported commodities, they had the power to raise prices to unreasonable heights. The control of currants was one of the chief motives in forming the Levant Company in 1581. Unlike the Merchants Adventurers, this company was organized on a joint-stock basis, with Elizabeth herself as one of the principal stockholders. Not satisfied with the profits from her dividends, she levied heavy custom duties on currants. This Levant Company constituted a monopoly of the most vicious kind. The Merchants Adventurers did not defend it; instead they tried to show that they were not in the same category.[1] They did not have joint stock, but each member traded on his own account. Thus they had at least a semblance of competition, although many observers believed that their tendency was to raise prices. Indeed, they were sometimes accused of making their chief profits through the sale of foreign goods in the home market rather than through the sale of England's commodities abroad. It was plausibly argued that when abroad they had to sell in the seasonal markets and therefore sold quickly, almost as soon as the goods were unloaded, whereas at home they could dispose of their imports at leisure and use the services of clever chapmen in their distribution.[2]

The complaint that they raised the prices of foreign commodities, however, was not very strongly urged against them. Some observers, especially among the clergy and the staunch protectionists, felt it was not wholly an evil to make people pay dearly for imported luxuries. They would have preferred that the "outlandish merchandise" should not come in at all. Moreover, there was the consolation that part of the extra cost was used (or was supposed to be used) for maintaining the navy. As a matter of fact, the goods imported by the Merchants Adventurers according to Wheeler's list,[3] do not include many that were bitterly attacked on the score of price, as were the currants, sugar, oil, and wine from the South. The Merchants Adventurers stoutly affirmed that they brought in commodities "good cheape."

The really vital complaint against the Merchants Adventurers was that they restricted the cloth industry. Certainly they furnished but a narrow channel for its outward flow. They were in a position to dictate to the clothiers the price they would pay, and it would be no marvel indeed if they used their power. In ordinary times, the accusations of the clothiers could be ignored. But when cloth was "at a stand" (standstill) the protests became loud and disturbing. Nor did

[1] See *infra* p. 428.

[2] See "A Discourse of Corporations" Harl. Mss. 4243, ff. 605 seq.(1587–89?), reprinted in Tawney and Power, *Tudor Economic Documents*, vol. III, p. 265 ff.

[3] See *infra*, pp. 337–8.

the cloth industry stop to inquire how much of the blame could justly be laid at the doors of the Merchants Adventurers. The stoppage in 1598 and the years following was no worse than some that had been experienced earlier, notably about 1550, 1564, and 1586. In 1550 a group of clothiers complained that the price fixed by the Merchants Adventurers meant a loss of one pound on each cloth. Other clothiers, however, defended the Merchants and declared that the real trouble was that there were too many in the cloth industry. Here, as in the struggle with the Hanse, the Merchants profited by the division of their enemies, and the crisis was safely passed. About 1564, when the Netherlands were closed to the Merchants Adventurers, the situation was relieved by opening new channels into Germany.

The depression in 1586–8 was perhaps the most severe of all. These were glorious years for England's naval history, but at the time the weavers had little interest in the exploits of Drake and Hawkins. Their suffering was acute, for the cloth industry was completely prostrated. Although the Merchants Adventurers were not primarily responsible for this condition, their monopoly was suspended. As Wheeler points out, the situation was not relieved. He naturally omits to mention the fact that the Merchants Adventurers boycotted the cloth market and that neither alien nor native merchant dared run the risk of taking up the cloth until they could be sure of getting in touch with a satisfactory market for it abroad. However, it was made clear that the Merchants Adventurers had a strangle hold on the cloth industry and there was no immediate alternative to the use of their service.

A part of their strength lay in excellent discipline. Nevertheless, they did not get along without some dissension. The New Hanse members who had gained admittance by virtue of the Act of 1497 frequently rebelled against the iron rule of the Old Hanse members—but were compelled to submit. The members from provincial ports were jealous of the dominance of London. More progressive merchants chafed at the "stints" or quotas assigned them and at the restriction to the mart-towns. Occasionally they carried their trade to inland cities in spite of the rules. To modern business men this would seem a logical way to widen the market and increase the demand. But the old conservative element held that the cloth was "embased" by these tactics; that the only sound way to maintain its price was to make the buyer come to the mart-town for it. This line of reasoning was quite in accord with medieval thought and with the long experience of the wool-staple; hence it was accepted by a large proportion of Englishmen, including many of the clothiers themselves. Some even carried it to its logical conclusion by arguing that the foreign buyers should be compelled to come all the way to England for the cloth. They evidently did not know that this scheme had been tried with the wool-staple, and had proved a failure. Several proposals were seriously made that a staple of cloth should be held at an English port. The boy king Edward VI is said to have worked out an elaborate scheme for a staple of cloth at Southampton. Elizabeth in 1573 received a proposal for a staple of cloth at Ipswich.[4] These schemes might have been more seriously considered if it had not been for the obvious impossibility of designating any one city for the staple without arousing the violent wrath of all the other ports.

The Merchants Adventurers must have been shrewd enough to realize that there were limitations to the distance which foreign buyers would travel for English cloth. Perhaps they dimly suspected that buyers would not travel so far for cloth as for raw wool. Yet they genuinely believed that their cloth was so indispensable to Germany and the Netherlands and the demand for it so constant that they could safely centralize their selling in one or two towns and in the hands of a small group of merchants without danger of losing trade. Hence, the fewer the merchants, the better for prices and profits. If this policy bore heavily on the cloth-makers, their remedy was likewise to limit their numbers. The clothiers did attempt this, but with less success, since they were not or-

[4] *A Project for Erecting a Staple at Ipswich*, by John Johnson and Christopher Goodwin, reprinted in Tawney and Power, *Tudor Economic Documents*, vol. III, p. 173 ff.

ganized on a national basis. Even if the clothiers had been equally successful in restricting numbers, the stoppage of trade would have been a serious matter. The output of their looms could not be curtailed immediately—and when it was curtailed it involved unemployment and hardship for the weavers. So the years following 1598 saw a rising tide of bitterness in the cloth industry that was largely directed against the Merchants Adventurers.

It is highly probable that they would have been even more harshly criticized if they had been able to preserve their monopoly in water-tight condition. This they could not do. Although the Germans would not receive the Merchants Adventurers as a company, they did accept cargoes of cloth that were brought into their ports. Some of these were brought by independent merchants (interlopers), but some were brought by merchants who had a membership in the Merchants Adventurers. This interloping trade into Germany really constituted a safety-valve for the Merchants Adventurers, but they were far from regarding it in that light. Instead, they tried by every means to prevent it. They induced the Privy Council to issue an order in 1598 designating Middelburg as the sole channel for all trade into the Netherlands and Germany, but the clothiers protested so violently that the order had to be rescinded. To-day we can only marvel at the temerity of the proposal that all cloth destined for Germany and the Netherlands should pass through this little town of Middelburg on the Isle of Walcheren. Even their own members refused to obey the Company's order to confine their trading to Middelburg.

It might be supposed that the Company would prefer to see this German trade handled by their own members rather than by independents. But they feared that the situation would result in a breakdown of their organization. Already their discipline was suffering. The members trading in Stade and other cities of the Empire were neglecting to pay the impositions of the Company on cloth and other English commodities. The usual machinery for collecting these could not be maintained in the German ports, nor could their courts be held there. Special measures had to be taken. A letter from Secretary Wheeler to the Newcastle fellowship (presumably sent to all other fellowships also) informs them of an act passed at a General Court of the Company at Middelburg, January 10th, 1600.[5] This act took notice of the violations of the Company's orders, and declared that sons and apprentices of those trading in Germany who failed to pay the impositions should not be admitted as members. Such a penalty, however, could hardly have been an adequate substitute for their usual procedure.

We are now in a position to appreciate some of the conditions that prompted the publication of an official statement by the Merchants Adventurers Company. They were in disfavor with the cloth industry and many independent citizens. They were unable to trade with Germany, and in that territory—theirs by chartered right—individual merchants were operating. If these interlopers continued to handle the trade successfully, England might well conclude that the regulated companies were unnecessary and burdensome. An ironical element of their plight was that while they were being denied their monopoly privileges, they were being classed with the vicious private monopolies that Elizabeth had created. It is unnecessary to recount in detail here the growth of that pernicious system. Everyone knows how Elizabeth had rewarded her favorites with monopolies in salt, wine, tin, oil, etc., until practically every article that came into the household had paid tribute on the way to Essex, Raleigh, or some other nobleman. The representatives of an aroused people had protested in 1597. Elizabeth had promised Parliament to mend matters but had procrastinated as usual. The intolerable nuisance showed no signs of abatement at the beginning of the new century.

It was understood that the first business of the Parliament of 1601 was to be the consideration of the monopolies. No one knew how far the Commons would dare to go in the defense of the rights of the people. The monopolies were

[5] J. R. Boyle and F. W. Dendy, ed., *Extracts from The Records of The Merchant Adventurers of Newcastle-upon-Tyne*, vol. I, pp. 109–10.

Crown prerogatives; to dispute the Queen's right to them would be little short of sacrilege. Yet the strength and the temper of Parliament were such that this was not wholly unthinkable. As events proved, the clash between Crown and people was to be postponed until the Stuarts were on the throne. The conditions that made it possible, however, arose under Elizabeth. Under her, England had taken several important steps toward democracy. The upper middle-class in particular had strengthened its position and had grown both in literacy and in independence of thought and action.

At earlier periods than this there would have been little reason why any private company should air its case in a public pamphlet. A private petition to the Crown was the simpler and more effective instrument. Now, however, the court of public opinion was not wholly confined to the Church and the peerage. A multitude of Englishmen had some voice and influence in national policies. If there were no other evidence of this, we could find proof enough in the fact that the *Treatise of Commerce* was published and circulated to several thousand persons.

CHAPTER VIII

THE CRISIS OF SIXTEEN HUNDRED AND ONE

THE threat of Parliament to abolish the monopolies at its forthcoming session might have been sufficient incentive for the publication of the *Treatise of Commerce*. The Merchants Adventurers could not afford to be classed with the vicious private monopolies that oppressed the people. But although they wanted to escape the opprobrium of the word *monopoly*, they wanted the profits of its reality. Yet at the very time they were getting the name they were in danger of losing the substance. In the early months of 1601 they were shaken by two blows that practically nullified their triumph over the Hanseatic League. And the blows came from Elizabeth.

If proof were needed of the fickleness of the Queen or of the fact that her support of the Merchants Adventurers was based on temporary expediency rather than national policy, she certainly furnished that proof amply. Her Privy Council resolved (March, 1601) to grant freedom of trade on the Elbe and Weser rivers, which meant chiefly at Hamburg and Stade. The interlopers, of course, were already operating there, but the decree gave them official sanction and status, contrary to the chartered privileges of the Company. Friis, citing Ehrenberg, says that this action was taken "in spite of all efforts of the government of the company, among which must be noted the vehement protests of Christopher Hoddesdon, the governor, and Wheeler's ably written defence."[1]

[1] Astrid Friis, *Alderman Cockayne's Project and the Cloth Trade*, p. 72. The passage cited in Ehrenberg reads as follows:

"Die Adventurers verteidigten ihren Stapelzwang in Middleburg mit allen Kräften, der Governor Hoddesdon durch Eingaben an die englische Regierung, der Secretary John Wheeler öffentlich durch eine Schrift, welche alle Argumente, die für das Monopol und den Stapelzwang der Compagnie sprachen, noch einmal meisterhaft zusammenfasste, und auch als historische Quelle von grosser Bedeutung ist. Es is die schon oft von uns citirte Schrift 'A Treatise of Commerce.' . . .

"Die Bemühungen der Adventurers waren

But this is an error of chronology. Wheeler's *Treatise* had not yet been written; the decree was one of the incentives for his writing it. He wanted to avoid further extensions of the interlopers' trade, and have them ousted from this territory as soon as possible. The other blow was more serious, for it shook the keystone of their business. Elizabeth granted to the Earl of Cumberland an unlimited license for the export of white cloth for ten years. By its terms he was permitted to transfer the exportation privilege to any party or parties he might designate. And no other licenses could be issued. Thus he could become the sole dictator of the cloth trade.

In some respects, Cumberland's grant was neither unprecedented nor unexpected. The Merchants Adventurers had a free license to export 30,000 white cloths annually. The remainder (amounting to an average of at least 30,000 more) they exported on licenses that they secured from the Queen, or bought from some favorite to whom she had granted them. When she rewarded Nottingham or Stafford (at no expense to herself) by a cloth export-license, the recipient of her bounty sold it to the Merchants Adventurers. They had to buy it to protect themselves. And although this form of petty graft was annoying, it was the sort of thing nearly all business men had to endure. All these earlier licenses had been for definite amounts—30,000 or 50,000 cloths usually, sometimes as high as 100,000. But Cumberland's license was unlimited. If this was graft, it was graft on a grand scale. What was to prevent him from selling a part of the license to them and an equal or greater part to other individuals or another company?

Cumberland's license appears to have been issued officially in August, 1601. But the grant had been made long before that, possibly before the decree of free trade on the Elbe and Weser. There was obviously a close connection between the two events, and the Merchants Adventurers learned of them at about the same time—probably in February, before either

vergeblich: der Handel mit Elbe und Weser wurde von der Königin im März 1601 freigegeben und bereits im folgenden Monat kamen abermals acht Tuchschiffe in Stade an." Richard Ehrenberg, *Hamburg und England im Zeitalter der Königin Elizabeth*, p. 209.

had become an accomplished fact. They certainly regarded the situation as desperate. For proof of this we are indebted to the diary of John Manningham, which tells of a meeting of their Court on March 2, 1601.[2] As the meetings of the Court were customarily held abroad, this was evidently a special meeting, called for emergency purposes. Manningham's account is as follows:

2 March, 1601

This day there was a great Court of Merchant Adventurers; two were sent from the Counsell [Privy Council] to sitt and see their proceedings at their Courts and to make relacion. At this Court two questions were moved.
1. Whether the Companie were able to vent all the clothes made in England if they might choose their place in the Lowe Countries, and be aided by hir Majestie for the execution of their orders? Resolved that they are able.
2. Whether they can continue a Company to trade if the Earle of Cumberlandes license take effect whereby he hath liberty to ship over what cloth he pleaseth, contrary to hir Majesties patents and graunts to the merchaunts? Resolved by handes that they cannot.

. . .

Their Courts consist of one Governor, one Deputy, a Secretary, and these sitt at a table raysed a little, and 24 assistants sitt about; the autority of these continues but six moneths; these speake, heare, and iudge of other men's speaches in Court. The greater part of the present at any Court carries the iudgement. (Mr. Hull, nar.)

Thus we see how grave the situation appeared to the officers of the Company, and how vigorously they resisted the encroachments on their chartered privileges. Very likely they realized, however, that their protests to the Queen would prove unavailing. Perhaps at this very meeting, or at a conference afterwards (with no representatives of the Privy Council present) they determined to state their case to the public in a printed pamphlet.

The *Treatise of Commerce* could hardly have prevented the issuance of Cumberland's license, even if it had been published in time. Elizabeth must have been under heavy obligations to her favorite. A limited license for fifty or a hundred thousand cloths, like those she had previously granted to others, would have been sufficient recognition of his beauty

[2] John Bruce, ed., *Manningham's Diary*, Camden Society Papers, 1868, p. 40.

and courage, and sufficient reward for such sentimental courtesies as wearing her old glove set in diamonds, in his hat, or acting as her champion at tourneys. Cumberland's license was unprecedented, not only in being unlimited, but also in omitting the usual clause that one cloth in every ten should be dressed and dyed. Although he paid her five hundred pounds a year for his license, this was but a fraction of its value. The balance must have been in consideration of some debt or service. Possibly the obligation was incurred in connection with Cumberland's numerous and generally unlucky privateering expeditions. On these he had captured some rich prizes, but rarely succeeded in bringing them back to port. His latest and most elaborate expedition in 1597–8, with no less than twenty ships, mostly fitted out at his own expense, had been a costly failure. Though he plundered the Canaries and captured San Juan, Porto Rico, he lost many men, and the Spanish treasure-fleet eluded him. As Elizabeth had previously compensated him for his misfortunes, she was doubtless doing so on this occasion—at the expense of the Merchants Adventurers. It must have been peculiarly vexatious to them to be placed at Cumberland's mercy. Not only did he represent the most objectionable characteristics of the cavalier nobility; he was also of the group of buccaneers whose exploits had reacted so unfavorably upon their trade and upon all English industry and commerce.

Cumberland may have had a more ambitious scheme than that of mulcting the Company, but if so it has never been brought to light. The idea that he was interested in the establishment of free trade can safely be dismissed. If he was instrumental in procuring the sanction of the interlopers on the Elbe and Weser, it was mainly in order to increase his power by widening the circle of those who were able and willing to buy parts of his license. But he undoubtedly preferred to sell his license at wholesale rather than at retail, and that could only be done to an organized campany. The Eastland Company would gladly have accommodated him, but this organization apparently received no encouragement.

There remains the possibility—though a faint one, unsupported by tangible evidence—that Cumberland's scheme was somehow connected with the fortunes of the newly organized East India Company. He was one of the leading backers of this enterprise. Its ships had not yet returned from their first long voyage, and the success of the venture was problematical. Cumberland may have had some hazy notion that this company could profitably engage in the settled cloth trade to Germany as a means of financing its new and speculative ventures to the East. Certainly he resisted for a long time the offers that the Merchants Adventurers made for his license. All these offers carried the proviso that they should have exclusive rights to ship under his license—a proviso they justly considered essential to their protection—but to this he would not agree.

Negotiations with Cumberland were protracted for months, during which he sold parts of his license to other parties. Finally, in 1602, they reached an agreement whereby the Merchants Adventurers were to have the exclusive privilege of using his license and were to pay him two shillings, two pence on each cloth they exported under it. This would total at least three or four thousand pounds annually—a very tidy sum for those days. Hence it may be said that indirectly the Merchants Adventurers helped to provide the capital for the young East India Company that was to become their successor as the dominant mercantile power of the world.

In the Spring of 1601, however, the Merchants Adventurers had only anticipations of what was to result from the Queen's unkindness. Doubtless these anticipations were fully as gloomy as the reality. Doubtless also the merchants pondered on the unwisdom of putting too much trust in Princes. They had just had a ghastly reminder of Elizabeth's fickle temperament in the execution of the Earl of Essex.[3] Once the petted darling of the Queen, he had lost not only her favor but also

[3] Among the large number of men who were imprisoned in February as suspects in the Essex Conspiracy but soon released for lack of evidence was one John Wheeler. It is not certain that this was the Secretary of the Merchants Adventurers; however, several other merchants were unjustly suspected and imprisoned, and our author may have suffered likewise. See *Acts of the Privy Council*, J. R. Dasent, ed., N.S., vol. 31, pp. 159, 186.

his head. Now that their Company had served her purposes were they also to be discarded? Perhaps it was not too late to appeal to her business sense to maintain them in their privileges.

Even if they managed to survive Elizabeth, the continuation of their monopoly would depend on the favor of her successor. His accession could not be far distant, for the Queen was now sixty-eight years old. They knew little about the Scottish James, but he was reputed to be a scholar and thrifty. It might be well to have him learn from a book how valuable the Merchants Adventurers were to the Realm, and how they enhanced the Crown revenue. And it might also be well if they had more friends at Court and in Parliament to work in their interests.

CHAPTER IX

MILLES' PAMPHLET ATTACK ON THE COMPANY

WHEELER had sufficient reasons for beginning his task of authorship in March, 1601. But he was conservative and hated "innovations"; he must have been reluctant to adopt the unheard of innovation of issuing a public defense of his company. With all the weight of logic urging him to this course, he may still have delayed until a relatively trifling incident—a mere pin-prick—goaded him to action. The pin-prick was supplied in April by Thomas Milles, in the shape of a pamphlet entitled *The Customer's Apology*.[1]

The "customer" indicated by this title was not a buyer of goods—the word was seldom used in that sense then—but a customs-officer. Milles was customs-officer for the Kentish Ports of Sandwich, Dover, Rochester, Milton, and Feversham.[2] His ostensible purpose was to explain the unfortunate situation of the custom-house officers, particularly those in the ports outside of London, and to secure for them proper recognition and treatment. Actually, however, he concerned himself less with defense than with attack. He attacked the Government for placing supervisors over the customs-officers; he attacked London for drawing to itself more and more of the trade; he attacked the Merchants Adventurers for monopolistic practices. *The Customer's Apology* was not a publicly distributed pamphlet. Milles did not even secure the requisite authority for publishing it, but had fifty copies privately printed and put in the hands of the Lords of the Privy Council.[3]

[1] The original title reads "The Custumers Apology," but the usual spelling in the text and in later titles is *Customer*.

[2] The principal members of the famous Cinque Ports are said to have been Sandwich, Dover, Hastings, Hythe, and Romney. Apparently Milles did not have jurisdiction over all these.

Milles was a singularly unfortunate man. He could hardly have chosen a more inauspicious moment for launching his shaft or a more tactless method. Some of his charges reflected directly upon the Privy Council; those that struck at the Merchants Adventurers were untimely, for the wings of this organization had just been clipped. Evidently the Lords of the Privy Council were not favorably impressed. One of these "understanding readers and wise in the highest authority" must have turned over his copy to the Merchants Adventurers for their attention.

Other evidence of a cold reception is furnished by the later publications of Milles which purported to be abridgments or summaries of *The Customer's Apology*. He issued three of these at different times,[4] but they differ materially from his original version. They are much milder in character and more like an apology, as we understand the term. (*Apology* in those days merely meant *defense* and did not connote humility.) More significant, they omit the objectionable charges against the Merchants Adventurers, as well as those that touched the Crown, and they contain implications that the author had been disciplined or reproved. The *Short Title Catalog of Books* lists almost a dozen items by Milles, nearly all of them pamphlets advocating "reforms." Such persistence perhaps deserved some reward. Apparently he never received it in his lifetime. Even posterity has been unkind to him, for some of the dates assigned to his works are incorrect in spite of his precautions to insure their preservation. About 1608 he deposited in the Bodleian his sole remaining copy of his masterpiece, *The Customer's Apology*, carefully annotated. In his subsequent abridgments he referred interested persons to the complete version "in Thesaurio Bodleyano." Yet this precious uniquity was catalogued as "n.d." and later assigned the date 1604 (presumably because it is bound with two other pamphlets, one of which bears that date).[5]

[3] "whereof there were but 50 printed 1601 & dispersed among the Ld of the Counsaille." (Marginal notes by Milles in the Bodleian copy.)

[4] *An Abridgement of the Customers Apology* (1609?); *The Customer's Apologie . . . here only abridged, paraphrased* (1609?); *An abstract, almost verbatim, of the customer's apologie* (1617?).

[5] The marginal notes by Milles are of later

Milles may have written his pamphlet simply to air his private grievances, or those of the Cinque Ports, but he gave grounds for suspecting that he was incited to write it by the interlopers. At any rate, he takes up the cudgels in their behalf. First he details their public griefs, in the form of heavy fees to Princes and collectors and a multitude of irregular exactions and fees to "searchers, controllers, surveyors, waiters, wayers, packers, scavengers, their deputies, clerks, servants (and such like). . . . In five or six years the payments in this kind do countervaile their stocks." The picture was doubtless only too true to be pleasant reading for the Privy Council. He then goes on to the private griefs arising from the dominance of London and the restrictions of the Trading Companies:

Privately they grieve, that amongst themselves Trades under Companies and Societies are drawn and abridged into a few men's hands; wherein, besides the wrong offered to the Law and general freedom of the land, even within themselves also, the wealthier and best grounded, by odds of stocks, restraints and other advantages, drive the weaker to the walls. That one Port ["London," pen-written by Milles] seems to give Law to all the rest, without warrant of Law, reason or Policy; the danger whereof, more see and lament than know how to prevent or remedy. That in all Ports extremities attend them driving them to this issue, either to quit their Trades altogether, or to worke it out by favour at one Porte or other, to the displeasure of the Prince, as if they conceald her Customs, when they get least by it, as may be observed in the falling of sundry, and decay of a great many.

Here he does not mention the Merchants Adventurers by name, but his reference is obvious. It will be noted that he virtually admits the existence of bribery and concealment of customs at some of the Ports as the only method whereby the independent merchants could exist.

In a later passage he attacks the Merchants Adventurers more specifically:

And in London more specially the Societie of Merchants Adventurers that sometime has been as curious to keepe and debarre men from their marttowns as now they seem violent to force all men thither. Least by their un-

date than 1601, but there seems no doubt that the pamphlet was one of the original and only complete copies printed in 1601.

quiet and uncertain *instruments* and form of proceedings they make good at home amonge themselves and within themselves, against themselves, that, strangers have feared written and forespoken, terming them a 'Private, Particular and Preventing Companie.'

Milles was fond of lengthy footnotes. In one of these, explaining the term "Merchants Adventurers," he includes his most offensive charges:

The argument of this discourse, being the advancement of customs, and the drift thereof, honour and peace to the Prince and her Kingdom; was resolvd at the first to depend efficiently on Traffic. That traffic consisted of four essential parts or pillars, *Matter*, *Persons*, *Place*, and *Order*. That to maintain Traffic and so consequently Customs, &c. Was to procure and cherish in all Matter *Goodness:* in all Persons, *Loyalty* and *Friendship:* in all Places, *Conveniency* and *Freedom:* and in all Order general *Equity*, the best rules whereof were only to be found in the *Certainty* and *Indifference* of the positive *Laws*, *Treatise* and *Contracts* of mutual Commerce. But the *Merchants Adventurers*, not knowing or not regarding these four essential grounds together, run away with Traffic as if it stood only in the choice of *Persons*, and by their uneven, uncertain and violent proceedings hold all men under to keep themselves above. Terming all Enterlopers that would live by the direct and set laws of Traffic, as if all were bastards, and scarce good Christians, at least no *Loyal Merchants* nor Friends, but they and their *Society*. And by a bare and idle pretence of the word Order and orderly transporting the *Credit* and *Cream* of the Land (Cloth) have brought the trade thereof to a kind of confusion, and themselves to such a Labyrinth: that besides the distress of the (Clothiers) with all their Dependants, and general Complaints at home (to their Ho. Lordships endless offence and trouble at the Council Table) the Commodity itself is impaired, abased and in a sort despised and the State withal dangerously divided and unkindly at Iarre with her ancient allies and best foreign friends.

Taken by itself, Milles' attack would hardly have been regarded as deserving serious consideration, much less the dignity of an official reply. But it brought into print the sort of charges that were being gossiped around and were inflaming public opinion against the Merchants Adventurers. The charges had to be answered. It was convenient to answer them as coming from such an unpopular source as a customs-officer.

It may be Wheeler was particularly enraged by the attack because of its author. Milles represented the Cinque Ports, whereas Wheeler was a Great Yarmouth man. This meant something in those days. The feud between Great Yarmouth and the Cinque Ports had lasted for centuries and had been full of violence, bloodshed, and the destruction of many ships. It was begun by the claim of the Cinque Ports to regulate the fishing trade of Yarmouth, and was ended in 1579 by an arrangement whereby Great Yarmouth had to pay annual tribute to the Cinque Ports. Wheeler must have witnessed part of the dispute or even participated in it, and must have felt bitterly the injustice of the outcome. The attack of a Cinque Ports man upon his honorable company of Merchants Adventurers might well affect him as a red rag affects a bull. Hence his castigation of Milles in the *Treatise of Commerce*[6] may contain an element of personal rancor. In reality, Wheeler and the Merchants Adventurers owed a debt of gratitude to Milles for acting as the spokesman of the discontented factions. Had the pamphlet come from some nobleman or even a cloth-maker it might have proved more embarrassing. But customs-officers have few friends at best. It was well known that some of them had been accepting bribes from the Hanseatic merchants—either substantial sums in money and plate, or trifling gifts like stock-fish (codfish) and Rhenish wine. Hence Milles presented a vulnerable target for Wheeler's counter-attack.

If, in addition, *The Customer's Apology* suggested to Wheeler the idea of a pamphlet as the most suitable medium for his purposes, his debt is even greater. It is entirely possible that the whole idea of the *Treatise of Commerce* was conceived after the appearance of Milles' work. At any rate a considerable part was executed after that time, although the reply to Milles became but a small and incidental part of the *Treatise*.

[6] See *infra*, pp. 209–211 and 382–384.

CHAPTER X

THE STRATEGY OF THE TREATISE

HOW much of the plan of the *Treatise of Commerce* is Wheeler's own and how much is due to the advice of others, we have no means of knowing. He obviously had co-operation from some one close to the throne, perhaps Secretary Cecil himself. Or he may have obtained State documents and letters through George Gilpin, his predecessor as Secretary of the Merchants Adventurers, who was now the Queen's agent, and well versed in the wiles of diplomacy. Then he and his associates made a careful analysis of the objectives to be accomplished, and arrived at somewhat the following conclusions: (1) The *Treatise* must convince discontented members of the wisdom of remaining within the organization and obeying its rules; (2) It must convince the leaders of the cloth industry that they are benefited by the system of having their products marketed abroad through the chartered companies; (3) It must convince Parliament that the Merchants Adventurers should not be considered a harmful monopoly; (4) It must convince the Queen that failure to support the Company would endanger the Crown revenue and embarrass the kingdom financially; (5) It must convince friends of the Hanseatics that it is useless to hope that they will be reinstated in England, and thus indirectly influence Hamburg to invite the Adventurers back; (6) It must increase public respect for merchants in general and the Merchants Adventurers in particular.

These objectives are not wholly unlike those of present-day corporations—especially public-service corporations. Great organizations of this kind are continually facing problems of influencing legislation and maintaining internal and external good-will. These they solve in a number of different ways, but commonly by lobbying, by secret propaganda, and by advertising. The Merchants Adventurers naturally used all the personal influence they could upon those they could reach. But personal contacts even among their own membership were relatively infrequent, especially at this time, and there were many other influential persons who could be reached only by the written or printed word. Newspapers did not exist in those days; handbills, posters and broadsides were inadequate to contain their message; hence a book was the logical medium for their propaganda.

Wheeler may have borrowed some of the methods of controversial writers on religious or economic questions. He certainly borrowed from an anonymous defense of London that appeared as an appendix to John Stow's *Survey of London* in 1598. The writer was described as a "Londoner born"; he himself says that in the reign of Queen Mary he was a young student at Oxford. His defense of London is said to have been written about 1578.[1] Wheeler may have read it in Stow or have had a copy of the manuscript himself. At any rate the early part of the *Treatise of Commerce* is patterned closely after this defense of London, and incorporates bodily several phrases, including the Latin quotations from Polydore and Cato; after the second section of the *Treatise* there is no evidence of borrowings from this source, but the writer may have assisted Wheeler or furnished him with material.

Having chosen his objectives and his medium, Wheeler went to work with businesslike energy. His duties compelled him to be in Middelburg, and there he dashed off the 40,000 words within a period of less than two months. Even allowing for the fact that a third of the material was copied from letters and documents, this speed of composition was remark-

[1] Stow's introduction to this appendix reads as follows:

"Now since that I have given you an outward view of this city, it shall not be impertinent to let you take an insight also of the same, such as a Londoner born discovered about twenty years gone, for answer (as it seemeth) to some objections that were made against the growing greatness thereof. The author gave it me, and therefore, howsoever I conceal his name (which itself pretendeth not), I think that they may take pleasure in the reading, as I doubt not but he did in the writing. Long may they (that list) envy, and long may our posterity enjoy the good estates of this city." Thoms' edition (1842) of Stow's *Survey of London*, p. 199. (Morley's edition does not contain this material.)

able. The printer, Schilders, had probably put much of the manuscript in type before Wheeler finished the last pages and signed the dedication on June 6, 1601. Thus he was able to deliver copies in London by August 14.

The London edition had probably been decided upon before the other was printed, for the same paper is used in both. Despite the large number of variants in spelling, the London edition is not a revised edition. Some small typographical errors were corrected, other than those the author himself had indicated in his page of *Errata*, but several important errors of fact were allowed to remain unchanged. Many new typographical errors crept in, including a few of major importance, due to the omission or insertion of a word. The presence of these, and the absence of a page of *Errata* to correct them, indicate that Wheeler did not see the London edition through the press and that this edition also was printed with the utmost speed. As has already been suggested, the London edition may have consisted of 2,500 or 3,000 copies. The fact that fewer specimens of the Middelburg edition than of the London are now extant seems to indicate that the entire edition was smaller. However, a large proportion of the Middelburg copies may have gone to the members of the Company from ports outside London. Not only would Middelburg be the logical place for distributing copies to them; the Middelburg imprint would tend to avoid the suggestion of London dominance, which was a sore point with them. On the other hand, the London imprint would make a favorable impression on members in that city and on the powerful companies and citizens whose support they needed.

The *Treatise of Commerce* was issued to its audience frankly as a piece of argumentative literature. There was no concealment of either its source or its purpose by pretending it was a work of history or of science, to be sold by the stationers. Hence it is more like modern good-will advertising than most corporate propaganda pamphlets later in the century. Perhaps if Wheeler had had more precedent, he might have used the subterfuges of secret propaganda. As it was, he chose the most direct and obvious approach to his object.

This fact, however, does not mean that he was lacking in subtlety. The dedication is enough to prove him a practical psychologist. It is addressed to Sir Robert Cecil, principal secretary to the Queen, and at that moment probably the most powerful man in the kingdom. Wheeler disclaims the intention of praising him, but manages to do so by eulogizing his father, the great Lord Burghley, who had died a few years earlier, and by adding that his own simplicity and Cecil's modesty forbade him to indulge in adulation. The method has since become hackneyed by frequent repetition, but Wheeler may have been one of the earliest to adopt it. This passage has considerable distinction, and the preceding passage, that declares that books are the worthiest monuments to a man's virtue, is not unworthy of Lord Bacon himself.

The careful craftsmanship of the dedication is not maintained throughout the entire *Treatise*. It was well enough planned, but the division into sections according to the benefits conferred by the Company led to confusing repetitions of material, and the hasty execution led to inaccuracies. Moreover, Wheeler was not an historian, nor was he writing for the benefit of future historians. Doubtless he had at least as much respect for the truth as the average propagandist, but the only parts of the truth that he cared to present were those that were favorable to his cause. Moreover, his misstatements may have been due to ignorance rather than intent to deceive.

Just what his sources of information were, other than the records of the Company and the recollection of the older members, is somewhat difficult to determine. No very extensive library could have been within his reach at Middelburg. His own book-shelf held a few of the classics, including Plutarch and Lucan, a few legal books, and at least three histories. Of the histories, he cites most frequently Sleidan's *Commentaries*.[2] He also refers by name to Carion and Polydore. These historians were all well known in England at the time. The works of the two Germans, Sleidan (John Philipp-

[2] John Philippson (known as Sleidan), *De Statu Religionis & Reipublicae Carolo Quinto Caesare, Commentarii.* (25 books, published in 1555.)

son) and John Carion, had been published in English as well as Latin versions, though Wheeler seems to have used the Latin versions of these. His citation from Carion is from the fifth book of his *Chronicles*, whereas the English version, published in 1550, contains only the first three books. This fifth book was not by Carion but by Gaspar Peucer, son-in-law of the great Lutheran reformer Philip Melanchthon. Indeed the whole chronicle that made Carion's name famous was not his work, but the work of Melanchthon, later added to by Peucer.[3]

The only one of these authorities that commands much respect to-day is Sleidan. This historian, Philippson, who took the name Sleidan from his birthplace, was born in 1506 and died in 1556. As the historian of the Reformation he enjoyed a considerable vogue in Protestant England in the sixteenth and seventeenth centuries. Translations of some of his works appeared as early as 1560 and there was still a market for a new English edition as late as 1689.[4] Polydore's work, although it passed through four editions between 1534 and 1570, has been called superficial and full of errors. However, he was not alone in sacrificing accuracy for the sake of interest. The chroniclers of the period, with few exceptions, interlarded their documented facts with wild tales based on hearsay. If we will compare Wheeler with his contemporaries who had better opportunities for gathering and sifting out the facts—for example, John Stow and the Frenchman De Thou (Thuanus)—we shall not be inclined to criticize him too severely on the score of credulity or unreliability.

We must also be lenient in judging his prose style. Accustomed as we are to the crisp, brisk movement of modern prose

[3] John Carion (1499–1538) was a mathematician and astrologer who wrote a chronicle of the world's history. Wishing to have it printed at Wittenberg, he submitted it to Melanchthon. Melanchthon wrote a new version and published it under Carion's name. Carion's version was also published in 1531. The Melanchthon version was translated into Latin in 1538. In 1562, a fourth book was added by Peucer, and, in 1565, a fifth. In 1572 Peucer made an edition of the whole work. This may have been the edition cited by Wheeler.

[4] *The General History of the Reformation of the Church (1517–1556) written in Latin by John Sleidan L.L.D. and faithfully Englished . . . by Edmund Bohun, Esq. London, 1689.* (This is considered the best English edition of the *Commentaries*.)

—particularly in business communications and advertisements, which are to-day the most dynamic of all forms of written messages—we are bound to find his style rather indigestible. The attempts to modernize it in this edition (pp. 313–459) by revising the spelling, punctuation, and paragraphing, have not been able to make it easy reading. However, its long sentences were characteristic of other writers of the time, particularly the men of affairs. Sir Walter Raleigh, Sir Richard Hakluyt, and Captain John Smith, with a much larger volume of literary output to their credit, are almost as difficult to read as Wheeler.

Wheeler's prolixity may be in some measure traceable to his association with legal documents. As Secretary of the Company he must have been compelled to write hundreds of communications of legal or quasi-legal character, and to read hundreds of others. This practice may have tended to develop exactness of phrase, but it did not tend toward readability. The multiplication of synonyms to cover every shade of meaning has its advantages in a contract, statute, or mandate, but it is not so useful in a stump-speech or in pamphlet propaganda. Wheeler is more stimulating when he doffs his legal wig and uses the homely expressions of the soil, such as "hold their clack."

His frequent introduction of Latin is also irritating to the modern reader. A few readers of his own day may have been unable to understand Latin, for in several important instances he gives an English translation along with it. Naturally it would have savored of irreverence to translate the Queen's Latin letters. Most of his audience could read his Latin as easily as his English. It was among the accomplishments of every educated person. With the merchant, as in the professions, it was not merely an accomplishment but a necessity. Wheeler was not a profound scholar, nor even "a learned Gent," as a successor later called him (see page 106), but he undoubtedly wrote many letters in Latin, similar to those from foreign cities which he appends to the *Treatise*.

It should be noted here that although many books published in England at this period were in Latin, the proportion rapidly decreased during the next half century. Most of the pamphlets later issued for propaganda purposes by various companies, such as Mun's *Discourse of Trade* and Parker's *Of A Free Trade*, contain little Latin or none at all. Its extensive use by Wheeler, however, cannot be accounted poor strategy. Those who could not understand it were impressed by it. Wheeler may have introduced some of his classical quotations partly for the purpose of increasing the respect of his readers for the learning and high estate of the Merchants.

To build respect and good-will was, as has been said, one of Wheeler's most important objects. The Merchants had already advanced considerably in the public esteem, but the stigma was not entirely removed from trade, even foreign trade on a large scale. It is generally supposed that the merchants held their heads higher under Elizabeth than they did in later days; at any rate, merchants later took a mournful pleasure in contrasting their unhappy situation with that of the Golden Age. Their laments may be discounted somewhat, for at every period trade (like farming) is "not what it used to be," and those engaged in it are always talking about its "decay." Nevertheless, Wheeler does give some evidence to support the reminiscences of his successors. Although his defense suggests that in his time a defense was needed, its tone is not humble. Moreover, he pictures England as a country in which business was a universal pursuit—"All the world choppeth and changeth, runneth and raveth after marts, markets, and merchandise."

The first section of the book, defending the "estate of merchandise," is the most philosophic in the *Treatise*. Wheeler shows himself in some respects ahead of his time, notably in his conception of the scope of business, when he says, "All that a man worketh with his hands or discourseth in his spirit is nothing else but merchandise." Doubtless he would have understood what a modern advertising man meant by "selling the idea." Wheeler mentions the slave-traffic in a tone which connotes disapproval. This traffic, which later became such a blot on the history of England and America, was at this time conducted mainly by Portugal for the benefit of Spain, although Hawkins and a few other English captains were engaged in it. Possibly Wheeler's object in mentioning it is to show that the practices of the Merchants Adventurers, however objectionable they might seem to be, were innocent by comparison with those of some of their contemporaries. It is more likely, however, that he was expressing his sincere conviction. He calls attention to the services of the merchants in politics and exploration and "for the opening of an entry and passage unto unknown and far distant parts." This reference is doubtless to Sebastian Cabot's Company, which was established in 1551 and made several voyages in search of a northeast passage to India. Although unsuccessful in this purpose, they did open up a new sea-route to Russia.

Progressive though Wheeler may have been in some of his views, he was a stand-pat conservative in business. He had absolute faith in established methods and detested innovations. "Innovation" was indeed a term of reproach to most people of his time. Most of them felt that antiquity was the best guarantee of excellence. Hence Wheeler is at some pains to show the great antiquity of the Merchants Adventurers, as well as the esteem in which they have been held by princes and potentates of past centuries. Having established this strong presumption in favor of the Merchants Adventurers, Wheeler is ready to show specifically why "it is most profitable for the Prince and Countrie to use a governed Companie and not to permit a promiscuous, stragling and dispersed trade. . . ." These terms "stragling" and "dispersed" and their synonyms continually recur whenever the author pictures the alternative to the orderly and governed trade of the Merchants Adventurers. His opponents, on the other hand, seem to have used such terms as "free trade" or "open trade"—terms which Wheeler naturally avoids.

His method of argument is that which we might expect from the practical business man. Instead of the economic theories and abstruse reasoning which were spun out at such length by Malynes and Misselden and other pamphleteers later in the seventeenth century, he cites his proof from practical experience and experiments, both by the English merchants and by their rivals, the Dutch and Portuguese. To practically every alternative to the company's methods that was suggested, his answer is substantially the same; namely, that it was tried and did not work. For example, the practice of confining the trade to one or two mart-towns seems inefficient to the modern mind, and so it seemed to many minds then. Wheeler points out that the attempt to carry the goods farther inland worked out badly in practice. Practically the only theories he gives are the homely axioms of merchants, such as the following:

> A Commoditie sought for at the Mart towns is more esteemed by the seeker thereof there than if it were brought home and offered to sell at his own doors; and the merchants proverb is *That there is twenty in the hundred difference between Will you buy? and Will you sell?*

It is easier for him to defend the methods of the Merchants Adventurers than to answer the charge that they were a dangerous monopoly. He is forced to a hair-splitting definition of a monopoly as "Monopoly is when one man alone buyeth up all that is to be got of one kind of merchandise, to the end that he alone may sell at his own lust and pleasure." For the rest his defense is of a sort that would be characterized nowadays as "flag-waving." He argues that the accusation is unworthy of belief because it comes from the enemies of England:

> As for the Monopoly, wherewith the M.M. Adventurers are charged, it is a mere slander, and injurious imputation, maliciously devised by the Hanses, to blear the eyes of the States and Princes of the Empire withall.

Surely any loyal Englishman would think twice before aligning himself with these unfriendly aliens whose object seemed to be, as Wheeler says, "through the side of the Merchants Adventurers to hurt and wound the State of England."

Probably no method of propaganda by private companies has been resorted to more frequently than that of identifying their private interests with the public interests of a nation. The method is still being used to-day and with less excuse than Wheeler had. It was certainly true that the chief charges against the Merchants Adventurers that were matters of public record had come from unfriendly foreign sources. What was more important, these charges had been answered by Queen Elizabeth and her ministers. With such high authority to speak in their defense, the Merchants Adventurers had little need of other arguments. Probably no corporation ever had a better basis for the "patriotism" appeal. Wheeler makes the most of it. Fully one third of the *Treatise* is devoted to the negotiations between the English Crown and the rulers of the Hanseatic Countries. The evidence must have been convincing at that time; in fact there have been few since then to question his assertion that the conflict was really between England and foreign nations.

Wheeler was too wise to introduce anything that might have suggested a lack of harmonious co-operation between the Crown and the Company. Elizabeth, as he pictured her, was a steadfast friend and supporter of the Merchants Adventurers, because their interests were the interests of England, and their enemies were the enemies of England. For the benefit of those who felt no particular animosity toward the Germans, he brings in a more dreadful bogey. Behind the Hanses he shows the sinister figure of Spain with the Papacy and the Inquisition. The part played by Spain in the charges against the Merchants Adventurers was not well established, but in those days Englishmen were ready to smell a Spanish plot in almost anything. As peace had not yet been declared, there was no direct commercial intercourse between the countries, and the Hanseatic merchants were at least profiting by the breach by sending their ships to carry on the interrupted traffic.[5] They were also giving aid and comfort to the enemy. Wheeler may have believed sincerely in the dangers he painted; if he did not, he gives an excellent imitation of sincerity.

Wheeler may have unintentionally cast some doubt upon the Queen's disinterestedness by showing how the Merchants Adventurers were a source of financial profit to her. How-

[5] L. R. Miller, "New Evidence on the Shipping and Imports of London, 1601–1603," *Quart. Journ. Econ.*, XVI, p. 740.

ever, this risk was unimportant compared to the necessity of proving to her that any encouragement of the interlopers would affect her revenues adversely. The "good round sums" that came into her coffers from the customs duties paid by the Merchants Adventurers were certainly one of the chief motives influencing her in their favor. By comparison, the "driblets" from the interlopers were not impressive; moreover, the thought that these straggling merchants evaded the duties in the small out-ports must have sorely tried her.

The strategy of Wheeler shows itself quite as admirably in the things he omits as in the things he includes. As already noted, he omits any hint of Cumberland's license or any other act of the Queen that suggested less than complete support of them. He omits any reference to the licensing system, whereby they were compelled to pay tribute to noble lords. He touches only lightly the fact that there was a group of discontented members within their own organization. Reading between the lines of his closing exhortation, we may see that he was urging the brethren to hold firm a little longer, for the Hanseatic organization was breaking up and they might soon expect to regain their former place in Hamburg and Stade.

Like the modern advertiser, Wheeler avoided, so far as possible, the darker side of his picture. He devoted a page to his colorful description of the Merchants Adventurers at Antwerp in 1549 when they were at the height of their glory. What a dramatic contrast he might have made by picturing the latter scenes of their stay there; for example, in 1576, when the Spanish soldiers were sacking the city. Then four of the members lay dead, and others were badly wounded. The remainder, huddled in the courtyard of their house, had to watch while their grey-haired Governor, Thomas Heton, pale and dishevelled, made obeisance to the conqueror. Their goods were confiscated; they had to redeem them two and three times over. Five thousand pounds was demanded as ransom, and since they could make up only half this sum by their money and plate, they had to remain prisoners while the remainder was brought from England.

But this was a situation to be described by other pens than Wheeler's.[6] It was not a part of his purpose to show that the Merchants Adventurers were subjected to perils and losses and indignities. He preferred to paint an imaginary picture of what would happen if the organization were broken up. In a sentence of unusual length, even for him, he declares that if all were set at liberty as some would have it, "It would in a few years come to pass that we should neither have privilege nor jurisdiction abroad, the friendship and kind usage of our neighbors would wax cold and faint; yea, we should go to the walls, be wronged and exacted upon everywhere, our country commodities would grow vile or come into the hands and managing of strangers, at whose courtesy also, or at least of a few Cormorants of our own Nation we should stand for that we have need of from abroad: by means whereof, the incomes and customs of the Prince would be sore diminished and the Navigation decayed; and lastly if there were occasion either at home of anything of importance to be done on the sudden for the defense of the Realm, the extraordinary help of the M.M. Adventurers would be lacking. . . ." This burst of eloquence may ring a little hollow to our ears. But three hundred and thirty years ago England was a comparatively young and struggling nation, by no means sure of her place in the sun. Wheeler's prophecies did not seem silly to his contemporaries. Those members of Parliament who were sceptical were to have proof of his contentions later when trade with Spain was resumed. In 1606 the English merchants trading there independently were so ill-treated that they had to petition Parliament for redress. Nor was this the only instance. The regulated trading Company was not ideal in principle, but it is questionable whether any other marketing method would have been more satisfactory at this period of England's history.

[6] See *The Spoil of Antwerp*, an anonymous pamphlet of 1576 attributed to George Gascoigne. Reprinted in *Tudor Tracts* 1532–1588, (vol. I in *An English Garner*, 1903). See also *A Larum for London*, a play based on this pamphlet and printed in 1602. It has been somewhat fancifully attributed to Marston and Shakespeare. (R. Simpson, ed., *The School of Shakespeare*, No. 1.)

CHAPTER XI

THE EFFECTS OF THE TREATISE

THE results of campaigns of propaganda and good-will advertising, even at the present time, are not easily weighed and measured. Hence we cannot hope to obtain a definite summary of the effects of Wheeler's piece of publicity more than three centuries ago. Yet a few bits of evidence are available from which we may venture to draw conclusions. We can scarcely doubt that the *Treatise of Commerce* received respectful attention; several of the extant copies have marginal notes, underlinings, and other signs of close study. The comments are not all favorable, but some of them came from avowed opponents of the Merchants Adventurers.

The most important of these annotated copies is in the Bodleian Library (4° Rawl. 261). This copy, one of the London edition, bears on the fly-leaf the signature "Emanuelis Demetrius" and the date, 1601. The same signature is significantly inserted on page 34 (corresponding to page 44 of the Middelburg edition), where Wheeler refers to a "stranger [foreigner] yet living in England" who was instigated by the Spanish Ambassador to summarize the grievances of the Low Country merchants in 1564. A third appearance of this signature is on page 36 (46 in Middelburg edition) where Wheeler mentions "their first and last (perhaps) consul." The copious notes are in another handwriting, presumably that of a secretary or close relative, but were no doubt dictated by Demetrius.

Emanuel Demetrius is one of the Latin forms of the name *Emanuel Van Meteren*, the other Latin form being *Meteranus*. Both forms, *Demetrius* and *Meteranus*, (and also De Meteren) appear in the known publications of Van Meteren. Van Meteren was a Flemish merchant and historian who was born in Antwerp in 1535, spent the great part of his life in London, and died there in 1612. He may have been a spokesman for the Flemish merchants in 1563–64, as Wheeler implies. Certainly he was an important official of their colony in London in the later years of his life. In advocacy of their cause and the cause of general freedom of trade, he published a tract, probably not long before 1601. No copy of this tract is known to exist to-day,[1] but we may safely assume that it contained much the same sort of attack on the Merchants Adventurers that was made by Milles in the *Customer's Apology*. Wheeler mentions Van Meteren by name in connection with Milles (see page 209).

The Flemish merchants, as already suggested, had long since ceased to be formidable rivals of the Merchants Adventurers, and Wheeler gave them scant attention. Possibly the decline of their trade provided Van Meteren with the leisure and the incentive to undertake his *magnum opus*, the *History of the Low Countries*, by which he is chiefly known today. This substantial work had already appeared in three languages before 1601.[2] Wheeler had probably read the Latin version *Historia Belgica*, by E. Meteranus, published about 1598. It contains a few passages that might have offended the Merchants Adventurers, but no specific references to the company by name.

In view of the part Van Meteren is accused of having played in the commercial warfare between England and the Low Countries in 1563–64, it is interesting to examine his own version of this affair. Naturally he mentions some facts that Wheeler conveniently omits. He complains of the cloth customs act of the time of Queen Mary (1557–58) and other discriminatory taxes and imposts by which the Flemish merchants were placed at a great disadvantage in exporting cloth and practically the whole of their trade was transferred to

[1] *Nouvelle Biographie Generale*, Paris 1861: biography of E. Van Meteren in vol. 35, p. 206.

[2] First edition in German 1593, two complete editions in German, 1596, Latin version, 1598, Flemish version, 1599. Van Meteren continued his work up to 1611, with four or five editions between 1605 and 1611; a final revised edition was published at Dordrecht in 1614, two years after the author's death. (From an article by Leonard Willems in *Biographie Nationale de Belgique*, 1897, vol. 14, pp. 615–620.)

English hands. The Flemish merchants bore this patiently for a time but at length in 1563 their grievances moved the Duchess of Parma to send an ambassador to England to secure relief; but in vain. On the contrary, the English Parliament prohibited the importation of many articles of Flemish manufacture, such as pins, knives, girdles, harness, gloves, and lace.[3] These fresh injuries to Flemish industry and trade led the Duchess first to prohibit the export of certain raw materials to England, and later to issue her proclamation prohibiting the importation of English cloth into Flanders. This embargo was ostensibly due to the prevalence of the plague in London, but it was generally understood that this was a pretext, and even Van Meteren does not put it forward as a basic cause. Other passages in the *Historia Belgica* might be cited to show that Van Meteren was hostile to the selfish policies of English trade and industry as exemplified by the Merchants Adventurers. On the other hand, he could not justly be accused of undue friendliness to Spain. The important point is that as a critic of Wheeler's *Treatise* he was by no means unbiassed. And, although he was not a good historian, he was much more familiar than Wheeler with the facts about the Low Countries, particularly Antwerp. We should probably be safe in accepting most of his corrections and emendations that relate to matters of fact.

Unfortunately these marginal notes in the Bodleian copy are difficult to decipher and understand. (A few of them are quoted in the textual footnotes later.) It is at least clear that

[3] "Praeterea vectigal cuiusque panni ex Anglia evehendi à mercatore extraneo, auxerant, ut mimimum Angeloti pretio; idque cum tanta vectigalium atque portoriorum inaequalitate, ut Anglia quibusdam vectigalibus liberi, quidam media tantum parte pendentes, Antwerpiae pannum Anglicanum sex florenis minoris quam Belgae, vendere potuerint. Ita pannorum negotiatio astutè mercatoribus Belgis subtracta, prorsus in Anglorum manus translata est. Et haec quidem certo temporis spatio tolerarunt Belgae, donec mercatorum crebris mota querelis Gubernatrix Parmensis Ducissa, anno 1563, Consiliarium Christophorum Assonuilium in Angliam has plurisque alias controversias & difficultates componendi causa, mittit; sed incassum: Quin contra, id fere temporis (Anglorum amplioris questus gratia) Anglicani Parlamenti statuto pleraque opeficum opera Belgica, nempe aciculae, cultri, fasciae, teniae, cingula, pluraque; id genus alia; ex Anglia fuere eliminata." (From *Historia Belgica* by E. Meteranus, 1598, Book II, p. 39.) See also Adam Anderson, *Origin of Commerce*, edition of 1801, vol. II, p. 120. Anderson, like Wheeler, alleges that Spain instigated the Duchess of Parma to declare the embargo on English cloth.

nearly all of them are adverse. Wheeler's assertions regarding persons and places in the Low Countries as well as the political and commercial relations of those countries with England are challenged again and again, sometimes with specific contradictions and sometimes with the bald "a lye." Van Meteren declares that Antwerp and Bruges were important commercial centers before the English came; that the good Duke Philip was never in England; that the Merchants Adventurers were not responsible for keeping the Inquisition out of Antwerp; that the merchants of other nations did not follow the English to Middelburg; and so on. Occasionally he indulges in even harsher accusations against the English, such as dishonesty and piracy. Without doubt, Wheeler was grossly inaccurate in his statements regarding Antwerp, Bruges, and Middelburg, and greatly exaggerated the influence of the Merchants Adventurers upon the life and prosperity of these cities.

It seems likely that Van Meteren contemplated the publication of another pamphlet refuting Wheeler's *Treatise*, and again attacking the Merchants Adventurers as a selfish monopolistic organization. If this were his intention, he abandoned it, either because he realized its futility or because he saw that it would only strengthen Wheeler's contention that the chief opposition to the Merchants Adventurers came from unfriendly foreign sources. Perhaps he introduced some severe criticism of Wheeler and his company into one or more of the versions of his history published in the Low Countries in the latter years of his life, but they do not appear in the final edition of 1614. Apparently the only direct reference to Wheeler this contains is a statement of the size and importance of the Company of Merchants Adventurers for which Wheeler's *Treatise* is cited as the authority.[4] This final edition, however, had been revised by a committee which included the learned Grotius, and any passages in which Van

[4] Emanuel De Meteren, *Historie der Nederland*, Dordrecht (1614) p. 394. (I have given this version only a hasty examination and it may be that some indirect or veiled references to Wheeler's *Treatise* have escaped me. I have not had access to any of the editions that appeared between 1605 and 1611.)

Meteren aired his grievances against the Merchants Adventurers would naturally have been eliminated.

If Van Meteren continued to oppose the Merchants Adventurers, he must have confined his publicity to his native country and his own language. In England he remained silent. Thomas Milles was not so discreet. In 1604 he renewed the attack he had begun in the *Customer's Apology* by bringing out another pamphlet with the following title-page: "The Customer's Replie/or/Second Apologie/that is to say,/An Answer to a Confused/Treatise of Publicke Commerce/printed and dispersed at Midlebourghe/and London, in favour of the private society/of Merchants-Adventurers/By a more serious Discourse/of Exchange in Mer-/chandise and Merchandising/Exchange/Written for understanding Readers/onely, in favour of all loyall/Merchants and for the advancing of traffick in England/At London/Printed by James Roberts, dwelling in/Barbican 1604/."

The Epistle dedicatory, addressed to Lord Buckhurst, Lord High Treasurer of England, Lord Henry Howard, warden of the Cinq-Ports, and Lord Cecil, Principal Secretary to the King's Majesty, consists of eight pages criticising Wheeler's *Treatise*. The following extract will serve as a fair example of the author's controversial talent and of his prose style—neither of which entitles him to very high rank as pamphleteer:

Right Honorable: Such hath been of late yeeres the successe of a like learned writer, who printing, a Treatise of public Commerce, in favour of the private Societie of the Merchants Adventurers, hath with much a-doe, and a heap of sillie words, (farre unfitting the gravitie of his Theame) endeavoured to persuade his Reader, that Trafficke rightly ordered, is the honor of Kings, and prosperitie of Kingdoms; And that Merchants in that respect were to be cherished, favoured, and encouraged in all Commonwealths. Quia Vita Civilis in Societate Posita Est, Societas Autem in Imperio Et Commercio.

It is strange to observe what strong apprehentions are able to worke in weake men's braines. For as a plaine simple man was sometimes persuaded, that if Pontius Pilate had not beene a Saint, the Apostles would never have suffered his Name to stande in the Creede: so this Treatise-Writer, by a strong imagination of the Merchant-Adventurers extraordinary deserts: seeing the admirable effects of the golden blessings of England, by turning Creekes into Ports, joining Ports into Townes, raysing

Townes into Cities, and enriching whole Countries with artificers and Trades, Marriners and Shipping, Applauding withall, their singular happines, and great good fortunes, to have the managing thereof within themselves. Commending their* dexterities in disposing diverting, dividing, mincing, abridging, restraining, and lastly confining the Store and Staple thereof within the walls of some one or two Townes for best Advantage in †Forraine-Countries culloured with the Title of their special Mart-Townes. And above all things extolling their excellent wits and absolute cunnings in moulding Laws by meere Discretion, to hold all men under, and themselves above.

(* The MMA boast themselves, to be able to make and divert a Trade at their pleasures, Page 25)

(† Marke this well by the way, for heerein lyes hid, the Pot of Roses)

Onely for sending or sayling crosse the Seas from Coast to Coast, without hazard of their Persons, or losse of their goods more than usuabl & ordinary. And for wearing‡ Chaines of gold about their Necks, Caps and greene Feathers, Hats and white Feathers, Buskins of purple Velvet, guilt Rapiers, Daggers, Bridles, Stirrops, Spurres, and such like, at Triumphs and publique meetings. But specially for feeding, maintayning, and setting§ thousands on worke beyond Seas, when God knowes the wants & heares the cryes at home: would faine persuade others (being bound to admire them himselfe,) That his Governors is for Skill the ||PILOT, for Gravitie the Judge, and for Wisedome the Oracle of all orderly Commerce. Their private¶ Decrees, above Common Lawes, and Forraine-Treatise. Theyr particular **synodes, above Generall Counsailes, and their ††Society a Communion of Saints. Pronouncing all that dislike, distaste, or distrust their Doctrine, for En Ter-LoPers. That is to say ‡‡Schismatics, Hereticks, and Infidels, unwoorthy to breathe Common-ayre or live in any Commonwealth. Concluding strongly withall, That these Men thus put in trust with the credite and Creame of the Kingdome, (our Cloth) must needes bee holden more loyall to their Prince, more serviceable to the State, more welcome to their Neighboars, and therefore more to be honoured, than any other Men, with a Name above all Names, of *Merchants-Adventurers*. With this and such like stuffe the Booke being confusedly fraught, (curius contrarium veresimum est,) might well have been suffered to have dyed in the birth, if withall it had not been mingled with assertions of obloquy & untruthes against Customers of the Out-Ports of the Realms.

(‡ Page, 154, 155, 156)

(§ At Antwerpe 20,000 about Anwerpe 30,000 In Flaunders, 60,000 page, 24)

(|| Pontius)

(¶ Talmud)

(** Synhedry)

(†† Synogogue)

(‡‡ All English Christian, and loyal Merchants, Crucifige)

The most significant fact is that three years had elapsed before this "reply" to the *Treatise of Commerce* was published. Why did Milles delay until 1604? Perhaps his former unlicensed pamphlet had so displeased the Queen and her ministers that he could not get authority to publish the new one. Some slight hint of this possibility is contained in the entry in the Stationers Register for 1604 which includes the condition, "if thought fit to be published." All that it proves, however, is that the necessary authorization had not yet been obtained.

A more probable explanation is that he did not consider the time ripe until King James was on the throne and the Merchants Adventurers were again being subjected to adverse criticism. Popular feeling against them had apparently subsided for a time; the *Treatise* may have had something to do with this. At any rate, Wheeler's book had not "died in the birth"—to quote Milles. He would have had little reason for attacking it in 1604 if it had not made a considerable impression—and a favorable impression—in 1601. And if any other adverse criticisms had been circulated in the meantime, Milles would certainly have used them to reinforce his own.

Milles' *Replie* may therefore be accepted as evidence that the *Treatise of Commerce* was well received. So may John Stow's reference to it in the *Annales* (see page 44), for Stow was no friend of the Company. What is more important, its chief objects were accomplished, one by one. It was in the hands of members of Parliament before the meeting in October. The Journal of the House of Commons for this year has, unfortunately, not been preserved. However, Heyward Townshend, a member, wrote a fairly complete account of the famous debate on the monopolies,[5] which was ended only when Queen Elizabeth graciously yielded to the desires of her people and promised to remedy the evil.

During the bitter debate, scores of commodities were named in which some nobleman enjoyed a personal monopoly: salt, starch, oil of blubber, vinegar, tin, even tobacco-

[5] Heyward Townshend, *Historical Collections*, pp. 230 ff.

pipes, which were mentioned somewhat jestingly. But the records fail to show that a single word was said against the Merchants Adventurers, and it appears that by common consent the monopolies of trading companies were excepted from censure. Whether Wheeler's *Treatise* was responsible for this separation between private monopolies and company monopolies is not certain, but at any rate the distinction was made. Perhaps this distinction may have been influential in helping to bring the Earl of Cumberland to terms. Perhaps the more favorable public attitude toward the Company may also have impressed him. As mentioned earlier, he did yield to them in 1602, and not long afterwards the trade of the interlopers in Germany was ended. Thus the Merchants Adventurers regained the position they had enjoyed at the beginning of 1601.

Then too, Wheeler received honors and financial rewards. At least one of the provincial fellowships, that of Newcastle, voted him a bonus of ten pounds for his "travell [travail?] and furtherance heretofore extended towards this Companie in the causes of the same."[6] As this was in April, 1602, the service indicated was probably the *Treatise*. However the entry shows that the Newcastle representatives, when paying Wheeler the ten pounds, were to solicit some additional favors. These they probably obtained, for the laws and ordinances codified in 1608 show some special clauses affecting the Newcastle fellowship. Wheeler was also mentioned prominently for an important diplomatic post. In 1603 he was elected a member of Parliament as one of the burgesses of the port of Great Yarmouth.

His presence in Parliament may possibly explain why he did not issue another defense in 1604, when the Merchants Adventurers faced another crisis. At this time, a bill was presented to open English trade to all free-born Englishmen. This bill was, of course, aimed primarily at the monopolies of the trading companies and, as the Merchants Adventurers was the largest of these, it bore the brunt of the attack. This

[6] J. R. Boyle and F. W. Dendy, eds., *Extracts from the Records of the Merchants Adventurers of Newcastle-upon-Tyne.* (Surtees Society) vol. 1, p. 112.

bill was considered by a committee of the House of Commons headed by Sir Edwin Sandys. As a burgess from an outport, Wheeler must have been a member of this committee, and could accomplish all that was possible by personal contact. After protracted hearings of the cloth workers, the merchants themselves, and other interested parties, the committee reported favorably on the Bill.

The report of the committee which purports to give both sides of the question forms a very interesting document.[7] As W. R. Scott says, it is a temptation to regard it as a unique example of a noble ideal which appeared almost too early. But he conjectures that Sandys was simply playing the usual politicians' game of condemning a company until he had gained admission, and then making its monopoly more rigid. When Sandys a few years later became Treasurer of the exclusive Virginia Company, he acted in the matter of the tobacco monopoly "exactly in the manner he condemns in the Governors of the company existing in 1604."[8] We may also be justified in doubting the accuracy of his report of the hearings. In the later case of the tobacco companies, the copy of the minutes shows Sandys' arguments at length and only brief summaries of the opposing arguments. This may have been his strategy in the House of Commons report of 1604.

Though the bill abolishing the trading monopolies was passed by the House of Commons, it was side-tracked in the House of Lords and never became effective. Lord Coke pompously declared that its purposes were good but the method of accomplishing them was not. It is possible that the Merchants Adventurers may have resorted to bribery on this occasion as they certainly did later in the reign of King James. At any rate, they weathered the storm.

That the Merchants Adventurers were popularly believed to have used a bribe of thirty thousand pounds in maintaining their monopoly seems to be implied by a passage in *Mi-*

[7] Reprinted in Bland, Blaine and Tawney, *English Economic History, Select Documents*, p. 443 ff.

[8] W. R. Scott, *Joint Stock Companies*, vol. I, p. 121.

chaelmas Term by Thomas Middleton. This play was published in 1607, but probably had been produced on the stage in 1604 or 1605. The satirical reference to the Merchants Adventurers is one of the very few that occur in Elizabethan drama, although their prominence and their unpopularity must have made them an inviting target. Middleton was more familiar with business affairs than most of his fellow-dramatists, and may also have been somewhat bolder.

The passage in question occurs during the scene in which Quomodo, a woollen-draper, assisted by his apprentice, Shortyard, is attempting to defraud Master Easy of his estate. Their plot is to induce Easy to become bondsman for a loan which Shortyard, disguised as another gentleman, is obtaining from Quomodo. Quomodo protests that he cannot supply the loan in cash and invites them to take two hundred pounds' worth of cloth instead, saying:

> There's no merchant in town but will be greedy upon it, and pay down money upo' the nail; they'll despatch it over to Middleburgh presently, and raise double commodity by exchange. . . .[9]

This method of obtaining loans was by no means uncommon, and after some parley the offer is accepted by Easy and Shortyard. Thereupon Quomodo inquires where they wish the cloth carried:

> Shortyard: Faith, to master Beggarland, he's the only merchant now; or his brother, master Stilliard-down; there's little difference.
>
> Quomodo: You've happened upon the money-men, sir; they and some of their brethren, I can tell you, will not stick to offer thirty thousand pound to be cursed still; great monied men, their stocks lie in the poor's throats.[10]

The "label-names" *Beggarland* and *Stilliard-down* may have no more than their obvious significance, but it seems likely that the latter symbolizes the well-known policy of the Merchants Adventurers, (shown by their acts and by the *Treatise of Commerce*) of keeping the Steelyard merchants out of the trade. It may be too fanciful to see in *Beggarland* a mask for *Cumberland; Eastland* is possibly a safer conjec-

[9] Thomas Middleton, *Michaelmas Term*, Act. II, Sc. III, ll. 212–215.

[10] *Ibid.*, ll. 255–260.

ture. At any rate, Middleton clearly implies that a closely allied group of merchants control the export of cloth, and maintain their monopoly by heavy bribes. The accusations, however, lose something of their force by coming from the mouths of the two arch-rogues in the play.

Later it appears that the cloth can only be sold at a ruinous loss, for the servant reports:

> The passage to Middleburgh is stopped, and therefore neither master Stilliard-down nor master Beggarland, nor any other merchant, will deliver present money upon 't.[11]

The assertion was a lie, of course, but was made plausible by the fact that there had been occasions when the presence of the Spanish men-of-war in the Channel temporarily prevented the sailing of the cloth-fleet to Middelburg. Now, however, peace had been made with Spain, and interruptions of this sort had ceased.

The Hanseatics had not yet given up all hope of returning to their old home in the Steelyard and about this same time (1604–05) they sent representatives to England to plead their cause to the King. But if they expected James to be more pliable than Elizabeth had been, they were disappointed. He was already on the payroll of the Merchants Adventurers, and gave the Germans so cold a reception that they must have become convinced that their former privileges would never be restored.

Some of the cities, notably Stade and Hamburg, were already chafing against the iron discipline of the League—or rather of Lübeck—that prevented them from making a trading contract with the Merchants Adventurers. Both of these cities were profiting from the visits of the interlopers, but this business was scattered and uncertain. Both remembered the prosperity that they had enjoyed as the mart-town of the Merchants Adventurers and longed to see that prosperity return. They had waited patiently for nearly ten years in the hope that the League might win its way back into England, but now that it was certain that this could not be done, they

[11] *Ibid.*, ll. 407–410.

saw no good reason for self-denial. The Merchants Adventurers continually dangled before them the rich prize of being designated the sole channel of trade into Germany, and they could not resist it.

Stade was first to come to terms (in 1607), but this city was only second choice with the Merchants Adventurers, and they had no hesitancy in jilting her when Hamburg became receptive to their proposals. In 1611, the Senate of Hamburg granted the Merchants Adventurers an ample charter of privileges, with the consent of the Emperor, but not of the Hanseatic League. This marked the formal resumption of trade relations with Hamburg although actually these relations had begun some time before.

Thus the long commercial warfare ended in a complete victory for the Merchants Adventurers. They now had an undisputed cloth-export monopoly for Germany and Holland and this monopoly was made more rigid and was more closely guarded against interlopers as time went by. John Wheeler died in 1610 or 1611, but not before he had seen a satisfactory outcome of his labors. Practically every object of his *Treatise* had been accomplished, and the Merchants Adventurers seemed to be more firmly entrenched than ever before in their history. He might well have been justified in believing that they could look forward to a long career of even greater power and prosperity.

CHAPTER XII

LATER HISTORY OF THE MERCHANTS ADVENTURERS

THE last important service John Wheeler rendered to the Merchants Adventurers was the compilation in 1608 of their laws and ordinances. The compilation was carefully transcribed on vellum and bound in a massive volume in 1611–12. Perhaps the reason for this costly transcription was the fact that the headquarters of the Company were being removed to Hamburg; however, we are justified in believing that it was a sort of memorial to Wheeler, who had recently died. At any rate, the time was ripe for crystallizing the "good orders" of the regulated company, which seemed to have been fully vindicated and in a fair way to be the permanent form of organization for foreign marketing.

At the moment, the prosperity of the Merchants Adventurers was at its peak. Their ancient enemies had all been subdued, their monopoly was fully protected, and they were back in the mart-town they preferred. But their period of prosperity was brief. New enemies at home were already plotting their overthrow, and within a few years they were again embroiled in a struggle that nearly ruined them and started them on a long decline from which they never completely recovered. The crisis was doubtless unexpected; certainly it was not foreseen by Wheeler in 1601. If he had been alive in the period from 1613 to 1615, he might have helped them to avert the calamity, but this is most unlikely. However, the one man who could and probably would have averted it had also died in 1612. This was Secretary Robert Cecil, Earl of Salisbury, who had been the wise and trusted counsellor of the King. The Merchants Adventurers, great and powerful though they were, depended on royal favor for their protection. This they could safely do, so long as Cecil was alive, for he was a good business man himself as well as a good friend of the Company. After his death they were at the mercy of the vain egotist who was called "the wisest fool in Christendom."

Cecil's hand is plainly to be seen in the conduct of King James toward the Merchants Adventurers during the early part of his reign, from 1603 to 1612. He never interfered with them but accorded them every support. After Cecil's death, the King was surrounded mainly by weak, venal men who were poorly qualified to restrain his folly, and who were mainly interested in their own advancement. And so he was able to put into execution the fatal project of exporting only dyed and dressed cloth instead of the "white cloth" that constituted the bulk of the trade to Holland and Germany. It is estimated that at this period about 80,000 white cloths were exported annually, as compared with 60,000 mentioned in Wheeler's *Treatise*.[1]

The project of exporting only dyed cloth is known as "Cockayne's Project," because Alderman William Cockayne persuaded James to adopt it. The idea, however, had been advanced many times before. The very fact that a statute prohibited the export of white cloths and that these were exported only under royal license suggests that some attempts had been made before to build up the dye industry in England. A gradual pressure in that direction is also indicated by the clause in private licenses to the effect that one cloth in ten should be dressed and dyed. This clause, however, had been omitted from Cumberland's license. Theoretically there was no reason why all the cloths should not be dyed and dressed before being exported, and the theorists were continually advocating this policy.

It is noteworthy that Wheeler's *Treatise* omits any reference to this dyed-cloth project. Even in his time, one complaint against the Merchants Adventurers was that by exporting white cloths they gave employment to workmen in foreign countries instead of giving the whole benefit to home

[1] *The Rise & State of the Fellowship of Merchants Adventurers of England* (Stowe MSS. 303 f. 99); also contemporary estimates presented to the Privy Council.

industry. Wheeler in fact boasts that 20,000 or more persons were given employment at Antwerp when the Merchants were there, and Milles is quick to seize upon this point as an argument against their methods. Reading between the lines, we may see one reason why the export of dyed cloth was impracticable. The welcome of the English merchants in the mart-town depended partly on the fact that they contributed greatly to the town's industries.

It is probable that in 1601 the dyed-cloth project was not being violently agitated. It was one of those things that kept bobbing up periodically. As far back as 1553, a lengthy petition had been addressed to Edward VI by William Cholmeley a dyer. His *Request and Suite of a True Hearted Englishman*[2] argued that England could dye cloth as well as her neighbors across the seas (by importing dyers from Flanders to do the work) and that great benefits would result. Cholmeley estimated a gain to the kingdom of 20s. on each cloth and declared that this would be a boon to the English workingman. He appealed to the boy king to adopt his plan as an act of charity, for: "If it be charitie to sucker a thousande, it is greater charitie to sucker many thousands."

Similar arguments were presented about 1605 by Sir Walter Raleigh in his *Observations, touching on trade and commerce with Holland and other nations.*[3] These "Observations" formed a private memorandum to King James; and, although James did not act upon them at the time, it is probable that he was touched by Raleigh's flattery as well as by the delicate suggestion that his own treasury would benefit. Raleigh estimated that some £25,000,000 had been lost to the kingdom within the past half century through permitting the export of undyed cloth, which was especially lamentable "considering that God hath . . . given your Majesty power to advance dressing and dyeing." Raleigh's estimates were absurd and his arguments flimsy, as Cecil was doubtless frank enough to tell the King. But soon after Cecil's death, James began to

[2] Reprinted in *Camden Miscellany*, 1853, also in Tawney and Power, *Tudor Economic Documents*, vol. III, p. 130 ff.

[3] Sir Walter Raleigh, *Observations touching Trade and Commerce* (1653).

consider this dyed-cloth project seriously. It had been advocated by other sources, notably by the artisan members of the London Company of Cloth Workers, who joined the Dyers Company in addressing a petition to the King.[4] The strongest and most persuasive advocate was William Cockayne, an Alderman of London, who was a leading member of the Eastland Company.

Miss Astrid Friis, in her brilliant study, *Alderman Cockayne's Project and the Cloth Trade*,[5] puts forth a plausible explanation for Cockayne's action. She sees it as the outcome of jealousy on the part of the Eastland Company and an attempt to break down the Merchants Adventurers' organization, rather than a *bona fide* attempt to export dyed cloth. Certainly this explanation has ample precedent in the history of guilds of the period. The Eastland Company did not have the privilege of exporting white cloth to their Baltic territory. They complained that the white cloth exported by the Merchants Adventurers to Holland and Germany was dyed and dressed there and that then a large part of it went on into Eastland territory, thus constituting unfair competition; the more unfair in that the Dutch stretched the cloth unduly. They had tried to get a part of Cumberland's license to export white cloths, but had failed. They had also failed in their attempt to force bills through Parliament restraining the export of white cloth by the Merchants Adventurers.

By 1613, Cockayne had succeeded in winning James over to the project. Not only did it seem to promise increased revenue for the Crown, but it contemplated a benefit to the Kingdom by transplanting the great dyeing industry of Holland. No one seems to have worried about the ethical or economic aspects of such a transfer; the only question was regarding its feasibility. The Merchants Adventurers knew it was not feasible. Cockayne must have known it also. Yet he assured the King that if the Merchants Adventurers would

[4] George Unwin, *Industrial Organization in the 16th and 17th Centuries*, p. 124.

[5] Miss Friis gives a comprehensive survey of the Project, and contributes materially to our knowledge of the Merchants Adventurers. She appears to have overlooked Raleigh's *Observations* although Anderson believed that Cockayne got his idea from Raleigh. See A. Anderson, *Origin of Commerce*, (1801 ed.), vol. II, p. 220.

not carry out the dyed-cloth project, others could be found who would.[6]

With this threat of annulling their privileges and replacing them with a new company, the King exerted pressure on the Merchants Adventurers to adopt the plan. Nevertheless, they stood firm in their refusal. Subscription books for the new company were opened and soon Cockayne could show (on paper) a most imposing total of capital resources. Meanwhile the Merchants Adventurers were vainly pleading their case before the Privy Council and in Parliament. Their representatives were able speakers and they had cogent arguments. The one argument that Holland and Germany would not take the English-dyed cloth was indeed sufficient, but they had others. They also detected the insincerity of Cockayne and his friends in the Eastland Company.

Parliament did not render a decision in the matter, and when Parliament was dismissed in 1614, the King had a free hand. The Cockayne group secured the favor of some members of the Privy Council by bribery, and the others were not strong enough to stand out against the project. Steps were taken toward the revocation of the Merchants Adventurers' charter—Lord Coke's legal mind was able to find technical grounds for this—and the new company began operations. The old Merchants Adventurers were invited to join but few of them cared to do so. The Eastland merchants became the dominating element in it and Cockayne became their Governor.[7] This company was usually called simply "the new company," much to their displeasure, for their official title was "Governor, Assistants and Fellowship of the King's Merchants Adventurers of the New Trade of London." Their charter, which they received in February 1615, was drafted by Sir Francis Bacon, and the preamble sets forth the King's "constant resolution" that "the reducing of the trade of white cloths which is but an imperfect thing toward the wealth and good of this our Kingdom unto the trade of cloths dressed and dyed might be the work of our time." Thus he

[6] Friis, *Alderman Cockayne's Project and the Cloth Trade*, p. 243.

[7] Friis, p. 281–83.

proposed to be an even greater benefactor than Edward III had been. From the beginning, however, the company made very little of the export of dyed cloth. It was a part of Cockayne's strategy that they should be permitted to export the white cloth as usual until affairs were running smoothly. Very likely he hoped that King James would abandon the dyed-cloth idea, but leave the new company securely entrenched in place of the old Merchants Adventurers. On this point, however, the King was stubborn. He had declared in writing that the export of dyed cloth was his purpose, and his pride would not permit him to abandon it.

In June, 1616, after the company had been in operation for a year, Cockayne gave a great banquet to King James, celebrating the "success" of the King's venture into business. Ben Jonson wrote an entertainment for the occasion. The King was presented with a bowl full of gold pieces. Cockayne was knighted.[8] The King may have believed for a moment that he had laid the foundation for a new English industry and contributed to the prosperity of the country. Actually at that moment the cloth industry was in a terrible state of depression. The whole cloth exports for the year showed a decline of nearly 40%—and only a small proportion of the cloths were dyed.[9] The Hollanders had refused to take the dyed cloth, and, angered by the attempt to force it upon them, they had started to build up their own weaving industry by offering bonuses for each new loom. Efforts to shut off the supply of raw wool from them had not been successful. The complaints of the cloth industry were increasing in bitterness. There was nothing to do but admit the failure and ask the old Merchants Adventurers to return to the trade. The new Company was dissolved, and the old one re-established at the beginning of 1617.

Ben Jonson's share in Cockayne's banquet should not be taken as evidence that he was in sympathy with that gentleman or his dyed-cloth project. Indeed there is ground for believing that Jonson bit the hand that fed him. Only a few

[8] *State Papers Dom. James I*, vol. 87, pp. 51, 57, 67. See also *Progresses of James I* by John Nichols, vol. III, p. 174.

[9] Friis, pp. 303–4.

months later he wrote *The Devil is an Ass*, which satirized, among other things, the schemes of "projectors" and the system of monopoly patents.

According to Kittredge, this play must have been performed in the latter part of October, 1616.[10] At this time the collapse of Cockayne's project was generally known and was an absorbing topic of conversation. Hardly a ship-load of cloth had gone to Middelburg since July. Under these conditions, many of the audience must have seen in "the great projector," Meercraft, a caricature of Cockayne, and in his great project "for the recovery of drown'd land" a symbolic representation of his attempt to wrest the dyeing industry from the Low Countries. Those whose friends had invested in the enterprise might well find a hidden meaning in such a passage as the following:

Meercraft:

> We'll take in citizens, Commoners, and Aldermen
> To bear the charge, and blow them off again,
> Like so many dead flies, when 'tis carried.
> The thing is for recovery of drown'd land,
> Whereof the Crowne's to have a moiety,
> If it be owner; else, the Crowne and owners
> To share that moiety, and the recoverers
> To enjoy the tother moiety, for their charge.[11]

Jonson's attack, of course, may have been aimed chiefly at the schemes for draining the Lincolnshire and Cambridgeshire fens. Editors have generally been content to accept this obvious explanation.[12] But there is no evidence that these schemes were the subject of active interest in London in 1616. If Cockayne's Project was thought by the public to be the object of Jonson's satire, we can readily understand why King James was displeased and why he asked Jonson to "conceal" the play (as Drummond reports he did). We can also understand why contemporary history and literature contain so few obvious references to this dyed-cloth project.

[10] G. L. Kittredge, "King James I and *The Devil is an Ass*," *Modern Philology*, vol. IX, No. 2, October, 1911.

[11] Ben Jonson, *The Devil is an Ass*, Act II, Sc. I.

[12] See W. S. Johnson, ed., *The Devil is an Ass*, Introduction, pp. lix, lx.

One publisher, however, considered this a suitable time for printing a play that had been in his hands for at least fifteen years. The play was *Englishmen for My Money, or A Woman Will have her Will*, written in 1598 by William Haughton, and produced in that year by Henslowe. Though of little intrinsic merit, it is significant because it was possibly the earliest of the so-called "comedies of London manners," and because it appealed to the same anti-foreign sentiment that Wheeler appealed to in the *Treatise of Commerce*. Doubtless it owed its inspiration to the circumstances surrounding the closing of the Steelyard. The Stationers Register shows its entry for publication by William White on August 3, 1601, just a few days before the entry of *A Treatise of Commerce*, but apparently it was withheld at this time, for no copies of earlier date than 1616 have come to light.

The play can hardly be classed as propaganda; it was merely a timely satire on foreign merchants in London. Three of these merchants—a Frenchman, an Italian, and a Dutchman—are represented as suitors for the hands of three sisters. They are favored by the girls' father, himself a London merchant of Portuguese birth, but the girls are determined to marry their English lovers. Of course they have their way, and in the process the foreigners—particularly the Dutchman—are made the butts of ridicule.

We cannot be sure that the play published in 1616 is exactly the same as that produced in 1598. Some authorities on Elizabethan drama have found reasons for believing it was revised. A slight corroborative hint appears in the fact that the minor but dignified character of an English merchant bears the name Towerson. Towerson was actually the name of a leading English merchant in 1616; in fact, he was a Deputy Governor of the old Merchants Adventurers and their leader in the fight against Cockayne. He could not have been very prominent in 1598 or 1601.

At the time the play was written, a German merchant would have been the logical target for satire, but of course a Hanseatic could not have been represented plausibly as attempting to marry an Englishwoman. Very likely the author considered a Dutchman a satisfactory substitute; his audience saw no great difference between the Germans and the Dutch, and called them all Dutch.[13] However, a few persons who were well informed regarding politics and commerce might consider the distinction vital. If the original version of the play burlesqued the Dutch, this alone may have been sufficient to cause a postponement of publication. It may well have seemed inadvisable in 1601 to risk offending the few friends that England still retained on the Continent, especially the few who were also good customers.

By 1616, the situation had changed. The Dutch had definitely supplanted the Germans as the most formidable commercial rivals of the English. The Cockayne fiasco had caused a breach in their friendly relations that promised to become wider as time went by. The moment was opportune for publishing *Englishmen for My Money*. It was evidently a popular success, for it was twice reprinted in later years. But if its publisher profited by the dyed-cloth experiment, he was among the very few who did. Business in general and the cloth trade in particular suffered a severe depression.

Although the return of the old Merchants Adventurers helped matters somewhat, it was impossible to revive the trade completely. Some of the members of the Company had retired; others had lost contact with the foreign market. Jealousies and animosities had been aroused that could not be completely allayed, and of course the new Dutch looms continued to operate. James had proved himself a failure as a business man. His own losses from Cockayne's project were partly offset by the twenty or thirty thousand pounds he exacted from the Merchants Adventurers for restoring their charter,[14] but the cloth industry of England had suffered a setback from which it was slow to recover, and the economic effects of which were wide-spread.

During the reign of James I, the Merchants Adventurers had a second narrow escape. After 1620 England suffered an-

[13] See also the translation of *The Emperor's Mandate*, *infra*, pp. 403–414.

[14] The price James had asked was fifty thousand pounds, and at one time the old Merchants Adventurers were willing to pay this, but the best testimony (Parker, *Of a Free Trade*) indicates that the actual amount paid was twenty or thirty thousand pounds.

other severe depression, accompanied by an alarming scarcity of coin. A special commission, in which Sir John Suckling was a leading member, found a variety of causes responsible for this. So far as the cloth trade was concerned, the decay was partly attributable to Cockayne's fatal experiment, and partly to the restricted market in Germany due to the Thirty Years' War. Again the proposal to open the trade was agitated in Parliament by various interests, including the Staplers, the interlopers, and the former adherents of Cockayne. The Merchants Adventurers were compelled to make easier terms for the admission of other merchants, and they were allowed only the trade in white cloth as an exclusive monopoly. They were also threatened with complete extinction by the Statute of Monopolies in 1623, but a special clause excepted the trading companies from the operation of this act. According to later chronicles of the Company, no benefits resulted from the freeing of the trade to the Netherlands and Germany,[15] but it was not until 1634 that the Company was restored to all its old privileges.[16]

During this trying period the Merchants Adventurers resorted to bribery to accomplish their purposes. The policy was not very successful, but perhaps it saved them from worse difficulties than those they experienced. At any rate it was necessary; the evil of bribery was so wide-spread that few men in high places remained untainted. Occasionally there was a wave of reform, like that which wrecked the career of Francis Bacon, the Lord Chancellor, in 1621. Hard times demand a sacrifice to propitiate the gods, and Bacon was a convenient victim. The charges against him were being investigated at the very time another committee was investigating the monopolies. Bacon confessed that he had received bribes and was punished by a heavy fine and by banishment beyond the verge of the Court (so that the King might not have to gaze upon his disgraced countenance again).

But Buckingham and other favorites remained in their places and continued their sorry business as usual. The censure of Bacon did not abate the evil of bribery or lessen the

[15] Stow MSS. 303, f. 99.

[16] Friis, p. 431.

amounts of tribute the Merchants Adventurers had to pay annually to the Lord Treasurer, the Archbishop of Canterbury, and other exalted personages. They also had to submit to the regular mulcting process involved in buying up licenses. As the royalty they paid increased, along with their taxes, customs duties, and gifts, the overhead charges on each piece of cloth became increasingly burdensome and tended to restrict what was already a declining trade.

So long as trade was growing, the Merchants Adventurers could submit with a reasonably good grace to the royal exactions. Under the Stuarts, however, the cloth export-trade continued to be poor. Charles I was insatiable in his demands for loans and as tactless and arbitrary in dealing with the Merchants as with others. On one occasion he ordered them to appoint as deputy at Delft, one Edward Misselden, who was not acceptable to them. Just why Misselden was unsatisfactory is not entirely clear. Like Wheeler, he had shown himself a champion of their interests by publishing a pamphlet entitled *The Circle of Commerce*. Perhaps Misselden's offence was merely in being the King's favorite; perhaps his religious zeal in support of Archbishop Laud's policies had made him unpopular; at any rate they were loath to accept him.

Then after Charles I was at odds with Parliament, he applied to them for a loan of some £20,000. Cautiously they inquired of Parliament whether they should grant it. Parliament said "No" and then asked to borrow £30,000 on their own account. The Merchants had had experience with Charles, and Parliament was an untried quantity. They chose Parliament. In the struggle that followed they were stalwart supporters of the Commonwealth.

As a matter of fact, they found the Cromwellian government as greedy in its demands as Charles I had been. Even though Parliament protected the monopoly with ever-increasing strictness, and further limited the membership by doubling the entrance fee, the Merchants Adventurers had to stagger under heavy financial burdens. However, they were loyal to the Commonwealth, and in 1656, their governor, Christopher Packe, was a prime mover of the "Humble Petition and Advice" to Cromwell to take the Crown.

This record probably did not work greatly to their advantage after the restoration of Charles II in 1660. It was not through any attitude of Charles, however, that they got into difficulties; it was rather because the burden of debts had made membership in the company less desirable. Unlike the East India Company, they had continued their existence as a membership organization, although by this time it was clear that a joint stock company was far better fortified against adversity.

In the spring of 1665 they suffered a severe blow when their Hamburg fleet was captured by the Dutch, who were then at war with England.[17] Then some of the fellowships of the ports outside London broke away from the organization, and carried on their trade independently, with apparent success. In 1689 their monopoly charter was suspended for three years, and as trade in their territory immediately showed an increase, it was clear that the Company of the Merchants Adventurers had outlived its usefulness. Merchants and clothiers joined in a petition to continue the free-trade policy, and it was continued.

Eventually the Merchants Adventurers reorganized as the Hamburg Company, but it was a relatively unimportant organization compared to the lusty young giant, the East India Company. The Hamburg Company continued until 1804 when the Napoleonic wars finally brought their long history to a close. Their exit from Hamburg, April 20, 1808, brought no tremors to the business center of London. During the last century of their existence, they are said to have had a total of 81 members altogether and those mostly from the same families.[18] Yet it is significant of the great prestige they had acquired in Europe that Napoleon considered them a far greater organization than they really were, and counted it as a great triumph when he drove them out of Germany.

[17] Pepys' *Diary*, May 31, 1665: "To the Change, where great the noise and trouble of having our Hambrough ships lost."

[18] W. E. Lingelbach, "The Merchant Adventurers at Hamburg," *Am. Hist. Rev.*, vol. IX, pp. 264 ff.

CHAPTER XIII

LATER PAMPHLET ADVERTISING OF THE SEVENTEENTH CENTURY

ONE indication that Wheeler's *Treatise of Commerce* was well received may be seen in the fact that his policy was speedily adopted by other business men. Up to his time, books dealing in any way with business had been few and far between; most of these few were dramas or other forms of entertainment, or else criticisms by clergymen and landowners. In the Stationers' Register for 1600, the only title that seems to suggest business is Shakespeare's *The Merchant of Venice*. In 1601, appeared Wheeler's *Treatise* and one other by a business man: Malynes' *Canker of England's Commonwealth*, a treatise on foreign exchange.

As the century advanced, an increasing number of business men used printed publicity. Milles, as we have seen, was a prolific and persistent writer. He continued to fight for Sandwich and the customs-officers. We might suppose that the overthrow of his old enemies the Merchants Adventurers, in 1615, would have gratified him. On the contrary, his latest version of *The Customer's Apology*[1] attacked the "new" Company for making a bad matter worse. This undated pamphlet must have been published in 1616 or 1617, although it refers to the original version as having been written eighteen years earlier. It could have had no effect, for the King's Company—the "new" Company—ended its short and disastrous career at the beginning of 1617. Possibly it was already extinct when Milles attacked it; that would be his usual luck.

There were other public officers, such as the Aulnegers and the Garblers, who, like Milles, wrote in behalf of the interests of their group. Some pamphlets advocated or criticised some

[1] Thomas Milles, *An Abstract almost verbatim of the Customer's Apologie*. (Br. Mus. assigns date as 1627; Hewins in *D. N. B.* conjectures 1619.)

particular policy or method. A considerable proportion, however, were defenses or eulogies of specific companies.[2] Not all of these can be classed as advertising. Some are anonymous, some do not reveal their purposes definitely; some seem to be merely the outpourings of an individual with a taste for public controversy. In those days, a man with the itch for publicity could not relieve himself by writing a letter to the *Times*. The pamphlet was his only outlet, and sometimes he did not bother with the formality of getting license to print. Possibly a number of such publications have been lost to posterity—not a serious loss, to judge by the specimens that have been preserved. The pamphleteers employed by the chartered companies and corporations were generally men of ability, and their productions are valuable to the economic historian. The Virginia Company and the East India Company were the most lavish users of publicity. The former sought to attract subscribers and emigrants for their venture; the latter sought to protect their profitable monopoly in the East.

The Merchants Adventurers had a much smaller output of printed propaganda—probably not more than half a dozen pamphlets altogether. None of these appeared in Wheeler's lifetime, although he has been credited with a brief anony-

[2] Some slight evidence of the extent to which advertising pamphlets were used as early as 1616 is furnished by Ben Jonson's play, *The Devil is an Ass.* Meercraft, the great projector, speaks of a scheme to obtain a patent

> "For serving the whole state with tooth picks;
> Somewhat an intricate business to discourse: but
> I show how much the subject is abused,
> First in that one commodity; then what diseases
> And putrefactions in the gums are bred,
> By those are made of adulterate and false wood;
> My plot for reformation of that, follows:
> To have all tooth-picks brought into an office,
> There sealed; and such as counterfeit them, mulcted.
> At last, for venting them, to have a book
> Printed, to teach their use, which every child
> Shall have throughout the kingdom, that can read
> And learn to pick his teeth by; which beginning
> Early to practice, with some other rules,
> Of never sleeping with the mouth open, chewing
> Some grains of mastick, will preserve the breath
> Pure and so free from taint . . . ."
>
> —Ben Jonson, *The Devil is an Ass*, Act IV, Sc. I.

mous undated pamphlet of a few pages entitled "The advantages of the Kingdome of England both abroad and at home by managing and issuing the Drapery and Woolen manufactures of this Kingdome under the Ancient Government of the Fellowship of *Merchants Adventurers of England*."[3] It is mainly a rehash of his *Treatise* with some passages quoted verbatim, but it is obviously by another hand and of a much later date.

About 1621, the Merchants Adventurers were in need of a defender. Along with the attacks in Parliament, they were assailed in a public pamphlet in behalf of the old Staplers, who were demanding a share of the cloth trade. This pamphlet entitled, *The Maintenance of Free Trade*, was by Gerard Malynes, a member of the Staplers Company. Malynes complained that all commodities of wool were now in the hands of the Merchants Adventurers and "it is come to be managed by 40 or 50 persons of that company, consisting of three or four thousand." This was an exaggeration, but the analysis of Miss Friis shows that unquestionably the trading members of the Merchants Adventurers were only a small proportion of the total number. Malynes asserted that as a result of this restriction and some other influences—such as the immoderate use of tobacco and the decay of the fishing industry—the balance of trade in England had become unfavorable and was causing the export of money.

Edward Misselden, a Merchant Adventurer, took it upon himself to reply in his *Circle of Commerce*, though it is doubtful whether this or his other pamphlets were authorized officially by the Merchants Adventurers. In any event, he did a very poor job. The bulk of his pamphlet is dull and of no great significance. He did make some attempt at increasing the interest by borrowing from literary methods. His title *The Circle of Commerce* is due to the story of Giotto and his perfect circle, with which he begins the dedication, but the story is poorly told and only distantly related to his subject. The rest of the long dedication is a florid eulogy of King James' financial minister.

[3] Br. Mus. Tracts on Wool, 816 m 14/79.

It may be that this dedication endeared Misselden personally to James and to Charles, who later tried to force his promotion, but it did not help the Merchants Adventurers very much in the crisis of 1623. At that time they were compelled to increase their "yearly presents to such Honourable Personages as they had received favours from."[4] The Lord Treasurer received 200 pieces of 22s. in gold and a piece of plate. Others who were "sweetened" were the Lord Duke of Buckingham, Archbishop of Canterbury, Lord Keeper, Lord President, Mr. Secretary Calvert, etc.

With these drains on their purse, it is not strange that the Merchants Adventurers indulged in little publicity during the reigns of James I and Charles I. Then too, the Stuarts were not particularly pleased to see appeals addressed to the people; and what was more important, the methods of the Merchants Adventurers at this time were not of the sort that could be exposed to the limelight.

It was not until 1648, under the Commonwealth régime, that the Merchants Adventurers officially issued another important pamphlet. Again, the immediate inspiration seems to have been a public attack, this time in behalf of independent merchants (interlopers) who wanted the foreign export market thrown open to all. This pamphlet, which is attributed to Nathaniel Brent, had the following title-page: "A Discourse consisting of/Motions for the Enlargement and Freedom/of Trade/Especially that of cloth and other/woollen manufacture, /Engrossed at present/

contrary to { the Law of Nature
the Law of Nations
and the Lawes of this Kingdome

by a company of private men who style themselves/Merchants-Adventurers/April 11, 1645. Na. Brent."

Brent was thoroughly familiar with the secret history of the company under the Stuarts. He revealed the unsavory details of its bribery, as mentioned above, and also the fact that since 1603 the King had received a rent of £50 a year from the company as well as half the fines they collected for

[4] Brent's *Discourse* (1645).

violations. He was somewhat shaky on dates, but otherwise his facts were substantially true. Along with these blots on the company record, Brent offered very cogent arguments against its monopoly system. Altogether, he showed himself the most formidable opponent in their history. His style is vigorous and lucid, and he dared to speak out freely.

The Merchants Adventurers had a stout champion in Henry Parker, the Secretary of the company. Although he did not reply to Brent until nearly three years later and made no reference to the attack, the connection is definitely suggested by his title-page: "Of a Free Trade/A Discourse/ Seriously recommending to our Nation the wonderfull/benefits of Trade, especially of a rightly Governed,/and Ordered Trade. /Setting forth also most clearly, /The Relative Nature, Degrees, and Qualifications of Libertie,/Which is ever to be inlarged, or restrained according/to that Good, which it Relates to, as that is more,/or lesse ample/Written by Henry Parker Esquire/τῆς πολυπραγμοσύγης Οὐδεν χενεώτερον ἀλλὸ./ Doing all things thou doest none:/Business too vast makes thee a Drone./London/Printed by Fr: Neile for Robert Bostock, dwelling in/Paul's Church-yard, at the Signe of the King's Head/1648."

Brent was evidently familiar with Wheeler's *Treatise of Commerce*, but Parker was not, as his dedication shows. This dedication reads as follows:

Dedication

To the
Right Worshipfull John Kenrick
Alderman of London, Governor of the Merchant Adventurers of England
To the Right Worshipfull Isaac Lee,
Deputy of the said Company of Merchant Adventurers residing at Hamburgh
To all other Deputies, Assistants and Members of the said Famous Company

Worthy Gentlemen:

If in this brief Argument (which here treats of your Charters and maintains your privileges) there be any thing beseeming an advocate of yours: I desire the intire advantage thereof may redound solely to yourselves. For indeed the merit of your Cause is such, as would require an able Orator: and when I first applied myself to serve you herein, I perceived your interest was the same as the common interest of all Merchants, and that could have no termination, but in the common interest of our Nation: But if there appear any Error, or Fayler in these papers: if the workmanship be found unworthy of the stuffe: I shall then desire of all my Readers, that the blame may be onely mine: and that none but myself may suffer the least disadvantage by my defects, and disabilities. I am certain all wise, impartial Judges will distinguish between that which is mine in this weak piece, and that which is yours: and if they cast some disdain upon me for my pleading your cause as I might; they will not proceed to a condemnation of your cause, for having no better pleader here than it is.

In Queen Elizabeth's dayes a Tract to this very purpose was printed by Mr. Wheeler (a learned Gent: that preceded me in this place) were that Tract now re-printed, perhaps our Times would be better satisfied in this Case. It came not to my sight, till after I had formed the lump of this, and given it all those rude lineaments almost, which it now bears: and I was induced then to persist in my resolutions of finishing this, and not of retroceding; the rather; because I saw my stile a[illegible]thod varied much from his: because the face of the times (which has great influence upon the State and fate of Merchandise) was not the same when He wrote, as it is now: because, his Tract was in bulk more than twice, as great as mine; because, He might give some light to me in some things, and I adde some to Him in other things; and so both might be more effectual for the ends proposed by both, then either; because, if He was more satisfactory in matters of this particular Company, I had some thoughts in myself, that I was more proper for the affairs of Merchants in generall. These reasons kept from abortion this Essay of mine at that time: for how long a space it was reprieved I cannot prognosticate: nor do I much regard how soon its fatall houre approaches, so the business which it aymed at may survive and prosper. Gentlemen, my reputation in this case may run some hazard, and stand or fall, as the vogue of this age pleases: yet my intention is to be judged of onely by you, therefore let that onely find your fair acceptation, and favourable construction, and that shall be a sufficient encouragement to

Your Worships obliged faithfull Servant

Hamb: Decemb 30, 1647 — Hen: Parker

It may seem strange that the Secretary of the company in 1647 had not been acquainted earlier with the defense that was written in 1601. But many executives of 1931 have never seen the publicity material their corporations issued in 1885. Parker's methods are largely borrowed from those of the East India Company, which had earlier borrowed from Wheeler.

Parker's *Discourse*, though less interesting and valuable than Wheeler's *Treatise*, is superior in some respects. Naturally it is easier reading; considerable progress had been made in English prose style in the half century intervening between them. Parker, however, was no clearer for the middle of the seventeenth century than Wheeler was for its beginning.

More significant is the difference in methods. Parker based his arguments for the chartered trading company on general economic grounds rather than the temporary situation. The weakness of Wheeler's *Treatise* in the eyes of his successors was that it depended too much upon the conditions of the moment. War-time propaganda loses much of effectiveness when the emergency is past. After the Spanish peril had become only a memory and the teeth of the Hanses had ceased to threaten, Wheeler's arguments were no longer valid. Parker, like most of his contemporaries, aimed to give his work longer life by basing it on permanent principles. He makes out a good case for the chartered company. He asserts that its solid organization is the only protection against unjust impositions by foreign governments. He questions whether there is any other way of assuring proper apprenticeship for the difficult art of selling, and reminds his readers that the art of selling cloth is just as necessary as the art of making it and is more delicate and difficult. He implies that some of the objectionable features are not the fault of the Merchants Adventurers; that, ever since Cumberland received his license, the company has been compelled to pay some nobleman royalties on a large part of their cloths, thus burdening the maker, seller, and buyer, without benefiting the Commonwealth.

Reading between the lines of Parker's and Brent's pamphlets, we may justly conclude that in their day the intrinsic evils of the trading monopoly were far less serious than the evils which had developed out of it. If the Government had chosen to administer it for the benefit of the cloth industry and the nation as a whole instead of as an instrument for their own greed, it might have been at least tolerable.

Parker's *Discourse* is the last important publication in the history of the company. After his time they published a few more leaflets and pamphlets, notably one about 1670, but these contained no new material of any significance. The old arguments of Wheeler and Parker are simply brought up to date and expressed in style suitable to the audience.

Even more than Parker, the writers of the East India Company based their arguments on economic grounds. They show some indications of Wheeler's influence, particularly in their appeals to patriotism. A few of the pamphlets—that dealing with the Massacre at Amboyne, for example—concentrated on the attempt to inflame national feeling; many others incidentally tried to arouse antagonism against the Dutch. More and more, however, they relied upon abstract exposition, particularly of the balance-of-trade theory. They had to do this in order to controvert the bullionist doctrine that the export of money was injurious to the nation, and that therefore the East India Company was a bad influence.

Thomas Mun in 1621 published *A Discourse of Trade from England*, in which he gave a far clearer exposition of the balance-of-trade theory than Misselden's. Later he developed his theory more fully in *England's Treasures by Foreign Trade* which, however, was not published until 1664. That it was considered worthy of publication then shows how little it was dependent upon temporary conditions for its effectiveness.

Toward the end of the century, the East India Company had other skillful controversialists like Child and Davenant—either in the company or hired for the purpose—to combat the verbal fire of their many opponents. They succeeded in winning public acceptance of their principles, but these "principles" are now discredited as largely fallacious. After all, these men were concerned more with the plausibility than with the soundness of their reasoning. As W. A. S. Hewins says:

Men wrote pamphlets, not because after a careful and impartial investigation they had discovered important principles which it was desirable that the world should know, but to defend the interests of some section whose interests were attacked, to support a project to which subscriptions were invited, or to urge some remedy for evils in the State. There was for the most part nothing wrong in this. We are in our own day inundated with publications of the same kind, but we do not rank them with scientific treatises. We must not expect an impartial view of the Merchant Adventurers from Wheeler, its paid secretary and advocate, or of the East India Company from Sir Josiah Child, first director and then chairman of the Company.[5]

The generalization applies to the antagonists as well as the protagonists of the companies. Each side had an axe to grind. The critics and attackers at any period may seem to be less biassed than the defenders, and doubtless they seemed so in the seventeenth century. But when we examine them from the vantage-point of the twentieth century, we find that they do not assay a much higher percentage of sincerity or truth than the defenders. On neither side do we find a prophet whose expression of economic theory is acceptable to-day.

The pamphlets of the East India Company have become far better known than those of the Merchants Adventurers and are still studied for their historical significance. They not only illustrate economic thought in the seventeenth and eighteenth centuries; they helped to influence it. Yet the chief job of the pamphlets of both companies was to advance the private interests of a profit-making corporation. The issues for which both fought have become dead issues. The only difference is that the issues of the Merchants Adventurers died much earlier.

[5] W. A. S. Hewins, *English Finance and Trade, Chiefly in the 16th Century*, p. xvi.

CHAPTER XIV

CONCLUSION

THE complete history of the Merchants Adventurers of England is yet to be written. In spite of the excellent research of Schanz, Ehrenberg, Lingelbach, Unwin, Lucas, Friis, and others, there are still many gaps that must be filled with conjectures. Even in these chapters dealing with that drama in which the *Treatise of Commerce* played so important a part, the words "probably" and "perhaps" have recurred with annoying frequency. If the missing facts (particularly the official records of the Company) are ever brought to light and marshalled together, it may be possible to form a just judgment of the place that this great organization deserves in history.

That place is still a matter of dispute, partly because of our imperfect knowledge, and partly because of the different view-points, political and economic, of the historians. The prevailing opinion is that they were instrumental in building up the national commerce of England and ultimately in developing its world empire. Cawston and Keane enthusiastically declare that they and the companies that they founded "secured the fairest lands of the earth for our race, laying the foundation of our great Colonial Empire, and thus have secured an undeniable claim to the gratitude of all succeeding generations of Englishmen."[1]

The German historians, Schanz, Ehrenberg, and Hagedorn, all see the Merchants Adventurers as the instruments of English national policy in world commerce. Naturally the struggle with the Hanseatic League looms large in their eyes, and they see the outcome not merely as the victory of one private trading company over another, but as the victory of

[1] Cawston and Keane, *The Early Chartered Companies*, p. 14. (A book written as propaganda for the Rhodesian Chartered Co.)

England over Germany. Some of them have a passing regret that the Hanseatic League did not triumph in the conflict and thus pave the way for a larger and more permanent triumph of German commerce. W. E. Lingelbach in his *Merchant Adventurers of England, Their Laws and Ordinances* seems also to believe that the Merchants Adventurers were the cornerstone upon which England built its commercial dominance. Ian Colvin in *The Germans in England* looks at the matter much as the Germans did, but from the opposite view-point. His book, however, published in the first year of the World War, is somewhat colored by animosity.

W. A. S. Hewins and George Unwin are inclined to dissent from these opinions. They see the Merchants Adventurers as a purely selfish organization; and they object to the identification of its interests with those of the nation. Unwin in his illuminating lectures in 1913 said:

> The triumphs of English policy, in so far as they consisted in strengthening the monopoly of the Merchant Adventurers, in setting up new monopolistic companies and in excluding the German merchants from their accustomed share in English trade, were won at the expense of national commerce and industry, and led immediately and unmistakeably to a period of prolonged depression.[2]

Unwin made a very searching analysis of the Company and its history, and no one is better qualified to express an opinion. Nevertheless, it is possible that he overestimated the evils of the organization and particularly gave them a greater part of the blame for the trade depression than they deserved. After all, they were merely exponents of the medieval-guild policy and their faults are the characteristic faults of the guilds.

Sir Charles Lucas in his *Beginnings of English Overseas Enterprise* takes a middle ground and one which seems more likely to be the final verdict of history. As he says:

> In these latter days, supposed to be days of greater moral scruple than their predecessors, we fix our eyes too exclusively upon the obvious shortcomings of chartered companies, the evil things which have soiled their history, the possibilities which they have offered for buying and selling the welfare

[2] Unwin, *Studies in Economic History*, p. 216.

> of lands and of men. We should see straighter, and interpret English history more correctly, if more was thought and more was told of these companies as the special means, whether good or evil, which the English, above all nations, devised and perfected, on their own peculiar English lines, for making an Empire.[3]

It is significant to note that the whirligig of time has again brought into being forms of export enterprise by cartels and other combinations not wholly unlike the Merchants Adventurers, and these with the support or sanction of national governments. It is too early to tell whether these forms of modified monopoly will breed the evils of their predecessors or will prove that the old methods of the Merchants Adventurers were not so indefensible as they seemed in the days of laissez faire.

Because the Merchants Adventurers were the first of the great chartered companies of England and the model for the others, they deserve a share of the credit—or blame, as the case may be—for what all of them accomplished. However, their own original contributions were few indeed. As we have seen, nearly every important feature of their organization and policies was borrowed either from the Merchants of the Staple, the Hanseatic League, or the guilds. They opened no important new markets or trade-routes; they colonized no lands. They have left behind few memorials of their greatness. Even the famous cloth that was for centuries the bone of contention between them and their European neighbors is no longer a familiar sight except, perhaps, in a few Dutch towns on market-days.

One commercial policy they seem unquestionably to have originated is the policy of publicity as exemplified in Wheeler's *Treatise of Commerce*. It seems fairly certain that this was an important factor in preserving the company and its monopoly privileges through a difficult period. Perhaps it would have been better if Wheeler had not written it; if the cloth trade had been permanently opened to all merchants; if foreigners had been given equal trading rights with Englishmen. We shall never know with certainty what the future

[3] Sir C. P. Lucas, *The Beginnings of English Overseas Enterprise*, pp. 146–47.

course of history might have been. Certainly the English trade-monopolies helped to shape events both in India and in America.

The policy of commercial publicity has continued to increase in importance with the centuries. Certain evils have become manifest; some of them are to be found in this pioneer essay in the field. Wheeler was guilty of boasting and exaggeration; he suppressed disagreeable facts; he may have used "manufactured" testimonials. But these faults seem to be almost inseparable from advertising, in spite of all efforts to purify it. And at least Wheeler believed sincerely in the merits of his cause and fought for it openly. If propaganda is to be carried on—and in any democracy this seems inevitable—propaganda openly avowed is less objectionable than secret propaganda. On this point there can scarcely be any difference of opinion.

Historical scholars who do not sympathize with Wheeler's cause or with his method respect the ability shown in the *Treatise*. Ehrenberg declares that in spite of its vainglorious tone the work is of great value. The modern specialist in advertising, publicity, sales promotion, and the other complex activities of commercial propaganda will (like Parker, in 1647) be able to "give light" to Wheeler in some things. But the better he becomes acquainted with the *Treatise* the more he will find in it to admire. He may well be proud to claim as a founder of his craft that stalwart old Elizabethan, John Wheeler.

Chronological Table of Significant Dates in the History of the Merchants Adventurers

1248 Brotherhood of St. Thomas Becket receives privileges from Duke of Brabant. (This assertion by Wheeler has not been verified.)

1272 *Edward I*

Edward I confirms privileges granted by his predecessors to German merchants from various cities.

1282 Contract between City of London and Hanseatic Traders.

1296 Earliest known charter granted by Duke of Brabant to English merchants trading in the Low Countries.

1303 *Carta Mercatoria*, or Charter of liberties granted by Edward I to foreign merchants in England.

1307 *Edward II*

1313 Statute of the Staple designating one foreign market for wool, etc.

1327 *Edward III*

1347 Cloth Customs Act (placing English merchants at a disadvantage in exporting cloth as compared with the Hanseatic merchants).

1353 Ordinance of the Staple (designating home staples).

1358 The English Merchants settle in Bruges.

1377 *Richard II*

1399 *Henry IV*

1404 Henry IV grants charter to English merchants in Prussia and Hanseatic territory.

1406 Henry IV grants charter to English merchants trading in the Low Countries (chiefly at Bruges).

1413 *Henry V*

1422 *Henry VI*

1435 English merchants expelled from Hanseatic territory.

1446(?) The English Merchants settle in Antwerp.

1447 Treaty affirms that English merchants are to have the same privileges in Hanseatic Cities that Hanseatics enjoy in England. (Disregarded by Hanseatic Cities.)

1463 William Caxton, Governor of English Merchants at Bruges.

1464 Edward IV

1464–6 Philip the Good, Duke of Burgundy, prohibits importation of English wool and woolen goods in his domains. English merchants hold marts in Utrecht.

1470–5 Edward IV grants extensive privileges to Hanseatic Merchants in England, including perpetual possession of the Steelyard.

1483 Edward V—Richard III

1485 Henry VII

1487 Statute prohibiting export of undressed cloth (thus making it necessary to secure royal license for exporting white cloths).

1493 Commercial intercourse with Low Countries suspended. The English Merchants remove to Calais. They establish another market at Middelburg.

1496 *Intercursus Magnus*, Commercial Treaty with Flanders. The English Merchants return to Antwerp.

1497 Act of Parliament recognizes monopolistic position of the Company of Merchants Adventurers by limiting the entrance fee to 10 marks.

1505 Merchants Adventurers receive their official title in a new monopolistic charter from Henry VII.

1509 Henry VIII

1512 Statute reaffirms prohibition of export of white cloth. Hanseatic violators punished.

1547 Edward VI

1552 Hanseatic privileges in England pronounced void. The Merchants Adventurers finance the crown.

1553 *Mary*

1554 Hanseatic privileges partly restored.

1557 Hanseatic privileges again curtailed.

1558 *Elizabeth*

1563 Embargo on English cloth drives Merchants Adventurers from Antwerp. They establish mart at Emden.

1564 Elizabeth grants new and enlarged charter to "Merchants Adventurers of England" covering Low Countries and a large part of Germany. She also grants them a license for export of 30,000 white cloths annually.

1568 Merchants Adventurers receive ten-year contract from Hanseatic City of Hamburg.

1574 Temporary settlement of troubles with Spain and Netherlands. Resumption of trade at Antwerp.

1576 The "Spanish Fury" at Antwerp temporarily interrupts the trade of the Merchants Adventurers.

1578 Hamburg, under Hanseatic pressure, refuses to renew contract with Merchants Adventurers. Hanseatic privileges in England again curtailed.

1581 Monopoly of Merchants Adventurers threatened by the Emperor. He prepares a Mandate of exile, but does not issue it.

1585 Merchants Adventurers leave Antwerp for the last time.

1586 Depression in cloth industry. Merchants Adventurers receive new charter providing protection against interlopers.

1587 Monopoly privileges of Merchants Adventurers temporarily suspended, but restored. They establish mart at Stade (Hanseatic City).

1588 The Spanish Armada.

1597 Merchants Adventurers exiled from Stade and Hanseatic territory by Emperor's Mandate.

1598 Elizabeth exiles Hanseatic merchants from England. The Steelyard is closed.

1600 East India Company chartered.

CHRONOLOGICAL TABLE OF DATES

1601 March: Privy Council decrees freedom of trade at Stade and Hamburg. Cumberland receives unlimited license for cloth export.
April: Merchants Adventurers attacked in Milles' pamphlet, *The Customer's Apology*.
August: Wheeler's *Treatise of Commerce* published.
Oct.–Nov.: Parliament debates the monopolies. The Merchants Adventurers are tacitly approved.

1602 Merchants Adventurers secure exclusive right to export under Cumberland's license.

1603 James I

1604 Freedom of Trade Act passed by House of Commons; blocked in House of Lords.

1607 Merchants Adventurers received again at Stade. Trade of interlopers restricted.

1608 Laws and Ordinances of Merchants Adventurers codified by Wheeler.

1611 Merchants Adventurers return to Hamburg as their chief mart-city. End of Hanseatic opposition.
John Wheeler dies.

1612 Secretary Cecil (Lord Salisbury) dies.

1613 Cockayne wins the support of King James for the dyed-cloth project. The Merchants Adventurers refuse to attempt it.

1615 The Merchants Adventurers lose their charter. Cockayne's new company, chartered as the "King's Merchants Adventurers," takes over the trade.

1616 The new company proves a failure. Cloth industry prostrated.

1617 The old Merchants Adventurers are restored to their former monopoly.

1620–21 General industrial depression. Merchants Adventurers again attacked in Parliament and through pamphlets.

1623–24 Statute of Monopolies passed, but trading companies are exempted. Monopoly of Merchants Adventurers limited to white cloths.

1625 *Charles I*

1634 The Merchants Adventurers are restored to their complete monopoly.

1641 The Merchants Adventurers side with Parliament against the King.

1643 Parliament permits the Merchants Adventurers to tighten their monopoly of the cloth trade by increasing the entrance fee.

1649 *The Commonwealth*

1656 The Governor of the Merchants Adventurers heads the delegation urging Oliver Cromwell to take the Crown.

1660 *Charles II*

1662 Entrance-fees for Merchants Adventurers reduced. They are in financial difficulties.

1665 The fleet of the Merchants Adventurers is captured by the Dutch.

1685 *James II*

1688 *William and Mary*

1689 The monopoly charter of the Merchants Adventurers is suspended. They resume operations as the Hamburg Company.

1808 Napoleon drives the Hamburg Company from Germany. Their career is ended.

PART ONE

FACSIMILE OF "A TREATISE OF COMMERCE"

A TREATISE OF COMMERCE, WHERIN ARE SHEWED THE COMMODIES ARISING BY A WEL ORDERED, AND RVLED TRADE,

Such as that of the Societie of Merchantes Adventurers is proved to bee, written principallie for the better information of those who doubt of the *Necessarienes of the said Societie in the State of the Realme of Englande.*

BY IOHN WHEELER, Secretarie to the said Societie.

MIDDELBVRGH,
By *Richard Schilders*, Printer to the States of Zeland.
1601.

TO THE RIGHT HO NORABLE SIR ROBERT CECILL KNIGHT, PRIN- cipall Secretarie to her *Maiestie, &c.*

THose which heretofore (Right Honorable), haue written of anie matter, and had opinion, that the publishinge thereof might doe good vnto others, haue vsed to Dedicate their Labours to some one, or other, vnder whose countenance, and protection the same might goe foorth, and bee the better lyked, and receyued of all men: Whiche is the cause that I haue made bolde to inscribe this TREATISE,

A 3 such

ſuch as it is, vnto your Honour, vpon hope of fauourable allowance, and Patronage, whiche I inſtantlie craue, and entreat, and with all, that in the readinge thereof, your Honour would vouchesauſe to remember, that it concerneth thoſe men, and that olde and auncientlie renoumpned Companie of MERCHAVNTES ADVENTVRERS, which was ſo well eſteemed of, and highlie fauoured by your late right Honorable Father, of woorthie memorie, vnto whome as God hath appointed your Honour to be a Succeſſour in manie excellent thinges of this life, whether wee regarde the Honourable Places, wherevnto you are called in the Gouuernement of the State, or the vertues, and qualities fitt for ſo waightie a callinge, wherewith you are endewed, So it may pleaſe your Honour to take vnto you this Succeſsion alſo, to witte, the dewtifull Obſervancie, and Promptitude, which the ſaid Companie alwayes ſhewed towardes your ſaid right Honourable Fathers ſeruice, and

and which they alſo ſtande readie, and deſirous to preſent, & performe vnto your Honour to their beſt power, and abilitie.

I am not ignorant alſo, that it is the manner of Writers, to fill vp the greateſt parte of their Præfaces with the praiſes, and cōmendations of thoſe, to whome they Dedicate their Trauailes, and ſurelie this Reward ſeemeth to bee dew vnto true Vertue, that the Memorie thereof ſhould bee conſecrated to Poſteritie, which can not be performed by anie Monument better, then by Bookes: And albeit, without all Gloſinge, or counterfeyting, I haue heere in verie deed a large fielde of your Honours prayſes offered vnto mee, yet becauſe my ſimplicitie not onelie abhorreth all Adulation, but with all all kinde of Fawninge, or flatteringe ſpeeche, and that your Honours ſingulare Modeſtie, is wonte, not to abide anie thing leſſe, then euen the modeſteſt commendations, I will lett paſſe the ſame, and come vnto the handlinge of the enſuing Treatice, which with my my selfe I humblie recommende vnto your Honours good fauour, and so beseeche the Almightie to blesse, and keepe your Honor. *Middelbrough* the vi[th] of Iune 1601.

Your Honors with his seruice at commandment,

Iohn Wheeler.

A Treatise of Commerce, wherein are shewed the commodities arising by a well-ordred and ruled Trade, such as that of the Societie of MARCHANTS ADVENTVRERS is prooved to bee, Written principallie for the better *information of those who doubt of the Necessarienes of the said Societie in the state of the Realme of England: By* IOHN WHEELER, *Secretarie to the saide Societie.*

Vita Civilis in Societate est, Societas in Imperio, & Commercio.

Commercio Gentes mari, montibusq; discretæ miscentur, vt quod vsquã nascitur, apud omnes affluat.

THERE be twoo pointes about the which the Royal office, and administration of a Prince, is wholy employed, to wit, about the Gouuernement of the Persons of men, next of Things cõvenient and fitt for the maintenaunce of Humane societie: wherein principally the civile life consisteth, and hath her being: And therefore the Prince that loveth the Policie, and ruleth by

B sage

ſage and good councell, is to conſtitute and appoint certaine Lawes, and ordinarie Rules, both in the one and the other of the abouesaid pointes, and eſpeciallie in the firſt, as the chiefeſt; which is cõverſant and occupied about the inſtitutiõ of the perſons of men in Pietie, civile converſation in maners, and facion of life, and finallie in the mutual dewtie of Equitie, and Charitie one towardes another: of the which my purpoſe is not to intreat, but ſomewhat of that other point, namely the gouvernement of Things convenient, and fitt for the maintenance of Humane Societie: whereunto mens actions and affections are chieflie directed, and whereabouts they beſtow and employe not onely the quickenes and induſtrie of their ſpirites, but alſo the labour and travaile of their handes, and ſides: that ſo they may drawe from thence either commoditie or pleaſure, or at leaſt wiſe therby ſupplie, helpe, & furniſh their ſeveral wantes, and neceſſities: From hence, as from a root or fountaine firſt proceedeth the eſtate of *Marchandiſe*, and then conſequentlie in a rowe, ſo manie, diverſe, and ſundrie Artes, as we ſee in the worlde. At which it ſhould ſeeme that man beginneth the train, or courſe of his life, and therein firſt of all diſcovereth not onlie the dexteritie and ſharpenes of his witt, but withall that naughtines & corruption which is naturallie in him: for there is nothing in the world ſo ordinarie, and naturall vnto men, as to contract, truck, merchandiſe, and trafficque one with an other, ſo that it is almoſt vnpoſſible for three perſons to converſe together

gether two houres,but they wil fall into talke of one bargaine or another, chopping, changing, or ſome other kinde of contract Children, aſſoone as euer their tongues are at libertie, doe ſeaſon their ſportes with ſome merchandiſe,or other, and whē they goe to ſchoole,nothing is ſo common among them,as to chaunge,and rechaunge,buye and ſell of that,which they bring from home with them : the Prince with his ſubiects,the Maiſter with his ſeruants,one freend and acquaintaunce with another,the Captaine with his ſouldiers, the Huſband with his wife, Women with,and among them ſelues, and in a woord,all the world choppeth and chaungeth,runneth and raveth after Martes, Markettes, and Marchandiſing, ſo that all things come into Commerce,and paſſe into Traficque (in a maner) in all times,and in all places: not onely that, which Nature bringeth foorth, as the fruites of the earth, the beaſtes, and living creatures with their ſpoiles,ſkinnes,and caſes,the metalles,mineralles,& ſuch like things, but further alſo,this man maketh merchandiſe of the workes of his owne handes,this man of another mans labour, one ſelleth woordes,another maketh trafficque of the skins,and blood of other men, yea there are ſome foūd ſo ſubtill and cunning merchantes,that they perſwade and induce men to ſuffer them ſelves to bee bought and ſolde,and we haue ſeene in our time enowe,and too manie, whiche haue made marchandiſe of mens ſoules : to conclude, all that a man worketh with his hand, or diſcourſeth in his ſpirit, is nothing elſe but

B 2 mar-

marchandise, and a triall to put in practise the Contractes, which the Legistes & men skilful in the lawes knew not to name otherwise thē thus: *Do vt des Facio vt facias.* the which wordes in effect comprehend in them all Negotiations, or Traffiques whatsoeuer, and are none other thing but meer matter of marchandise, and Commerce. Now albeit this affection be in all persons generallie both high and low, yet there are of the notablest, and principallest Trafficquers which are ashamed, and thinke scorne to bee called Marchantes: whereas in deede Marchandise which is vsed by way of proper vacatiō, being rightlie considered of, is not to be despised, or accoumpted base by men of iudgement, but to the contrarie, by manie reasons and examples it is to be prooved, that the estate is honorable, & may bee exercised not only of those of the third estate (as we tearme them) but also by the Nobles, and chiefest men of this Realme with commendable profite, and without anie derogation to their Nobilities, high Degrees, & conditions: With what great good to their States, honors, & enriching of themselues and their Countreis, the *Venetians*, *Florētines*, *Genoueses*, and our neighbours the *Hollanders*, haue vsed this trade of life, who knoweth not? or hauing seene the beautie, strength, opulencie, and populousenes of the abouesaid Cities, and Prouinces wondreth not thereat? Was not this the first steppe, and entrie of the Kinges of *Portugall* vnto the kingdomes, and Riches of the East? *Solon* in his youth, gaue him selfe to the feat of Merchan-

Cōmendation of Marchandise.

chandise, and in his time saith *Plutarch* (bringing *Hesiodus* for his Authour) there was none estate of life reprochfull, neither Art, or occupation, that did put difference betweene men, but rather which is more, *Merchandise* was accompted an honourable thing, as that whiche ministred the meanes to haunt, and trafficque with Barbarous Nations, to procure the friendship of Princes, and to gaigne experience in many matters: in so much (sayeth hee) that there haue been Merchants, which were founders of great Citties, as he was that founded *Marseilles* in France: The wise *Thales Milesius* did also exercise Merchandise, likewise *Hippocrates* and *Plato* defrayed the charges of a voyage, whiche hee made in *Egypt*, with the monie which he got there by selling of oyle: So that it appeareth, that not onely a Prince may vse this kinde of men, I meane Merchantes, to the great benefite, and good of his state, either for forreigne intelligence, or exploration, or for the opening of an entrie and passage vnto vnknowen and farre distant partes, or for the furnishing of monie, and other prouisions in time of warres, and dearth, or lastly, for the seruice and honor of the Prince, and Cou͂trie abroad at all times requisite, and expedient, but also this kinde of life may be exercised and vsed with commendation, and without losse of one jote of honor in those, who are honorable, or of eminent degree, as aforesaid: Whereunto I adde this further, that without Merchandise, no ease or commodious liuing continueth long in anie state, or common- Plut. in vita Solonis.

B 3 wealth,

wealth, no not loyaltie, or equitie it selfe, or vpright dealing. Therfore herein also, as in the former point, good order and rule is to be set, where it is wanting, or where it is alreadie established, there it ought to be preserved: for the maintenance of so necessarie, and beneficiall an estate in the common Wealth, by constituting meet and well proportioned ordinãces ouer the same, & ouer those things, which are thereupon depending, betweene the Marchantes, and those things, which are marchandized, or handled likewise with cõvenable, and well appropriated Magistrates, and overseers for the maintenance, and execution of the said ordinances. For it is very certain and true, that *sine imperio nec domus vlla, nec Civitas, nec Gens, nec Societas, nec hominum vniuersum genus stare, nec rerum natura omnis, nec Mundus ipse potest, &c.*

The peaceable, politike, and Riche Prince King *Henrie* the seventh, well marking the trueth hereof, and perceiuing that as in former times, so in his, manie disturbances, grievances and damages had befallen to, and among the Englishe Merchantes his subiectes, trading into the lowe Countries, *ob defectum boni Regiminis*, tooke order for the same, as well by confirming the auncient Charters of his Predecessours, Kings of England vnto the Societie of M. M. Adventurers, as also by adding thereunto newe, whereby he so strengthned, and enlarged the authoritie, and Priviledges of the saide Fellowshippe, that euer since the same hath florished in great prosperitie, and wealth, and out of it (as out of a plentifull Nour-

Nourcerie) haue sprong and proceeded almost all the principall Merchants of this Realm, at least such Companies, as haue arisen since, haue for the most part, fetched their light, patterne, and forme of policie and trade from the said Societie to the inestimable good and commoditie of this Realme, our natiue Countrie: so that to change this course were to returne to the olde cõfusion, and disorder, and withall to bereave the lande of so necessarie and seruiceable an estate, as *Merchandise is.*

Whatsoever is commendable, or is said of the best founded Companies, or Merchauntes in generall, maketh also for the Companie of Merchantes Adventurers speciallie: howbeit these things are perticularlie for our purpose to be considered in this Cõpanie: *The first Institution: The Auncient estimation it hath had: The state and Gouvernement of it, and such benefites, as growe to the Realme by the maintenance of it.*

Of the first Institution of the Fellowshippe or Companie of Marchantes Adventurers, and the causes thereof.

ARCVS Cato, a prudent Councellour, and a good husband in deed, saith: *Quod oportet Patremfamilias vendacem esse non emacem:* And who knoweth not, that we haue no smal need of manie things, whereof foreign

reign Countreis haue great store, and that we may well spare manie thinges, whereof the saide Countries haue also need: Nowe to vent the superfluities of our Countrie, and bring in the Commodities of others, there is no readier, or better meane then by merchãdize: and seeing we haue no way to increase our treasure by mynes of golde, and siluer at home, and can haue nothing from abroad without monie, or ware, it followeth necessarilie, that the abouesaid good councell of *Cato* to be sellers and not buyers, is to be followed, yet so, that we carrie not out more in valew ouer the seas, then we bring home frõ thence, or transporte thinges hurtfull to the State, for this were no good husbandry, but tẽdeth to the subversion of the lande, and deminishing of the treasure therof, whereas by the other wee shall greatlie encrease it, the trade being caried, and managed vnder a convenient Gouvernement, and orders, and not in a dispersed, loose, and stragling manner: the practise whereof we may see in this Realm almost these 400 yeares together: First in the Staple, and Woolle trade, and next in that of the M.M. Adventurers, and Clothe trade. And King *Edward* the thirde thought it not enough, to bring the working, and making of Cloth into the Realme, except when the same was indraped, he with all provided for the vent therof, in forreigne partes, to the most benefite, and advancement of that new begun Art, and therefore whereas the abouesaid Companie (though then otherwise tearmed then nowe) in the yere *1248*. had obtained Pri-

The brotherhood of Saint Thomas Becket of Canterbury.

Privileges of *Iohn* Duke of *Brabant*, the said King cõfirmed the same for the substantial Gouvernment of the saide Companie in their trade.

In the yeare 1399. the Art of making of Clothe being growen to good perfectiõ within this Realm, King *Henrie* the Fourth first prohibited the invection of foreigne made Cloth, and gaue vnto the saide Companie a verie beneficiall, and ample Charter of priviledges, confirmed by Act of Parleament for the same purpose and intent, as his predecessor King *Edward* the third had done before him: whose example the succeedinge Kinges *Henrie* the fifth, and sixt, *Edwarde* the fourth, and *Richard* the thirde followed, ratifying and confirming their Predecessors doeings on this behalfe: the next in order following King *Henrie* the seauenth, like a wise and provident Prince, well marking, and considering howe necessarie, and serviceable the estate of *Merchandise* was vnto this Realme, not onely liked and confirmed that, which the aboue-rehearsed Kinges had done before him, but also greatlie enlarged and augmented the same by three seueral Charters, and by other his gracious, and Roiall favours from time to time, not onlie towardes the saide Companie in generall, but withall to diuerse Merchantes in particular: *Mercatores ille sæpenumero pecunia multa data gratuitò iuuabat, vt Mercatura (Ars vna omnium cunctis aquè mortalibus tum commoda, tum necessaria) in suo Regno copiosior esset.* Polidorus in vita Hẽrici septimi. And when vpon variance fallen out betweene him and the Archduke *Philippe*, he had drawen, as wel the

C said

ſaid Companie, as that of the Staple out of the lowe Cuntries, & placed them at *Calice*, he gaue vnto them within the ſaid Towne as large, and beneficiall priuiledges, as they before had enioyed in the ſaid lowe Countreis, which were verie large, and favourable, entituling them by the name of MARCHANTS ADVENTVRERS. And albeeit in this Kinges dayes, as alſo in the raign of King *Henrie* the Fourth, the like complaint, as of late, was made by the Clothiers, Woolle-growers, Dyers, &c. againſt the Companie of M.M. Adventurers: yet after dew examination of the ſaide complaint, the iſſew procured great favour to the ſaide Companie, and gaue occaſion of the enlarging of their former Charters, with an expreſſe reſtraint of all Straglers, & Entermedlers, that might diſturbe, or empeach their trade: and wheras alſo the *Eaſterlinges* at this time had entred into the ſaid trade, the foreſaid prudent Prince King *Henrie* the ſeuenth, did not onelie ſtraightlie inhibite them ſo to doe, but alſo tooke recognizāce of twētie thouſand markes of the Alderman of the Steelyarde at London, that the ſaid *Eaſterlinges* ſhould not carie anie Engliſh Clothe to the place of Reſidence of the M.M. Adventurers in the lowe Countreis, or open their Fardelles of Cloth in the ſaid Countries, to the preiudice of the ſaid Companie, by putting the ſame to vent there, which they were not wont to doe.

In the time of the raigne of King *Edward* the ſixth, *Iohn Tulle*, *Iohn Dimock*, and others, brethren of the ſaid Companie, enformed the Biſhop of *Elye*, at that time

time Lord Chāūcellour, of matter against the Companie, but their bill being brought to the Councell-boord, and examined, it was finallie ordred, that the said Complainantes should submit themselues vnto the obedience of the Companies orders, and paye certaine fynes, which the Lordes then laide vppon them, besides that two of the principallest found to be the Ringleaders of the rest, were committed to the Fleet, there to remain, till such time as the Companie of M.M. Aduenturers should sew for their release: And albeit the said persons renewed their cō-plaintes, in the first yeare of Queene *Maries* raigne, and did put vp a bill to the Parleament house, against the Companie, yet the same being answered by the said Companie, was reiected, and cast out of the Parleament house. Since the time of King *Henrie* the seauenth, the succeeding Princes, Kinge *Henrie* the eight, of famous memorie, King *Edward* the sixth, & Queene *Marie*, haue continued, confirmed, and enlarged the abouesaide Charters and Priviledges, but aboue all other, our most gracious Soveraigne, that now reigneth, Queene *ELIZABETH*, hath shewed her gracious, and fauourable affection towardes the saide Companie, in not onelie confirminge the letters Patentes, and Charters of her most Noble Graundfather, and of other her Highnes Predecessours aboue-mentioned, but also in adding therevnto other more large, and beneficiall Priviledges of her owne. For whereas the M.M. Advēturers about the beginning of her Maiesties raigne, by diuerse re-

C 2 straints

ſtraintes, Edictes, and Proclamations made and ſett foorth by the Gouvernours and Commaunders of the low Countries, were empeached, and prohibited to trade into the ſaid Countreis, contrarie to the auncient Entercourſes, and the Priviledges to the ſaid Companie graunted of olde time, and conſequentlie were occaſioned to ſeeke, and erect a Trade in the partes of Germanie, which they did with their great charges and travaile for the vent of the Commodities of the Realme, her Highnes calling to remembrance this and other faithfull and acceptable ſeruice at ſundrie tymes done by the ſaid M.M. Aduenturers in diuerſe the great and waightie affaires of her Maieſtie and Realme, & minding the encreaſe and aduancement of the ſaide Merchantes, as much as anie her progenitours, (as her Highnes profeſſeth in the ſaid Charter) it pleaſed her ſaide Maieſtie in the ſixt yeare of her Raigne, to giue and graunt vnto them thoſe gracious and ample Priuiledges, which the ſaid Companie now enioyeth, and afterwardes vpon new occaſion the trade of the ſaid Companie being much empeached by the wrongful intermedling of vnfree perſons in the ſame, it pleaſed her Maieſtie by a new Charter, and letters Patentes vnder the great ſeale of Englande, in the eight-and-twentieth yere of her Raigne, to prouide againſt ſuch iniurious, & vnorderlie intruſion, acknowledging the ſeruices done to her Highnes by the ſaid M.M. Aduenturers, and pronouncing them to haue bene, and to bee very beneficiall members to the generall ſtate of of the Realme, and Common Wealth of Englande: which notable testimonie of so incomparable a Princesse after so manie yeres experience and tryall, may alone, if there were none other, serue for a full & sufficient *Apologie* of the abouesaid Companie of M.M. Aduenturers, against all the privie, & open, foreign, and domesticall gain-sayers, slaunderers, and oppugners of the same, and withall for a certaine, and infallible argument, that for the vent of Wooll, and woollen wares (the principall commodities of the Realme) it is most profitable both for the Prince and Countrie, to vse a governed Companie, and not to permitt a promiscuous, stragling, & dispersed trade, whereof I shall haue occasion to saye more, when I come to shew the benefites, which doe arise vnto the Common Wealth of Englande, by the maintenaunce of the aboue-said Companie, and the Gouuernement therein vsed.

Of the Auncient estimation which the Companie of Merchantes Adventurers *hath had.*

BY that which hath been aboue said of the Institution of the Fellowship or Companie of M.M. Aduẽturers, is partlie shewed in what estimation the said Cõpanie hath been hetherto, with the Kings, and Queenes of

C 3 this

this Realme, from the raigne of King *Edwarde* the thirde, a ſufficient motiue, and reaſon, as may be wel thought for the preſent and future ages, to haue the ſaide Companie in no leſſe eſtimation, and liking: but this is not all, for if wee would but looke out of England to our neighbours in *Germanie* and the low Coũtreis, we ſhould ſee the M. M. Aduẽturers many ages together ſought for, welcomed, embraced, cheriſhed, and vſed in as good, yea oftentimes in better tearmes, then the Naturalles of the ſaide Countries them ſelues, as appeareth by the auncient Charters, large, and beneficiall priviledges, and exemptions graunted to the ſaide Companie by ſundrie Princes, States, Citties, and Common Wealthes of high & lowe Dutcheland, ſince the yeare of our Lord 1296. to this our tyme, which are yet extant to be ſhewed to the great honour, and benefite of this our natiue Countrie, & the Princes thereof from tyme to time: For thereby we haue not onely opened a paſſage, & entrie into foreigne States, and Countreis, but alſo by our gainfull & beneficiall trade, haue made them the faſter friendes to the State of the Realme of Englande, and the Engliſh Nation, beſides the great wealth and commoditie which hath ariſen thereby to the common wealth.

After the taking of *Calice* by King *Edward* the third, the Earles, and people of Flaundres, for the better aſſuraunce and ſafetie of their State, procured a league and Entercourſe with the Kinges of Englande, and their Merchants: whereby the ſaide Earles & people found founde in short time such profite and commoditie, that *Lewes* Earle of Flaunders, in the yeare 1358. gaue, and graunted to the English Merchantes so large and ample Priviledges, and freedomes, that no Nation in Europe had the like in that Countrie at that time, by reason whereof, and that the adventure by sea and by lande into Flaunders was verie short, and easie, and almost without daunger, the Companie settled them selues in the Towne of *Bridges*, and stapled their commodities there: Whiche once knowen, and blowen abroad, Merchantes out of all partes of Europe, resorted thether, and made their habitation there, which appeareth by the houses at this day standing, which beare the names of the Citties, and Countreis, whence the said Strangers were, So that in few yeares all the Townes in Flanders, especiallie *Bridges*, were growen to such wealth, and prosperitie, that the fame thereof went almost thorough the whole earth, and at this daye, although their great opulencie, and concourse of Merchantes be altogether failed, yet in manie Countries of Christendome, and out of Christendome, all the Netherlanders carie the name of Flemminges, and the lowe Countries of Flanders. After this, when the Flemminges through wealth, and fulnes of bread, did forgett their bounden dewtie to their Prince, and withall grew to a proud desdain & contempt of all Merchants straungers, and in particular of the Englishe, by whom they had receiued their chiefest good and wel-fare, the Companie remooued from *Bridges* to a Town

Companie of M. M. Aduenturers at Bridges.

Companie of M.M.Adventu. leaue Bridges and repaire to Middelbourgh.

a Towne in Zelande called *Middelbourgh*, where they are nowe at this present residinge, whether all other Nations followed them straight: Since which those of *Bridges*, feeling the smart of their follie, haue manie tymes made sute & meanes to draw the Englishe thether againe, and in mans memorie, they profred a great summe of monie vnto the saide Merchantes, with offer of more ample Priviledges, and immunities, then ever they had before in *Bridges*, or anie where else, yea in a maner they profered a blancke to tye them to what the Englishe thought good, to haue the trafficque againe in their Towne, which verie fondlie, when they had it, they could not keepe. This Towne of *Middelbourgh* stood so neare the sea, that the Ditches, and low places round about it, being continuallie full of salte, and filthie oaze for want of a freshe Riuer, or current, to cleanse the same, bred such stynche, and noysome savours, that the Englishe vsed to a holesome, and sweet ayre in their own Cuntrey, were troubled with grievous agewes, and other sore diseases, & for their healthes sake, were forced to leaue the said Towne, about the yeare of our Lorde 1444. at which tyme *Antwerp* beeing but a poore, and simple Towne, standing in *Brabant*, made great sute to the Companie, to repair thether, which they finallie vpon offer of very large and beneficiall Priviledges, obtayned. In whiche Towne of *Antwerp*, and the Town of *Bergen op Zoom*, likewise in *Brabant*, the Cōpanie euer since hath for the most parte continued, saue that (as aforesaid) in the

the time of King *Henrie* the seuenth, they were vpon occasion remoued to *Calice* for a time, till that by the earnest intercessiō of the Ladie *Margarete* Dutches of *Savoye*, they repaired againe into the low Countries, first to *Middelbourgh*, the afterwards to *Antwerp*, where they were ioyfully, & honorably receyued, & entertayned by the Magistrate, & chiefest Citizens of the Towne, comming foorth in solempne procession to meete, & welcome the said Merchants, as by the Recordes of those times sufficiently appeareth: & heere by the way it is not much from our purpose, to insert somwhat of the state of *Antwerp*, at the first cōming thether of the Companie, wherein a man shall see that, which almost is incredible: *Philippe* surnamed the *Good*, Duke of *Burgundie*, and of *Brabant*, *&c.* gaue Priuiledges to the Companie vnder the name of the English Nation, by which name the said Companie euer since hath been most commonlie knowen in the low Countreis, whiche happened in the yeare 1446. Which Priviledges the Towne of *Antwerpe* confirmed the sixt of August in the abouesaid yere, giuing to them besides a large house, which is nowe called the old *Burse*, and afterwardes by exchaunge, another more goodlie, spacious, and sumptuous house, called the Court of *Lier*, which the Companie enioyed till the saide Towne was yeelded vp to the Duke of *Parma*, in the yeare 1585. At the aboue saide first Concordate, & Conclusion of Priuiledges with the Town of *Antwerp*, or not long before, there were not in all the Towne aboue foure Marchants, Estate of Antwerp at the Companies first comming thether.

D and

and thoſe alſo no adventurers to the ſea, the reſt of the Inhabitantes or Towneſmen were but meane people, and neither able, nor ſkilfull to vſe the feat, or trade of Merchandiſe, but did let out the beſt of their houſes to Engliſh-men, and other ſtraũgers for Chambers, and Packhouſes, contẽting them ſelues with ſome corner for their profites ſake: but within few yeares the concourſe, and reſorte of forreigne Merchantes to that Towne was ſo great, that houſe-roome waxed ſcant, Rentes were raiſed, Tolles, Axcyſes, and all other dewties to the Prince and Town wonderfullie encreaſed, and the *Antwerp*-men themſelues, who in few yeares before were but meane artificers, or liued by huſbandrie, and keeping of Cattaile (whereof one *Gate* of that Cittie to this daye beareth the name) and had but ſix ſhippes belõging to their Towne, and thoſe for the Riuer onely, that neuer went to ſea, began to growe exceeding riche, ſo that ſome fell to the trade of Merchandiſe, and others employed their ſubſtance in building, then their olde rotten houſes couered with thatche; were pulled downe, their waſte grounde, whereof there was ſtoar within the Towne, was turned into goodlie buildinges, and faire ſtreates, and their ſhipping encreaſed accordinglie: thus proſpered not onelie thoſe of *Antwerpe*, but all other Townes, and places thereabouts, ſo that in our memorie that now liue, the ſaid Town was growen to ſuch wealth, ſtrength, and beautie, as neuer none the like in ſo ſhort a time, and no marvaile, for within the compaſſe of fiftie yeares

De Coe Poort.

yeares, an house that was woorth but fortie Dallers a yeare, grew to bee woorth three hundred Dallers a yere, And an house that was lett out for sixtie Dallers, came afterwardes to bee lett for foure hundred Dallers, yea some houses in *Antwerpe* were lett for 600 some 800. Dallers a yeare rent, besides their Hauens for shippes to come and lade and discharge within the Towne: their publike stately buildinges, and edifices erected partlie for ornament, and partly for the ease & accõmodating of the Merchant, were so costlie, and sumptuous, as he that hath not seene, and marked them well, would not beleeue it: to say nothing of the fortification of the Towne, which is such, that the charges thereof would trouble the richest Prince in Europe: but as the Poet *Lucane* said,

A Daller is three shillinges sterlinge.

Invida Fatorum series summisq; negatum stare diu.

So it fareth at this day with *Antwerpe*, for it hath within these few yeares suffered verie great chaunge and alteration, and more is like to doe, if it long continew shutt vp, and without trade and trafficque vnder the yoak of the Spaniard, and the feare of an impregnable Castle stuffed with souldiers, a scourge, & plague to that, and to all free Citties: thus much by the way of *Antwerp*, the late Pack-house of Europe, & of the state thereof, when the English Marchants first repaired vnto it, and of the great wealth it grew vnto in a verie short time, whereof the saide English Merchantes with their gainfull, and beneficiall trade were a great cause, and meanes, whiche principallie

D 2 made

made them to be so much regarded and esteemed in the said Towne, and by the Princes & Gouvernours thereof from time to time, as well appeareth, among other proofes, by this one recorded by *Sleidane*, and remembred by some that yet liue: The Emperour *Charles* the fifth would haue brought the *Inquisition* into the Towne of *Antwerp*, in the yeare 1550. wherabouts there was much adoe, and great question, & neither by the sute of the Towne, nor by anie Intercession, or request of their friendes could the saide Emperour be diuerted from his purpose: at the last it was shewed him, that if the *Inquisitiō* were brought in, he would driue the Englishe Merchantes out of that Cittie, and out of the whole low Countreis also, the consequence whereof when he had well considered, he chaunged his minde, and so the Cittie of *Antwerp* was saued from the Inquisition, which they so much feared, and by no sute, or meanes besides were able to put from them: of such estimation and accoumpte were the Merchantes Aduenturers with that Mightie and Prudent Emperour, and of suche credite and reckoning haue they been from time to time at home with eleven Kinges, and Queenes of this Realme of Englande, and abroad with the Citties of *Bridges* in Flanders, *Antwerpe*, & *Berghen op den Zoom* in *Brabant*, *Middelburgh*, and *Zie̓riczee* in *Zeland*, *Amsterdam*, and *Dort* in *Hollande*, *Vtrecht* the chiefe Cittie of a Prouince of that name, & with the Dukes, Earles, Lordes, and Rulers of the abouesaid Citties, and Prouinces lying within the low Countreis, auncient

Sleidanus 21. libro Commentariorum.

Inquisition in Antwerp left of for the M. M. Advēturers sake.

cient friendes, and Confederates with the Crowne of Englande: And in *Germanie* with the Townes of *Hambroughe*, and *Stade*, and the Earles of *East-friesland* since the yeare 1564. till this daye, at whiche tyme they obtayned Priviledges of the Ladie *Anne* Countesse of *Oldenburghe*, and her sonnes *Edgard* and *Iohn*, wherein they call the Companie of Merchants Adventurers, *Inclitam illam & celebratam passim Anglicorum Mercatorum Societatem*. In all which places, and Countreis the foresaide Companie haue so demeaned themselues, that thereby they haue reaped great loue, credite, fame, and commendation, and haue left behind them a longing for them againe in those places, where they once resided, or helde their Martes, and procured a desire of them in many places, where they neuer were: whiche appeareth by the honorable Testimonie giuen of the Companie by the aboue saide Townes, and forreigne Princes abroad, and is otherwise well knowen to those, who knowe anie thing of the doeings of our neighbours. And latelie when through the malicious, and iniurious working of a fewe of the *Hanse Townes* instigated and holpen forward by the King of Spaines ministers, a parte of the saide Companie was put from the Towne of *Stade* in the yeare 1597. and were forced to retire out of the Empire, the Townes of the vnited Lowe Countreis, eleuen or twelue in number, of the best scituate, each striving to be preferred, like so manie Riuales or Competitors, offered themselues in most friendlie, and hartie sorte, and invited

D 3 the

the saide Companie to reside with them vpon promises of such fauour, and Priviledge, as ought neuer to be forgotten: but hereof possibly enough: Let vs now looke into the Estate, Policie, and Gouvernement of the said Companie, wherby we shall plainlie see the causes and reasons of the loue, estimation, and credite which it hath purchased abroad, and so the sooner beleeue that, which hath aboue been sett downe, and affirmed.

Of the State, and Gouuernement of the Companie of Merchantes Aduenturers, and of such benefites as grow to the Realme by the maintenance therof.

THE Companie of Merchants Adventurers consisteth of a great number of wealthie, and well experimented Merchantes, dwelling in diuerse great Citties, Maritime Townes, and other partes of the Realme, to witt, in *London, Yorke, Norwitche, Excester, Ipswitch, Newcastle, Hull, &c.* These men of olde time linked and bounde them selues togither in Companie, for the exercise of Merchandise, and sea-fare, trading in Clothe, Kersye, and all other, as well English as foreign Commodities vendible abroade, by the which they brought vnto the places, where they traded, much wealth, benefite, & com-

commoditie, and for that cause haue obtayned manie verie excellent, & singular Priviledges, Rightes, Iurisdictions, exemptions, & immunities, all which thôse of the aforesaid Fellowshippe equallie enioye after a well ordered manner, and forme, and according to the ordinances, lawes, and customes denized, and agreed vpon by common consente of all the Merchantes, free of the said Fellowshipp, dwelling in the aboue mentioned Townes, and places of the Lande: the partes, and places which they trade vnto, are the Townes, and Portes lyeing betweene the Riuers of *Somme* in *France*, and the *Scawe* in the *Germane* sea: not into all at once, or at each mans pleasure, but into one, or two Townes at the moste within the abouesaide boundes, whiche they commonly call the Mart Towne, or Townes: for that there onelie they stapled the commodities, whiche they brought out of Englande, and put the same to sale, and bought such foreigne Commodities, as the lande wanted, and were brought from farre by Merchants of diuerse Nations, and Countreis flockinge thither, as to a faire, or markett to buye and sell. And albeit through the troubles, and alteration of tymes, the M.M. Adventurers haue been forced to change and leaue their olde marte Townes, and seeke new, (as hath been partlie touched before) yet wheresoeuer they seated them selues, thither presentlie repaired other Straungers, leauinge likewise the places whence the English Merchants were departed, and planting them selues where they resided: so that as long

The companie of M. Advêturers is able to makê & diuert a trade.

long as the Companie continued their Mart, or Staple in a place, so long grew, and prospered that place: but when they forsooke it, the welfare, and good estate thereof seemed withal to departe, and forsake it, as in olde time hath been seene in *Bridges*, and in our tyme in some others, and no marvaile: For diligent inquirie being made in the yere 1550. by the commandement of the Emperour *Charles* the fifth, what benefite, or commoditie came to his State of the low Countreis by the haunt, and Commerce of the English Merchantes, it was found, that in the Cittie of *Antwerp* alone, where the Cōpanie of M. M. Adventurers was at that time residing, were at least twentie thousand persons fed & mainteyned for the most part by the trade of the M. M. Adventurers: besides thirtie thousand others in other places of the low Countries likewise maintayned and fed partlie by the said trade, partly by endraping of Clothe, & working in Wooll and other commodities brought out of England. In confirmation wherof, I haue heard auncient Merchants say, That at the time when the aboue said Companie was entierely resident at *Antwerp*, a little before the troubles which fell out in the yeres 63. & 64. there were fed, & mainteyned in the low Countreis sixtie thousande soules (and some haue saide a great manie more) by the English trade, and by the Wares bought in the low Countreis to be caried into England, which no doubt was the cause, that the Princes of the low Countreis haue been so favourable to the aboue saide Cōpanie, & so loath to forgoe or or loose them, as knowing that therewithall they should loose a verie faire flower of their garlande, yea a sure roote, and foundation of their wealth. For on the one side, such is the valew, profite, and goodnes of the English Commodities, that all Nations of these partes of Europe, and elswhere, desire them, and on the other side, the English Merchants buye vp, and carrie into Englande so great a quantitie of foreigne wares, that for the sale thereof, all straunge Merchauntes doe, and will repaire vnto them. Now what these Englishe commodities are, and how they be so profitable, may appeare by the particulars following:

The profites arisinge by the M. M. Advēturers trade & residence beyonde the Seas.

First, there is shipped out yearely by the abouesaid Companie, at least sixtie thousande white Clothes, besides coloured Clothes of all sortes, Kersyes short, and longe, Bayes, Cottons, Northern Dosens, & diuerse other kindes of course Clothes: the iust valew of these sixtie thousande white Clothes can not well bee calculated, or sett downe, but they are not lesse woorth (in mine opinion) then sixe hundred thousande poundes sterling, or English monie.

The coloured Clothes of all sortes, Bayes, Kersyes, Northern Dosens, and other course Clothes, I reckon to arise to the nūber of fortie thousand Clothes, at least, and they be woorth one with another foure hundred thousand poundes sterling, or English monie.

There goeth also out of England, besides these Woollē Clothes, into the low Coūtries, Wool, Fel,

E Lead,

Lead, Tinne, Saffron, Conyſkins, Leather, Tallow, Alablaſtre ſtones, Corn, Beer, & diuers other things, amoũting vnto great ſummes of mony: By al which commodities, a number of labouring men are ſet on work, & gaign much monie, beſides that which the Merchaunt gaineth, which is no ſmall matter. Hereunto adde the monie which Shippers, and men that liue vpon the water, gett by fraight, and portage of the foreſaid Cõmodities from place, to place, which would amount to a great ſumme, if the particulars thereof were, or could be exactlie gathered: hereby in ſhort may be ſeene, howe great and profitable the Companie of M. M. Aduenturers trade hath been, and is in the places, where they hold their reſidence, beſides the profite raiſed vpõ the Chambers, Sellers, and Packhouſes, which they muſt haue for foure or fiue hundred Merchants, whereby Rentes are mainteyned and kept vp, and the great expenſes otherwiſe, which the ſaid Merchants are at for their diete, apparell, &c. to ſaye nothing of the Princes, or Generalities profit, and reuenues by their Tolles, Convoyes, Impoſtes, Axcyſes, and other dewties, whereof there can be no certaine notice had, but to ſhewe the greatnes thereof, let this one ſigne ſo long agoe, ſerue for all, That *Philippe* the *Good*, Duke of *Burgundie*, and firſt founder of the order of the *Golden Fleeſe*, gaue the foreſaid Fleeſe for a liuerie, or badge of the ſaid Order, for that he had his chiefeſt Tolles, Reuenues, and Incoms, by Wooll, and Woollen Cloth: Thus you haue ſeene what profit is raiſed by ſtrangers,

Carion. 5. Libro.

gers, vpon the English trade, it followeth to shewe, what the M. M. Adventurers buye for returne, of straunge Nations, & people frequenting their Marte Townes, and bringing their Countrie commodities thether.

Of the Dutche, and Germane Marchantes, they buye Rhenish Wine, Fustians, Copper, Steele, Hemp, Oinion-seed, Copper & Iron Wyre, Latten, Kettels, and Pannes, Linnen cloth, Harnas, Saltpeter, Gun-powder, all things made at *Norenbergh*, and in summe, there is no kinde of ware, that Germanie yeeldeth, but generallie the M M Adventurers buye as much, or more thereof, then any other Nation. Germane wares.

Of the Italians, they buye all kinde of silke wares, Velvittes, wrought, and vnwrought, Taffitaes, Sattins, Damaskes, Sarsenettes, Milan fustians, Clothe of golde, and siluer, Grograines, Chamlettes, Satin, and sowing silke, Organzine, Orsoy, and all other kinde of wares either made, or to be had in Italie. Italiane wares

Of the Esterlinges they buye Flaxe, Hemp, Wax, Pitche, Tarre, Wainscot, Deal bordes, Oares, Corn, Furres, Cables, and Cable yearne, Tallow, Ropes, Mastes for shippes, Sope-ashes, Estrigd wooll, and almost what soeuer is made, or groweth in the East Countries. Esterlinge wares.

Of the *Portingales*, they buye all kinde of Spyces, and Drugges: with the Spanish and Frenche, they had not much to doe, by reason that other Englishe Merchantes haue had a great trade into France and Spaine, and so serue England directlie from thence Portingale wares.

E 2 with

with the commodities of those Countries.

Netherlanders wares

Of the low Countrie Merchantes, or Netherlanders, they buye all kinde of manufacture, or handworke not made in Englande, Tapestrie, Buckrams, white threed, incle, Linnen clothe of all sortes, Cambrickes, Lawnes, Mather, and an infinite number of other thinges, to longe to rehearse in particular, but heereby I hope it sufficientlie appeareth, that it is of an exceeding valew, which the M. M. Aduenturers buye, & carrie into England, in so much, that I haue heard it crediblie reported, that all the Commodities, that come out of all other Coũtreis, besides Englande, were not wonte to sett so manie people on woorke in the low Countreis, as the Commodities, which came out of England onely did, neither that anie other two of the greatest Nations, that frequented the said low Countreis for trade, did buye, or carie out so much goodes in valew, as the Merchantes Adventurers: The knowledge, and consideration whereof hath made them thought woorthie to bee made of, cherished, & desired by Princes, States, and Common Wealthes, and it would not hurt the state of the Empire a whytt, to holde friendshippe, & entertayn so profitable a Companie, and Trade, as this, whereby great multitudes of their poore people, might be sett on worke, and gett their liuing, and in processe of tyme grow riche thereby, as the men of *Antwerpe*, and others of the lowe Countries haue done, which by the practises of the Pope, and King of Spaine, & the vnreasonable dealing of the *Hanses*, is is in a manner kept from them. The root, and ſpring of all this almoſt incredible Trade, and Trafficque hath had his increaſe, and proceeding from the politike Gouuernement, Lawes, and Orders deviſed, and obſerued of olde time in the ſaid Companie, as aforeſaide: eſpeciallie ſince the raigne of King *Henrie* the ſeuenth, by the ſpeciall order, cōmandement, and encouragement of the ſaide Noble Prince, one day ſtill being a Schoolemaiſter vnto the other, and men by experience, vſe, and knowledge of foreigne People, and their facions, orders, and kinde of dealing, growing dailie, and from time to time to an exacter courſe, and greater perfection of matters, and vnderſtanding of their own eſtate, and what is fitteſt for the vpholding, and maintenance thereof: Theſe ſaide ordinances conteine in them all kinde of good Diſcipline, Inſtruction, and rules to bring vp youth in, & to keepe them in order: ſo that the Marchants Adventurers dwelling in the aboue mentioned Citties, and Townes of the Realme of Englande, ſende their yong men, ſonnes, and ſervauntes, or Apprentices, who for the moſt parte are Gentlemens ſonnes, or mens children of good meanes or qualitie, to the Marte Townes, beyonde the Seas, there to learne good facions, and to gaigne experience, and knowledge in trade, and the manners of ſtrāūge Nations, thereby the better to knowe the world betymes, and to be able, to goe through with the ſame, to the honor, and ſervice of their Prince, and Countrey, and their owne wel-fare, and advauncement in the com-

E 3 mon

mon Wealth, whereof a verie great number haue shewed them selues, and at this daye manie are, verie notable, and beneficiall members: Besides, the said Companie hath a Gouvernour, or in his absence, a Deputie, and foure and twentie Assistentes in the Marte Towne, who haue Iurisdiction, and full Authoritie as well from her Maiestie, as from the Princes, States, and Rulers of the low Countries, and beyond the seas, without Appelle, prouocation, or declination, to ende and determine all Ciuile causes, questions, and controversies arising betweene or amonge the Brethren, Members, and supposites of the saide Companie, or betweene them and others, either Englishe, or Straungers, who either may or will prorogate the Iurisdiction of the saide Companie, & their Court, or are subiect to the same by the Priviledges, and Charters thereunto graunted.

By the saide Gouvernour, and Assistentes are also appointed, and chosen a Deputie, and certaine discreete persons, to be Associates to the saide Deputie in all other places cōvenient, as well within, as without the Realme of Englande, who all holde Correspondence with the Gouvernour of the Companie, and chiefe Court in the Mart Towne on the other side the Seas, and haue subalterne power to exercise Merchauntes lawe, to rule, and looke to the good ordering of the Brethren of the Companie euerie where, as farre as may bee, and their Charters will beare them out.

Further, the saide Companie entertaineth godlie and

and learned Preachers with liberall stipendes, and other benefites : Hath also Treasurers, Secretaries, and other needefull Officers, the end of all which is: *The seemelie and orderlie Gouvernement and rule of all the members, partes, and Brethren of the saide Companie wher-soeuer in their Trade, and seat of Mercandise. Secondly, The Preseruation of Amitie, and the Entercourse betweene the Realme of Englaned and their Neighbours and Allies, and the Preventing of Innovations, griefs, wronges, and exactions contrarie to the same. Thirdlie, The great Vent, Advancement, and keeping in Estimation of English Commodities, and the bringing in of foreigne Commodities good cheape. Fourthlie, The Maintneance of the Navigation. Fifthlie, The Encrease of the Queenes Incomes, and Customes. Sixthlie, and lastlie, The Honor, and Service of the Prince, and of our State and Countrey, at home, and abroad.*

Benefites & Commodities arising by the Cõpanie of Merchantes Advẽturers.

Now that all these benefites, and commodities arise by the Companie of Merchantes Adventurers, I hope by, and by, plainlie to shew, and with-all to proove, That by the saide Companie, all the abouewritten pointes are better performed, and brought to passe, then if all were sett at libertie, as some haue desired, & consequentlie that without the said Companie, few, or none of the foresaid Benefites, or Cõmodities will bee so well raised or redounde to the State, and Common Wealth.

Of

Of Rule, and Gouvernement, the first point and Commoditie arising by the united Companie of Marchants Adventurers.

I Shall not neede to say much in commendation of good Gouvernement, & Policie, as having before touched the same in parte, and shewed howe needfull, & requisite it is also in matter of Commerce, Trade, and the feat of Merchandise. Now that the Companie of Merchantes Adventurers hath for this Point been auncientlie famous, and highlie praised, and esteemed of Straungers, as well, as of those of their owne Countrie, and so continueth to this day (although much disturbed, and disquieted by newe Tulles and Dimockes) I thinke no man doubteth: so that I take it as graunted, that the State, and Common Wealth heereby reapeth more profite, then if men were suffred to runne a loose, and irregulare course without order, commaund, or oversight of anie: whereby manie griefes, hurtes, dissentions, and inconveniences, besides no small dishonour to the Prince, and State would in shorte tyme arise, as heeretofore they haue done for want of sage, and discreete Gouvernment, of which Remedie seeing the foresaid Companie is sufficientlie provided, and that it hath been by the experience of so manie Ages, and the allowance

ance of eleuen Princes of the Realme approued, me thinkes, it were an offence, and wrong vnto the State offred to goe about to alter, or hinder the same: *atque ita Cornicum oculos configere.*

That the Amitie, and Entercourse betweene the Realme of Englande, and their Neighbours, and Allies, are cherished, and all Innovations, griefes, wronges, and exactions contrarie to the same, are prevented by the Maintenance of the Companie of Merchants Adventurers.

THERE hath been of olde tyme, very straight alliance and amitie betweene the Kinges of *Englande*, and the Princes of the low Countreis, especiallie since the gouuernement of the saide Countreis came to the handes of the Dukes of *Burgundie*, and among the saide Dukes, betweene King *Henrie* the fifth, and *Philippe*, surnamed the *Good*, Father to *Charles* surnamed the *Warriour*, which *Charles* was slaine before the Towne of *Nancy*: This Duke *Philippe* had almost from a childe been brought vp in the Court of Englande, so that betweene the saide King, and him, and their subiectes, was a verie firme league, friendshippe, & entercourse, the causes wherof, and of the former Amitie, and League betweene

F the

the Kinges of England frõ King *Edward* the third,& the said Princes of the low Coũtreis,are reckoned to be three principallie. First the aide of the said Kings in the pursuite of their iust title to the Crowne of France. Secondlie, The saufer keeping of *Calice*, and the territorie thereabouts in the possessiõ of the said Kinges: And thidlie, The nearenes of *Flanders*, *Brabant*, *Holland* and *Sealand* vnto the Realme, and the commodious scituation thereof for the vent of English Commodities,in which Provinces the English Merchauntes were at that time settled. This neighbourlie league grounded vpon the aboue saide causes hath constantlie continued euer since, but more nearely was confirmed betweene King *Henrie* the fifth, & the abouesaid Duke of *Burgundie*, who liued in the yeare of our Lorde 1420. so that since that tyme it hath neuer been broken, but at the death, or chaunge of any Prince,on eache parte hath been renewed, confirmed, and sometimes augmented, and namelie betweene King *Henrie* the seuenth, & King *Philippe*,sonne to the Emperour *Maximiliane*,and Father to *Charles* the fifth Emperour, and for the maintenance, and cherishing of the saide league, and entercourse, it is well knowen to those which are conuersant in Historie of things past, that since the winning of *Calice*,by King *Edward* the thirde,in the yere 1347. the Kinges of Englande haue with great Armies by lande,and Fleetes of shippes by sea,invaded the Realme of France,in the quarrel and for the ayd of the house of *Burgundie*, as well as for their owne parti-

particular claymes,and right,&especially King *Henrie* the fifth, as appeareth by diuers writers of those times, and since,but to lett passe so old matters, and only to rehearse somewhat of that,which hath been done in the memorie of men yet living, or not long before, I will in brief recount some speciall proofes of that abouesaide,giuing this note by the way, that as the Kings of Englande, and the Dukes of *Burgundie* were ioigned in league,and friendshippe,so were the Frenche,and Scottes,that when soeuer England had warre with France, Scotland had the like with England,so that the Kinges of England haue had alwayes double warres with the Frenche and Scottes togeather, and haue beene forced from time to time to keepe two Armies,sometimes three at once in the fielde.

Aydes giuē by the Kings of England to the house of Burgūdie

In the yeare 1492.King *Henrie* the seuenth,in fauour and ayde of *Maximiliane*, Archduke of *Austrich*, & sonne to the Emperour *Frederick* the fourth, who had maried the Ladie *Marie*, daughter & sole heire to *Charles* the Warriour,slaine before *Nancy*,as aforesaide, and against whom almoste all the Townes in Flaunders rebelled, and tooke armes, and with the ayde of the Frenche, besieged the Towne of *Dixmuyde*, the saide King sent ouer the Lord *Dawbenye*, and the Lord *Morley*, with an armie vpon his owne charges into *Flanders*, who raised the foresaide siege, and slew eight thousand Frenche men, & Flemings in the place, taking all their prouision,& ordinance: and in the yeare following, when *Nieuporte*, a Town

F 2 lying

lyeing vpon the Sea-coast of Flanders, was besieged by Monsieur de *Cordes*, a Frenche man, with twentie thousand Frenche and Fleminges, and that one of the principallest Towers or Bulwarkes of the saide Towne was entred, and helde by the enimie, yet by the valiant resistence of such English men, as were within it, and fresh supplie sent by the foresaid King, the foresaid *Cordes* was forced to leaue the said Town with shame, and losse of manie of his men, & much provision. In the same yeare also, the saide Kinge *Henrie* the seuenth sent an armie by sea vnder the cõduct of the Lord *Pominges*, to the ayde of the saide Archduke *Maximilian*, against the Lord of *Raven-steyn*, Geneall of the Rebellious Fleminges, who had taken the Castell and Towne of *Sluse* (the onelie Hauen and Porte to the seas of that olde and famous Towne of *Bridges*) but the Lord *Pominges* recouered the said Castell by force, and deliuered it to *Albert* Duke of *Saxonie*, generall for the foresaid Archduke: By the saving of which Castle, and the aboue saide towne of *Newporte*, the whole Earldome of Flanders was saued out of the handes of the Frenche Kinge, who otherwise, without the ayde of King *Henrie* of Englande, had ioyned the same to the Crowne of France. In the yeare following, the saide Kinge *Henrie*, in revenge of the great scorne and iniurie done to the abouesaid Archduke by the Frẽch King, partly in returning home the Ladie *Margaret*, daughter to the saide Archduke, who was affianced, and after the maner of great Princes, by Deputies maryed to to the said Frenche King, and partlie by getting in craftie sorte the Ladie *Anne*, the onely heire of the Dutchie of *Britanie* from the said Archduke, to whō shee was maried, entred France with a great Armie, where the saide Archduke promised to meete him with another armie on his parte, and although the saide promise was not kept, yet the said King proceeded on his purpose, besieged *Bullen*, and finally constrayned the French King to seeke peace of him, and to giue him a great summe of monie, with the which (and great spoile gott by his people) he returned into England, to his high honour, and praise, without once seeing or hauing anie helpe at all of the saide *Maximiliane*.

In the yere 1512. at which time the French King made warres with *Fernando* King of Spaine, and inuaded his Countreis by lande, King *Henrie* the eight (of famous memorie) sent an aide of tenne thousand men by sea into Spain, vnder the leading of the Noble Lord, the Lord *Thomas Grey*, Marquis *Dorset*, at the request of the aboue-mentioned *Maximilian* then Emperour, whose only sonne and heire *Philippe*, had maried *Ioan* the daughter, and heire of the aboue said *Ferdinando*: Twoo yeares after this, the saide King *Henrie* in fauour and defence of the yonge Prince or Infante of Spaine, *Charles*, grandchilde to the aboue saide *Maximiliane*, and afterwardes Emperour himselfe, went ouer in person with a mightie armie into France, and besieged the strong Towne of *Terwin*, which finallie was yeelded vnto him, maugre the

F 3 whole

whole power of Fraunce, after he had discomfited, and ouerthrowen in battaile the French armie, slaying eight or tenne thousande in the place, and taking prisoners the Duke *de Longueville*, the Marquise *Retelois*, and besides 240. Lordes, Knightes, and Gentlemen of name and honour: In whiche battaile the aboue saide Emperour with at least fortie or fiftie of the Nobilitie of the lowe Countries, serued vnder the Kings Standerd, receyuing wages of him, and wearing the redd Crosse, or Cognizance of England, after the rendring ouer of *Terwin*, the saide Kinge brought his armie before the Citie of *Tonrnay*, or *Dornick*, at that time tearmed the Maiden Citie, (for that it neuer had been wonne by Prince) but Kinge *Henrie* gott it, and having taken order, for the sure keeping thereof, returned the way that he came, being a long marche of 63. miles with great glorie, and honour into Englande, and in the meane while the Duke of *Norfolke*, and his sonne the Earle of *Surrye*, had discomfited an armie of fiftie thousand Scottes, vnder the leading of their King *Iames* the fourth, who was slaine in the fielde with fourteene thousande of his people, whereof manie were of the Nobilitie, besides 12 Earles, 20 Lords, 40 or 50 Knightes, and manie Gentlemen, taken prisoners.

In the yeare 1514. the said King *Henrie* the eight did sende a bande of 1500. choise souldiours, vnder the leading of the Lord *Clinton*, vnto the ayde of the Ladie *Margarete*, Regent of the low Countries, against the Duke of Gelderlande.

In the

In the yeare 1530. a perpetuall peace was agreed vpon, and sworne at *Parise* in France, betwixt the Emperour *Charles* the fifth, the King of England, & the French King, during their three lives: and which of the three should first violate, or breake this peace, the other two were bound to sett vpon him, as their open and ioint enemie: this peace was firste broken on the French Kinges parte, by reason of a quarrell betweene the Emperour, and the saide King, whereupon the King of England, for his oath and promise sake, sent ouer into France a great Armie, vnder the leading of the Duke of *Suffolke*, and prepared a great Fleet of shippes by sea, to anoye the saide Countrie, and by this meanes drewe the Scottes against him: for the Duke of *Albanie* in ayd of the Frenche, entred England, and began to spoile the borders thereof, against whom the Earle of *Surrye* was sent, who forced the Scottes to retyre, to their losse, and dishonour, and entred Scotland at their heeles, burninge, and spoyling the Countrie afore him, and returning with great pray, and bootie.

In the yeare 1543. the said King *Henrie* the eight, sent ouer Syr *Iohn Wallop*, and other Gentlemẽ, with a band of six thousand mẽ, to the ayd of the foresaid Emperour *Charles*, when he went to *Landersey*: and in the yeare 1545. the saide King in person with two Armies went ouer into Fraunce, in ayd of the saide Emperour *Charles*, at which tyme hee besieged, and tooke *Bullen*: but how ill the said Emperor kept promise with the said King, and afterwards without his know-

knowledge, or privitie, made peace with the French King, I shall not neede to say much, as being partlie freshe in mans memorie, and partlie commended to writing by such, as liued in those dayes.

Sleidanus Libro sexto.

In the yeare 1557. Queene *Marie* in favour of her husband King *Philippe*, and by his procurement, and meanes, made warres vpon Fraunce, sending ouer an armie by sea, vnder the Lorde *Clintone*, highe Admirall of England, into *Britanie*, where they landed, spoiled, and burnt a great way into the Countrie, And another armie of tenne thousand men by lande, vnder the Earles of *Penbrooke, Bedforde*, & *Rutland*, by whose helpe King *Philippe* gott the stronge Towne of S[t] *Quintins*, and had his wil of the French King: but the English by these warres, and breaking peace with Fraunce for King *Philippes* sake, lost the Towne of *Calice*, which the predecessours of the said Queene, had kept in spighte of all France 210. yeeres before that time: What other privie helpes Queene *Marie* gaue vnto her saide Husband, few or none can tell, but it is tought, he had many an hundred thousande poundes from her, that all the worlde knewe not of. These warres haue the Kings of Englande taken in hande, and these aydes from tyme to tyme haue they giuen to the house of *Burgundie*, besides great, and vnknowen summes of money lent, in so much, that in the opinion of men of knowledge, and experiēce, it cost the Realme of England three skore tymes an hundred thousand poundes at least, in the quarrel and defence of the Princes of the said house, within

within the compaſſe of 76. yeres after that *Maximiliane* maried with the Ladie *Marie*, daughter to *Charles* the *Warriour*, and heire to the ſaid houſe: to ſaye nothing of that which happened before, and nowe of late hath fallen out ſince the troubles in the low Countries, in all which the Kinges, and Queenes of England, haue ſhewed themſelues faithful, & friendlie Princes, and good Neighbours, and Allies to the the ſaide low Countries, and truelie & readilie haue holpen, & ſtood by the Princes thereof in their greateſt need, and extremitie: whereas we can not read, that thoſe of the houſe of *Burgūdie* euer made warres againſt Scotlande, or Fraunce in helpe of the Kinges of Englande directlie: neither were they, or anie of them euer required thervnto, but once, and that was in the dayes of King *Edward* the ſixt, being then but eight or nine yeres of age, and at ſuch time as he had both warre with Scotland, and Fraunce at once, and beſides was troubled with a great rebelliō of his ſubiectes at home, for which cauſe a ſolempne Embaſſage was ſent to the Emperour *Charles* the fifth, who laid before the ſaide Emperour, the feeble eſtate of the ſaid King *Edwardes* infancie, and tender yeares, & the commotion of his ſubiectes, euen vpon the neck of the warres, and troubles with Fraunce, and Scotlande, putting the ſaide Emperour in minde of the great Armies, which at ſundrie tymes had been ſent out of England in ayd of his Father, and Graund father, and alſo of the daungerous, and chargeable warres begunne, and taken in hande by King *Henrie*

Embaſſage to the Emperor Charles the fifth from King Edward the ſixth.

G the

the eight, the ſaid Kinges Father, for the quarrell of the ſaid Emperour alone, as then but an Infant alſo, and vnder yeares: they did not lett further to tell him of the great paines, and travell taken by the ſaid King *Henrie*, with his friendes the Princes Electors, and others of Germanie, at the requeſt of the ſaide Emperour, to preferre him to the Imperiall Crown, and Dignitie, which he now poſſeſſed, and perhaps might elſe haue miſſed: Laſtlie, they prayed the ſaid Emperour, to remember the auncient, and faithfullie continued Amitie betweene the Emperour, and his Predeceſſours Dukes of Burgundie, and the Predeceſſours of the ſaide Kinge *Edwarde*, and that the warres, which he now had with Scotland, & France, was for none other cauſe mooved, then in maintenaunce of the ſaide Amitie, and in defence of the Quarrell of the houſe of *Burgundie*, and at the requeſt of the Princes thereof onelie: But, as the ſaid Emperour had dealt before with Duke *Frederick* of *Saxonie*, by whoſe meanes eſpeciallie he attayned to the Emperial Dignitie, ſo he did the like with King *Edward*, for clean forgetting all olde, and new friendſhippes, he gaue the Embaſſadours vncourteous woordes for the alteration of the Religion by their Kinge, and would doe nothing except the ſame were chaunged againe to the olde: Wherevpon they beſought the ſaid Emperour, that he would at leaſt be pleaſed, to take into his handes, and keeping the Towne of *Bullen*, not long before gott from Fraunce by King *Henrie* the eight, and that but for a tyme, till the ſaide King

King *Edward* had quieted the troubles with his subiectes at home: but this he would not yeelde vnto neither, except the King would change his Religiō, which the King, and his Counsell (hauing the feare of God before their eyes) vtterlie refused, choosing rather to loose earthlie thinges, then heauenlie, and therefore seeing the Emperour would neither giue ayde him selfe, nor suffer anie munition, or souldiors to goe out of his land into England, no not so much as an armour (as I haue hearde) that one of the Embassadours had bought for him selfe at *Bruesselles*, a peace in the yeare 1549. was concluded with France and Scotlande, with the restoring of *Bullen*, & vpon other conditions according to the tyme: this peace fell out but litle to the profit of the Emperour, for in the yeare 1551. began the great warres betweene him, and *Henrie* the Frenche King, wherein the *Burgundians* fealt the want of their olde trustie Friendes, and Allies the King of Englande, and his people. And vndoubtedlie, if the Kinges of Englande had not continuallie ayded, and assisted the house of *Burgundie*, and the low Countreis, they had both been Frenche before this daye, or if the Frenche Kinge might haue been sure of England, and without feare thereof bent his whole forces by sea, and by lande against the House of *Burgundie*, and *Spaine*, neither should the Emperour haue gott so much advantage, as he did against the French King, neither haue been able to haue troubled Germanie, and the Germane Princes, nor other Princes, States, and Countreis, as

G 2 he

he did, neither ſhould he haue gotten ſo much poſ-ſeſsion, and Dominion in *Italie*, and other places, as hee gott, neither laſtlie ſhould his ſubiectes haue obtained ſo great wealth, and ritches, nor ſo much knowledge by lande, and by ſea, as they haue done. For ſurelie, he, and his people may thanke the Kings of Englande for all theſe thinges: for the ayde of the ſaide Kinges, and the trafficque, and reſorte of the Engliſhe Merchaunts haue been the principal cauſes thereof, and therefore great reaſon had the Dukes of *Burgundie*, to ſeeke the friendſhippe, and Amitie of the Kinges of Englande, and to cheriſhe, & augment the ſame by Treaties, and Entercourſe from tyme to tyme, which are yet continued in force: and where-of the foreſaide Companie of M. M. Adventurers haue ſo good notice, recorde, & vnderſtanding, that vpon anie occaſion whatſoeuer, they haue them rea-die, thereby to defend the Right of the Realme, and ſubiectes thereof, againſt ſuch as would either will-fullie, or vnawares breake, & violate the ſame, which ought to remaine as ſacred, and vntouched, for the preſeruation of mutuall friendſhippe, and Amitie betweene both Nations, which oftentimes for want of dew care, and prouiſion on this behalfe in tyme, might turne into open ennimitie, and alienation of good will, not without daunger of warre in the end, if ſome men might haue their willes: As in the yeare 1564. *Don Giraldo Deſpes* Embaſſadour for the King of Spaine in England, at the inſtance of the Cardi-nall *Granvelle*, dealt with a ſtraunger, yet livinge in England,

Don Giral-do Deſpes.

Englande,& wel knowen there, to drawe out a summarie of all the doleances of the low Country Merchantes, promising redresse therein, or to bringe the matter to an open warre, whiche whether the saide straunger did, or not, I can not iustlie saye, but it is like enough his busie head considered, and hee hath conceyued no small discontentement of olde, that thinges goe not, as he would faigne haue them in Englande for his owne particular fancies sake, and employment, without regardinge the alteration of tymes, or breach of Amitie, which might fall out betweene her Maiestie, & the States of the vnited low Countries for that cause, so hee might come to his purpose: For immediatelie vpon this followed that violent proceeding of the Dutches of *Parmae*, in banishing of Englishe Clothe, and Commodities out of the low Countries, by meanes wherof, the Commerce, and Trade for a tyme surceased, not without perill of warre betweene the Princes, and their people. The Companie therefore of the M.M. Adventurers are a great obstacle to the raising and bringing in of new, and vnwonted Tolles, Impostes, exactions, and grievances, which otherwise the subiects of the Realme of Englande, their Shippes, and goods, would be charged with, and oppressed, contrarie to the treaties of Amitie, and Entercourses, to the empouerishing of the saide subiectes; & the hinderance of the Navigation, whiche commeth to passe by meanes, and helpe of their common purse, & by officers mainteyned to keepe register of all things needfull

G 3 full

full, and to defende these common causes from time to time, when anie Innovation, or straunge exaction is brought in, tending to the hurt, and hinderance of the Merchantes, Mariners, &. sea faring men, and consequentlie to the dammage, and preiudice of the whole state: and this a perticular man is not able to doe, for either his purse, or meanes will not reach vnto it, or else being loath to spende his monie, and tyme, or to hinder his affaires, and trade hereaboutes, will rather yeeld vnto a wronge, whereby it cometh to passe by litle and litle, that the auncient rightes of the Realme, are either lessened, or infringed, & that, which ought not to bee suffered, vnwonted tallages, taxes, and impositions, are leuyed vpon the subiect, to his great grievance, & empouerishing, and to the bringing of the Trade into straungers handes onely: a thing of longe tyme practised, and laboured for by them, and chieflie prevented, and withstoode by the Companie of M. M. Adventurers, which hath stirred vp the Easterlinges, and some Merchants of *Antwerpe*, of late dayes against them, the Easterlings continewe still in their pride of heart, and indurate malice, the *Antwerpians*, and their new-borne Colledge (the troubles groweing vpon them) were forced to be quiet, though within these three yeares, their first and last (perhaps) Consull, and Secretarie haue sollicited the States Generall of the vnited Provinces with their Complaints, and accusations, to embrace, and renew their olde quarrelles, and pretences, and to sett vp on foote againe their decayed Consulate,

in

in recompēce of the good seruices heretofore done, (which I could wishe examined for that they vaunt them selues thereof) and for the great benefite, that may hereafter redounde, to the saide vnited landes, by the same, as they would haue the said States beleeue. The true purpose, & drift whereof is nothing else (as I saide) but to eate the Adventurers out of their trade, as they of *Antwerpe* heeretofore did the Merchauntes of other Nations, *Portingalles*, *Italians*, *Dutches*, or *Germanes*, & others, whereby they greatlie enriched themselues, their Prince, and Countrie, which finallie turned to the hurt, daunger, and disquieting of all other Princes, and States, as hath appeared by the doeings, and practises of the late King *Philippe* of Spaine, and his Confederates: And to shewe that this which I haue saide, is true, I will by the way more perticularlie rippe vp this matter.

The Antwerpeners eate the Marchants of other Nations out of their trade.

First for the *Portingall*, we knowe, that like a good simple mā, he sailed euerie yeare full hungerlie (God wotte) about three partes of the Earth almoste for spyces, and when he had brought them home, the great ryche purses of the *Antwerpians*, subiectes of the King of Spaine, engrossed them all into their owne handes, yea oftentimes gaue money for them before hande, making thereof a plain *Monopolie*: whereby they onely gaigned, and all other Nations lost. For that the spyces, being in few mens handes, were sold at such rate, as they listed, to their own private lucre, and gaign, and to the hurt, and damage of all others.

The *Italians*, Englishe, and Germane Merchantes, were

were wont to haue a verie profitable, and good trade into Italie with Kersyes, and other Englishe, and foreign Commodities seruing that Countrie, but a litle before the troubles of the low Cuntries, the *Antwerpians* were growen into that trade, and were become the greatest Dealers that way, and further, to *Alexandrta, Cipris, Tripolie in Siria*, and other remote places, seruing the same more then anie other, with linen Cloth, Worsteds, Sayes, Tapestrie, and other Netherlandishe Wares, by meanes whereof the said Italians, Englishe, & Germanes were forced to leaue that trade, or to doe verie litle.

The *Dutch*, or *Germane* Merchantes had the whole Trade in their owne handes, of all Commodities brought to *Antwerpe* from other places, that serued Germanie, buying vp all them selues, and caryeing them to the Townes, and Martes in their own Coũtrie: But in a few yeres the *Antwerpians* had also wholie gott that Trade, and the Germanes in a manner, did nothing, for the other in all Martes, and Faires in Dutchlande, bare the chiefest swindge, and serued the same with Commodities of all Landes, and of all sortes, so that looke what the Germane vsed to gett, that they gott, eating as it were, the bread out of his mouth.

As for the *Easterlinges*, they had begunne a Staple of their commodities at *Antwerpe*, but in the opinion of wyse-men, if it had longe continued, it would haue eaten out cleane, & consumed their Merchants and Mariners from the seas, as they began not a litle

to be

to be diminished by those of *Amsterdam*, and other, but new vpstart Townes in *Holland*, with their great number of Hulkes, & other shippes: of the Spanish trade, and Merchantes of Spaine, because they were King *Philippes* subiectes, there is not much to be said, but yet the *Antwerpians* had meanes, to gett a good fleese from them too: for the Merchauntes of *Antwerpe*, beeing of great wealth, were able to sell these commodities, which best serued Spaine, and the *Indies*, at longe dayes of payement, & by meanes therof did sett them at such highe, and deare pryces, that when the dayes of payment came, and the Spaniard lacked his returnes, to keepe credite with, hee was forced to runne vpon the Exchaunge, or Interest, till his provision came in, by which time his gaynes was consumed by vsurie, and many tymes some of the principall: besides, they solde the Spaniarde their worst wares, and caried the choycest them selues into Spaine, whether they traded more, thẽ al the Spaniardes in the lande did. For the trade of the Merchauntes of Fraunce: there hath been often warre betwene that Countrie, and the Dukes of *Burgundie*, as hath bin aboue partlie touched, by meanes whereof, there hath been much colouring of goodes betweene the one Princes people, and the other, and that so ordinarilie, and cunninglie, that the *Antwerpians* aboue all the Merchauntes besides, were as privie, expert, and skilfull in all the Frenche trickes, and indirect trades and conveyances, as the Frenchmen them selues, by reason whereof, in tyme of peace, the

H French

Frenche Merchauntes were much endamaged, and hindred: for the *Antwerpians* serued *Germanie*, *Spaine*, *Portingall*, *Eastlande*, and their neighbours of the low Cou͂tries, with such things, as the French men themselues vsed to sell, and vent in those places: now lett vs looke a while into England, and take a view, what the *Antwerpians*, and other Netherlanders, principallie those of *Antwerpe*, haue done there, and you shall finde that not past 80. yeares agoe, there were not in all *London* about twelue, or sixteene lowe Countrie Merchantes, and amongst them, not past fower of anie credite, or estimation. For the Merchaundise which they then brought into Englande most, were stone pottes, brushes, puppettes, and toyes for children, bristles for shoemakers, and such other pedlery ware of small valew, and sometimes a litle fishe, and three or foure pieces of linen Cloth, but in lesse then the compasse of fortie yeares following, there were in *London*, at least one hundred Netherlandish Merchantes, the most parte whereof were of *Antwerp*, and thether they brought all kinde of wares, whiche the Merchauntes of *Italie*, *Germanie*, *Spaine*, *Fraunce*, and *Eastlande* (of all whiche Nations there were before that tyme diuerse famous, and notable riche Merchants and Companies) vsed to bring into England out of their owne Countries directlie, to the great damage of the saide straungers, and of the Naturall borne English Merchauntes, whiche Englishe Merchantes and their trade also the saide Netherlanders (but especially those of *Antwerpe*) as much as in them laye,

laye, euen then sought, and practised ro destroy, and ouerthrow, and since haue been manie yeares about it, which in good time was discouered, and by the diligence, and trauaile of the Merchantes Aduenturers principallie, not without their great cost, and charge hath been hetherto withstood, and prevented, & so will be still so long, as that Companie continueth on foot, let the other repine, and mutter at it, as much as they list, and seeke to crosse, and hinder the Adventurers, wheresoeuer they can procure audience with their vnseasonable Remonstrances, spitefull Declarations, and harshe Complaintes, to the raising vp, as much as in them lyeth, of the like stirre, and disagreement betweene her Maiestie, and the States of the vnited Netherlandes at this time, as happened in the yeare 1563. vnder the gouuernement of the Dutchesse of *Parma*, Regent for the late King *Philippe* of Spaine, at that time in the low Countries: when as through the complaint of the Merchantes of *Antwerpe* principallie, and of others of the said low Coũtries, against the raising of the Custome of Clothe, & of foreign Wares brought into England, and speciallie against an Act of Parleament made for the setting of her Maiesties people on worke, by vertue whereof foreign wares, as Pinnes, Kniues, Hattes, Girdles, Ribbin, and such like, were forbidden to be brought in readie wrought, to th'intent, that her Highnes subiectes might be employed in making thereof, the saide Dutchesse of *Parma* by proclamation forbadd the carying into England of anie kinde of matter, or

H 2 thing,

thing, wherewith the said wares might be made, and banished out of the low Countries all *Manufacture*, or handie-worke, as Bayes, &c. made in Englande, Clothe, and Kersye onely excepted, which also shee afterwardes forbad to be brought in vpon payne of confiscation, vnder shew, or pretence of infection, (for that the plague had raigned verie sore in *London* and other places of the Realme that sommer) but in verie trueth the right cause was, for that shee could not haue her will in the aboue-mentioned pointes, and tooke that time of mortalitie, and wante of trade in Englande, to be the readiest, and fittest opportunitie to attayne therevnto. So that finallie the M. M. Adventurers, after they had kept their Clothes, and other goods aboorde their shippes in the Riuer of *Thames*, and *Scheld* fiue monethes together, & might not be permitted to lande them at *Antwerpe*, were at length forced to departe with the same vnto the Town of *Embden* in Eastfriseland, where they obtayned Priviledges, & Contracted for a free Commerce with the two yonge Earles *Eggard* and *Iohn*, and the Ladie *Anne* Countesse of *Oldenburghe* their Mother, Anno 1564. who neither feared, nor founde anie contagion in the Englishe, and their Commodities, and by this meanes brake the violence of the foresaid Dutchesses intention, erecting their trade in the abouesaid Towne, and leauing *Antwerpe*, and the low Countries, wherevpon King *Philippe*, and his Ministers grieving sore, that they could not haue their will of her Maiestie, and her Highnes subiectes, and that

that they must forgoe so profitable a Milche-cowe, as the English trade was vnto the low Countries, an Edict or Proclamation was sett forth in the Moneth of Maye of the aboue-saide yeare, That no person in the saide low Cuntries, should haue, or vse any trade with the Englishe at *Embden*, buy anie Cloth, or Englishe Woollen commoditie of them, or carie them anie wares vpon paine of confiscation of the same: then the which dealing what could be more iniurious, or enemy-like in time of opē warres? But herein the saide King not onely shott at the state of England, but withall he endammaged other Nations, and particularlie those of the Empire, as though no Countrie-Merchants ought to trade any where, but in his Countries, and when, and where, and with whom it pleased him, thereby to holde all the whole trade of Merchandise in his Netherlandes alone, forbidding vpon paine of losse of goodes the Imperiall Merchantes, as well as others, from occupying, buying, or selling within the limites of the Empire, as though he had been Emperour him selfe, and more then Emperour: In which point hee touched verie neare the toppe & heigth of the Emperiall Crowne, and Dignitie, in that being but Duke of *Burgundie*, and in that respect but a subiect of the Empire, hee tooke vpon him peremptorilie, to commaunde, restrayne, forbidde, and iniuriouslie to breake the old, and auncient freedomes, and liberties of the Empire freelie yeelded, and so longe Religiouslie mainteyned, and kept as well towardes all the subiectes, as to-

prohibition of al Trade with the Englishe by K. Philippe.

H 3 wardes

wardes all the friendes, & Allies of the same, amongst which Friendes the Englishe haue been continually not the least, or last, as fetching their originall out of the saide holy Empire : At length when the King of Spaine, for all the instigation of his Netherlanders, and popish Ministers, sawe, that hee could not preuaile, and were at a stand, he and they were glad, and fayne to come to a provisionall agreement, and to accept of such Priviledges, and liberties, as the saide Netherlanders enioyed in England in the last yeare of Queene *Maries* raigne : whiche was the yeare of our Lord 1558. and to call in all those foresaid Placcates, Edictes, and Prohibitions made against the Englishe, and bringing in of Englishe wares.

And although in the yeare following, and the yere 1566. a diete was helde at *Bridges*, for the taking vp, and compounding of all variances, difficulties, grieuances by certaine Embassadoures sent from both Princes, yet nothing was concluded, the Customes about the which the first, and moste question grew, were for all the Netherlandishe Merchantes wrangling, and importunitie continued, as hauing been erected in Queene *Maries* dayes (King *Philippe* their naturall Prince being maried to her) and the former agreement made in the yeare 1564. betweene the Queenes Counsell, and Don *Gasman de Silva*, Embassadour for the abouesaid King, stoode, and so remayned in force till the yeare 1568. when as the Duke of *Alua* in the low Countries, and Kinge Philippe throughout Spain caused the persons, & goods of of the English Merchantes, to be arrested, and stayed, vpon this occasion: it happened in the aboue-saide yeare 1568. that a great shippe of *Biscaie*, and foure Pinasses which the Spaniards call *Assabres*, were chased by certaine men of warre belōging to the Prince of *Condé* into the hauē of *Plimmouth*: in which great shippe were the valew of two hundred thousand pistolettes, which monie the Spanishe Embassadour at that time in England, *Don Giraldo Despes*, required to haue deliuered vnto him, as belonging to the Kinge his Maister, with consent to conveigh the same to *Antwerpe* vnto the Duke of *Alua*, which was graunted him, but while he attended order from the saide Duke, about the saufe sending of the said monie, her Maiestie came to the knowledge, that it did not belonge to the King of Spaine, but vnto certaine Merchauntes of *Genua*, & that the Duke of *Alua*, needing monie, meant to seaze vpon the same, and turne it to the Kinges vse. Which the owners fearinge, chose rather, that it should remain in the Queenes handes: wherevpon her Maiestie caused all the monie to bee landed, saying that shee would borow it of the Italians, with their good will, and liking, and so preserue it from the Frenche, who threatened to fetche it by force out of the Hauen, where it laye. The Duke as soone as he had knowledge heereof, suddenlie commaunded all the Merchauntes Adventurers to be arrested at *Antwerpe*, and caused them to be kept safe in the Englishe house, with a companie of Dutch souldiers: he commaunded also the shippes and goodes of

The Duke of Alba arresteth the persons and goodes of the English in Antwerp & elsewhere in the low Countreis.

of all the Englishe Merchantes, as well at *Antwerpe*, as elsewhere, to be attached, and inventarised, which he afterwardes solde to *Fernando Frias*, a Spaniard, and others, to the vse of the King of Spaine. When her Maiestie vnderstood of this hastie, & vnadvised dealing of the Duke of *Alua*, shee gaue leaue vnto her subiects for their Indempnitie, to arrest the Netherlanders, and their goodes in Englande: By meanes of these generall arrestes on both sides, the trade of the M.M.Advẽturers ceased at *Antwerpe*, but for the sale of the Commoditie of the lande, they presentlie contracted with the Town of *Hamberough*, and there helde their Martes onely for a time: The Duke of *Alua* on the other side, to hinder the Trade, and consequentlie to hurt the state of Englande, the last daye of Marche 1569. by straight proclamation forbad all dealing with the Englishe, either in carying them any wares, or buying of them Englishe Commoditie to bee brought into the lowe Countreis, appointing for the more seuere execution heereof certaine spyes, or promoters, among the which, as principall, was Doctour *Storie*, of whose shamefull, and well deserued punishement, and end, there is yet freshe memorie: but these differences, and troubles were afterwardes in the yeare 1574. at a Diete helde at *Bristowe* taken vp, and agreed, and the Entercourse was renewed, and confirmed in such maner, as was concluded at *Bridges* in the yeare 66. to the high honour and commendatiõ of her Maiestie, who medled not with one penie of the arrestes goodes, but gaue the same the same wholy ouer vnto her subiectes, in recompence of their losses in the lowe Countries, and honorablie contented the owners of the monie (about the which the Question and trouble first rose) for the same: whereas to the contrarie the King of Spaine neuer recompenced his subiectes for their damages, but as is saide, converted all the English Merchantes goodes which he found in the low Countries, or in Spaine, to his owne vse, without hauing the least cōsideration of the losse of anie man. By the abouewritten discourse we may perceiue the sleightes, practises, and industrie of the *Antwerpians*, and Netherlanders, to drawe the trade of all Nations into their owne handes, the proud, vnneighbourlie, yea ennimilike Edictes, & Proscriptions of the Dutchesse of *Parma*, vpon the vnreasonable complaintes, and demaundes of her Merchantes, no doubt egged on by the Cardinall *Granvelle* in hatred of the Religiō professed in England: the rashe and vnadvised arrestes, and detayning of the persons, and goodes of the M. M. Adventurers, and others in the lowe Countries, and Spaine by the King, and the Duke of *Alua* the *Heroicall* courage; wisedome, and equitie of our gracious Queene in defence, and reliefe of her subiectes wronged, and spoiled in barbarous sorte, contrarie to reason, and against the Entercoyrs, and Treaties sworne, and established betweene both the Nations, and the Princes thereof: And lastlie, the great care, and travaile of the M. M. Aduenturers in middest of all these troubles, & their exceeding great losses, and

I hinde-

hinderances to seeke, and procure a place, Firste at *Embden*, then at *Hamborough*, for vent of the Commoditie of the Realm, and maintenance of the trade, whereby so manie liue, the ouerthrowe, and destruction whereof, hath been the principall marke, and purpose of all the aboue-mentioned Complaintes, Edictes, Proscriptions, and Arrestes, and is nowe at this day of all the violent machinations, & workings of the King of Spaine, and his Ministers, and fauourers (to which partie the *Hanses* adioigne them selues with might and mayn) thinking thereby, to stirre vp some notable commotion, trouble, ot disorder in the State of Englande, and so the sooner to bring to passe their longe purposed bloodie, and treacherous practises against the precious life of her Maiestie, (whom the Lorde longe preserue amongest vs) and against the true Religion, and Church of Christ planted in her Highnes Dominions, and in steede thereof to sett straungers ouer vs, and to reestablishe Poperie, and so lastlie, bringe the whole Englishe people, and subiectes of her Maiestie, into miserable slauerie of bodie, and Conscience, vnder an vngodlie and superstitious Nation, from the whiche the Almightie God in mercie keepe vs, and our posteritie, that wee may see peace in our dayes, and that there may be rest in the Church vnto the end of the worlde: But to returne to my purpose.

That

That the better and greater vent and advancement of English Commodities, and the bringing in of foreigne Wares (good cheape) is procured by the Companie of Merchants Adventurers.

THE next benefite which ariseth to the Prince, and State by the maintenance of the Companie of M. M. Adventurers is, The better and greater vent, and advauncement of Englishe Commodities, and the bringing in good cheape of foreigne Wares. Which to be so, not onely that which hath passed heeretofore, but also freshe experience hath sufficientlie manifested: for first it is plaine, as hath been aboue touched, that in tymes longe paste, and euen of late yeares, the M M. Adventurers did settle them selues in some one Towne of the low Countries, and there stapling the Woollen Clothe, Kersyes, and other the commodities of the Realm of England, in good and merchantlike order, and vnder good & prudent Gouuernement, did atende the Merchantes straungers, whiche should repaire vnto the saide Towne, (commonlie tearmed the Mart Towne) to buye the saide Clothes, Kersyes, &c. or to sell, or barter vnto the Merchaunt Aduenturer such foreigne commo-

I 2 dities

dities, as were most fitt, and necessarie for the Realm of Englande, by meanes whereof great numbers of Merchauntes of *Eastlande, Germanie, Italie*, and almost out of all the Townes, and Provinces of the lowe Countries resorted to the Mart Town: and there in moste ample, friendlie, and Merchantlike maner did trafficque, and deale with the saide M. M. Adventurers, whereby the English Commodities were kept, and holden in singulare credite, and estimation, and all kinde of foreign wares were returned, & brought in at reasonable, and low prices, not onely to the good of the common Wealth of Englande in generall, and the benefite of the M. M. Adventurers in particular, but also to the great satisfaction, contentment, and good liking of all the aboue-saide foreign States, and people, in so much, that some great personages, drawen with the verie reporte of the seemlie dealing, cariage, and orders of the Companie of M. M. Aduenturers, haue repaired to the Marte Town, to beholde, and see the same.

This course deriued from common reason, and approoued by *Experience*, (the surest Doctor in the schoole of Mans life) manie yeares togeather hathe been obserued, & continued in the abouesaid Companie, as a principall point, and one of the mayne postes, and pillers of the same: For first, it cannot be denied, that to advaunce anie thing, and to make it of price, and estimation, is to bring it in request: secondlie, to bring it in request, is to drawe a concours & multitude to desire it: and lastlie, the best meanes, to to drawe a Concours and multitude, is to appointe a certen place, whether men may commodiously resorte, where also if they may finde, not onely that whiche they desire, and haue neede of, but withall may vent that, which their Countrie bringeth forth, and hath plentie of, it is a double cause, and allurement to invite them to such concourse, and flocking together. From this reason is the order, and institution of the Marte-Towne so longe, and so seriouslie practised, and maintayned by the M. M. Aduenturers, which to be soundlie, & well grounded, I think no man will gain-saye, next late experience, as well at home, as abroade, hath taught vs, that when another course was liked of by some, and that diuerse of the Companie had disbanded them selues, and held not the foresaid commendable, and Merchauntlike course, but erected vnto them selues a private, irregulare, and straglinge trade, the commoditie of the Realme lay vnvented, or grew to bee embased, and solde at lower prices, then before: for when as about fourteene yeares past, in the 29th yeare of her Maiesties Raigne, the Wooll-growers, Clothiers, Weavers, and others liuing vpon Cloth-making, wanting their accustomed commoditie, gaines, and woorke, made a grievous complaint thereof, it was thought to be the onelie expedient to remedie this sore, to giue libertie to all her Highnes Subiects, and others, to buye, and transporte Clothe accordinge to the limitation of the lawes, any grantes, or Priviledges by her Maiesties prerogatiue heeretofore to the M. M.

Complaint of the wooll growers & Clothiers for want of Trade.

I 3 Ad-

Aduenturers graunted notwithſtandinge: yet wee ſawe, that the maladie was neuer a whitt the better, but rather grew worſe, and worſe, in ſomuch that the poore people in *Wiltſhiere*, and *Gloceſterſhiere*, livinge wholy vpon Clothe making, in great numbers were readie to growe into a mutinie for this cauſe, to the ſingulare reioycing of the enemies of her Maieſtie, and in particulare of the *Hanſes*, who deſire nothing more, then the ouerthrowe of the M. M. Aduenturers, and their Trade: thereby finallie intendinge to diſturbe the peace of the whole Realme. At length when all men expected nothing elſe, but an abolliſhment, and diſſolving of the abouesaid Companie, as the ſole, and onely cauſe of all this griefe, the ſetting vp of the Steelyarde againe, and the equalling of all the ſubiectes, and others in the Realme, in tranſporting, and carying out of Clothe. None of all theſe thinges fell out, but to the contrarie, thoſe of the ſaid Companie were ſent for, and after they had been heard, and had made knowen the true cauſe of the abouesaid ſoare in deed, they were willed to proceed in their Trade, with promiſe of aſſiſtence, and countenaunce from my Lordes, and others of the Counſcill, which aſſuredlie their Honors would not haue donne, if that they had ſeene, that the late innovation, or libertie had brought foorth, or was likelie to bring foorth the promiſed effect, or that without the ſaide Companie of M. M. Adventurers ſo great a quantitie of the Woollen cōmodities of the Realm, could be vented, as in former tymes, when the ſaide M.M.

M.M.Adventurers were mainteyned,and backed in their full Priviledges and Rightes.

THe Marchantes Adventurers were at this time encombred with no ſmall difficulties: for that neither of their Mart-Townes(*Embden* & *Middelborough*) were verie ſaufe,or fitt for the vtteraunce of their Commodities, neither knew they, where to finde a place cõvenient for that purpoſe: for at *Middelborough*, partlie through the continuall loanes of great ſummes of monie, vpon the necke one of another required at their handes,without warrant or authoritie from her Maieſtie, and partlie thorough the feare of daũger they were put in by the Earle of *Leiceſter*,then Gouvernour of the vnited Provinces,the Trade was in a manner wholy damped, and diuerſe of the principalleſt of the Companie in that place, almoſt in flying manner, with-drew them ſelues,and their goodes into Holland: At *Embden* on the other ſide, thinges were in no verie good tearmes, by reaſon of the Duke of *Parmaes* prevaylinge in the Provinces next adioyning, and that the States ſent their men of warre into the Riuer of *Embs*, whereby the trade by lande grew exceeding perillous,and by water troubleſome and chargeable: ſome alſo to mend the matter,ſticked not to put into mens mindes a ſuſpicion of the Count *Egdard* of *Eaſtfriſelande*, as a ſecrete Pentioner,and fauourer of the King of Spain, and ſure it is, that his chiefe Officer *Ocko Freez*, then Droſſart of *Embden*, ſhewed him ſelf by many ſignes and

& actions, very much enclined to the Spanish parte: The *Hanses* also in the yeare 1582. at an Assemblie of the Empire at *Ausburghe*, by fauour, and assistence of the Spanish ministers, and of the Princes, and Prelates of the Romish Religion (the most part whereof were at the devotion of the house of *Austritche*) had vpon their complaintes, and iniurious informations obtained a Decree, for th'expelling of the Trade, and residence of the M. M. Adventurers out of the Empire, and otherwise by new occasions of losses, sustained at sea by English men of warre (though nothing were done to them contrarie to the law of Nations) were sore incensed, not onely against the said M.M. *A*dvēturers, but also against the whole English name, so that there was little or no hope, or likelyhoode to finde anie friendshippe, or good entertaynement at their handes.

Commissioners sent to treate with the Hamburgers of new Priuileges.

The Companie all these difficulties notwithstanding, taking new courage, and moued in dewtie towardes her Maiestie, and their Natiue Countrie, In the yeare 1587. sent their Commissioners Syr *Richard Saltonstall*, Knight, at that tyme their Gouvernour, & Doctor *Giles Fletcher*, a Ciuilian vnto *Hamborough* with foure shippes loaden with Cloth, to trie the mindes of that people, and whether they could procure a residence in that Towne againe (whether they were invited by letters of the 19. of August, 1586. from the Senate,) The *Hamburgers* notwithstanding their saide letters, by the instigation of the Duke of *Parma*, who at this time was wholy intentiue time in a manner to the matters of England, and had inckling of a commotion doubted among the commons there, for want of worke (the appeasing or encrease whereof much depended vpon the M.M. Adventurers Trade, and therefore sought by all meanes to disturbe it) held them selues very nyce, and coye, and hauing daily in their Counseill Doctor *Wesendorp* of *Groeninghe*, sent thether by *Verdugo*, Gouuernour of *Westfriselande* for the Kinge of Spaine, delayed, and dallied with the foresaid Commissioners, so that after much labour spent, nothing in the ende was concluded: for the *Hamburgers* beeing certified by the abouesaid Doctor *Wesendorp*, of the great preparation in hande, and the invasion intended by the King of Spaine against Englande, of the happie successe whereof, he promised and presumed much, and of the which the *Hamborghers* (it should seeme) conceiued no smal hope, vpon euery dayes newes either confirmed, or recalled that, which before hand with much a doe, had been passed, and agreed vppon betweene them, and the M.M. Aduēturers Commissioners, excusing this their light dealing sometime by the vnwillingenes of their Commons, (whose consentes as they saide they could not obteyne) otherwhiles by want of authoritie frō the rest of the *Hanses*, without whose privitie and liking they might not conclude any such thing, and yet they had written the contrarie in the abouesaid letter: in these words, *Neque tamen ad has nostras privatas Cōsultationes reliquarum Civitatum Confœderatarum consensum requirendum*

K *arbi-*

arbitramur: So that in fine the Commissioners being wearied with these delayes, and finding that at *Stade*, a Towne not farre distant from *Hambourgh*, the trade might be well seated, thether they repaired, and procured a Residence, and Priviledges there in the moneth of Semtember 1587. This Towne of *Stade* is an auncient free towne of the Empire, in the territorie of the Archbishoppe of *Breme*, who as Protector of the Towne, hath a Tolle there, but no other commaund. It is scituate from the riuer of *Elb* about two English miles, out of the which is a Creek called the *Swinge*, which ebbeth and floweth vp to the Towne, and is able to carie a shippe of four skore or an hundred tonnes, and maketh a saufe, and quiet harbour for shipps in all weathers: The Town standeth vpon the maine land of *Germanie*, on the hether side of the Elb, a dayes iourney from *Bremen*, three dayes iournie from *Embden*, as manie from *Cassell* in *Hessen-land*, two dayes iournie from *Lunenburgh*, and from *Hambourgh* six houres: verie neare, and convenient for *Westfalia*, *Freeslande*, and the partes thereabouts: in the winter season, and alwayes farre better, & commodiouser then *Hamborough*, for transportinge, and sending of goodes to and fro the abouesaid townes, and partes of Dutcheland. In this Towne therefore lying so commodious, and fitt for trade, though old and vnfrequented, the Companie at their own great costes, and charges, by their abouesaide Commissioners, obtayned Priviledges with the allowance, and good lyking of the Archbishoppe, and Chapter of *Breme:*

Scituation of the Town of Stade.

Priuiledges obtayned at Stade.

Breme: and there they found great, and quicke vtteraunce of their Commodities at good rates, and prices, Marchauntes resorting thether from all partes, for in the whole Towne of *Stade* was not one Merchaunt before the Companies of M. M. Advēturers coming thether, but they liued generallie all the inhabitantes thereof vpon tillage, feedinge of cattell, swine, and other husbandrie, the Towne also with the houses and buildinges thereof, was almost vtterlie decayed, and growen ruinous, but in the tenne yeares that the Cōpanie resided in that Town, there was a straunge alterarion, so that it grew in deede to be another Towne in regard of that it was before, & as the estate of *Stade* mended daily, so the Trade encreased, till the publication of the Emperours *Mandate* in the yeare 1597. the ende of which *Mandate*, a blind man may see to be none other, then through the sides of the M.M. Adventurers to hurt, & wound the State of England, that is by the subuersiō of that Companie, to stoppe the vent of English Clothe, by the which so manie thousandes are fedd, and sustained in the lande, and must want, if the Trade faile, to repossesse the *Hanses* with their olde antiquated, and obsolete Priviledges no way sufferable by the Prince or State, and to gratifie the Capitall Enemies of this Realme: And therefore I could wishe all the well-willers, and louers of the common wealth, and state of Englande, and all the good subiectes of her Maiestie, that through Envie, or misconceipt, they seeke not, or procure the decay, or hinderance of the

K 2 aboue

aboue saide Companie, least vnawares they ioyne handes with the common Enemie, who seeketh not onelie the subuersion of the saide Companie, but also of this whole Realme, from the which the Lorde in mercie preserue vs.

By that which hath been aboue sett downe, I doubt not, but it alreadie in parte appeareth, how true it is by late experience at home, that the Commoditie of the Realme can neither so wel, nor in so great quantitie be vented by anie other course, as by mainteyning the M.M. Aduenturers in their Trade, and Priuiledges: for further proofe whereof, and that foreigne wares are by this meanes brought into the lande at the more reasonable rates, let vs see what hath happened abroad, and consider the particulare doeinges of some Fellowes, and brethren of the said Companie.

Norebergh Traders, & traders out of the Mart Townes.

In the yeare 1584. and a few yeares before, some of the Companie had found out, and vsed a trade to the Towne of *Norenberghe*, and other partes of Germanie, contrarie to the old good orders of the Companie, especiallie that, whiche forbiddeth trade out of the Marte Townes, ordayned for the keeping in credite, and better vent of English Commoditie, and bringing in of foreign Wares good cheape, & at reasonable prices: So that where the trade was before tymes in the Mart Townes betweene Englishe, and foreigne Merchauntes, it was now growen (especiallie in the Towne of *Embden*) to bee betweene English,

glish, and English Merchantes: Those whiche vsed this Trade, to excuse their doeinges alleadged, that they did transporte, & carrie from the Mart Townes as great a quantitie of Clothes, Kersyes, and other woollen commodities, and at as good prices, as the Merchaunt straunger did, or would doe, and that they brought to the Mart Townes, as much foreign Ware, and that as good, and as good cheape, as the straunger Merchauntes could doe, and therefore, if the M.M. Adventurers were not of an envious disposition, they could bee content, that their owne Countriemen, and brethren, should rather gaigne, then Straungers. Heerevnto it was aunswered: That although all this were true, and graunted, (as it was not, for that much might be excepted there-against) yet all men of sound reason, & vnderstanding, might easilie see, and perceiue, that a Commoditie sought for at the Mart Townes, is more esteemed by the seeker thereof there, then if it were brought home, and offred to him to sell at his owne doores, and the Merchauntes proverbe is (*That there is twentie in the hundred difference betweene, will you buye? and you sell?*) And therefore, admitt that these Traders to *Norenberghe*, did transporte from the Marte-Townes, as manie Clothes, Kersyes, &c. as the straunge Merchantes did, or would doe, yet could not the saide Clothes, Kersyes, &c. beare such price, and estimation in *Norenbergh*, and other partes of Germanie, being there offered to sell by Englishe, as they would doe, if they were to bee solde by straungers, or the

K 3 Natu-

Naturalls of the place, for the aboue written reason: the like might bee said, and vnderstoode of foreigne Wares, that the same would bee bought, as good cheape at the least in the Mart Townes, as they are to be bought at the strāgers own doores: besides it was founde, that, as some sortes of silke wares were in a greater quantitie, then heeretofore brought by the saide *Norenberghe* Traders into England, so were the same wares much falsified, and empaired in respect of their former goodnes, and substance, since the beginning of the saide newe and disordered trade and dealing: ouer and aboue all this, who knoweth not that the Merchauntes straungers are either ignorant for the most parte, or haue not so perfect aduice from tyme to tyme, as the English Traders had, how Englishe, and foreigne commodities rise and fall in Englande? By reason whereof, there is more advantage in selling to the saide straungers, and in buyinge of them, then in dealing with the English Norenberge traders: for that they, or their friendes are weekelie in the Cloth-market at London, and so may, and no doubt doe take knowledge, what pryce euery sorte, and kinde of Clothe, and Kersye beareth, and then, being throughlie acquainted with the Exchange, do calculate the reckoninge of the orderlie Merchaunt Aduenturer, & share him such gayne as liketh them, and, when they bring their foreigne Commodities to the Marte Townes, knowing before hande, what is in request in Englande, they either sell the same at excessiue prices, or as they list themselues, or shippe them

them into England, & often reſerving the beſt wares to them ſelues, doe barter, and ſell the refuſe in the Marte Townes: to conclude, they buye foreign wares at *Norenberghe*, and elſe where vppon credite, for the current anſwering whereof, (as is well to be proued) they ſell their Engliſh Clothes, and Kerſyes, at vile, and baſe pryces, ſo rayſing their gaignes vppon foreigne wares, and caſting away the commodities of the Realme: and thus the ſtraunge Merchauntes are put from their accuſtomed trade with the M. M. Adventurers in the Mart-Townes for Engliſh commoditie, and the Marchauntes Adventurers from buying of foreigne wares at the ſtraungers handes, as much as lyeth in the ſaide Norenberghe Traders. Laſtlie where as it was ſaid by them, that, if the Merchaunts Adventurers were not of an enuyons diſpoſition, they would bee content, and wiſhe that their Country-men, and brethren ſhould rather gaigne then ſtraungers: The M. M. Adventurers are herein wrongfullie charged, for they can be very well content, to ſee their Countrie men (much more their Brethren) to thriue, and gaigne, but when as ſuch gaigne (reachinge alſo but to a fewe) is much more hurtfull to the common weale of England, & to the generall body of the Companie of M. M. Adventurers, then beneficiall to the ſaid few perſons, traders to *Norenberghe*, and other places out of the Marte Townes, there is no reaſon, but that it ought to bee forbidden, and cutt off: for ſuch priuate and vnwonted trade betweene Engliſh, and Engliſh in the Mart Townes,

Townes, and ſuch ſtragling by free, and vnfree Engliſhe vſed in Germanie, and the Townes of the low Countries out of the Mart Townes, is ſo vnſeemlie, vnmerchantlike, and farre differing from the auncient, laudable, and right Engliſhe manner of the M. M. Adventurers our predeceſſours in former tymes, and is ſo offenſiue to all foreigne States, and people, as nothing can be more: and hath bene well ſeen, and perceiued in the *Hamburghers*, and Earle *Edgard* of *Embden*, who where much diſpleaſed with the diſordered trade at *Norenberghe*, and elſewhere: ſaying, that they had giuen the Adventurers leaue to trade with all kinde of foreigners in their Citties, but had no meaning, that their Citties ſhould bee vſed as through Faires, by trading from thence into other partes of the Empire, thereby to hinder the repaire of foreigne Merchantes to the ſaid Citties: the ſaide Earle went further, & compelled ſuch Engliſhmen, as traded to *Norenberghe*, to pay Tolle, not onely for ſuch Clothes, Kerſyes, and Engliſhe wares, as they ſhould tranſporte, and cary from *Embden*, but alſo for ſuch foreign wares, as they brought frō other partes vnto *Embden*, to the great preiudice of the State, and of the M. M. Adventurers, who by priuiledge were before free of all Tolles, and exactions whatſoeuer either inwardes, or outwardes, and ſurely it may be preſumed, that the *Hanſes* deriued that their falſe ſlaunder of the companie of M. M. Adventurers, in charging them with *Monopolie*, from none other head, or grounh then from this diſordred trade vſed be-

betweene a few vnbridled, and private Englishe, and English within the Marte Townes, and without the Marte Townes into the Partes of Germanie, whereby they shew an exorbitant, & vnsatiable desire, and greedines of gaigne, as not content with a reasonable trade in the Mart Town, but incroaching, as it were, vpon the whole trade of those partes, and of other men which can not choose, but be a great ey-sore, & offence to all foreign, and straunge Merchauntes. Nowe although I hope by this tyme it sufficientlie appeareth, that the gouuerned, & well ordered trade of the M.M. Advenrurers Companie, is farre to bee preferred before a dispersed, stragling, & promiscuous trade, so that it needeth no further proofe, or demonstration, yet because some men holde this to be against the libertie of the subiect, and thinke, that the Adventurers by their orders restraine or limite the Clothe Market at home, it shalbe necessarie for these mens satisfaction also, to saye something further of this matter. First, it is true that *Bonum quo communius, eo maius:* and it were to be wished, that there were enough for euery man, but that wil neuer be: furthermore, he looseth a piece of his libertie wel, that being restrained of a little, fareth better in that estate, then if he were left to his owne greedie appetite: for wee haue seene by experience, that many men in our time leaping from their shoppes, & retayling, wherein they were brought vp, and gathered great wealth, and taking vpon them to be Merchauntes, and Dealers beyond the seas, haue in few yeres growē poore,

L or

or so decayed in estate, that they might well haue wished, that they had neuer left their former trade, and vocation, but suffered others quietlie to enioye their priuiledge, and disgested the losse of a little scrappe of libertie, hurtfull to them selues, and rightlie bestowed vpon others for such seruices, desertes, and considerations, as no other subiect neede to envie them for the same, or to be agrieued thereat, except they will challenge the Prince of partialitie, or not to haue a dew care of the Subiect, or say that the preferrement, or exemption, whiche one man hath more, and before another in the common wealth, is against the libertie of the subiect, and so bringe in an ilfauoured confusion, or intollerable equalitie, by vsurping vpon other mens rightes, and patrimonie so dearelie obtained, and with their great, and excessiue charges, & trauaile mainteyned certen hundred yeares together, as the freedome, which the Companie of M.M. Adventurers enioyeth, hath been. But (I pray you) let vs see, what would followe, if these men had that, which they so much desire, and contende for, surelie nothing elsе, then that, whiche hetherto we haue seene to haue fallen out: neither can there anie better ende come thereof, then heretofore of the like. For example: The Englishe had at the *Narue* in *Liefland*, a profitable Trade, and good sales for their Countrie commoditie a good while together, till at length in the yeare 1565, a number of stragling Merchauntes, resorting thether out of this Realm, the trade was vtterlie spoiled, in so much that many

The pedlarlike dealing of the English straglers at the Narue.

many of them went about the Towne with Clothe vpon their armes, and measures in their handes, and solde the same by the *Arsine*, a measure of that Coũtrie, to the great embaling of that excellent Cõmoditie, the discredite of our Nation, and the finall enpouerishing, and vndoing of manie of the said stragglers, which being made knowen to her Maiestie, and her Highnes right Honourable priuie Counsell, order was taken at the next Parleament, that the Town of *Narve* should bee comprized within the Charter of the *Muscovie* Cõpanie, to prevent the like pedlarlike kinde of dealing euer after, and the makinge vile of the principallest commoditie of the Realme. Which one example, among other, may serue for verification of that, which hetherto hath been saide against the stragling, and single Merchantes trade in Woollen commoditie, wherein further may be noted that which by experience is founde true, that in the vngouerned single trade, the first commer marreth the market for him that commeth after, and at his returne making haste (as his maner is) to prevent those which followe, hee setteth vp his wares at an high price, whiche afterwardes are hardlie pulled downe to a lower rate: the which is otherwise in the gouuerned trade of the Merchauntes Adventurers: for cõming together, and at one instant to one market, at their Mart Towne, where they are priviledged with conditions, and exemptions to their owne liking, and for the furtherance of the Commerce, sufficient order is taken for the preventinge one of another,

L 2

ther, and keeping in estimation of the commoditie of the land without vsing anie such indirect dealing for this purpose as the *Hanses* haue falselie imagined, and as impudentlie published, whereas the single, & stragling trader, wanting all the abouesaide helpes, and meanes, lyeth open to sundrie wronges, inconveniences, and grievances, whiche to straungers are incident, and common in straunge places, and thereby are made subiect to manie exactions, new tolles, and excessiue paymentes, and charges for one cause or another, and consequentlie are soone empoverished, & driven from their trade by the foreign Merchaunt, or after they haue made the foreigne Merchauntes acquainted with the trade, are eaten out by them: whiche also would happen to the M. M. Adventurers, if they were not so vnited, and held together by their good gouuernement, and by their politike, and Merchauntlike orders.

Here it may be obiected, that the more buyers there are, the quicker sales, and higher pryces, and therfore if all others, as well as the Merchantes Adventurers, might transporte Clothe, the more would be solde, and the prices would be the higher: To this I haue sufficientlie aunswered before, and proued the contrarie by experience, fetched from the 29 th yeare of her Maiesties Raigne, when as all, both English, and straungers, that would, were by letters patentes directed from her Highnes to the Lorde Treasurer, enabled to buye, and transporte English Clothe, and for that the Charter of the Citie of London should not

be

be in the way,or an hinderaunce heerevnto (by reason that vnfree men are therby restrained from buying and selling within the saide Cittie, and that the ordinarie markett-place at that time for Clothe was in Blackwellhall) the signe of the *George* at *Westminster* in the Kings streat was appointed a market place, for such Clothiers to resorte vnto, as would take the libertie of the aforesaide Letters-patentes, but what followed thereof. I could neuer yet learne,that one wayn load of Clothe was vnladen at the saide place, neither, that the Steelyarde Merchauntes, nor anie of her Maiesties subiectes so enabled,as aforesaid,did euer take benefite by the same for fourtie Clothes, one man yet liuing onely excepted, who since (as I haue heard)hath often protested,that in buying 200 Clothes,he lost a good summe of his principall, and no mervaile, seeing those, who had serued, and had been brought vp in the trade of a Merchant Adventurer manie yeares together,could hardlie make one of one, such was the longesomenes of Returne, and the badnes of the tyme at that instant, through the coniunction of manie difficulties not heere inserted, besides those whiche haue been aboue touched: So that, not the want of buyers was the cause of the complaint of want of worke, and trade at that time, but rather the aboue said causes. For it is verie well knowen,that the Companie of M. M. Adventurers is sufficient,and able enough, and ouer many to buy vp,and vent all that Cloth, and those sortes of woollen commoditie made, and endraped within the

L 3 Realm,

Realme, wherewith they vsuallie deale, and whiche are vendible in the Countries, whether they trade beyond the seas: for they are not so fewe as 3500. persons in number enhabiting London, and sundrie Cities, & partes of the Realm, especially the townes that lye convenientlie for the sea, of whiche a verie great manie vse not the trade, for that it suffiseth not for all, but are costrayned to get their liuing by some other meanes: and to the ende that those, which are traders may be equally, and indifferentlie cared and foried for, and that the wealthie, & richer sorte with their great purses may not engrosse the whole commoditie into their owne handes, & so some haue all, and some neuer a whitt, there is a stint, and reasonable proportion allotted, and sett by an auncient order and manner, what quantitie either at once, or by the yeare euery man may shippe out or transporte, which he is not to goe beyonde, or exceed: Which whole stint, and proportion, if it were shipped, or transported out of the lande, would amounte vnto yearelie the double quantitie of all the Clothe of those sortes made in the Realme, whiche the M. M. Adventurers deale in, whereby it is euident, that this stinting is not a restraint, or limitation of the Cloth-markett (as some of late haue misconceiued) but rather an œconomicall, and discreete partition, or approportioning amonge the members, and Brethren of the Companie, of the commodities, and benefites of the same: so that the wealthier sort are not forgotten, but withall are kept from engrossinge the whole trade

8500. Freemen of the Companie of M. M. Adventurers.

trade, contrarie to the vse, and maner of a well ordered common wealth, or familie, wherein all are prouided for, and not some starued for want, whilest others are swollen vp to the eyes with fatt, and plentie: *For it is merie in Hall, where beards wagge all*, according to that olde right Englishe Prouerbe of our Auncestours, who full well vnderstood, what belonged to good house keeping, and practised the same better then in these our dayes is vsed, the more the pittie.

That the Navigation of the Realme is mainteyned and advaunced by the Companie of the Merchants Adventurers.

SINCE the erection of the Companie of Merchauntes Adventurers, and of other Companies trading *Rusia, Eastlande, Spaine, Turkie, &c.* the Navigation of the Realme is merveilouslie encreased in number of good shippinge, and of able, and skilfull Maisters, and Mariners, in so much, that whereas within these threeskore yeares, there were not aboue foure shippes, besides those of her Maiesties Navie Roiall, aboue the burthe of one hundred, and twentie tonnes, within the Riuer of *Thamis*, there are now at this daye to be founde pertayning to London, and other places lying vpon the saide

saide Riuer, a great number of very large, and seruiceable Merchaunt shippes, fitt as well for the defence of the Realme (if need were) as for trafficque, wherof a good parte are sett on worke by the saide Companie of M.M. Adventurers: the reason whereof is, that this, and other Companies transporting at once, or at one instant, a great quantitie of goodes, and wares, and being to make returne of the same in foreigne cõmodities, doe goe in Fleetes, or with great and warlike vessellcs, well furnished, and this maner of going in fleet to the Marte Towne tendeth to the sanfetie, and preseruation of the shipping, and goods of the subiectes of the Realme, which amount to a great valew, and would helpe the enemie, and hurte our state very much, if it shuld come into his hands, being thereby able to defende them selues frõ spoile and violence, so that since the troubles began with Spaine, not one shippe sett out by the Companie of M.M. Adventurers, hath been taken by the enemie, whereas the single Merchaunt goeing where, and when he listeth, and not able to sett a good shippe on worke, casteth how to come of good cheape, and either shippeth in straungers, or prouideth him selfe of small vessolles, and pinkes to serue his turne for small quantities of wares, and fitt to flie, or runne awaye, if he should chaunce to meete with the enemie, and yet he is many times snapped vp, and made a pray to the Dunkerkers, and other sea rovers, both to his owne, and the publike hurt, as we haue oftentymes knowen of late yeares, whereby it appeareth, that

that the Navigation of the Realme is mainteyned, advaunced, and encreased by the vpholdinge of the Companie of M.M. Adventurers, and of other later Companies also.

That the Queenes Customes and Incomes are augmented by the mainteyning of the Companie of Merchantes Adventurers.

THE like reason is for the increasinge of her Maiesties Customes, and Incomes, as is for the Navigation: for if the good, and serviceable shipping of this Realm be mainteyned, bettered, and increased by the great trade, and trafficque of the said Companie, and if that greater quantities of Clothe are transported, and vttered by them in foreigne partes, then if all were free, and sett at large, as hath been aboue plainlie, & throughlie prooved, it followeth necessarilie, that their saide vnited trade is more advātageable, & yeeldeth more ample, and certayne profite, and encrease to her Highnes Customes, then a single, stragling, or loose trade by anie meanes can doe: The Custome also, which the said Companie payeth, commeth in yearlie, and at certain times in round summes, and payementes, whereby the turn of the Prince, and State is the better serued vpon anie occasion of need of mō-

M nie;

nie: whereas the paymentes of the single Merchants come in by driblettes, and small parcelles: and heervnto the good orders of the saide Companie, are no small helpe, especiallie in transportation, or shipping outwardes, for that the most parte of the Commodities, which the Merchauntes Adventurers carie out of the Realme, beeing shipped in appointed shippes at *London*, the saide Companie haue there certaine overseers, by whose order, and appointment they shippe that, which they shippe, and when the goods ariue on the other side of the seas, there are also officers, who attend, & take view of the Packes, Fardells, and other parcelles of commoditie landed, presenting, & enforming of such, which they finde to haue shipped in other maner then was appointed them to shippe, or not to haue entred, & paid their Custome and dewties rightlie to her Maiestie, who are subiect to great penalties, and forfeitures for the same: this course deuised, for the better collection of an Imposition leuied by the Companie vpon Clothe and other thinges for the maintenance, and vpholding of the saide Companie, doeth not only the better make knowen vnto them, but also vnto her Highnes officers of the Customehouse, what euery man shippeth away, so that by this meanes the Custome is the truelier, and fuller payed, whereas the stragler shipping his Clothe, and other commoditie in couert maner, hugger mugger, & at obscure portes, hath more aduantage, and meanes to defraude her Maiestie of her dewties, and rightes, then those which shippe at *London*,

don, & other great Porte Townes, either by falſe entryes, colouring of ſtrangers goodes, and corrupting the Cuſtomers, and other officers, who, for the moſt parte, being needie perſons in thoſe ſmall, & remote Portes of the Realm, are more ready to take rewards, and cloſelier may doe it, then the officers of the Cuſtomes at the Porte of London: to ſaye nothing of the great quantitie of foreigne wares brought into the Realme by the M.M. Adventurers, the Cuſtom whereof is better, and trulier paide, then if the ſtragler, or ſtraunger had the importation or payement thereof, or of the like quantitie, and if the Recordes were ſearched, no doubt, but it would ſo be founde: For it was not without ſome cauſe, that heeretofore we haue ſeene ſo great fraternitie, familiaritie, kindnes, and inward friendſhippe betweene the Officers for her Maieſties Cuſtomes, and ſtraungers, and that the ſaid Officers, aboue all others, nowe wiſhe them againe ſo hartilie, & call ſo lowd for them, as though now the State were daungerouſlie diuided, and vnkindlie at iarre with her auncient allies, and beſt foreigne friendes, and therfore time to prouide againſt a deſolation, which the land is readie to fall into (for want of theſe deare Allies, and kinde Friendes forſooth) whileſt no man is foũd, that layeth it to heart, and bringeth them in again: Surely this is well preached for ſtockfiſh, and Rheniſh wine, &c. the Alderman of the Steelyarde, and *EMANVEL van Meteren* haue great cauſe to giue them thankes, but not her Maieſtie, or the State: the reaſons I haue ſufficient-

Cuſtomers of the out-Portes, bacbyte the M. M. Adventurers.

M 2 lie

lie laide open, and shewed in this Discourse, whereunto I referre the indifferent, and discreete Reader. As for those Strangers, who haue termed the Companie of M.M. Adventurers *A Private, Particulare, and Preventing Companie*, or haue written, or forespoken in that sorte of the said Companie, if it bee so, as these Customers say, they haue thereby well shewed their skill in *P P.* and that they are not only straũgers to our State, and common Wealth, but withall privie vndermyners, & maligners of the good therof: and let these Customers, while they warne other men, be wise, and warned them selues also, least by their too too much leaning vnto, and favouringe of such Straungers, they prooue not in the ende badd Customers to her Maiestie, and consequentlie corrupt, and vnnaturall members of their Countrie and State: and withall let them vnderstande, and be well assured, that the M.M. Adventurers both know, and regarde the essentiall partes, groundes, and pillers of Trafficque, and of olde tyme haue put them in practise, and yet at this day doe quietelier, better, & certainlier obserue, and mainteyne them, then the Customers of the out Portes (I feare me) doe their office: Lastlie, where they saye, that the M.M. Adventurers by a bare, & idle pretence of the woord *Order*, and Orderlie transporting of the Credit, and cream of the Lande *(Clothe)* haue brought the trade thereof to a kinde of Confusion, and them selues into such a Laberinth, that besides the distresse of the Clothiers, with all their dependentes, and generall complaints plaintes at home (to their Honourable Lordshippes endles offence, and trouble at the Counsell table) the commoditie it self is empaired, abased, and in a sorte dispised, &c. Surely either their intelligence hath deceiued them, or they shew thē selues to be caried with a malicious spirite; for who knoweth not, that the Trade of the M.M. Adventurers is not in a bare or idle pretence, and shew, but in very deed the most orderly, & best framed trade that may be? True it is, that some straungers & others (possibly of these Customers, Familiars & Friends) haue by opē, & couert means at home, and abroad endevoured, and done their best to bringe the saide Trade to some notable confusion, & those of the Cōpanie into a laberinthe to the empairing, and embasing in deed of the commoditie of the land, but, thankes be to God, and our alwayes gracious Ladie, and Queen, they haue not yet had their willes, neither shall they (I hope) though these od Customers tooke parte with them neuer so much: and therefore they may well holde their Clack, and be content like subiectes with that, which those in highest authoritie haue so longe found good, & decreed shalbe so in their wisedoms, and not take vpon them like controllers, to check the doeings, which either of ignorance they vnderstand not the ground, and reason of, or through malice or vnnaturall affection towardes straungers more, then their owne Country-men, doe misconceyue, and misreporte of: but, because I haue often made mention of the *Hanses* in this discourse, it shall not by the

M 3 way

way bee amiffe, to fhewe what thefe *Hanfes* are, and what hath paffed betweene this State, and them in mans memorie.

Original of the Hanfes & their doings in England.

The *Hanfes* or Eafterlinges, as they are commonly called, are people of certain free townes in Dutcheland, either lyinge vpon the Sea, or fome navigable Riuers, and were in olde time twoo and feuentie in number, as they fay: wherof *Lubeck* of the Wendifh, *Brunfwick* of the Saxone, *Dantzick* of the Pruffe, and *Cullen* fince it was of late yeares receyued into this confederacie of the Weftfalifh townes (for into thefe four partes or names they are diuided) were, and are the chiefeft: thefe townes, by reafon of their fcituation, and to put a diftinction betweene them, and other free townes of the Empire, were in old time called in Dutch *Aen zee fteden*, or Townes on the fea-fide, or for breuities fake *Anfefche*, or *Hanfefche fteden*, & in our language *Hanfe ftedes*, or *Hanfe-townes*: thefe Townes having vnited them felues for the fea trade, and comerce, were full of good, and great fhippinge and had an exceeding great trade, and trafficque in all the Eaft Countrie-wares, and cōmodities, to wit, Corne, Stockfifhe, Waxe, Hemp, Steel, Maftes, Firpoles, Dele-boordes, Pitche, Tarre, Soape-afhes, &c. ferving diuerfe landes, and places there withall, and with their fhippinge in time of neede, by meanes wherof they gott vnto them felues large Priviledges and immunities, to their great benefite, advantage, and enryching, & in our time they had their houfes, or places of refidence in this Realme, at *London*, in *Nor-*

Norway at *Berghen*, in *Russia* at *Nouogrode*, and in the low Countries at *Antwerpe*, whether they remooued from *Bridges*: each of these Houses had their Chief, or Alderman, & Assistentes with a Secretarie, Treasurer, Steward, and other necessarie officers, but all of them helde correspondence with the Towne of *Lubeke*, as head of all the *Hanse* Townes. These Aldermen, and Assistentes had power to exercise Merchauntes lawe, among them selues in their house; at *London* called the *Steelyard*, so named by reason of the steel, which they in great quantitie brought thether to sell, and is a verie large, and spacious house, lying vpon the Thamis side, for that they were enioigned to dwell all in one house. Among other their Priviledges in Englande, one was, That they might carie out, and bring in their Wares, and Merchandise for an old Custome of one and a quarter vpon the Hundred, and thereby were exempt from all personall, or Reall charge, or contribution, whiche all other Merchauntes are subiect vnto, saue that in time of neede, they were enioigned to repaire, and helpe to keepe one of the Gates of London, called *Bisshoppes gate:* Now in King *Edward* the thirdes time, Woolle was the best Merchandise of this Land, and the Custome thereof the chiefest income, which the Prince receyued, as amounting yearelie to the summe of 65. or 70. thousand poundes: which was muche in those dayes. And we read that in the yere 1355 there was graunted by a Parleament to King *Edwarde* the third, Fiftie shillinges vpon each sacke of Woolle to be be caried out of the Realme in six yeares, so that the saide King might dispende every day one hundred Markes, which in six yeares tyme, amounted to fifteene hundred thousand poundes, reckoning for an hundred thousand sackes of Wooll a yeare transported, 50 shillinges vpon each sacke: This woolle was for the most parte vented in the low Countries, and there wrought, & endraped into Clothe, but in processe of tyme the Draperie, and Arte of makinge of Clothe was brought into this Realme, and the *Hanses*, who before time bought all their Clothe in the lowe Countries, and so caried them vpwardes, did now buye much Clothe in England, & transported the same cōtinuallie vpon the olde small Custome, which at the first was sett so low for the furtherance of the new begunne Draperie, and Arte of making of Cloth, but at length it being growen very great, and the Wooll trade almost wholie decayed, it was found, that the Prince, & State lost exceedinglie, by the passing out of Cloth vpō the said small custome, and therefore in Queene *Maries* dayes, after her mariage with King *Philippe*, in the yeare 1557. and by his meanes the custome of Cloth, Kersye, and other Woollen commoditie, besides foreigne Wares, was, raised frō 14. pence to 6 shillings 8. pence the Cloth, to be payed by English men, and 13. shillings and 4. pence by straungers, transporting the same: by meanes whereof the Custome of Cloth endraped within the Land, was brought to be equall with the Custome of Woolle, when it was moste, and when the said

said Wooll was caried out vnwrought, and was draped in the low Countries: against this the *Hanses* opposed them selues, pretendinge their priviledges so long agoe graunted, and by many Kings confirmed vnto them, as they saide, but for that in the yere 1550 vnder King *Edward* the sixth, vpon dew examinatiō of their pretended Priviledges, there were manie defectes, and faultes found therein, & for that the *Hanses* for diuerse abuses, and falsehoodes in colouring, and freeing of foreigne goods, or such, which ought not to enioye the libertie of the *Hanses*, beeing none of their vnion, or confederacie, and for other causes had been by a Decree of the Councell adiudged to be fallen from their saide Priviledges, parte whereof were presentlie resumed, & called in, especiallie that, which cōcerned the carying out of woollen Cloth, they obtayned no remedie all that Kings dayes, but since they haue been offred great fauour, as by that, which followeth, shall appeare: But not content heerewithall, they made their often complaintes to the Emperours Maiestie, of the wrong done them, in seazing of their Priviledges in England: First in the yeare 1564. at which tyme the English Clothe was banished out of the low Countries by the Dutchesse of *Parma*, for the causes heeretofore expressed in this Treatise, and that the M.M. Adventurers helde their Martes at *Embden*, and afterwardes in the yeare 1582 at an Assemblie of the Empire at *Ausburge*, charging the said M.M. Advēturers, that they had taken away the said *Hanses* priviledges in Englande, to the ende, Some of the Hanses calumniation against the M. M. Adventurers.

N that

that they might haue the whole Cloth trade in their owne handes, and so by their *Monopolish* dealinges, make Clothe deare in the Empire: setting also pryce before hand of that, which they sell, & of that, which they will buye, and so committing open *Monopolie:* Wherevpon the Emperour wrote vnto the Earle of *Embden*, commanding him, to banish the M. M. Adventurers out of his Countrie, as Monopolishe persons, & hurtfull to the Epmire. The Earle discreetlie considering that her Maiestie might, & could easilie aunsweare the slaunderous complaintes of the *Hanses*, chargeing her Highnes with wrong done vnto them, as shee did, by her Letters sent to the Emperor in Aprill 1581. by Maister *George Gilpin*, at that tyme Secretarie to the Companie, and that the said M. M. Adventurers were now in his Towne of *Embden* no more to be accompted *Monopolians*, then they were heeretofore in *Antwerpe*, and of late at *Hambrough*, during their Residence there tenne yeares together, and vpwardes, did not only not put the said Decree, or Commaundement of the Emperor in execution, but tooke vpon him by his Oratour at *Spieres*, to defende the trade of the M. M. Adventurers in the Empire, and to iustifie the entertainement of them into his Countrie, wherein Doctor *William Muller*, at that time Chauncelour to the said Earle, and since *Sindicus* of *Hambrough*, was a chief Councelour, or Actor: so that the Emperor, for that tyme, was well satisfied with the Earles doeinges, and aunswer, and the saide M. M. Advẽturers continued their trade at *Embden*, till

till that by the Duke of *Parmaes* too neare, and badd neighbourhood, and other vrgent causes they were forced of necessitie, & for the better vent of the commoditie of the Realme; to seeke a new place, and finallie to agree with the *Staders*, as is aboue at large rehearsed : howbeit the *Hanses* heere ceased not, but persisted in their former pursuites, and complaintes, till the yeare 1597. at which tyme the saide *Hanses* were much endammaged at sea by Englishmen of warre, who by vertue of a proclamation sett foorth by her Maiestie, tooke manie shippes of the Easterlinges goeing into Spaine with Corne, Ammunition, and furniture for shipping, all which was made good bootie, and prize, whiche doeing caused the *Hanses* to haue the better audience in their cōplaints, the yeare before by *Don Francesco de Mendoza*, Admirall of *Aragone*, in the name of the King of Spain, and the Archduke *Albert* highlie recommended to the Emperour, and earnestlie sollicited vnder pretext of withstanding, and chastising of Pirates & sea Robbers: to the forwarding of this busines holpe not a litle, that in May, and Iune 1597. *Florence* Earle of *Barlamont*, Doctor *George Westendorpe*, and *Iohn van Niekercken*, Counsellors, were sent vnto the Kinge of *Denmarke*, and to the *Hanse* Townes, and namelie to the Towne of *Lubecke*, on the behalfe of the King of Spaine, and the Archduke *Albert* : these Embassadours, comming to the said Towne of *Lubecke*, did in writing declare the auncient friendshippe betweene the house of *Burgūdie*, and the *Hanse* Townes, & how

N 2 much

much the ſaid King had advaunced, and recomme-ded their cauſe vnto the Emperour, touchinge their Priviledges in Englande, by the meanes of his Em-baſſadour *Don Guillame de St Clement* reſident at *Pra-ghe:* They alſo complained, that the *Hanſe* Townes vſed ſo ample trade with the Kings Rebelles (as they tearmed them) in the low Cūtries, by meanes wher-of they, and the Queene of England were the more emboldened, and ſtrengthned againſt the ſaid King, wherefore they required, that the *Hanſe* Townes would for a time forbeare all trade whatſoeuer with the ſaid Rebelles, that thereby they might the ſooner be reduced vnder their Kings obedience, but if they feared to doe this, by reaſon of the league betweene *Englande*, *France*, and the *States* of the vnited Provin-ces, then they required, that they would alſo deale, and trafficque with the Kinges true and loyall ſub-iectes in the Hauens of *Callice*, *Gravelinghe*, *Dunkerck*, *Nieuport*, *Sluyſe*, and *Antwerpe*, as well as they did with the *Hollanders*, otherwiſe their trade might bee well accompted for Partialitie, rather then Newtralitie, promiſinge further, that the ſaide *Hanſes* ſhould diſ-charge their goodes, buye, ſell, and make returne in the foreſaide Hauens, without any payment at all of Tolle, Impoſt, Licence, or other charge whatſoeuer, and further ſhould be aſſured, and warranted by the Archduke *Albert*, from all dammage, or loſſe: Theſe Embaſſadours alſo ſeemed to bee much grieued for the iniurie, which they ſaid the Queene of England did vnto the *Hanſes*, in takinge frō them their ſo aun-

cient

of he required reparation, and restitution, and that the trade Westwardes might remaine free, and open to those of *Polone*, otherwise his Maister the Kinge should bee forced, to vse such meanes, as thereby neighbourlie freedome, & restitution might bee obtayned. This was in brief the effect of the saide Embassadours speach, whiche with a verie loude voyce hee deliuered in the Latine tongue: Whereunto it pleased her Maiestie to make him a short aunswere, and quicke for that tyme, referring him for further answere to certaine of her Highnes Honourable privie Counseill, to witte, the Lorde *Burghley*, late high Treasurer deceased, the Lord high Admiral, Sir *Iohn Fortescue*, and Sir *Robert Cecill* Secretarie: to whome after the said Polish Embassadour had deliuered his speach, which hee made before the Queene in writing, and excused his rough kinde of speaking, shewing that by his Commission signed, and sealed by his King in the assemblie of the States of *Polone*, hee was thereunto enioigned, he receyued the aunswere following in the name of her Maiestie, which properlie pertayning to the matter of the *Hanses*, and aunswering fullie, and verie pertinentlie the question made by them about their old priviledges, I haue thought meet to insert in this place.

The said Honorable Personages therefore tolde him, that her Maiestie, vnderstanding of his cōming into Egland, was right glad thereof, as sent from the King her brother, for whom not longe since she had by

Aunswere made on her Maiesties behalf vnto the aforsaid Embassage.

by her Intercession obtayned, First a trewce, and afterwardes a peace of the great Turck, when the saide King, and his State were oppressed with sore warre, which peace he yet enioyeth, to the great good, and benefite of his Kingdome, and therefore now expected, not onely a remembraunce of the saide good turne, but also dew thankes for the same, for that neuer since she had receyued any from him: her Highnes had giuen him gratious audience, and read the King his Maisters Letters willinglie, wherein shee saw nothing but that which ought to proceed *A Rege fratre, ad Reginam sororem charissimam*, but said they, you chaunging, as it should seeme, the person of an Embassadour, began a longe speach, and turned the same almost into a sermone, the which notwithstanding, her Maiestie heard with patience, signifyinge vnto you onely in a few wordes, beseeming the Maiestie of a Prince, how vnworthily you in your Oration had layed the faute of manie thinges vpon her Highnes, and with how great equitie in deede shee hoped, that her Actions would bee well liked of all men, & so dismissed you, to receyue further answer, according to your negotiation of vs her Counseillours, who are best witnesses of all her doeinges almost these fourtie yeares, as well with the Kings her friendes, as with her enemies, although we know no Prince in Christendome for enemie, but the King of Spaine onely, whose cause you verie seriouslie handled in your speech. First therefore wee required to see your Oration in writinge, to the ende, that wee might

might giue such answere therevnto, as were conuenient, & for that you haue shewed vnto vs your cõmission sealed, and signed by the Kinge of *Polone* (as appeared vnto vs) in the assemblie of that kingdom, whereby we haue plainly perceiued, that you haue vttered nothing in your oration, which you had not order to declare, therefore wee can in no wise blame you for any thinge by you said, although her Majestie looked not for any such matter. Concerning the pointes of your complaintes, wee obserue them to be these: First you say, that your King perceiueth, that his subiectes haue not onely not receiued any new benefite from her Maiestie, but are partly depriued of those, which proceeded from her highnes progenitors, and were cõfirmed vnto them, & partly are in a maner excluded frõ all Nauigation, or Trade in this Realme: The second point conteineth a grieuous complaint of your Kinges subiectes against the proclamations sent vnto them, by the which all trafficque into Spain is forbidden them, and consequentlie that their shippes haue bene in hostile manner taken by the Queenes men of warre, and the goodes therein made prize, and confiscated, and finally you required in the Kings name restitution of the said goodes, or reparation of the damages, and iniuries (as they terme them) receiued, and that they bee not hereafter hindred in the foresaid trafficque which by the common law ought to bee free to all men, otherwise such meanes of necessitie must bee vsed, whereby they may gett satisfactiõ by the ayde

O and

and helpe of the saide Kinge: these being the chief heades, or pointes of your Embassage, and of that which your K. requireth, her Maiestie hath thought good to answear therevnto sincerely, and according to the treuth of the matter in this manner: First, that your King is not rightely enformed concerning the first point, in that it is said that his subiectes are partly depriued of their priuileges, & partlie shutt out from all trade almoste in this Realme: for where there is mention made of his subiectes, as subiectes of the Kinge of Polone, this doubt may arise, what kinde of people the subiectes are, because they must be vnderstood either to be subiectes of the Dukedome of *Prussia*, or else to bee cōprised vnder the name of the *Hanses*, who haue no certaine seat, or place whence they are: for other then the subiectes of the Dukedome of *Prussia*, and the *Hanses*, as Merchantes of Germanie residing at *London*, the Queenes Maiestie neuer vnderstood, that there were any that pretended any priuiledge of Comerce aboue or before other Merchantes of all Europe: And whereas they complaine as subiectes of the Kinge of Polone, that they are depriued of their priuiledges, and almost excluded from all Trade in this Kingdome: First concerninge the right of their priuileges, question was made almoste fiftie yeares agoe in the time of Kinge *Edward* the sixth of the validitie of their former priuileges, and then the saide Priuileges were rightelie iudged void, and forfeicted for the manifest breach of the conditions thereof, and since the saide *Hanses* could

could neuer proue, that they had iniurie done them in the said reuocation: notwithstanding all this they had graunted vnto them in their Trade into this Realme, and in the payement of their Customes more libertie, then any Merchantes of whatsoeuer nation through all Europe, yea by especiall grace, & fauour they were made equall, and had, as much freedome giuen in their Trade, and in the payement of the Customes of their Merchandises, as the naturall borne subiectes of this Realm, accordinge to the true meaning and intent of their priuileges from the beginning: and if they haue not accepted of this, which by great fauour was offered vnto them, and so haue forborn their Trade in this Realme, the fault is in themselues, neither can it be rightly saide, that they are excluded (as it should seeme by the Kinges wryting that hee is informed) but rather admitted & retained with the same fauour, as the very mere subiects, & naturalls of the Crown of England are, then the which benefite what can be greater? Vnles, contrary to all humane lawe, the Queene should haue more care of them, then of her proper subiectes and howe absurde, yea howe detestable this should bee, wilbe made manifest, if it bee but considered, what the office of a good Prince is in the rule, and administration of his kingedome: for if in regarde of his Kinglie office a Kinge be compared to the Husband of an house, or to the Pastour of the people, or (as he is said to be in the diuine scriptures) to a foster father of the people committed vnto him, who except hee

O 2 were

were ſtarke madde, would call that Prince a good father, or huſbande of the houſe, which ſhould haue more care of another mans familie then of his own? Or a good Paſtour, or Sheepheard, whiche neglecting his own flocke, ſhould looke better to another mans then his owne? or woorthie of the name of a Nurſing, or foeſter King, which ſhould neglect his owne children, & nouriſh other mens children with his milke? And ſo theſe thinges may be well applied to the preſent cauſe, and queſtion in hande, for if the *Hanſes* ſhould haue better conditions, then the proper ſubiectes of the Kingdome, it would plainly followe, that the Prince of this Realme ſhould doe his owne naturall ſubiectes very great iniurie, contrarie to the law of Nature, & mans law; for by this meanes his ſubiects ſhould become poore, or rather deſtitute of all honeſt, and profitable trafficque, and Navigation, and the *Hanſes* ſhould growe opulent, and poſſeſſe the whole trade of the Realm, as Monopoliſtes of the whole kingdome. And by theſe reaſons, well waighed, it manifeſtlie appeareth, that thoſe, whom the King calleth his ſubiectes, doe moſt falſelie complaine, that they are excluded from lawfull trade in this Lande, when as freelie they may trade, and with the ſame conditions, as her Maieſties meere Engliſh ſubiectes may doe, and with farre better then all other Merchauntes, In ſo much as that they are preferred before all the neighbour people of this Realme, *French, Scottes, Fleminges, Hollanders*, & the reſt of the low Countrie Merchantes, and before all

all the people of Dutchelande, the said *Hanses* onelie excepted. Wherefore her Maiestie is perswaded; that when the King of *Polone* shall vnderstande these reasons, he will change his opinion, the like shee expecteth at the handes of the Senatours of that Kingdome, if these things be aright imparted vnto them: For the complaintes of the *Hanses* are so vniust, and vnreasonable, that it may be doubted, whether the accustomed forme of iudgment in matters of doubt were obserued by the abouesaide Assemblie in this cause, or that credite was giuen to the Cōplainantes, the matter but slightlie examined, or that place was giuen to their importunate prayers, and requestes: For her Maiestie hath that opinion of the supreme authoritie, and dexteritie of the Senatours of *Polone* in their proceedinges in the Assemblies of the saide Kingdome (which commeth not to the King by enheritaunce, but by election, and consent of the saide Senatours) that it seemeth absurd, and not likelie to be true, that they in their publike assemblie would decree any thinge against the Maiestie of suche a Queene, whose like Christendome hath not had in this age, nor anie other happier in noble Actes, or in length of raigne, or superior in Princelie vertues, and yet that the same her Maiestie should be vniustlie accused, and without being heard, blamed, is a thinge not to be taken in good parte: for this amonge priuate men, was alwayes accompted vnreasonable, much more being done against a Queene of so great Maiestie, which hath so well deserued of the King, &

O 3 his

his Kingdome. For it is apparant, that certain yeares past, the warre which the Turke had prepared against the said King, and kingdome, by her Highnes intercession, ceased, and peace was graunted to the King, and his Realme, by the benefite whereof they to this daye enioye quietnes, and peace in that kingdome: The like good turne the Queene did in the yere 1553 to the Kinges Father *Iohn* King of *Sweden*, when as he, as well by his Embassadours the Lorde *Enicke* of *Wissenbroughe* his Cosin, *Andrew Kithe* Counseillour and *Raschias* his Secretarie, as also by letters sent vnto her Maiestie, earnestlie entreated her Highnes, to sende an Embassage into *Muscouie*, to make intercession for a peace betwene the said King, and the *Muscouite*, whiche shee without delay willinglie performed, and by her persuasion drew the *Muscouite* to make peace with the said King vpon indifferent, and reasonable conditions: Which two excellent benefites done by her Maiestie, the one to the Father, the other to the sonne, and to their kingdomes are therfore rehearsed, because that in remembraunce thereof, a better, & more courteous course of proceeding might iustlie haue been expected from the King, & from the Senators of his Kingdom, then by your Oration (it appeareth) was by them determined: In so much, that if at the beginning of your instructions, it had not been sett downe, that your commission was decreed vpon in the Assemblie of the Realme, it might haue been suspected, some pointes of your saide Commission, not to be lyked, were composed

posed by some Spaniards, and slaunderous Iesuites, of whiche Iesuites it is said there is a great number spred through manie partes of the Kingdome of *Polone*, whose malicious raylinges, are often cast out in publike places against her Maiestie, and this Kingedome, without cōdigne punishment, or any reprehension at al: and therfore it may be the more likelie to be true, that they as sworne men to the Kinge of Spaine, together with the Spaniardes of late enterrayned by the King, and heard in the publike Assemblie of the Realme, haue procured this Embassage with these kinde of Commissions in fauour of the Kinge of Spaine.

The second point of your Embassage conteyneth a request for free Nauigation, or trade into Spaine, which we deeme to be such, as the Kinge of Spaine him selfe hath lately in serious manner recommended for him selfe: for this prohibition was not sett foorth by the Queenes Maiestie before shee was of necessitie compelled therevnto: least the Kinge of Spaine, open enemie to this Realme, should bee furnished with Armes, Shippes, and Ammunition with such facilitie, & in such great aboundance, as he was from the Maritime partes of Germanie, by meanes whereof hee might mainteyne longe warre against this Realme, so that if he could not gett these aydes, and helpes, it is manifest that he should bee forced to leaue of warre, and offer peace not onely to this Realme, but also to others, against whom hee most vniust-

vniustlie maketh warre, whereas therefore it is plain, that this Kinge of Spaine, being an enimie to this Realme, is furnished, armed, and strengthened to continue vniust warre with shippes, victuall, and other warlike prouisions out of certaine Citties vnder *Polone*, and other maritime Citties of Germanie, in what sorte can her Maiestie (being oppressed by the Spaniard with vniust warre) tollerate or suffer that such orders, and helpes so openly, and so copiouslie should be caried to the said King her enemie for the cōtinuance of the warre against her? And although you manie times repeated it, that the said her Highnes prohibitions were contrarie to the lawe of Nations, it is straunge, that you would alleadge this against the law of Nature, when as by Nature it selfe, it is ordained, that euerie man may defende him self against force, which law not written, but borne with vs we haue not learned, but receyued, and drawen from Nature it selfe, besides it is prouided by the auncient lawes, that it may be lawfull, to forbid, yea to lett, and hinder, that no man minister armes, victuall, or any thing else, whereby the enimie may be holpen to make warre, as by this one, wherewith manie other agree, you may perceyue: *Cotem ferro subigendo necessariam, Hostibus quoque venundari vt ferrum & frumentum & Sales non sine periculo capitis licet:* Neither may it heere be omitted, that this prohibition is plainlie contayned in diuerse Articles of the Charters, giuen to the *Hanses* by the Kinges of Englande, and first in the Charter of King *Edward* the first King of

ff. lib. 39. tit. 4. de Publicanis.

of Englande, in these wordes following: *Licebit prædictis Mercatoribus quô voluerint tam infrâ regnum, & potestatem nostram, quàm extrâ mercantias suas ducere, seu portari facere, præterquam ad terras manifestorum, & notoriorum Hostium Regni nostri*: the verie same clause, and promise is in expresse wordes conteyned in the Charters of *Edward* the second, and *Henrie* the sixth Kinges of England, which exceptions so oftentimes repeated, by so manie Kinges, ought to admitt no reason to the contrarie, especiallie on those mens behalfe, who challenge their right by vertue of the said Charters onely: but we should haue had no neede to propounde these our reasons vnto you, but that we supposed you were ignorant howe this question, of prohibiting ayd to be giuen to the King of Spain, for making warre against vs, was handled about two yeares agoe before your King in his Counseil, when as certaine Merchants, or Mariners of *Danzick*, complained of the like prohibition, and had obtayned an Edict against her Maiesties people, which Edict being oppugned with many reasons by our Embassadour Doctor *Parkins* heere present, was abrogated, & made void, so that there followed no execution vpon the same, but the *Danzickers* were dismissed: which happened in the yeare 1595. so that to treat further of this matter, wee should seeme to doe that, which is alreadie done: yet wee doe not denie, that which is alleagded by some on your behalfe, that these prohibitions are hurtfull to your people, for that while the same are in force, they cannot with

P their

their profite sell their Corne, and many other things growing in their country: but for this is an easie remedie, if your people would bringe a great parte of the goodes by her Maiestie prohibited into this Realme of England, where it should bee lawfull for them to sell the same with all fauour, and with their great gaigne, and carie another part thereof into the low Countries and Fraunce, or into Italie, so it bee done without fraude, and that the same come not into the Spaniardes Countrie: and by this meanes they may carie out and transporte all their goodes saufe, to the greater benefit of the subiectes of *Polone*, then otherwise, which might bee prooued manifestlie by diuerse examples, and presentlie by this, that by carying their commodities into the other Countries besides Spain, they should avoide the arresting of their shippes, whiche happeneth euery yeare in that Countrey: so that many tymes, to their great charge, they are compelled to rigge their shippes, & fitt them for warlike vse, and so with eminent daunger to hazard the losse of shippes, and men in fight at sea, as too often the *Danzickers*, & others haue prooued: and euen this present sommer, it is knowen, that the Cõmaunders of the Spanish Nauie haue hunge vp and drowned in the Hauen of *Ferole* manie Mariners, Maisters, and Pilotes of shippes pertayninge to the Maritime Cities of the *Hanses*, for that they went about to deliuer them selues, and their shippes from violent, & constrained bondage: For the avoyding of the like losse, and dammage, her Maiestie this last

yeare

yere by publike writing sett forth in Dutch, French, and Latine tongue, declared, and gaue warning, that if there were any shippes of foreigne Nations by any meanes, either with, or against their willes, deteyned in the Spanishe armie by Sea, at that tyme readie to invade Englande, it should bee lawfull for them, for their safetie, to withdrawe them selues out of the said Armie to ours, or to departe home quietlie to their owne Portes, without any damage to be done vnto them by her Maiesties people : and it is certaine that manie shippes, as well of *Danzick*, as of *Hamborough*, were founde deteyned by the Spaniardes amongest their shippes, which the Englishe men of warre did their beste to saue from burninge when they did sett fire on the Spanishe Navie : and if the Kinge of *Polones* Counsellours had knowen of this writing, it had not been congruent, that without mention of such a benefite done to the Kinges subiectes, they should prosecute these matters in the worser parte : neither can we here passe ouer in silence, that before her Maiestie did put the foresaid prohibitions in execution, shee many wayes made it knowen, as well by publike letters, as also by Admonition of the East countrie Merchauntes, that shee now was of necessitie compelled for the defence of her Realme against the King of Spaine her open enemie, to forbidde the transporting of Armes, Victuall, and other things into Spaine, wherewith the said King might set foorth and furnish his Navies, and Armies, and without the which he could not possiblie continew the warre a-

P 2 gainst

gainst this Realme. Besides all this for the iustifying and defence of the saide her Maiesties prohibitions, it manifestlie appeareth, that the verie like haue been often made by other Kinges, & namely by the King of *Polones* Father *Iohn* King of *Sweden*, & by *Sigismond* King of *Polone*, graundfather to the King, that nowe is, who by force tooke much Merchandise from her Maiesties subiectes, for that they were to bee caried into *Muscouie*, which many honest Englishe Merchauntes, hereby brought into pouertie, haue cause to remember. The like was also oftentymes done by the Kings of *Sweden* to the subiects of *Denmarke*, who would haue traded into *Muscouie*: And for confirmation heereof we can shew the authentique commissions of the said King *Sigismonde*, giuen to his Admirall *Otto Mannickes* the 25th of May 1566. and others of the 12th of Marche 1569. to *Asmo Genrick*, & the like to *Hans Necker*, Captaines of his, to whom authoritie was giuen vnder the said Kings hand, and seale, to intercept, take, spoile, & make hauocke of all those, which by way of Merchandise, or otherwise, should carie into *Muscouie* Powder, Ordinance, Saltpeter, Victuall, or anie other kinde of ware tendinge to warlike prouision. There bee also letters extant, written in verie earnest maner by the saide Kinge *Sigismond* vnto her Maiestie, dated in Marche 1568. wherein by manie argumentes hee shewed, that the Trafficque, or Nauigation into *Sweden*, & the *Narue*, forbidden to all men in generall, was most iust and lawfull, and by that meanes had prouided, that his ene-

enemies the *Muscouites* should not be furnished, and armed not onely with armes, weapons, and ammunition, but with other greater matters, which might help his enimie, & to that end he writeth, that he had sett a watch in the sea of men of warre, with commaundement that if anie mā against their will would trade into *Muscouie*, they should take, and seaze vpon him, & all his goodes: of this prohibition the Coūsellours of *Polone* can not bee ignorant, neither was that wise and prouident Kinge heerein to bee reprehended: And after that these reasons were deliuered vnto the said Embassador, he was asked whether anie thing could be iustlie opposed against them, wherevnto he answered, that he had none authoritie to dispute of these matters, but onely to lay foorth, that which he had in commission, and to require an aunswere therevnto: the saide Councellours therefore thought it not fitt to vse any longer speache on that behalfe: But to conclude auouched for a full answere of all that hath been by the saide Embassadour propounded, that seeing it is manifest that this deed of her Maiestie is allowable, not onely by the law of Nature to defende her selfe, but also by the expresse Ciuile lawe, and examples of the Kings of *Sweden*, & *Polone*, especiallie by diuerse Charters of the Kinges of England, therefore her said Maiestie could not be rightlie accused either of iniustice, or Iustice denied in anie her doeinges, for as (saide they) shee hath alwayes professed (taking the omnipotent GOD the searcher of heartes to her witnes) it was neuer in her

P 3 mynde

myndeto cōmitany thing against the sacred rule of Iustice, so shee wilbe ready to giue eare to anie complainant, either her own subiect, or straunger, and by her officers to doe iustice to the said plaintife, according to equitie, and reason: the which shee will also performe towardes you, if you shall recōmend anie expresse cause of any subiect of the kingdom of *Polon*. For her Maiestie is so ready, to giue answer to *Pisman* of *Danzick*, who (as it is saide) followed you from thence, for the prosecutinge of certaine his sewtes for iustice, that if you did not in such haste vrge your departure, wee her Maiesties Counselours, before your departure, should haue authoritie, to heare, and determine his said sewtes, according to reason, and equitie: And to make an end of this longe, yet necessarie aunswere of ours to your obiections, for that many of the thinges published in your Embassage, may by imputation be taken in ill parte against the honour, and dignitie of her Maiestie, all which by our saide aunswere are plainly proued to haue proceeded from your Kinge ill informed, her Maiestie with good reason doeth expect, that when her aunsweres shall before the Kinge, and the Senate of his Realme be compared with the complaintes of the Complainers, the saide Senate will prouide, that the trueth of her Maiestes Actions bee no lesse publikelie by some means repaired, and restored, then the contrary hath bene attempted by false accusations, and the Kings publike Embassage, that so it may appeare, that the Kinge hath that regarde of the preseruati-

seruation of mutuall freendshippe, as her Maiestie doth expect from a Prince that is her confederate,& brother: this aunswere was made by their Honors abouesaid on the 13th day of August 1597. at *Greenwitch*, with the which the said Polishe Embassadour departed, and heerein the question betweene the Englishe, and the *Hanses* is fully laide open, and aunswered, and their malice against the State of the land plainly discouered: so that it were more then time, that they were restored, and satisfied in their vnreasonable pretences, as some without dew consideration vnaduisedly desire. About this time, to witt, the first of August 1597. the Emperour continuallie called vpon by *Don Guillelmo S. Clement* ordinarie legder for the Kinge of Spain at *Prage*, and stirred vp as well by the abouesaide Embassages, as by the importunate, & clamorous sollicitations of the *Hanses*, permitted a Mandate, or Edict to bee published, and sett vp in the Empire, the tenoure whereof ensueth, taken out of a translation of the saide Mandate into the Netherlandishe tongue, and printed *cum Privilegio* at *Brusselles*, to the greater and more enormous iniurie, and reproch of her Maiestie, & her Highnes Actions, and of the Companie of M. M. Adventurers, as no doubt their meaninge was, that were the authours & doers thereof, and consequentlie to make the whole English nation, and name the more odious, and condempned of all men, thereby also openlie iustifying, and making lawfull all the vniust, and vnlawfull attemptes, and practises of the King

Kinge of Spain and his ministers against her saide Maiestie, Realme, and people.

The Emperours Mandate against the M. M. Aduēturers.

Wee *Rudolph* the seconde, by the grace of God Elect Romane Emperour, &c. to all and singulare Princes Electours, Princes Spirituall, and temporall, Prelates, Earles, Barons, &c. sende freendshippe, fauour, and all good: Heretofore in the time of our right welbeloued Grandfather, and Father the Emperours *Ferdinand*, and *Maximilian* (of famous memorie) as also in the time of our Raigne ouer the Empire, the Confederate Dutche *Hanse* Townes, and some others thereby interessed, many yeares together, and at sundry times, and tydes not onely at our Court, but also at former meetinges of the Empire, especially at *Ausbourghe* in the yeare 1582. and at *Regensbroughe* in the yeare 1594. last past, haue in complayning wise declared and shewed: That they three hundred yeares agoe, and aboue had obtayned & gotten notable priuileges, immunities, freedoms, and exemptions within the Realm of England, partly by the especiall grace, and fauour of the Kinges of that Lande, and partlie with great summes of monie for the good, and commoditie of the holy Empire, and the members of the same, and for the aduancement of the generall Trade, and Comerce, which priuiledges, &c. they haue held, & enioyed till now, not without their great, and notable charge, as hauing bene graunted, approued, and confirmed by fourteen Kings of Englande succeßiuely, and in the yeare

Falsis narratis tacita & suppressa veritate.

yeare 1470. by foreknowledge, and consent of the States of the Lande, both spirituall, and temporall, made of the force, and nature of a perpetuall, and irreuocable contract: wherevpon they helde their residence and Officers within the cittie of *London* in an house, or counter called (the Dutche Guild hall) where they vsed to buye Clothe of the subiectes of the Crown of Englande, and caryed the same from thence into Dutchelande, by meanes whereof Englishe Clothe was to be bought *good cheape* throughout all the said Country of Dutcheland, frõ whence also on the other side a Trade was driuen with all kinde of wares seruing England, to the no small profitt, and gaigne, as well of vs, as of the subiectes of the Empire, aud of the Crowne of Englande: Whiche notwithstanding certaine couetous Companies of Merchauntes, whereof some call them selues Merchauntes Aduenturers, seekinge their owne priuate gaine and lucre, are spronge vp in the saide Realme, who by bad meanes haue wrought and practised, to the great, & notorious hurt and damage of the foresaide *Hanses*, and haue taken vpon them to bringe in manie vntollerable innovations, contrarie to the aboue said olde Customes, Priviledges, & perpetuall contract obtayned, and purchased with the great costes, and charges of the saide *Hanses*: So that it is come to passe, that the Queene of Englande nowe raigning, will not any longer endure, or cõfirme the said *Hanses* Priuiledges, and perpetuall contract, and

Notwithstãding this good cheap the Lantgraues of Hessen had at one time out of Englande 600. Clothes for their Liueries: which they would not haue boght there if the Hanses had solde Clothe so good cheap as here is said.

Q nowe

nowe finallie the last yeare to the further, and more intollerable grieuance of the foresaide *Hanse* townes (specialllie for that they founde it not reasonable nor fitt to yeeld vnto the saide M. M. Adventurers a Residence according to their desire at *Hamborough*) hath wholy forbidden, and cutt off all priviledged trade, both within, and without the saide Realme of England, thereby the better to strengthen the trade of the foresaid Adventurers Companie, and to bringe their Monopolish trafficque into a full course, and trayne with English Clothe, & commoditie in such forme, and manner, as the Staplers Companie haue drawen the trade of English Wooll into their owne handes onely, whiche nowe is apparent, in that the *Hanses* can not enioye their Priuiledges, & well purchased trafficque, whereas on the other side, the Englishe Adventurers Companie encreaseth in number, to witt in Dutchelande, firste at *Embden*, where they were receiued by the Earle of *Eastfriselande* that then was, and afterwardes in other places more, and now presentlie at *Stade*, within the Archbishopricke of *Bremen*, where they haue settled the Clothe trade, and haue drawen vnto themselues onely other commerces, and commodities whiche the Dutche Merchauntes in former times vsed to enioye, and farther to the preiudice of the *Hanse* townes, haue erected an especiall Societie, Staple, Colledge, Confederacie, and alliance, by meanes whereof they haue not onely made diuerse and sundrie Monopolish prohibitions, treaties, and accordes hurtfull to the common

mon wealth of the holy Empire, against vs, & against the Right, and ordinance of the saide Empire, and against all vse of Merchauntes, but also haue raised Clothe, and other wares accordinge to their owne willes, to such a dearenes, " that the pryce thereof is almost as high againe, as it was wont to be when the *Hanses* might vse their Priviledges. Besides the saide Englishe Adventurers doe not sell their Clothes after they haue been wett, and put in the water without retching, or stretching, as it ought to be by the policie, constitutions, & penale statutes of the Holy Empire: and for that the same hath been left *vnpunished a long tyme, other Merchauntes, which buye Clothe of the saide Adventurers doe take occasion of the like badd example: Finallie, through the drift and dealing of these Adventurers, the Dutche Merchaunt hath the best of his trade taken from him, omittinge heere howe that the Queene of Englande " with armed hand hath presumed, or advanced her selfe to cause the Merchauntes Adventurers shippes to be convoyed from *London* to *Stade*, thorough the Dutche sea, and within ours, and the Holy Empires Iurisdiction, & commaundement: and besides, hath sett vp, and published all kinde of Edictes tending to the hinderaunce, and empeaching of thē freedome of the sea, and Navigation, togeather with arrestes

How came it to passe thē that diuerse Factours, and Seruants of sundrie the Princes Electours, & Lordes of the Empire, bought their liuerie clothes of ẏ Merchants Advēturers at such time as the Hanses might ship clothe out of Englād as good cheap as the Merchantes Advēturers?

* There are none who desire a reformation in this point more then the M. M. Advēturers.

" Vnto this the Hamburgers gaue occasion by exacting a tolle by forcible hande laying their men of warre before the Swinge for that purpose: Defensio autem non tantum omni iure est permissa, sed etiam pro defensione rerum & bonorum alium non modo vulnerare sed & occidere licet, & is qui illicitè exactam gabellam soluere recuset, neque Deum neque homines offendit.

Q 2 which

which haue followed vppon the ſame, by meanes whereof the *Hanſe* Townes, and other our ſubiectes, and the ſubiectes of the Holy Empire, are forced to forſake, and leaue vnfrequented the foreſaide free Navigation throughout the whole " Weſtern ſea, and in the *Ems* ſtreame, and partlie in the Eaſterne ſea, and elſwhere, forwhich cauſe the foreſaid *Hanſe* Townes, and others thereby intereſſed, haue called vpon vs, and the Holy Empire, and in moſt humble manner haue prayed, and beſought vs, to haue conſideration of all theſe matters, & to giue them heerein ayd, and aſſiſtance.

" Vnto this ſee her Maieſties aunſwear made to the Poliſh Embaſſador.

For aſmuch then, as we founde, that theſe com. plaintes, and grievances were of very great waighte, and importance, and ſeeing that by our neighbourlie, and friendlie writing to the Queene of England we haue but ſmally prevailed, and laſtlie, for that we haue little profited with our Emperial Mandate and ordinances heeretofore ſett foorth, againſt the Reteiners of the ſaide M. M. Adventurers, but to the contrarie, perceyuing that for the defence, and iuſtifying of theſe matters, all kinde of Diſputations, excuſes, queſtions, & delayes were mooued & brought foorth, it ſeemed to vs verie neceſſarie, before all other things, for our more aſſurance of the trueth on this behalfe, to cauſe a diligent, and perfect information to be taken, " whether the Engliſh Adventurers Companie did vſe anie trade or *Monopolies* contrarie to our, and the Holy Empires ordinances, which being

" It were reaſon the M. M. Adventurers

ing done, it was founde by the Deposition of not a fewe credible persons at *Francfort* vpon *Meyn*, in the Lent Marte 1581. and by other information on this behalfe taken, that all, that is aboue written, clearely appeared, and that which is more, that the foresaide Adventurers Colledges were heretofore forbidden, and banished out of *Danzick* in *Prussia*, as also out of some places of the low " Burgundish, & other Coũtries: wherevpon hauing with our selues waighed the whole matter, according to the importãce therof, and considered, that these things concerned not onelie the *Hanse* Townes, but also all the subiectes, and Merchauntes of the Holy Empire, the further proceeding therin was deferred to a generall Assembly of the Empire, holden at *Ausbrough* in the yeare 1582: against wch we caused the Acts & Propositions concerning the same, to be sent vnto all the Princes Electours, to the ende, that they might the Ripelier, and better consider vpon the same, and afterwardes we laide the matter in deliberation of all the States of the Holy Empire, who after mature Counsel, and bethinking, gaue vs their advice, and opinions vpon the same, praying vs with all, that seeing there was no meanes to obtayne at the foresaid Queene of Englandes handes the full restitution of the foresaide *Hanses* priviledges, hereditarie agreement, and contract, and that in the meane while the Englishe Adventurers Companie vsed, and went forwarde with an hurtfull *Monopolie*, against all right, and reason, that we would with publike Edictes, forbid the foresaide

were heard what they could oppose to this deposition.

Howe the M. M. Adventurers were banished out of the Burgundishe lowe Countries, appeareth before, and if they bee not now banished out of the Empire by the practise of the same men the Spanishe Ministers, let the wise judge.

Q3

ſaide Merchauntes Adventurers their trade by water, and by lande, throughout the Holy Empire, and the Iuriſdiction, and Commaund of the ſame: And further, that we would ſtraightlie charge, and vppon great penalties enioigne euery State, whom it might concerne, not to permitt the ſaide M. M. Aduenturers, or their Conſortes, Confederated Companies, Factours, and ſervauntes, to haue recourſe, or anie commõ trafficque in any place within the holy Empire, but rather to expell, defende, and forbidde the ſame, vpon paine of our indignation, and loſſe of all Royalties, Fiefes, Rightes, and Iuriſdictions, which to the diſobedient on this behalfe might appertaine, or belonge, either vnder vs, or the Holy Empire. And if ſo bee, that contrarie to this our Emperiall commaundement, the Engliſhe Merchauntes Aduenturers, or their Factours, or ſervauntes, ſhould be ſo bolde, as to vſe, or dryue anie trade either in buying, or ſelling of Engliſhe Clothes, Wooll, or other wares what ſoeuer, at any place within the holy Empire, that then each Magiſtrat and Ruler within his Commaund, or Iuriſdictiõ ſhould be holden where the ſaide bought or ſolde goodes may be found, and where ſuch trade is vſed, preſently to ſeaze vpon, and confiſcate the ſaide forbidden goodes, as by the contentes of the adviſe, and determination to vs at that tyme deliuered at *Auſburghe* on the behalfe of the Electors, Princes, and States of the holy Empire, more at large appeareth: howbeit wee proceeded not to the publication of the ſaid Mandates, but nothwithſtanſtanding that the Deputies of the Hanſe townes earneſtly inſiſted, to haue a finall concluſion of this matter, wee firſt of all ſought by all gentle meanes, to induce, and moue the Queene of Englande, for the confirmation of good neighbourhood, to giue vs, and the Empire, as alſo the *Hanſe* townes contentment in the aboue-written complaintes, and grieuances, without compelling vs for that cauſe to vſe any ſharper meanes, or remedie: and to that end we gaue her Ambaſſadour, at that time being at *Auſbroughe*, to vnderſtand, through what vrgent and neceſſary occaſions the foreſaid Mandate was concluded, and reſolued vpon by vs, and the States of the holy Empire, and with all to offer that, whenſoeuer it ſhould like the Queene of Englande, to ſuffer the matter to be brought to a freendly treaty, and communication, and to that end ſhould appoint her Embaſſadours with full commiſſion, that wee then on the otherſide would bee willinge, to depute alſo certain perſonages of qualitie, and countenaunce, before whom both parties ſhould appeare at ſome conuenient place within the Empire, and lay forth their doleances, and griefes, and ſo growe to a compoſition, and determination in all reaſon, and with a true and faitfull hearte and meaninge: Wee alſo admoniſhed, and finallie moued the *Hanſe* Townes to their great coſte, and charges, to ſende a particular Legation into Englande vnto the Queene, where after they had preſented our letters of Interceſſion, which wee gaue them with them, a friendlie agreement,

ment, and composition was required, but they could not effect, or profite anie thinge on this behalfe, but receyued of the Queene a cleane contrarie answear. In the meane while, the Adueturers, with their Monopolishe trade, and dealinges encreased more, and more, and multiplied in the Empire, and ouer, and aboue this, the Englishe did vnto the subiectes of vs, and the holy Empire in the open sea, great violence, and damage: which discommoditie beganne, continued, and encreased whole twelue yeares longe, to witte, from the Assemblie at *Ausburgh*, 82. to the Assemblie last held at *Regensbroughe*. 94. to the preiudice, and contempt not onely of our Emperiall Intercessiõ, but also of the writing of the *Hanse* townes, and of the many wayes sought for friendlie appointment, in so much, that the *Hanse* Townes, at the last holden assembly at *Regensbrough*, againe complained on this behalfe, and we, considering the manifest necessitie of the cause, layd the same a freshe in deliberation, and consultation with the Electours, Princes, and States which ther appeared, and with the Coũsellours, Ambassadours, & Deputies of the Princes: which appeared not personallie at the said assembly. And forasmuch, as it was founde, to bee against all right, and reason, that the *Hanses* should bee spoyled in the Realme of Englande of all their Iust tittle, hereditarie agreement, and Priuileges gotten, as aforesaide with their great coste, and charges, and that on the other side the Marchauntes Adventurers with their Conventicles, Companie, and trayne, without anie any [a] permiſſion of vs as preſently raigning Romane Emperour, and ſupreme head of the holy Empire, yea that which is more, contrary to all former receſſes, & Mandates, ſhould *de facto* intrude themſelues, and goe through with their trade, to the notable loſſe, and damage of all the States of this Empire, great, and ſmall, and to the bringing in of a dearth in Clothe, and woolle, and by their Monopoliſhe practiſes (which according to the conſtitutions of vs, and the holy Empire deſerue great puniſhement) to goe about to weaken, and ouerthrow the auncient, and honeſt trade of Merchaundiſe vſed amonge the laudable Dutche Nation: without making mention in this place of the outrage, force, & violence, which the foreſaid Engliſh haue committed, with manifold robberies, & ſpoilings at ſea, to the daungerous conſequence, and preiudice of the Iuriſdiction, and ſuperioritie which pertayneth, and belongeth vnto vs, and the holy Empire in the ſame: therefore in the foreſaide aſſemblie of the Empire, it was with one voice, and conſent concluded, and reſolued, and of vs by the Electors, Princes, and States required, that if ſo bee (notwithſtandinge all the great paynes and charges hetherto in vaine beſtowed) at our newe inſtance, and requiſition, with deduction of all the circūſtances thereto neceſſarie, the Queene of England would not let the *Hanſe* Townes enioye their Priviledges free, certaine, and whole, as heretofore of old they had them, and would not alſo ſuffer the Commerce, and trade open, and vnmoleſted, that then we

R should

[a] Contractus ſunt de Iure Gentium liberi: & vt liberi ſunt ita etiam ignorante Magiſtratu ex generali legum conceſsione cū quouis non hoſte liberè & licitè exercentur.

should in deed assiste the *Hanse* Townes, as the faith-full subiectes of vs, and the holy Empire, and should cause the aboue-mentioned Mandate agreed vppon at *Ausborough* 1582. to be published, and put in execution against the hurtfull Monopolishe Companie of the M.M. Adventurers, without any fauour, dissimulation, or composition: whiche consultation in such maner by the Electours, Prince, and States in generall, with one consent propounded, at former Assemblies, and now againe renewed, were according to right and reason confirmed, and ratified, and consequentlie the fifth of Iuli 1595. wrote vnto the foresaide Queene louinglie, and neighbourly requiring her a new, and setting before her eyes the fore-saide reasons, with manie other motiues thereto seruing, that shee would cause the old, and continuall complaintes, together with the oppressions, and damages of the foresaid *Hanse* Townes to cease, but we receyued such an answere vnto this our writing, that thereby it may sufficientlie bee perceyued, that our hetherto longe vsed patience is not onely receyued with small thankes, but with all, the said Queene presumeth, to asscribe vnto her selfe some interest heerein, & to drawe the same into consequence, as though by our deferring of the publishing of the saide Mandates, the intrusion of the foresaid M.M. Adventurers were allowed, or that, as if it stoode in the liking, choice, will, and power of the Queene, to take from the foresaide *Hanse* Townes their dearlie purchased Libertits, and hereditarie accorde, and so well not, that

that in anie other place then in England (where shee may be Iudge and partie) that anie treatie be held on this behalfe, and besides requiring, that her subiectes according to their owne good likinge, and pleasure, may haunt, liue, & exercise their Merchandise within the Empire of the Dutche Nation, which for vs, and the Empire it falleth altogether greeuous, and verie contumelious to dissemble any longer: therefore then, whereas we in regarde of our Emperiall office, and place, cannot any longer delay to put in execution the foresaide consultations, and Decrees of the yeares 82. and 94. for the furtherance of the common welfare, and for necessities sake, especiallie seeing the Monopolies, and preiudiciall, dangerous, and vnlawfull forestalling (which as is abouesaide, are vsed among the English Aduēturers Companie) by testimonies, and other credible informations, are altogether open, and manifest, and not onely, according to the common written lawes, but also accordinge to the published constitutions of the Empire, are forbidden vpon great penaltie, and punishment, to witte, losse of goodes, and chattell, and banishement out of the lande.

Therefore is it, that we prohibite, banishe out, and proscribe all the forenamed Englishe Merchantes, to witt, the whole Companie of the M. M. Adventurers, together with their hurtfull dealings, traffickes, and contractinges out of all the holy Empire, so that such hurtfull Commerces, and dealinges of the Englishes Adventurers, with the conventions, compactes,

R 2

pactes, and alliances on this behalfe made, from this time forwarde shalbee forbidden and made voide, without that any man by himself, or any other shall, or may hereafter exercise, or practise the same: ordayning therefore, and commanding expressely by our Romishe Emperiall power, and authoritie, accordinge to the resolution of the Electours, Princes, and States of the Empire agreed vpon, renewed, and approued, that vpon paine of the ban, and proscription of vs, and the holy Empire, all and euery Merchantes, & dealers in Englishe Clothe (to the Companies of M. M. Adventurers any wayes allyed or associated) together with their Factours, Agentes, Atturnyes, and Seruants, that within three monthes after the publishing, and setting foorth of these presentes, they departe, and remoue without further delay, or opposition out of the Rule, cōmand, and lande of vs, and of the holy Empire, as also of the Electours, and common States, and specially out of the towne of Stade, scituate in the Archbishoprick of *Breme*, & out of all other partes, and places, where they commonly haue their residence, and conventicles, or exercise their Trade: and that from hence forwarde they wholy, and entirely abstaine, and forbeare from all recourse, and Commerces howsoeuer they may bee called, by water, and by lande, openly, or priuilie, throughout all the whole Empire. And further wee giue commandement to all Princes Electours, Princes, States, and subiectes of vs, and the holy Empire, vpon the forfeicture of all their Royalties,

alties, Fiefs, and other rights, and dewties obtayned of vs, and the holy Empire (which euery one whosoeuer shall dare wilfully to doe here against *ipso facto* shall forfeict) that they vnto the saide Englishe, naminge themselues Merchantes Adventurers, their Societies, Companies, Factouis, and Seruantes, no where in the holy Empire, by lande, or by water, doe giue, yeald, or permit any open, or secrete conveighance, passage, help, or other fauour, but the same doe altogether lett, and prohibite: And, if so be that the Englishe Adventurers, their adherents, factours, or seruantes boldly shall goe forward, or proceed, contrary to this our Emperiall Mandate, and Commandement, either in buying, or selling of Clothes, and Woolle, or with exercisinge any other Commerces, howsoeuer they may bee called, in any quarter or place of the holy Empire, in such case, herebyauthoritie and power is giuen, and earnestly is enioigned, and required, that all Magistrates, and Rulers, vnder whose commande, or Iurisdiction such place immediately doeth lye, and where such kinde of trade is vsed, or where such bought, or solde goodes may be found, to apprehend the persons without delay, and to arrest, and confiscate the forbidden goodes. And further it shall not be lawfull for any Magistrate, or Ruler in the Empire, to giue Convoy, or Saufeconduict with whatsoeuer woordes, meaning, colour, or clauses the saide Convoyes, or saufeconduictes, may be conceiued, or sett downe, to the Englishe Adventurers Companies, Merchantes, or dealers, neither

R 3 shall

shall they be conducted, or conuoyed by any Magistrate, or Superiour in the saide Empire: And in case that the Magistrat, or Superior shalbe heerein negligent, or slacke, & that we, or our Procurour Fiscaell shalbe thereof advertised, then our will is, that the said Fiscaell (according to our commaundement to him in earnest maner alreadie giuen) on this behalfe, to advertise the Magistrate, or Superiour, where the said Merchauntes, and Dealers dwell, or reside, and admonishe the same such Englishe trade foorthwith out of hande to forbid: and if so bee the saide Magistrate, or Superiour, doe not so within the prefixed tyme, we will on our Emperiall Courtes parte, or otherwise our foresaid Fischale shall haue full power, right, and authoritie to proceede to the execution of this our Emperiall Mandate, and by vertue of his office presentlie to call in question the disobedient, without all fauour, or dissimulation, as the necessitie of the cause shall require, without that it shalbe lawfull for the aforesaid misdoers to alleadg, or produce any exceptions, or declinatorie delay in any maner what soeuer. And for that it is lawfull, and permitted to euery man to giue information against the Transgressours, therefore whosoeuer firste shall informe the Magistrate, where offence is made of the saide offence plainlie and truelie, or in case of negligẽce in the said Magistrate, our Fiscale, he shall haue the fourth parte of the offendours goodes, wherein also he shalbe assisted, & holpen by the foresaid Magistrate, or Superiour, or in default thereof by vs, and our

our Emperiall Chamber right, & by all other States of the Holy Empire: according to this let euery mā take knowledge, how to demeane him selfe: Giuen in our Royall Castell at *Praghe*, the firste day of the moneth of August Anñ 1597. of our Romish Kingdome the two and twentieth yeare, of *Hungarie* the 25th, & of *Bohemia* also the 22th. Subscribed *Rudolphus* Paragraphed *I D. W. Freymondt, ad Mandatum Sacræ Cæsareæ Maiestatis proprium*, And signed *An. Hanniwalt*: and the priuie seale of the Emperours Maiestie was printed vpon the same in forme of a *Placcart* or *Edict*.

These are the woordes of the Mandate, which I haue fullie and truelie sett downe, to the end that it may the better appeare, what the causes were of the said Mandate, and what good freends the *Hanses* are to the state of England. Cōcerning the causes, I note them to be three in number: First, *The taking away of the Easterlinges Priviledges in Englande*. Secondlie, *The doeings of the English men of warre at the Sea*. And thirdlie, *The Monopolie vsed by the Merchantes Adventurers*. To the first twoo causes her Maiestie at sundrie times hath sufficientlie answeared, and namely by her Letters written to the Emperour in the yeares 1585. and lastlie by the answeare giuen to the Polish Embassadour, as aboue at large is set downe. As for the Mononopolie, wherewith the M. M. Adventurers are charged, it is but a meere slaunder, and iniurious imputation, maliciouslie deuized by the *Hanses*, to blear the

the eyes of the States, & Princes of the Empire withall, and to drawe them vnder colour of complayning on the M.M. Adventurers, as Monopolishe traders, to ayde, and assiste the saide *Hanses*, to recouer their Priuiledges againe, and to mainteyne them therein, contrarie to all reason against the English Nation, as I doubt not anone most plainly, & clearely to proue.

Her Maiestie beeing informed of the abouesaide Mandate, sent Maister *Iohn Wrothe*, & Maister *Stephen Lesieur*, with letters to the Emperour, and diuerse of the Electours, and Princes of Germanie, declaringe her Highnes opinion of this proceeding as an vniust practise and doeing of the *Hanses*, and therefore required, to haue the said Mandate reuoked, or suspended, but beeing vncertain, what would follow herevpon, it seemed good vnto her Maiestie in the mean tyme, to direct a commission to the Maior, and Sheriffes of the Cittie of London, in maner following.

Cōmission directed to the Maior & Sheriffes of London against the Hanses by her Maiestie

ELIZABETH by the grace of God, Queene of Englande, Fraunce, and Ireland, Defendor of the faith, &c. To our righte trustie, and wellbeloued the Maior, and Sheriffes of our Cittie of London, greeting. Whereas there hath been directed a Commaundement, by the name of a Mandate, from the Romane Emperor to all Electors, Prelates, Earles and all other Officers, and subiectes of the Empire, reciting sundrie complaintes made to him by the allied Townes of the Dutche *Hanses* in Germanie, of diuerse diuers iniuries comitted against them in our Realm, and likewise vpon complaint made by them against the Companie of M.M. Adventurers, without hearing anie aunsweare to bee made to the saide *Hanse* Townes in disproofe of their complaintes, the same being most notorious vniust, and not to be mainteyned by anie trueth, And yet neuertheles by this Mãdate the English Merchantes, namely the M.M. Adventurers are forbidden to vse anie traffique of Merchandise within the Empire, but are commanded to departe from thence vpon great paines, and to forbeare openlie, and secretlie, from all hauens, & landing places, or to vse anie Commerce by water, or by lande in the Empire, vpon paine of apprehension of their persons, & confiscation of their goodes, with sundrie other extreeme sentences pronoũced against our said subiectes: heereupon, although wee haue sent our letters expressely to the Emperor, and to the Electors, and other Princes of the Empire, declaring our opinion of this proceeding, to be vniustlie prosecuted by the saide *Hanse* Townes, and therefore haue required to haue the said Mandate either reuoked, or suspended, yet beeing vncertaine what shall follow herevpon, wee haue thought it agreeable to our honour, in the meane tyme, to commaunde all such as are here within our Realme, appertayning to the saide *Hanse* Townes, scituated in the Empire, and especiallie all such, as haue any residence in our Cittie of London, either in the house commonly called the Steelyarde, or in any other place elswhere, doe

S for-

forbeare to vse any maner of Traffique of Merchandise, or to make anie contractes, and likewise to departe out of our Dominions in like sorte, as our subiectes are commanded to departe out of the Empire, vpon the like paines, as are conteyned against our subiectes in the said Mandate. And for the execution of this our Commaundement, wee will, that you the Maior of our saide Cittie of London, & the Sheriffes, shall foorthwith repaire to the house, called the Steelyarde, and callinge before you such, as haue charge therof, or doe reside there, to giue them knowledge of this our determination & commandment: Charging them by the 24th of this moneth, (being the day that our Merchauntes are to departe from *Stade*) they doe departe out of this our Realm: charging them also, that they giue knowledge thereof to such, as bee of any of the *Hanse* Townes, belonging to the Empire, remayninge within any parte of our Realme, to departe likewise by the saide day. And you the Maior, and the Sheriffes, calling vnto you twoo of the Officers of our Custome-house, to take possession of the saide house the said 24. day, to remaine in our custodie, vntill we shall vnderstande of anie more fauourable course taken by the Emperour, for the restitutiō of our subiects to their former lawfull trade within the Empire, & this shalbe your warrant for the execution of the premisses. In witnes whereof we haue caused these our letters to bee made patent, witnes our self at *Westminster*: the thirteenth of Ianuarie in the Fourtyeth yeare of our Raigne.

Raigne. In this state the matters haue honge euer since, the M.M. Adventurers still expecting a Diete, or general assemblie of the Princes, and States of the Empire, in hope that by her Maiesties gracious intervention for them, the aboue said Mandate may be either abrogated, or suspended, and they restored to their former trade, & Priuiledges in the Empire, for without such an assemblie this can not bee done, (as appeareth plainlie by the answear of the Emperour, and Princes vnto those letters whiche it pleased her Highnes to write by the abouesaid Maister *Wrothe*, & M[r] *Lesieur*) & on the other side the *Hanses* still labouring, to haue the abouesaide Mandate extended and retched farther then the contentes thereof will bear, to witt, that all Englishmen generallie, & all English wares should be banished, and forbiddē the Empire: for that otherwise they see, that they loose their labour, and cost, & the Merchantes Adventurers finde meanes, to continue their trade, & to vent the commodities of their Countrie in Germanie, maugre all that their aduersaries, and ill willers can doe, though not in that sorte that were conuenient, but because you shall see, what cause the *Hanses* haue to cōplaine in such clamourous manner, as they doe of iniuries done them in this Realme, I will giue you the view of a Decree of the Right honourable priuie Counsell, giuen at *Westminster*, the 24th day of Februarie in the sixth yeare of the raigne of King *Edward* the sixt, in these wordes following.

Decree against the Hanses in the Raign of Kinge Edward the sixth.

In the matter touching the Information exhibited against the Merchantes of the *Haunse*, commonlie called the Merchauntes of the Steelyarde, vpon good consideration, as well of the said Information, as also of the aunswere of the said Merchaunts of the Steelyarde, and of such Recordes, Writinges, Charters, Treaties, Depositions of witnesses, and other recordes, and proofes, as hath been exhibited on both parties, it was founde apparaunt to the Kings Maiesties priuie Counsell as followeth.

First, it is found, that all liberties, and priuiledges pretended to be graunted to the said Merchantes of the *Haunse*, be void by the lawes of the Realme, forasmuch as the same Merchauntes of the *Hanse*, haue no sufficient Corporation to receiue the same: It appeareth also, that such graunt, and Priviledges, as the said Merchauntes of the *Haunse* doe claime to haue, doe not extende to anie persons, or townes certaine, and therefore vncertaine, what persons, or whiche townes should enioye the saide Priviledges: by reason of which vncertaintie, they haue, and doe admitt to be free with them whom, & as many, as they list, to the great preiudice, and hurt of the Kinges Maiesties Customes, and yearelie hinderance of twentie thousand poundes, or neare thereabouts, besides the common hurt to the whole Realme. It appeareth also, that if the pretended grauntes were good by the Lawes of the Realme, as in deede they bee not, yet the same were made vppon condition, that they should not avowe, or colour anie foreignes goodes, or or merchandises, which cōdition the said Merchants of the *Hanse* haue not obserued, as may appeare by office founde remayninge of recorde in the Kinges Maiesties Excequer, and by other sufficient prooues of the same. It appeareth also, that one hundred yeares, and more, after the pretended priviledges graunted to them, the foresaide Merchauntes of the *Hanse* vsed to transport no Merchandise out of this Realm, but onely into their owne Cuntries, neither to bring into this Realm anie wares, or merchandise, but onlie such, as were commodities of their owne Countries: where at this present they doe not onely conveighe the Merchandise of this Realme into the base countries of *Brabant*, *Flaunders*, and other places near adioyning, and there sell the same, to the great dammage, and subversion of the laudable order of the Kings Maiesties subiectes tradinge those parties for Merchandise, but also doe bringe into this Realme, the Merchandise, and commodities of all foreigne Countries, contrarie to the true meaninge of the grauntes of their Priviledges, declared by the auncient vsage of the same: by meanes whereof the Kinges Maiestie hath not onely lost much in his Customes, but also it is contrarie to the condicions of a Recoignisance, made in the tyme of King *Henry* the seuenth. It appeared also, that like as the Priviledges heretofore graunted to the saide Merchauntes of the Steelyarde, being at the beginning reasonably vsed, were commodious, and much profitable vnto them, without anie notable, excessiue, or enorme preiudice

S 3 to

to the Royall estate of this Realme, so nowe of late yeares, by taking of such, and so manie as they list into their Societie, and by bringing in the commodities of all other Cuntries, as carying out of the commodities of the Realme into all other places, their said pretensed Priuiledges are growen so preiudiciall to the King, & his Crowne, as without the great hurt thereof, and of the whole estate of this Realm, the same may not be longe endured.

Item, in the tyme of King *Edward* the fourth, the saide Merchauntes of the *Haunse* forfeited their pretended Priuiledges, by meanes of warre betwixt this Realme, and them, wherevpon a treatie was made, and agreed, that the subiectes of this Realme should haue like liberties in the lande of *Prusse*, and other places of the *Haunse*, as they had, and ought to haue vsed there, And that no Impostes, new exactions, or other prestes should be sett vppon their persons, or goodes otherwise, or by other meane, then before ten, twentie, thirtie, fourtie, fiftie, yea an hundred yeares agoe, and aboue had been, or were sett, which hath been, and is daily much broken, and speciallie in *Danzick*, not onely by prohibitinge English men freelie to buy, & sell there, but also in leauying vpon them certaine exactions, and impositions, contrarie to the said Treatie: And notwithstandinge, that diuerse requestes haue been made, as well by the Kings Maiesties Father, as by his Maiestie, for the present redresse of such wronges, as haue been done to the English Merchants, contrarie to the said Treatie, yet no no reformation hath hetherto ensewed. In consideration of which the premisses, & such other matters as hath appeared in the examination of this matter, the Lordes of the Kings Maiesties priuie Counseill, on his Highnes behalf decreed, That the Privileges, Liberties, and Franchises, claymed by the foresaide Merchauntes of the Steelyarde, shall from hence foorth be, and remayne seazed, and resumed into the Kinges Maiesties handes, vntill the said Merchantes of the Steelyarde shall declare, and proue better, and more sufficient matter for their claime in the premisses, saving, and reseruing vnto the saide Merchantes of the Steelyarde all such, and like liberties of comming into this Realme, and other the Kinges Dominions, buying, selling all, and all manner of trafficke and trade of Merchandise in as large, and ample maner, as any other Merchauntes straungers haue, or of right ought to haue within the same: This order aforesaid, or any thing herein conteyned to the contrarie notwithstanding. This decree was firmed by *T. Ely Chauncellour: Winchester: Northumberlande: Bedforde: Westmerland. Shrewsburie: E. Clinton: T. Darcie: N. Wutton:* and *W. Cecill:* By the contentes whereof, a man may plainlie see, that what so euer happened to the *Hanses* in Englande, they them selues gaue the occasion thereof, and therefore had no iust, or lawfull cause to complaine: Notwithstanding Queene *Marie* by the way of Recesse, the lande being full of troubles, reuoked this Decree, and restored the *Hanses* to their former Priuiledges, in the moneth of Aprill

Queen Marie reuoketh the foresaid decree.

prill Anō. 1553. at which tyme the *Hanses* had their Commissioners in Englande about a Treatie offred by King *Edward*, and accepted by the *Hanses* after the abouesaid resumption, wherevnto shee was induced for two reasons: the one was, for that the *Hanses* Cō-missioners promised, that their inordinate trade, forbidden by the lawes of the lande, and their too too much frequenting the low Cuntries, should be left: The other was, for that by meanes of the daungerousnes, and hardnes of the tyme, the abouesaid Decree of the resumptiō of the *Hanses* Priuileges, could not be dealt in: but this promise of the Commissioners not beeing performed, the saide Queene in the yeare 1556. caused her foresaid Reuocation to bee altered, and by a Decree restrayned the *Hanses* trade intothe lowe Cuntries with Clothe, and their bringingin of anie other foreigne Wares, then those of theirowne landes only, suffering them notwithstanding in other pointes, to vse their pretensed Priuiledges, and afterwardes, by mediation of Kinge *Philippe*, yeelding to a further Moderation, with condition, that the *Hanses* within one yeare next ensuinge, should sende their Commissioners into England, to conferre, treat, and conclude with her Hignes Coūsellours, in what sorte their Priuiledges ought to bee taken, and vsed: A whole yeare passed, & fiue weekes besides without anie newes, or tydings of any Commissioners, and to requite the manifold fauours they had receyued, they at an assembly of the *Hanses* at *Lubeke*, published an Edict against all Englishe men, for-

Revocation of the fore-said reuocation.

forbidding all Trade, or Commerce with them, and staying the carying out of Corne, which was prouided for the seruice and necessitie of the Realm: yet for all these indignities, the said Queene was contented, that Commissaries on both partes should meet in England, and agree vpon, and sett down a certain, and immutable maner of Trade to be helde, and obserued on both sides: but the *Hanses* were so farre from acceptinge of this gracious offer, that they wholy refused it, as by a petition of theirs exhibited to King *Philippe*, the third of Iune 1557. appeareth, wherein they declare the cause of that their refusall to be for that they could not haue in this Realm any other Iudges of their cause, but such as were suspect, not sparing, or excepting the Queene her selfe, of whose good will, and fauour., they had receyued so often experiēce, and triall. In these tearmes the *Hanses* Priviledges stood all Queene *Maries* dayes, after whose decease her Maiestie, that now is, succeeding, & finding them as they were left without anie other ground or foundation, then the Princes fauour, and good pleasure, yet at the sollicitation of *Suiderman*, & others, Commissioners from the *Hanses*, her Highnes was contented, that a meeting, and communication should be helde in the yeare 1560. whereas the *Hanses* stood, and insisted vpon their old treaties, and those appointed by her Maiestie propounded certaine other Articles, intituled, *A moderation of the old Priuiledges*, with this clause of singulare fauour, *Neque tamen excellentissima Regina propter hanc Moderationem*

Matter passed betwene her Maiestie & the Hanses.

T ab

ab vllo superiori legitimo Iure vlla ex parte recedi vult, sed saluum ius, saluas actiones, saluam denique reliquā omnem in hac Commercij causa materiam, & sibi ex altera parte, & suis successoribus, & ex altera parte Confœderatis Ciuitatibus, & eorum posteritati reseruat: But the *Hanses* Commissioners not liking thereof, the Treatie brake vp without anie effect: In which tearmes the matter hunge till the yeare 1572. at which tyme new Commissioners from the *Hanse* Townes, comming into England for other causes, they renewed their former sewt, and petition: whereunto they receiued this answeare, That cōcerning the Custome of their goods there should nothing more be exacted of them, then was propounded to the former Commissioners in the yeare 1560. all this while her Maiesties subiects were depriued of all priuiledge, and in diuerse of the *Hanse* Townes hardly, and extremely vsed, as at *Dansicke, Deuenter, Campen*, and *Swoll*, to the great hurt and hinderance of the Trade, and because the *Hanses* vnmeasurably frequented the Cittie of *Antwerpe* with Englishe Commoditie, the M.M. Adventurers were forced to drawe themselues wholy to the said Citty, and leaue *Berghen op Zoom*, where they vsed to keepe twoo Martes in the yeare: But finally the saide Adventurers were constrayned to leaue *Antwerpe* also, and to seeke another place, as hath bene aboue rehearsed, so that in the yeare 1567. they obtayned priuiledges for ten yeares of the town of *Hamburghe*, with this condition thereunto added. *Quod elapsis supradictis annis concessio dictorum Priuilegiorum renouaretur nuaretur, & continuaretur in infinitum, si interim non cederet in ciuitatis sua damnum, vel dispendium:* That the ten yeares time beeing expired, the foresaide Priuiledges should be renewed, and continewed for euer, if in the meane while no hurt, or damage happened to their Cittie thereby: But for all this when the ten yeares were almost complete, and run out, the *Hamburgers* signified to the M. M. Adventurers, that the time of their Priviledges expired, and that by a Decree of the *Hanse* Townes made at *Lubeke*, they were enioyned, not to graunt to the said Adventurers any longer priviledges, pretendinge the cause to bee, for that in Englande the saide *Hanses* were restrayned of their auncient liberties, and that daily new exactions were imposed vpon their goods, contrarie to former treaties, which done the said *Hamburgers* passed a decree the 20th. of Iune 1578. whereby they abrogated all former liberties graunted to the said Advẽturers, and ordained, that after a prefixed day sett downe in the saide Decree, they should not enioye anie other priviledge, or immunitie, then anie other straungers in the said Cittie: which assoone as her Maiestie, and her honorable Counseill vnderstood, they requited the *Hanses* with a like Decree, which yet was suspended till the 25th of Iulie 1579. at which tyme her Maiestie, not receyuinge any satisfaction at the *Hanses* handes, but to the contrarie vnderstanding, that the saide *Hanses*, at an Assemblie at *Lunenburghe*, the second of Nouember 1579. had sett foorth an Edicte for the leuying of 7 ½ vpon the hundred of all goods

T 2 brought

brought by Englishe men into their territories, or caryed out of the same, her highenes vpon this occasion commaunded the like decree to bee made, for the taking of the like summe vpon the goods of the *Hanses*: and in this estate the matter stood on both partes, till that by a petition put vp by the Alderman of the Steelyarde, this last decree of 7½. vpon the hundred was suspended for four monthes, but the first, because it depended vpon the restraint of Trade of her Maiesties subiectes, the Lordes of the Counsell thought not good to suspend, or reuoke the same, till the contentes thereof were satisfied, and fulfilled: And thus I haue briefly, & truely sett down what hath passed, and in what state at this daye the whole controuersie between her Maiestie, and the *Hanses* standeth: by the discourse whereof I doubt not, but it plainly appeareth, that (as aforesaid) the *Hanses* haue no iust, or lawfull cause to complain, for that they haue themselues beene the cause of all that happened: For first, the resuminge of their Priuiledges in Kinge *Edwardes* dayes, proceeded of this, that they freed, & coloured mens goodes, that were none of their Societie, and for other causes aboue rehearsed. Secondlie, when as Queene *Marie* had reuoked that, which had been done by her Brother, shee her selfe at length revoked the said Revocation, for that the *Hanses* had broken promise with her, in continuing an vnlawfull trade in the low Countries, whereby shee lost in her Customes within the space of eleuen monethes, more then 9360 pounde sterling

The Hanses them selues are the cause of the restraint of their Priuileges in England.

ling, besides the damage sustained by her subiectes in their trade, and when as shee offred a meetinge for the deciding of all cōtrouersies, the *Hanses* vtterlie refused the same, & would none of it. Thirdly, her Maiestie that now is, whē shee came first to the Crown, commaunded, that the *Hanses* should be vsed, as well (yea in some pointes better) then her owne subiects, but they in recompēce of this fauour, not prouoked with anie new occasion, commaunded, that the exercise & trade of Merchandise graunted to her Highnes subiectes by the *Hamburgers, cum clausula perpetuitatis* should be broken of, and disannulled: and afterwardes, when her Maiestie required a reformation of this their Decree, they in steede thereof imposed that exaction of theirs of seuen & three quarters vpō the hundred: And so with their new Impositions, their refusing of a meeting, & cōferenee in England, their abusing of their libertie in the lowe Countries, by doeing manie things to the preiudice of her Maiestie, and subiectes, by diminishinge the reuenewes of the Crown, by colouring other mens goodes vnder the pretence of their Priviledges, they were finallie depriued of their liberties, & immunities at the pleasure of her Highnes, yet alwayes were more friendly vsed, then anie other the subiectes of the Princes in Amitie, and league with her Maiestie, for the which they neuer shewed any sparke of thankefulnes, but haue from time to time vniustlie accused her Highnes to foreigne Princes, and States, her Maiesties louing friendes, and Confederates, and to this

T 3 day

day with much clamorousnes& importunacie leaue not off to doe the same, without respect to the person, and qualitie, of so excellent and gracious a Princesse, and doeing that, which is farre vnbeseeminge their state and condition, but if they thinke to gett anie thing hereby in the ende, they are much deceyued in mine opinion, their way to speede is, to proceede *cum precatione & supplicatione*, and not by way of force, and compulsion: *Magnorum siquidem Principum & Regum heroicis animis natura videtur insitum, quod flecti, & duci, non cogi velint.*

Defence of the M. M. Advēturers against the Hanses slaūder of Monopolis.

The third cause wherevpon the foresaid Mandate of the Emperours is grounded, is, *The Monopolie vsed* (as is saide) *by the Merchauntes Adventurers*: which to be a false, and iniurious slaunder, & surmize, needeth none other demonstration, then the true sence, and definition, of the woorde *Monopolie* it selfe: *Quum Monopolium sit quando vnus solus aliquod genus mercaturæ vniuersum emit, vt solus suo arbitrio vendat*: *Monopolie* is, when one man alone buyeth vp all that is to bee gott of one kinde of Merchandise, to the end that he alone may sell at his owne lust and pleasure. Which well considered, hath no communion, or agreement with the trade, and practise of the Companie of M. M. Adventurers, and the Townes where the saide companie haue resided, or are resident in at this day, doe knowe, and can witnesse, that those of the saide Companie haue vsed, & doe vse an honest, vpright, and lawfull trade *Emptionis, Venditionis, & Permutationis*:

nis: which by all lawe is permitted, *vita enim nostra sine contractibus, & commercijs, subsistere nequit*, not onlie with Clothe, but also with all kinde of wares, and Merchandises, So that, whatsoeuer is free, and at libertie to buye, & sell, the same by no reason, or right construction can be accompted a *Monopolie*: neither haue the Adventurers the sole transporte, and trade inwardes, and outwardes of Englishe Clothe, and other Wares, but it is well knowen, and notorious, that all the Members of the *Hanses*, & not onely they, but also all the subiectes of Vpper, and low Germanie, and all other straungers in league, & amitie with the Crowne of England, may, and doe at their libertie and pleasure, buye, and cary out of the Realme al sortes of Clothe, and Englishe wares, and may, and doe bring in, and sell their own countrie commodities without empeachment, or hinderance, payinge such dewties, and customes, as they ought to paye: besides there are diuerse other Companies of Merchauntes, who are priviledged to transporte Cloth, &c. out of the lande into foreigne partes, and Cuntries, as well as the Companie of M. M. Adventurers, which they doe in great quantitie: Moreouer, the Companie of M. M. Advẽturers hath no banke, nor common stocke, nor common Factour to buye, or sell for the whole Companie, but euery man tradeth a-part, and particularlie with his owne stocke, and with his owne Factour, or servaunt: wherevpon it necessarilie followeth, that forasmuch, as the M M. Adventurers haue not (as aforesaid) the sole dealing,

ling, and traffike alone in their own hands, either in Englande, or on the other side the seas, and that *Monopolij definitio cum suo definito* in the least parte agreeth not, the said companie by no sound reason, or argument can be charged to bee anie such Monopoliers, or priuate gaine, & lucre seekers, as the *Hanses* would make the world beleeue they are, neither is it to bee thought, that by the saide M. M. Adventurers the saide *Hanses* are brought to such apparaunt losse, and hinderaunce, as by their complaintes they beare the Emperour, and States of the Empire in hand. Concerning that, which they alleadge, that the said companie haue their Gouuernement, and officers, keepe Courtes, and Assemblies, make lawes, impose mulctes and penalties, and shippe at sett tymes, & with appointed Fleetes, out of which they would inferre a Monopolie: It needeth none other aunswear, then I haue alreadie made in this treatise, wherein is truelie, and plainly declared the practise, and manner of the Companie of Merchants Aduenturers in all the abouesaide pointes, and withall shewed the good, that commeth to the State, and common Wealth thereby, and howe farre it is out of the compasse of *Monopolie:* A fault not only forbidden, but also worthilie to be punished in all well gouerned common wealthes, *Imò honestorum Principum subditis indignum:* Besides, it is more then straunge, that the *Hanses* haue the face to condemne that in others, as vnlawful, and Monopolish, which them selues both in Englande, and euery where else, where they now haue, or haue had

had their Residence, or Counters continually practised: for who knoweth not, that they had their Aldermen, or Consuls, Treasurers, Secretaries, Assistentes, and other officers, and kept their meetinges, Courtes, and Assemblies, and vsed Merchantes law among them selues? And if it were lawfull, and free for them so to doe, why may it not be as lawfull, and free for the M.M. Adventurers to doe the like? But (say the Hanses) the Merchants Aduenturers in their Courtes doe sett the prices of their own Wares, and of other mens, ordayning not to sell, or buye otherwise, or at other rates, or prices, which is plaine *Monopolie*, this how true it is, I appeale to the consciences of the verie *Hanses* them selues, and of all other Merchauntes, with whom the saide Companie doe deale, whether this be a trueth yea, or no: Besides, I may boldlie, & with a good conscience affirme, that neither I in all the time of my seruice, neither the oldest man living in the saide Companie, can saye, that euer it was knowen, or heard, that any such matter of setting pryce was once mentioned in any Court, or assemblie of the said Companie: neither in deed was there euer any such matter, but euery mā rather studyeth to keepe his feat and trade as secrete to him selfe as he can, for feare of his fellow, least being espied, it might be taken out of his handes: and further, it is a thing abhorred, and condemned by the lawes of the Realme, and therefore, if the Companie of M. M. Adventurers could euer haue been iustlie accused of the said cryme, they should not haue escaped

V so

ſo longe without deſerued puniſhment: laſtlie, the verie ſtate, and policie of the ſaid Companie, cannot abide, or brooke anie Monopolie, as being directlie, & *ex diametro*, contrarie, and an ouerthrowe to that *Oeconomie*: ſo carefullie prouided for, and preſerued by the good lawes, & orders of the ſaid Companie: whereby there is a diſtribution of the benefites, and commodities of the Companie to all the members of the ſame, ſo much, as is poſſible with great prouidence, and equitie ordained, ſo that euery man, that will, or is able, may participate thereof, ſo farre, as they will extende: Whereas if it were otherwiſe, the meaner ſort ſhould not be able to liue by the richer: for theſe in ſhort tyme would with their great purſes and meanes drawe all the trade inwardes, and outwardes into their own handes, and (as vpon the Bankers in ſome places) all mens credites ſhould depend vpon their ſleeues, as hauing power to giue credite to whom they liſt, to ſell, or keepe vp their wares, at their pleaſure, & to rule the markettes, as they thinke good: whereby it would come to paſſe, that a fewe ſhall gaine, and growe mightie, and exceeding wealthie, and all the reſt ſhall haue nothing to doe, and in ſhort time be brought to extreeme miſerie, and pouertie: but the gouerned trade of the ſaide Companie is heere in the way, ſo that you ſee how farre it is from trueth, or likelihood of trueth, which is obiected againſt the Companie of M.M Adventurers on this behalfe, as beeing rather an vtter enemie, then a freend, or liker of that greedie, & inordinate courſe: as as appeareth partlie by that abouesaide, and more euidently as well by the testimonie of straungers of diuerse Nations, as also by Attestations, vnder the seales of great and famous Citties (whereof some are of the *Hanses* them selues) which I haue sett downe, not onely for the credite, commendation, and iustifying of the saide Cõpanie, but withall for the more manifestation of the trueth of that, which hath been abouesaide. And first, the Senate of *Hambrough*, at such tyme, as they caused to bee denounced to the Companie the expiration of their Priviledges, did in their Insinuation the nineteenth of Iuly 1577. expreslie put these wordes: *Quæ quidem Denunciatio non eo animo fit, quod Societas Mercatorum, quæ se honestè in hac Ciuitate gessit, & integritate sua bonorum virorum beneuolentiam meretur, Senatui nostro molesta, & grauis sit, verum solummodò, vt pactis satisfiat:* And afterwardes, *Etenim si inclita Societas Mercatorum florentissimi Regni Angliæ diutiùs in hac Ciuitate commorari, mercaturam exercere, & hoc nomine noua pacta posteaquam priora expirarunt cum spectabili Senatu inire in animo habeat, Senatus officio suo, & æquitati non deerit.* Whereby it appeareth in what estimation the said Senate held the Companie of Merchantes Adventurers, in that they not onlie commended them for their honest cariage, and integritie, but also offer them further fauour, and entertainement in their Cittie after the ending of the former priviledges, which were agreed vpon but for ten yeares, yet with this Addition, *Quod elapsis supradictis annis concessio dictorum Priuilegiorum renouaretur,*

Testimonie of strangers and whole Citties on the Companies behalf against the slaunder of Monopolie.

V 2 *& con-*

& continuaretur in infinitum, si interim non caderet in Ciuitatis suæ damnum, vel dispendium : Now that the said Cittie receiued neither losse nor damage by the Cōpanie of Merchauntes Adventurers, the aboue written woordes of honest cariage, and integritie, proceeding from the Magistrates themselues in the same Cittie doe sufficientlie beare witnes, and since that time also more particularlie the saide Senate of *Hambroughe* doeth touche that point of *Monopolie* in a letter written to the Gouernour and Generalitie of the said Companie in August 1586. wherein they say, that although they cannot denie, but that there were complaintes made vnder that name of *Monopolie* to the Emperour, and Princes Electours, *tamen nostra cum suffragatione, & approbatione easdem institutas esse cōstanter negamus* : *Ideoq́; quum hæ Actiones ex aliorum potiùs suffragijs, quàm ex nostra voluntate, & arbitrio dependeant, non dubitamus, Magnificentias, & Dominationes vestras diuersorum discrepantes intentiones, & sententias maturiore iudicio discussuros*: so that in this point a man may see they agreed not with the rest of their fellowes, whose doinges they disclaime as hauing no voice or allowance of theirs. Likewise the late Lord *Egdard*, Earle of *East-friselande* in a letter by him written in aunsweare of a Mandate from the Emperour, the 26th of Iuly 1580. concerning the abouesaide slaunder of *Monopolie*, and Monopolishe trade vsed in *Embden* by the English, hath these woordes : *Now what soeuer is free to all men, and forbidden to none, & when as this tēdeth not to the priuate commoditie of one, or of some few*

few singulare persons, nor goeth vpon anie one sorte of Wares (as hee had shewed that the Trade of the M.M. Adventurers did not) *whether this be a Monopolie, or Monopolish trade, that referre I most humbly to your Maiesties consideration, besides the Title of Monopolies in the lawe declareth, whether it be so yea, or no: it was therefore neuer my meaning, or thought to graunt vnto the English, or anie other such Monopolish trade, but such, as the law permitteth to all men: And in verie deede there is no such Monopolishe trade vsed at Embden, and I therein referre my selfe to anie iust proofe, and all both straungers, and others, which vnderstande these doeinges, can heerein witnes the same with mee:* This testimonie of the Earles, the Senat of the town of *Embden*, confirmed by an Attestation vnder their common seale, bearing date the 28 th of Iuly 1582. the true copie whereof, & of other the like vnder the seales of the Citties of *Antwerpe*, *Middelburgh*, and *Stade*, I haue sett downe at the ende of this Treatise, whereby I doubt not, but al the world may perceiue that the Imputation of *Monopolie* to the Companie of M.M. Adventurers, is but a malicious, iniurious, and altogether false slaunder, deuized by the *Hanses*, (as I saide before) to drawe the Emperour, and Princes of Germanie, to assist them in the obtayninge of their vniust pretences, and vnreasonable demaundes in England, to the dishonor of her Maiestie, and hurt of the whole State, as much as in them lyeth, which God defend that they should haue their willes in. Lastlie, to knitt vp this point, I will adde hereunto as a golden *Coronis* of all that hath been saide, the iudg-

V 3 ment

Her Maiestie cleareth the M. M. Adveturers of Monopolie.

ment of her Highnes our most gracious Soueraigne, and the true defence of the saide Companie in certaine her Maiesties letters to the Emperour, and diuerse of the Princes of Germanie: and namelie in one to the Emperour written in Nouember 1595. the eight of the said Moneth, in these woordes: *Monopolium porrò de quo Hanseatici subditos nostros criminatur, calumniæ potius, quam veræ accusationis rationem præ se ferre videtur, ab ipsis enim Imperij subditis, qui Londini resident, diligenter inquiri iussimus, si quid solidi de iniquis subditorum nostrorum negotiandi rationibus referre possent: illi verò ingenuè responderunt, se nihil ea de re in commissis habere, acturos tamen se quamprimum per literas cum suis Maioribus, quumq; demùm quid responsi acciperent, id totum fideliter relaturos: quæstionem præterea ea de re cum subditis nostris institui mandauimus, Illi verò authenticis scriptis edocent, negotiandi ipsorum rationes à plurimis Ciuitatibus in Belgio, Prussia, atque alibi vti honestissimas probari, atque quum duæ Imperij Ciuitates sint, quæ eum nostris maximè negotiantur, Lubeca, & Hāburgum, illarum altera publicis literis, vt nostri ostendunt, testata est, ipsorum Negotiationem ab omni Monopolij suspicione vacuā esse, seq; illius obiectæ criminationis participes nunquam fuisse: vbi verò Hanseaticorū institores plura ea de re ex Dominorum suorum expectata in scriptis cōmissione opposuerint, se quoq; pluribus in scriptis responsuros humiliter obtulerunt.* This whole letter, for that it conteyneth matter woorthie the knowledge concerning the *Hanses*, I haue added vnto the ende of this Treatie: Her said Maiestie in an other letter to the Emperour, dated the 20 th of December

cember 1597. sent by Maister *Iohn Wrothe*, after her Highnes had complayned of the vnorderlie settinge foorth & publishing of the Emperors Mãdate for the reasons in the said letter at large set down, hath these words following: *Quæ si paulò attentiùs Maiestas vestra ratione animoq; ponderasset, & ea quæ literis nostris anno 1595mo. mensęq; Nouembri conscriptis sunt comprehensa collatione cum vestris literis mense Iulij facta, diligentius considerasset (de quibus literis vel factiosorum hominũ machinationibus vos cælatos esse, vel à quibusdam ex ijs qui vestræ Maiestati sunt à Consilijs non optima fide vobiscum actũ esse magnopere suspicamur) nobis certè persuasissimum est, vos hanc rationem tam iniquam Edicti contra nos, subditosq; nostros vestro Imperio haudquaquam subiectos, promulgandi nunquam fuisse suscepturos, sed potius repudiaturos has commentitias Hanseaticorum querelas : quibus quidam præter eorum merita par, atque eadem libertas in Mercaturis apud nos faciendis, quæ nostris hominibus conceditur, oblata est: denique facturos fuisse, vt actiones nostræ remotis partium studijs, fictisq; delationibus ad rationis normam & æquitatis, ac iustitiæ ponderibus examinarẽtur.*
And in letters at the same tyme written to the Princes of Germanie, and sent by the said Maister *Wroth*, & Mr *Stephen Lesure*, to wit, to the Administratour of *Saxonie*, to the *Palsgraue* vpon the Rhine, the Elector of *Mentz*, and diuerse others, her Maiestie writeth in these woordes : *Eodem porrò Edicto nonnulla in priscam quandam subditorum nostrorũ Societatem (quam Adventurariorum vocant) obiecta commemorãtur, atque ex ijsdem proscriptionis veluti sententia infertur, qua & ex Imperij finibus*

nibus discedere, atque ab omni intra eosdem emendi ac vendendi vsu abstinere iubentur: quæ quidem res admiratione digna videtur, maximè quũ literis nostris ad Imperatorem mense Nouembri, anno 1595. à Comitiys quæ Ratisbonæ nonagesimo quarto habebantur datis ad singula Edicto hoc repetita abundè responsum, ac firmissimis rerum momentis satisfactum fuerit, quo sanè credendum nobis erat Cæsaream Maiestatem biennium penè silentio interposito rationibus à nobis allatis acquieuisse. Quod si quid adhuc dubij superesse visum fuisset, & Iustitia, & Regiæ nostræ dignitatis ratio, quam sub diuino numine absolutam gerimus, pro amicitia saltem nostra quàm sanctè hactenus cum Imperio coluimus, aut per literas, aut per internuncium aliquem nobis exponendum illud postulasset: Nunc verò hunc in modum sub silentio ex improuiso, etiam Typis exposuisse quæ ad nostram iniuriam (ipsa quoque in subditos nostros Iustitia violata) faciunt, indecorum omnino fuisse arbitramur: omniũ enim opinione iniquum meritò habendum viros probos nunquam auditos, aut vocatos ex maleuolorum obiectis calumnijs, nec probatis, & ne quidem ritè examinatis proscriptionis sententia, etiam contra ipsam sacri Imperij libertatem mulctasse.

Thus you see what the opinion of her Maiestie and of others hath been of the Companie of M. M. Adventurers touching *Monopolie*, whereof they are slaũdred by the *Hanses*, whiche I doubt not is sufficient, though not possible to stoppe the mouthes of the said *Hanses*, yet to convince them of vntrueth, & malicious forgerie on that behalfe.

That

That the Maintenance of the Fellowshippe of Marchantes Adventurers hath been and is for the Honour and seruice of the Prince and State at home and abroad.

Ll that which hath been afore at large sett down, tendeth in effect to the proofe of this point, as if it would please the diligent Reader to remember the same, & lay it together, would be soone perceyued For whereas I haue said, and shewed that the Merchauntes Adventurers, as subiectes of this noble Realme, haue procured at the handes of foreigne Princes and States many ample, and beneficiall Iurisdictions, Priviledges, Liberties, exemptions, & immunities, by vertue whereof they haue erected a good, and cōvenient gouvernement, for the rule, and ordering of them selues, and their Trade, and exercise ciuile Iurisdiction beyonde the Seas: that the saide M.M. Adventurers are a meanes of the preseruation of the Amitie, & league betwene this lande, and the said foreigne Princes, and States, that they advaunce the pryce, and vent of our countrie commodities, and bring in foreigne wares good cheape, that they are a maintenaunce of the Naviga-

X tion,

sion, and encrease of the Customes at home, who seeth not, and confesseth that all these thinges are to the high honour of the Prince, and notable seruice of the State and Common Wealth? Besides all this, some of the Princes of this lande haue knowen so well, howe to vse this Companie, and to make their vttermost benefite of them, that besides that the said Companie haue at sundrie times vpon vrgent occasions giuen their credites for the loanes of great summes of monie beyond the seas, for the seruice of the State, diuerse of the Gouuernours, and others of the said Cōpanie, haue in particulare not been wanting, according to their dewtie, to doe their Prince good, and commendable seruice many times in the affaires of the State. Further at the change of Princes, and receyuing in of new, at triumphes for victories, and Coronations, the said Companie haue not forgott the honour of their Prince, and Cuntrie, but haue spent and laid out great summes of monie this way, so that at some one Princes receyuing in, they haue consumed aboue twoo thousande Frenche Crownes in shewe or triumphal Arches, and namelie of the late King *Philippe* of *Spaine*, at his entrie into the Cittie of *Antwerpe* in September 1549. at such tyme, as his Father the Emperour *Charles* the fifth, transferred vnto him all his Seignories, and States in the low Countries: besides that Maister *Iohn Sturgeon*: at that tyme Gouuernour of the Companie was at the receyuing in of the said Prince accompanied with thirtie Merchantes of the Companie on horse-back

back all in a liuerie of Purple veluit in grain coates, and paned hose embrodered full of siluer waues, like the waues of the sea: their Dublettes, and drawinge out of their hose purple sattin, their Hattes of purple veluit with golde bandes, faire brouches, and white feathers: and each of them a chain of golde about his neck of great valew: buskins of purple velvitt, their Rapiers, Daggers, Spurres, Stirropps, & Bridles all gilt: the furniture of their horses was of purple veluit, Sadles, and Trappinges, &c. embrodered with golde, and green silke, and white, and green feathers on their horse heades: they were attended with three skore Lackies, apparailed in white veluitt ierkins cutt, embrodered with siluer twist, green sattin dublettes, with hose, and buskins of the same, purple veluitt Cappes, and green Feathers: behinde them roade the abouesaid Gouernour vpon a white English gelding, in a longe purple veluit growne, lyned with purple sattin: a black velvitt coat, and cappe with a fair brouche therein, and a chain of golde about his neck: his Dublett, and Hose, with the trappinges of his Horse were, as the other of his Companie wore, he was attended on by six Lackies on foot, and three Pages on horseback apparailed as aforesaid: In which their doeing, they shewed themselues for the honour of their Prince, and Cuntrye nothing inferiour to the Merchantes of other nations, namely the Germanes, Easterlinges, Italians, Spaniardes and Portugalles, and surmounting some of them in costly apparaile, furniture of themselues

X 2 and

and their horses, and in other preparation, to entertaine the said Prince, whereby they wanne great honour, and commendation to themselues, and the whole Englishe name: to say nothinge of the late Duke of *Alansons* entertainment into the said cittie of *Antwerp* in the yeare 1581. at which time Maister *Christopher Hoddesdonne* then, and nowe Gouernour receiued the saide Duke with four skore Merchantes of the saide Companie, all on horseback in very seemly, and decent sorte, apparailed in blacke veluitt, and most of them with chains of golde about their neckes, for the which the saide Gouernour and Companie receiued thankes, and commendation from her Maiestie, and the Lordes of the Counceill, whereof some were beholders of that abouesaid, and made honorable reporte thereof vnto her Highenes at their returne home. In deedes of Pietie, and Charitie they haue not also been wanting, as well appeared by the foundinge of Chappelles in olde time at *Brigdes*, and *Middelbrough*, and since in mainteyning the exercise of Religion amongst them in all the places of their residence hetherto, yea euen amonge those, who could not well away with the same: as also by their Christianlike care, and prouision for the poore, the comfort whereof many a distressed persone, souldiers, and mariners, &c. of our Nation haue found, and daily finde: besides their liberalitie is knowen to a great manie, who heretofore haue tasted the same, especially those, who haue, and doe receiue yearely pentions from them, partely in rememmembrance, and gratification of passed seruice, and partlie for their better relief, maintenance, & sustentation in their olde dayes as also in learning and otherwise: herevnto may be added the great, and continuall charges, which from time to time they haue been at, and still are in these troublesome tymes, through the manifolde disturbance, remoouing, and alteration of the Trade about the procuring of new Priuiledges, and residence for the better vent, and vtteraunce of the Commodities of the Realme, and maintenaunce of the Commerce, and trafficque in foreigne partes: And when for the defence of the Realme, shippes haue been to bee made out, it hath cost them notable summes of money, as by their accomptes thereof doeth appeare: all which could not haue been done, but by men vnited into a Societie, or Companie, as would bee too too evident if once all were sett at libertie, as some would haue it: for thẽ it would in few yeares come to passe, that we should neither haue priviledge, nor iurisdiction abroad, the freendshippe, and kinde vsage of our neighbours would waxe colde, and faint, yea we should goe to the walles, bee wronged, and exacted vpon euerie where, our Countrie commodities would growe vile, or come into the handes, & managing of straũgers, at whose courtesie also, or at least of a few Cormorantes of our owne Nation, we should stande for that wee haue neede of from abroade: by meanes whereof, the incomes, and Customes of the Prince, would be sore diminished, and the Nauigation de-

X 3 cayed,

cayed: and lastlie, if there were occasion either at home of anie thing of importance to be done on the suddaine for the defence of the Realme, the extraordinarie helpe of the M. M. Adventurers would bee wanting, and in foreigne partes, if there were neede, either of money, or other prouision for the seruice of the Prince, and State, no man would bee founde, and so neither credite, nor meanes would be founde or had to serue the turne with all, neither any man to doe anie thinge for the honour of the Prince, and Countrie, howsoeuer necessarie, or vrgent the occasion may be, either generall, or particular: all which I doubt not will be well considered of, and waighed by her Excellent Maiestie, and those whiche vnder her Highnes haue the ordering, and gouuernement of the affaires, and state of this noble Realme, that so the common wealth may prosper, & encrease in honour, and flourishing estate, & that those, which trauaile, and take paines to this ende, and haue from tyme to tyme been found profitable members, may be cherished, and mainteyned in their well doeinge, and encouraged to proceede, by vouchsaufing them gracious countenance, and favourable ayde, and assistance in their causes, and by vpholding them in the full and quiet fruition, and vse of their Priviledges, Charters, and Rightes giuen heeretofore with so good consideration, and hetherto continued, to the high Honour of her Maiestie, and the generall good of this Realme, as I hope in this treatise to haue plainlie, and euidentlie prooued, to the reasonable satis-

satisfaction of all that loue not nouelties, or haue no outlandishe appetites: especiallie of those in honorable, and eminent place, for whose informatiō principallie I vndertooke this labour, humbly prayinge that it may be well accepted, and bring foorth such good, as is thereby meant vnto her Roiall Maiestie, and the whole lande, with all the members thereof, the continuall happines, and prosperitie wherof the Almightie graunt, by whom Princes raigne, & without whom nothing is happie, or perdurable. And you true hearted Merchantes Advēturers, for whose sake I haue written this treatise, faint not in your orderlie, and hetherto wel continued course vnder the fauour, and protection of so gracious and excellent a Princesse, which you haue oftentimes proued, and seene, and by the ayd and Direction of so Honourable, and Wise a Counceill, as that of her Maiesties, of whom you may be well assured, to receyue all necessarie, and reasonable assistance in your honest, and commendable exercise, and feat of Merchaundise, mainteyne the credite and honour which you haue gotten abroade, continew in well doeing, keepe you to your auncient orders, and *Policie*: Preserue vnion and concorde amongest you diligentlie and carefullie, *& valeant qui dissiduum inter vos volunt*, note them notwithstanding, and looke vnto them betymes, for there are daungerous persons, louers of them selues, and enemies to your good, and the well fare of your Societie, wherein they, and the *Hanses* iumpe together and agree: for neither the one, nor the other would

would haue you to be a Cōpanie, for that is in their way, and restrayneth the ones inordinate gourmandise, and thirst after private lucre, onely regardinge the tyme present, and nothing at all the posteritie, (which is a pestilent & pernicious humor in al common wealthes) and keepeth the other from praying vpon the common wealth of this Realme, & hauing their will of the state: as for the saide *Hanses* slaunderous complaintes, and accusations of *Monopolie* forged without groūd of trueth, it shalbe for your credite to aunsweare, where they shalbe ashamed of their doeinges, and at length blushe, *vendere tam vanos circum Palatia fumos*: which you may easilie doe, and without anie great charge: And for the *Hanses* them selues, neither they, nor their meanes are so great, that the State need greatlie to feare them, for if we will but consider the causes, that made them of estimation, and accompt in olde time, namely, the multitude of their shippinge, and sea trade whereby they stored all Countries with the Easterne commodities, and serued Princes turnes in tyme of warre, & of vse of shipping: wee shall finde that they haue in a manner lost both the one, and the other long agoe in comparison of that it hath been, and is now at this day with them: And if her Maiestie should forbidd all trade into Spaine after the example of other Princes, they would in short time be quitt of the rest: for that trade is their chiefest support at this instant, and might be taken frō them: if it so were thought meet vnto her Highenes, and the Lords, and others of her Hono-

Honorable Councell: Besides of the twoo and seauentie confederate *Hanse* Townes, so much spoken, and vaunted of, what remayneth almost, but the reporte, and those which remayne, & appeare by their Deputies whē there is anie assemblie, are they of one minde? or are they able, but with much adoe, to bring vp the charges and contributions necessarie, & incident for the defence, and maintenaunce of their league, Priviledges, and trade in foreigne partes, and at home? surely no: so that it appeareth, that they are not the men they haue been, and therefore although their stomackes, & malice no doubt be bigge enough, yet we need not much to regard, what they can doe, for most of their teeth are out, & the remayner are but loose, and scattered: much better therefore were it for them, to seek the recouery of her Maiesties fauour, and grace by some other more decent course, and meanes, then they haue of late practised, *Precatio & supplicatio* were fitter for them, and would become them better, as I said before, let them remēber the difficulties, which some of the *Hanse* townes are alreadie brought into by their neighbor Princes, & what yet hāgeth ouer some other of their heades, for the preuenting or remoouing of the like, whereof the verie opinion of the good will, and friendshippe of her Highenes would not bee a little auailable, and may profite much heereafter: Wherefore like wise men, knowing their fault, and errour, let them shape another course, for this, whiche they hetherto haue runne will not bringe them there where they would

Y faign

faigne be: And when all is done, and that they haue ſpent their monie, and wearied the world with their importunate complaintes, and out-cryes, doe they thinke that they ſhal recouer their priviledges in Englande by forcing her Maieſtie, or the State? I ſuppoſe they are not ſo ſenſeles: As for the trade in Clothe out of England, which they ſo much contend for, I am of opinion if the matter were well examined, that the ryotouſnes, and vnfaithfull dealing of their ſeruauntes, and factours, the advẽture of the ſea, and charges, when they ſhipped, and helde the Steelyarde at London cõſidered, they did more profite by buycing of the M.M. Adventurers at *Embden*, and *Hambourgh*, eſpeciallie the Merchauntes of *Hambourough*, then by fetching of Clothe them ſelues out of Englande: But let that bee, as it may bee, I muſt confeſſe, that the auncient freendſhipp, & Cõmerce betweene the Realme of Englande, and the *Hanſes* (howſoeuer they bee now decayed) ought not altogither to be forgotten, that ſo by ſome good, and indifferent meanes and agreement the Trade, & Amitie betweene the two moſt noble Dutche, and Engliſh Nations might be made firme, and ſtable, and the auncient, and friendlie neighbourhoode confirmed againſt all humane Chaunges, and Chaunces, which are vncertaine, and variable: yet ſo, that ſtrãugers be not preferred before the Naturall borne ſubiecte, who at all times is, and muſt be readie to ſerue his Prince, and Countrey with his perſon, & goodes at home, and abroad, when the ſtraungers, & ſtraung helpe

helpe wilbe farre off, and to seeke: And therfore the demaund of the *Hanses* in this behalfe is very absurd, and vnreasonable, *Nam sitientibus nostris agris alienos irrigare, stultum esse Leges ducunt, & ordinatam Charitatem incipere à seipso, etiã Theologi admittunt*: wherewith I will conclude this *Treatise*, hopinge that therein I haue sufficientlie declared, and made knowen that, which I tooke vpon me at the beginninge, namelie, *The Commodities of a well ordered Trade*, such as I doubt not, I haue proued that of the Societie, or Cõpanie of M.M. Adventurers to bee, and the *Necessarines of the said Societie* in this florishing *State*.

Quem Deus incolumem servet, faxitq; perennem.

That so the members, and partes therof may continuallie, and daylie more and more prosper, and growe vp in the same, to the honour of God, their Prince, and Countrie.

Copie of a letter from her Maiestie in aunswear of a letter receiued from the Emperour in high Dutch, whereof the Mandate maketh metion, but much differing from the contentes of this copie.

ELIZABETHA Dei gratia Angliæ, Franciæ, & Hiberniæ Regina, fidei defensor, &c. Serenissimo Principi ac Domino Domino RODOLPHO, Romanorũ Electo Imperatori semper Augusto: Regi Hungariæ, Bohemiæ, Dalmatiæ & Slauoniæ: Archiduci Austriæ: Duci Burgundiæ, Styriæ, Carinthiæ & Wirtinbergæ: Comiti Tyrolis, &c. Fratri & Consanguineo nostro charissimo, Salutem rerumq; optatissimarum fælicissimũ incrementum.

Serenissime Princeps, Frater & Consanguinee charissime, Literæ Serenitatis vestræ decimo quinto Iulij datæ, & illæ quidem Germanicè conscriptæ (quod sanè primo aspectu, cum id genus idiomatis hactenus inter nos haud vsitatum sit, dubitationem an cõmentitiæ essent non leuem ingessit) sub finem Octobris redditæ nobis fuerunt, quas quidem ex subiecta materia ad Hanseaticorum instantiam editas animaduertimus. Illi verò dum absoleta quædam Priuilegia in Regno nostro sibi ipsi vendicare perperam decreuissent Anno octuagesimo secundo in Imperialibus comitijs Augustæ Vindelicorum habitis, Mandatum (vt hisce serenitatis vestræ literis habetur) de communibus Imperij ac Dominiorum vestrorum

strorum commercijs perturbandis extorserunt: & iam nuper anno nonagesimo quarto in Deputatorum conuentu Ratisbonæ, de ipsorum damnis Mari per Thalassos nostros (vt queruntur) illatis, deq; Mercatorum nostrorum in Imperio negotiandi rationibus (quas illi odiosa appellatione Monopolia vocitant) nonnullis allegatis & deductis, Mandati illius Augustani vim atque executionem postularunt. Hac occasione serenitas vestra pro mutua Amicitia nostra (quam amantissimæ Sororis affectu libenter amplectimur) scribendum hoc tempore duxit; nosq; hisce suis amicè hortatur, vt de eiusmodi malorum remedijs cogitemus, quibus fine querelis imposito, omnia in florentissimo Amicitiæ statu conseruentur.

Eo certè animo in serenitatem vestrã totumq; ipsius Imperium semper fuimus, vt arctissimæ Amicitiæ iura cum eadem perpetuo tueri, atque inuiolatè colere statuerimus; quam quidem animi nostri propensionem, vti pro re nata sæpiùs testatissimam reddere hactenus studuimus, ita deinceps mutui amoris nostri officijs nunquam deerimus. Ad Hanseaticorum querelas quod attinet, communes querelarum rationes subire illas necesse est: vt nempè quà minùs rectè instituta reperiantur, seipsis concidant. Atqui de memoratis Priuilegijs sæpè iam aliàs responsum est: illa ipsa ante Inaugurationem nostram collapsa, atque ex allegatis & probatis publico at summo Regni nostri Iudicio (à quo nullum Appellationis forum agnoscitur) penitùs euersa atque abolita fuisse. Nos verò alia nonnulla vt temporum rationes ferebant, aliquamdiu Hanseaticis cõcessimus; donec ipsi peculiari ipsorum decreto, subditos nostros tum Hamburgæ cum Stade residentes, nulla dignitatis nec amitiæ nostræ ratione habita, nulla ex causa,

Y 3 no-

nobisq; omnino non præmonitis, temerè exturbarent. Post aliquanto cùm à serenitate vestra commēdatitias in fauorem illorum accepissemus, ad easdem omnino apud nos negotiandi rationes, quibus ipsi nostri subditi vtuntur, illis in gratiam serenitatis vestræ concedendas, satis nos inclinatas sæpè ostendimus; nihil tamen illi eo in genere hactenus à nobis petierunt. Nunc igitur serenitas vestra cui Deus optimus maximus populos subiecit, multo rerum vsu edocta quæ nam sint sceptra tenendi rationes, ipsa secum perpendat, an ijs aures præbendæ sint, qui vetusta priuilegia Iuris ordine semel abiudicata, & iam olim penitus deleta, quæ mutati ab priscis temporum atque hominum mores non ferunt, è cineribus suscitare multa importunitate satagunt? Quis enim esset rerumpub. status, si quæ iam olim iustis de causis antiquata oportuit, ad preces cuiuspiam in vsum denuò reuocarentur? Neque vero alicubi consuetum est, neque ratione vlla ferendum videtur, vt Alienigenæ in earum rerū vsu quæ Regnorum sunt propriæ, Indigenis præferantur: quin potius singularis beneficij loco ducitur, si pares fiant: id quod nos Ciuitatibus Imperij si quæ petiuissent, iādudum ob singulare Amicitiæ nostræ studium, benignè concedere statueramus.

Interim verò quibuscunque Imperij subditis, in Dominijs nostris liberè versandi, & more exterorum negotiandi facultatem nunquam negauimus. Domum propriam in Metropoli nostra, vbi suis moribus viuerent, ex gratia illis semper permisimus: ita quidem vt Iure conqueri non possint, se vti denunciatos hostes apud nos habitos vnquam fuisse. Quod vero de damnis acceptis inferunt, ita se habet. Cùm superioribus hisce annis bello Hispanico implicari cœpissemus, more aliorum Principum, bellica præsidia hostibus intercludedam, denda, quantum in nobis fuerat decreuimus: eaq; de re Vicinas Ciuitates præmonuimus: atque si qui inhibita hoc belli tempore in Hispaniam transportare niterentur, eosdem veluti auxiliatores atque hostium complices, aliqua ex parte habendos, atque inhibitorum confiscatione mulctandos declarauimus: his actis Classiarij nostri in plurimas Hanseaticorum Naues rebus inhibitis onustas inciderunt: Nauibus verò ac Nautis ex indulgentia dimissis, bona tantum inhibita Iure belli ac Regni nostri institutis fisco commiserunt. Quæ quidem illorum Damna, (de alijs enim nihil nobis constat) mulctæ nomine Iure optimo illata nullo æquitatis colore restituenda veniunt.

Monopolium porrò de quo Hanseatici subditos nostros criminantur, calumniæ potiùs quàm veræ accusationis rationem præ se ferre videtur: ab ipsis enim Imperij subditis qui Londini resident, diligenter inquiri iussimus, si quid solidi de iniquis subditorum nostrorum negotiandi rationibus referre possent. Illi verò ingennè responderunt, se nihil ea de re in commissis habere: acturos tamen se quamprimùm per literas cum suis maioribus. Cumq; demum quid responsi acciperent id totum fideliter relaturos. Quæstionem præterea ea de re cum subditis nostris institui mandauimus: illi verò authenticis scriptis edocent, negotiandi ipsorum rationes à plurimis Ciuitatibus in Belgio, Pruscia, atque alibi vti honestissimas probari. Atque cùm duæ Imperij Ciuitates sint, quæ cum nostris maximè negotiantur, Lubeca & Hamburgum, illarum altera, publicis literis (vt nostri ostendunt) testata est, ipsorum negotiationem ab omni Monopolij suspicione vacuam esse: seq; illius obiectæ criminationis participem nunquam fuisse: Vbi verò Hanseaticorum Institores, plura

ea

ea de re ex Dominorum suorum expectata commissione, in scriptis opposuerint, se quoque pluribus in scriptis responsuros humiliter obtulerunt.

Ad Augustanum denique de cõmercijs inhibendis mandatum quod attinet, non satis intelligimus, qua ratione Imperij Principes rectè informati, de priuilegijs aut alijs quibuscunque ad Iura Regni nostri, ab Imperij Legibus semper absoluti, pertinentibus, cognitionem suscipere potuerint: neque sanè videmus quibus documentis eam in sententiam adduci possent, vt commerciorum inhibitionem Imperio; Serenitati vestræ, sibi ipsis, aut Imperij Ciuitatibus, vtilem fore arbitrarentur. Quamobrem Mandatum illud vti obreptitie impetratum, Iure optimo hactenus suspẽsum fuisse, ac deinceps suspendendum esse meritò existimamus. Interim vero ne quid mutua amicitiæ nostræ desit, Imperij subditos qui in Dominijs nostris fortè versabũtur, more solito benigna protectione nostra clementer tuebimur: atque si Lubeca, Hamburgum, aut alia serenitatis vestræ Ciuitas, ipsius nomine gratiam à nobis submissè postulauerint, qua negotiandi rationes maiori ipsorum commodo instituendas cupiant, Serenitatis vestræ commendationem plurimum apud nos momenti habuisse facilè intelligent: nos vicissim amanter petimus, vt parẽ gratiam subditis nostris in ipsius Dominijs clementer impertire serenitas vestra non grauetur. Eidemq; interim fœlicia omnia à DEO Optimo Maximo precamur. Datæ è Regia nostra Richemũdana octauo Nouembris, Anno Domini 1595, Regni vero nostri xxxvij.

Serenitatis vestræ Soror & Consanguinea

ELIZABETHA.

Atteſtation of the Cittie of *Antwerp*, on the Companies of M.M. Adventurers behalfe.

Niuersis & singulis nostras præsentes literas testimoniales visuris vel audituris, Burgimagistri & Scabini Ciuitatis Antuerpiensis in Ducatu Brabātiæ, salutem. Cum pium sit ac rationi consonum Veritati testimonium perhibere, præsertim si pro conseruandę alterius Iure requiramur, Hinc est quod obnixè rogati ex parte Magnificorum Dominorum Gubernatoris, Assistentiū, & communium Mercatorum nationis Anglicæ, præsentibus hisce fidem facimus & attestamur dictos Mercatores nationis Anglicæ qui pluribus ab hinc annis in hac nostra Ciuitate Antuerpiensi residerunt & adhuc resident, honestam, licitam, & Reipub. vtilem semper exercuisse negotiationem, & etiamnum adhuc exercere in emendis, vendendis, & permutandis mercimonijs alijsq̃ legitimis Cōtractibus ineundis, neque vllum fecisse discrimen inter Mercatores cum quibus contraherent cuius illi essent nationis, dummodo soluendo & spectatæ fidei forent, quibus interdum præsente, interdum ad tempus credita pecunia Pannos, Carseas, aliasq̃ Merces suas promiscuè semper vendidère, & adhuc vendunt. In quorum fidem hasce literas sigillo huius Ciuitatis ad causas muniri fecimus. Datum die decima nona mensis Aprilis, Anno Domini Millesimo quingentesimo octuogesimo secundo.

Z Atteſta-

¶ Atteſtation of eight and twentie Merchauntes in *Antwerp* of ſundrie nations concerninge the Companies orderly Trade and clearnes from Monopolie.

VNIVERSIS & ſingulis præſentes literas inſpecturis ſiue audituris, Burgimagiſtri, Scabini & Conſules Ciuitatis Antverpiæ ſalutem, Notum facimus ac harum ſerie teſtamur, Quod die infraſcripto ad inſtantiam magnificorum Dominorum Gubernatoris, Aſſiſtentium & communium Mercatorum nationis Anglicæ in hac Ciuitate reſidentium coram nobis comparuerunt D D. Ludouicus Guicciardini Flor̄etinus, Carolus Lam Franchi, Ioannes Angelus Vergano, Gaſpar Reuelaſco, Lambertus Lamberti, Simon Taſſa, Bartholomeus Luquini, Bartholomeus Balbi, natione Itali, Domini Iacobus de Pardo, Petrus de la Pena Hiſpani, Domini Ferdinandus Ximenes, Rodrigo de Vega, Ludouicus Ferdinandes, Simon Rodrigues Portugallenſes ſiue Luſitani; D D. Ioannes Putz, Iacobus Lange, Ieremias Gennis Germani, Domini Theodoricus de Moy, Ludouicus de Becque, Iacobus van Teweruen, Gualterus Schot, Henricus Moons, Daniel de Lommel, Arnoldus Boudewijns, Nicolaus Rampart, Henricus van Homſſen, Ioannes v inden Steene, & Iacobus Schot, Ciues & Incolæ huius Oppidi, omneſq; Mercatores, Burſam eiuſdem Oppidi frequentantes, Viri fide digni, nobiſq; probè cogniti, Qui medijs illorum iuramen-

ramentis solemniter præstitis iurauerunt & affirmauerunt primo ad id iuridice citati prædictos Mercatores Nationis Anglicæ, tam in hac Ciuitate Antuerpia, quā alijs locis vbi negotiantur, Iustam, licitamq; negotiationem exercuisse, & adhuc exercere, neque quantum rescire potuerunt eosdem Mercatores professionem fecisse fœnerādi vel dandi pecunias ad vsuram aut Monopolijs vsos fuisse, verùm è contrario eosdem semper exercuisse & indies exercere iustam negotiationem, consistentem in emendis, vendendis, & permutandis mercibus alijsque legitimis Contractibus ineundis. Itemq; præfatos Mercatores Anglicos illorum Pannos, Carseas, aliasq; merces omnibus & quibuscunque Nationibus Christiani Orbis sine discrimine vendere, prout etiam dicti Deponētes nunquam rescire potuerunt, quod dicti Mercatores inter se aliquas erexerint Ordinationes aut Statuta, quibus suis Pannis, Cariseis, aut alijs mercibus certum præfigant prætium, quo & non minoris diuendi debeant, Quinimo ipsorum negotiationem semper fuisse & esse liberam, Præterea Mercatores Anglicos in hac Ciuitate Antuerpiensi & Embdæ, aut alibi locorum residentes pro magna parte diuersos habere Ministros & Institores, & separata Domicilia & Magazena, vt plurimum seorsum & separatim negotiando pro lubito alij præsente alij ad tempus credita pecunia, itemque alij maiori, alij minori prætio, vel etiam cōmutatione mercium, & alias, sine dolo malo, In cuius rei testimonium, sigillum ad causas huius Ciuitatis Antuerpiæ præsentibus apponi fecimus, Die decima nona mensis Aprilis, Anno Domini Millesimo quingentesimo octuagesimo secundo.

Z 2 Attesta-

Attestation of the Towne of Embden in East-friseland, on the behalfe of the Companie of M. M. Adventurers.

VNIVERSIS, & singulis cuiuscunque Ordinis, & Dignitatis has nostras literas visuris, siue cognituris. Nos Consules, Senatores, atque Magistratus vrbis Embdæ sitæ in Frisiæ Orientali sub tutela sacræ Cæsareæ Maiestatis, Domini nostri clementissimi, & Sacri Romani Imperij existente Comitatu post debitam, & demissam salutis, atque obseruantiæ nostræ significationem, notum publicè facimus, ac testamur: Quum Ornatissima Anglica Natio aliquot annos in hac Ciuitate commorata varij generis mercimonia exerceant, & per suum Secretarium, ac Procuratorem doctum, & ornatum virum Dominum Iohannem Moer, à nobis in pleno Senatu Testimonium de ratione Negotiationis, & Mercatus sui petierint, minimè id quidem officij, quantum nobis constat, eis recusandum putauimus: Quamobrem pro certo affirmamus, ac testamur publicè, quod dictæ Anglicæ Nationis Mercatores, eorumq; ministri, & negotiorum gestores (quos Aduenturarios vocant) quatenus nobis cognitum est, quam diu apud nos fuerunt, sese semper honestè, & legitimè in suis Contractibus, & Negotiationibus gessisse, & adhuc gerere, honestum, liberum, ac licitum mercatum in Pannis, Cariseijs, alijsque mercimonijs emendis, vendendis, & permutandis exercere, atque

173

atque tractare, neque aliter agere, quàm probos, & idoneos Mercatores, & Negotiatores agere par est, & decet. Proinde quum Magistratus officij sit ad id requisiti, veritati ferre testimonium, nostram quoque mentem ea de re publicè profitendam censuimus. In cuius rei confirmationem sigillum nostrum ad causas scienter appendimus: Anno Domini suprà sesqui millesimum Octuagesimo secundo, vigesimo octauo die Iulij.

Atte-

An Attestation of fourteene Merchaunts in Stade of sundrie places on the Companie of M. M. Adventurers behalfe.

VNIVERSIS ET SINGVLIS præsentes has literas visuris vel audituris, quocunque dignitatis, honoris, & eminentiæ gradu fuerint, Nos CONSVLES & Senatores Reipub. STADENSIS, Archiepiscopatus Bremensis, post debitam officiorũ nostrorum oblationem & honorificam salutationem notum facimus, publicèq; attestamur, quod ad instantiam Magnifici, spectabilium & discretorum Domini Thomæ Ferrers, Regiæ Maiestatis Anglicæ Agentis, & hactenus apud nos Præfecti aliorumq; Assistentium & Mercatorum Anglicorum Adventurariæ Societatis, per aliquot annos in nostra Ciuitate residentium, & iam tandem abitum fauente Neptuno, dudum sperantium, coram Nobis comparuerunt legitimè iudicialiterque citati spectabiles & honesti viri, fideq; digni testes & Bursam Forumq; nostræ Civitatis quotidiè frequentantes, Domini Iohannes Calandrinus Lucensis Italus, Bartolomæus Pels, Wilhelmus Bartolotti, Iacobus de Greve, Antonius Boots, Hieronymus Hester, Simon de Beck, Matthias de Kestelt, Antuerpienses, Franciscus Boudewin Buscoducensis, Wilhelmus de Bari, Dornacensis, Antonius Engelbrecht, Aquisgranẽsis, Antonius Geir, Coloniensis, Iohan-

hannes Philippus Stamler, et Georgius Mauritius, Augustani, satisque & sufficienter de veritate dicenda admoniti, stipulato, sub fide datarum dextrarum, in vim & ad effectum corporalis iuramenti, quod se desuper re ipsa præstare, si requirantur, non gravari affirmabant, deposuerunt & attestati sunt, sibi quam notissimum seq; ipsos expertos esse, Adventurarios mercatores Anglicæ nationis, huc vsque in nostra Civitate residentes, & iam ad abitum paratos, non Pannos modò, Cariseias, Baiettas, sed & alias varias & diuersas merces ex Anglia huc advectas, quibuscunque orbis Christiani incolis, absque vllo discrimine Nationis aut Religionis, vendere, & vicissim qualiacunque bona, sibi placentia, ab alijs redimere aut in solutũ accipere atq; hinc in Angliam remittere solere, itemq; omnibus omnino Mercatoribus similiter liberum esse, suas merces in Angliam deportari, ibiq; vendi, aliasq; quascunq; denuò emi & in Germaniam atq; alias quascũque regiones, soluto solito telonio transvehi procurare, atque hanc Anglos Adventurarios Mercatores legitimam iustamq; negotiationem in emendo & vendendo aliisque licitis contractibus ineundis non minus atque alios quoslibet negotiatores in nostra Civitate hactenus exercuisse, nec sibi notum esse, aut se vnquam audiuisse, quod Angli Mercatores, hactenus apud nos residentes, professionem fœnerandi pecuniásve ad vsuram dandi fecerint, multò minus pacta aut statuta inter se constituerint, quibus se invicem obstrinxerint, aut suas merces certo precio, quod citra pœnam mutare nefas esset, vendendas aut alienas similiter emendas: sed è contra, omnibus esse cognitum, eiusdem bonitatis signique Pannos, Cariseias, Baiettas, aliaq; quæcunque mercimonia apud plurimos Anglos Adventuraturariæ Societatis Mercatores, in diuersis Tabernis & Domicilijs separatis existentes, tam Dominos quam Factores, aut famulos siue institores, vno & eodem temporis momento, reperiri, eaq; non vno, sed diuersissimo pretio, ad duas, tres, quatuor, quinque, & plures etiam libras, & sic nunc maiore, nunc etiam minore prætio, præsente, vel ad tempus credita pecunia, datis obligationibus, vel factâ merciũ permutatione, provt cuiusque res tulerit, emi, atque pariter alias merces diversimodo illis vendi posse, nec vnquam ad notitiam suam peruenisse aut se rescire potuisse Anglos Adventurariæ Societatis Negotiatores, quovsque hic Stadæ vixissent, de Monopolio iure & legitimè accusatos, multò minus vnquam à quoquam convictos fuisse. Absque omni dolo, malo, fraude, & sinistra machinatione. In cuius rei testimonium præsentibus solitum nostræ Ciuitatis Secretum appendi scienter iussimus. Datæ a. d. IIX. Mensis Februarij, Anno salutiferæ nativitatis unici Domini & Redemptoris nostri IESV CHRISTI, millesimo quingentesimo nonagesimo octauo.

Attesta-

Atteſtation of the Towne of Middelbrough in Zeland on the behalfe of the Companie of Merchauntes Adventurers.

VNiuerſis & ſingulis noſtras præſentes literas teſtimoniales viſuris, vel audituris, Burgimagiſtri, Scabini, Senatoresq́; Ciuitatis Middelburgenſis in Comitatu Zelandiæ Salutem: Quum pium ſit, & rationi conſonum veritati teſtimonium perhibere, præſertim ſi pro conſeruando alterius Iure requiratur, hinc eſt quòd obnixè rogati ex parte magnificorum Dominorum Gubernatoris, Aſsiſtentium, & cōmunium Mercatorum Nationis Angliæ, & Aduenturariæ Societatis præſentibus hiſce fidē facimus, & atteſtamur, dictos Mercatores Nationis Angliæ, qui pluribus abhinc annis in hac noſtra Ciuitate Middelburgenſi reſiderunt, & adhuc reſident, honeſtam, licitam, & Reipub. vtilem ſemper exercuiſſe Negotiationē, & adhuc etiamnum exercere in emendis, vendendis, & permutādis mercibus, aliiſq́; legitimis contractibus ineundis, neque vllum feciſſe diſcrimen inter Mercatores, quibuſcum contraherent cuiuſcunque eſſent Nationis, dummodo forent ſoluendo, & ſpectatæ fidei, quibus interdum præſenti, interdum credita pecunia Pannos, Cariſeias, aliaſq́; merces ſuas promiſcuè ſemper vendidere, & adhuc vendunt: Atteſtamur præterea nunquam nobis notum fuiſſe, aut audiuiſſe vnquam, quòd dicti Angli Mercatores Aduenturarij hactenus apud nos reſidētes profeſsionem fœnerandi, pecuniaſq́; ad vſuram dandi fecerint, multò minus pacta, aut ſtatuta inter ſeſe conſtituerint, quibus ſe inuicem obſtrinxerint, aut ſuas merces certo prætio, quod citra pœnam

A a mutare

mutare nefas esset, vel aliter vendendas, aut alienas similiter emendas, sed è contrà omnibus esse cognitum, eiusdem bonitatis signiq; Pannos, Cariseias, aliaq; quæcunque mercimonia, apud plurimos Anglos prædictæ Societatis Mercatores, in diuersis tabernis, & domicilijs seperatis existentes, tàm Dominos, quàm Factores, aut famulos, siue Institores vno, & eodem temporis momento reperiri, eaq; nō vno, sed diuersissimo prætio ad duas, tres, quatuor, quinque, & plures libras, & sic nunc maiori, nunc minori prætio, præsenti, vel ad tempus credita pecunia, datis obligationibus, vel facta mercium permutatione, prout cuiusque res tulerit, emi, atq; pariter alias merces diuersimodo illis vendi posse: Nec vnquam ad notitiam nostram peruenisse, aut nos rescire potuisse, Anglos Aduenturariæ Societatis prædictæ Negotiatores, quousque hic Middelburgi vixerunt, de Monopolio Iure, & legitimè accusatos, multò minus vnquam à quopiam cōvictos fuisse, absque omni dolo, malo. fraude, & sinistra machinatione. In cuius rei testimonium alterius Secretatiorum nostrorum manu Instrumentum hoc subsignari, nec non sigillum ad causas apponere iussimus, vt in simili negotio apud nos est consuetum: Actum septimo die mensis Iulij Anno Domini Millesimo Sexcentesimo.

Schotte.

Faultes escaped in printing.

Folio. 1. Lin. 13 for mare, read mari fol. 4. lin. 22. for honors read honor. fol. 5. lin. 8. for in, read into. Fol. 23. lin. 6. for denized, read deuized. fol. 26. lin. 21. for reuenues, read reuenewes. fol. 31. lin. 15. for seauenthly, read sixthly. Fol. 36. lin. 14. for Geneall, read Generall fol. 33 lin 26. for 1414, read 1514 fol 40 lin 21 for tought, read thought. fol. 49. lin. 8. for these, read those. fol. 50. lin. 10. for about, read aboue. fol 52. lin. 21 for Eggard, read Egdard. fol 54. lin. 17. the woord [and] wanteth. Idem lin. 26. for Gasman, read Gusman. fol 65. lin. 7. and lin. 13. for Wesendorp, read Westendorp. fol. 67. lin. 5. for Companies, read Companie. fol 69. lin 22. the word [will] wanteth. fol. 72. lin. 30. for grounh, read ground fol. 90. lin 9 for Epmire, read Empire. fol. 95. lin. 29. for Egland, read England. fol. 119. lin. 25. for faitfull, read faithfull. fol. 122. lin. 8. for Prince read Princes. Ibidem lin. 30. for libertits, read liberties. Ibidem lin 30. for well, read will. fol. 150. lin. 29. for Treatie, read Treatise. fol. 152. lin. 26. for possible, read possibly. fol. 154 lin. 22. for shew, read shewes. fol 155. lin. 28. for growne, read gowne. fol 159. lin 25 for diffidium, read dissidium. Idem lin. 27 for there, read they. fol. 164. lin 24. for absoleta, read obsoleta. fol. 165 lin. 30 for amitiæ, read Amicitiæ. fol. 166 lin. 30 for qræsidia, read præsidia fol. 167. lin. 11. for restienda, read restituenda. fol. 169. lin. 2. for Companies, read Companie.

In the Title, for Commodies, read Commodities.

fol. 151. lin. 17. for quidam, read quidem. Ibid. lin. 21. for examinaretur, read examinarentur.

PART TWO

EDITED TEXT OF "A TREATISE OF COMMERCE"

PART II

EDITOR'S PREFACE

THE text that follows is that of the Middelburg edition, which seems slightly more accurate than that of the London edition. The corrections indicated by the page of *errata* have, of course, been incorporated, but otherwise the only change from the original version (which is shown in facsimile on pp. 121–305) is the modernization of spelling, capitalization, punctuation, and paragraphing. As the forms of these in the Middelburg edition differ considerably from those of the London edition, they may safely be attributed more to the printers than to the author; hence it cannot be said that my version does any violence to his intention.

Generally speaking, I have attempted to make the spelling consistent, but where the original edition spells a word in two forms that are equally sanctioned by modern usage (e.g. *honor* and *honour*) I have declined the responsibility of choosing between them. Proper names that are consistently spelled in the same way (e.g. Bullen for Boulogne) have usually been left unchanged; those that show variants have usually been changed to the form that appears most frequently.

The original version capitalizes words lavishly. In one conspicuous instance I have allowed the capital to remain. This is on the word *Cloth*, which had a much more specific and limited meaning than it has to-day. The people of that time did not dignify all kinds of woven fabrics by the name *Cloth*; they reserved this word for a definite variety, closely resembling the broadcloth of modern times. It was a smooth, lustrous woollen fabric, so highly finished that the warp and woof were indistinguishable, and was not only beautiful but extremely durable. The white Cloths, so frequently mentioned, were merely lengths of this fabric in its undyed, undressed state.

A noticeable feature of the original punctuation is the frequent use of the colon. A number of these colons have been allowed to remain, even where they would not be sanctioned by modern usage.

Where marginal captions in the original are of a topical nature they have been considered as sub-heads, and are displayed as such in the edited text. A few that seem to be comments by the author have been treated as footnotes, and are inserted at the bottoms of pages, set in nine-point type, to distinguish them from the editor's footnotes which are in seven point.

The Latin letters appended to the *Treatise* have here been replaced by English translations by Professor Thomas W. Edmondson of New York University. The Latin passages in the body of the text have been allowed to stand, but are accompanied by translations in the footnotes, wherever these are necessary. Obsolete words and phrases are also explained in the footnotes. The other footnotes are mainly to clarify the statements and allusions of the author.

A TREATISE

OF COMMERCE, WHEREIN ARE SHOWED THE COMMODITIES ARISING BY A WELL ORDERED, AND RULED TRADE,

Such as that of the Society of Merchants Adventurers is proved to be, written principally for the better information of those who doubt of the *Necessariness of the said Society in the State of the Realm of England,*

BY JOHN WHEELER, Secretary to the said Society.

MIDDELBURGH,
By *Richard Schilders,* Printer to the States of Zeeland.
1601.

To the Right Honorable Sir Robert Cecil, *Knight, Principal Secretary to* her Majesty, &c.

THOSE which heretofore (Right Honorable) have written of any matter, and had opinion that the publishing thereof might do good unto others, have used to dedicate their labours to some one, or other, under whose countenance and protection the same might go forth, and be the better liked and received of all men. Which is the cause that I have made bold to inscribe this Treatise, such as it is, unto your Honour, upon hope of favourable allowance and patronage, which I instantly crave and entreat; and withal, that in the reading thereof, your Honour would vouchsafe to remember that it concerneth those men and that old and anciently renowned Company of Merchants Adventurers, which was so well esteemed of, and highly favoured by your late right Honorable Father, of worthy memory, unto whom as God hath appointed your Honour to be a successor in many excellent things of this life (whether we regard the honourable places, whereunto you are called in the government of the State, or the virtues and qualities fit for so weighty a calling wherewith you are endued) so it may please your Honour to take unto you this succession also, to wit, the dutiful observancy and promptitude, which the said Company always showed towards your said right Honourable Father's service, and which they also stand ready, and desirous to present and perform unto your Honour to their best power and ability.

I am not ignorant also, that it is the manner of writers to fill up the greatest part of their prefaces with the praises, and commendations of those to whom they dedicate their travails,[1] and surely this reward seemeth to be due unto true virtue, that the memory thereof should be consecrated to posterity, which can not be performed by any monument better

[1] Works.

than by books. And albeit, without all glozing[2] or counterfeiting, I have here in very deed a large field of your Honour's praises offered unto me, yet because my simplicity not only abhorreth all adulation, but withal all kind of fawning or flattering speech, and that your Honour's singular modesty is wont not to abide anything less than even the modestest commendations, I will let pass the same, and come unto the handling of the ensuing treatise, which with myself I humbly recommend unto your Honour's good favour, and so beseech the Almighty to bless and keep your Honor. *Middelburgh* the VIth of June, 1601.

Your Honor's with his service at commandment,

John Wheeler.

[2]Flattering.

A TREATISE OF COMMERCE,

wherein are showed the commodities[1] arising by a well-ordered and ruled trade, such as that of the *SOCIETY of MERCHANTS ADVENTURERS* is proved to be. Written principally[2] for the better information of those who doubt of the necessariness of the said Society in the state of the Realm of England: By JOHN WHEELER, Secretary to the said Society

Vita Civilis in Societate est, Societas in Imperio, & Commercio.[3]

Commercio Gentes mari, montibusque discretæ miscentur, ut quod usquam nascitur, apud omnes affluat.[4]

THERE be two points about the which the Royal office and administration of a Prince is wholly employed: to wit, about the government of the persons of men; next of things convenient and fit for the maintenance of human society, wherein principally the civil life consisteth and hath her being. And therefore the Prince that loveth the policy, and ruleth by sage and good counsel, is to constitute and appoint certain laws, and ordinary rules, both in the one and the other of the abovesaid points, and especially in the first, as the chiefest; which is conversant and occupied about the institution of the persons of men in piety, civil conversation[5] in manners and fashion of life, and finally in the mutual duty of equity and charity one towards another. Of the which my purpose is not to intreat,[6] but somewhat of that other point, namely the government of things convenient and fit for the maintenance of human society, whereunto mens ac-

[1] Benefits; profits. [2] "Principally" is omitted from the London edition.
[3] *Civic life lies in fellowship; fellowship in government and trade.* Milles quotes this same maxim with slightly different wording (see *supra*, p. 81) as if to correct Wheeler's version. I have not been able to trace the quotation to its original source.
[4] *By commerce, peoples widely separated by sea and mountains are brought together, so that whatever is produced anywhere is distributed to all.*
[5] Conduct. [6] Treat; discourse.

tions and affections are chiefly directed, and whereabouts they bestow and employ not only the quickness and industry of their spirits, but also the labour and travail of their hands and sides: that so they may draw from thence either commodity or pleasure, or at leastwise thereby supply, help, and furnish their several wants, and necessities. From hence, as from a root or fountain first proceedeth the estate of *Merchandise*, and then consequently in a row, so many, diverse, and sundry Arts as we see in the world.

At which it should seem that man beginneth the train or course of his life, and therein first of all discovereth not only the dexterity and sharpness of his wit, but withal that naughtiness and corruption which is naturally in him. For there is nothing in the world so ordinary and natural unto men, as to contract, truck, merchandise, and traffic one with another, so that it is almost unpossible[7] for three persons to converse together two hours, but they will fall into talk of one bargain or another, chopping,[8] changing,[9] or some other kind of contract. Children, as soon as ever their tongues are at liberty, do season their sports with some merchandise or other, and when they go to school, nothing is so common among them as to change and rechange, buy and sell of that which they bring from home with them. The Prince with his subjects, the master with his servants, one friend and acquaintance with another, the captain with his soldiers, the husband with his wife, women with and among themselves, and in a word, all the world choppeth and changeth, runneth and raveth after marts, markets, and merchandising. So that all things come into commerce, and pass into traffic (in a manner) in all times, and in all places: not only that which Nature bringeth forth, as the fruits of the earth, the beasts and living creatures with their spoils, skins, and cases,[10] the metals, minerals, and such like things, but further also, this man maketh merchandise of the works of his own hands, this man of another man's labor, one selleth words, another maketh traffic of the skins and blood of other men; yea there are some found so subtle and cunning merchants that they persuade and in-

[7] Impossible. [8] Bartering. [9] Exchanging. [10] Hides.

duce men to suffer themselves to be bought and sold, and we have seen in our time enow and too many, which have made merchandise of men's souls. To conclude, all that a man worketh with his hand or discourseth in his spirit is nothing else but merchandise, and a trial to put in practise the Contracts which the legists[11] and men skillful in the laws knew not to name otherwise than thus: *Do ut des, Facio ut facias:*[12] the which words in effect comprehend in them all negotiations or traffics whatsoever, and are none other thing but mere matter of merchandise and commerce.

COMMENDATION OF MERCHANDISE

Now albeit this affection be in all persons generally, both high and low, yet there are of the notablest and principallest traffickers which are ashamed and think scorn to be called Merchants; whereas indeed merchandise which is used by way of proper vocation, being rightly considered of, is not to be despised, or accounted base by men of judgment, but to the contrary by many reasons and examples it is to be proved that the estate is honorable, and may be exercised not only of those of the third estate[13] (as we term them) but also by the Nobles and chiefest men of this Realm with commendable profit, and without any derogation to their Nobilities, high degrees, and conditions. With what great good to their States, honor, and enriching of themselves and their Countries, the *Venetians*, *Florentines*, *Genoese*, and our neighbours the *Hollanders*, have used this trade of life, who knoweth not? Or having seen the beauty, strength, opulency, and populousness of the abovesaid Cities and Provinces wondereth not thereat? Was not this the first step and entry of the Kings of *Portugal* unto the kingdoms and riches of the East?

PLUT. IN VITA SOLONIS

Solon in his youth, gave himself to the feat[14] of merchandise, and in his time saith *Plutarch* (bringing *Hesiodus* for his

[11] Those skilled in the written laws of the Roman Civil law.
[12] *I give so that you may give; I perform so that you may perform.*
[13] The Commons. [14] Occupation; business.

author[15]) there was none estate of life reproachful, neither Art, or occupation, that did put difference between men, but rather which is more, *Merchandise* was accounted an honourable thing, as that which ministered the means to haunt,[16] and traffic with barbarous nations, to procure the friendship of Princes, and to gain experience into many matters: insomuch (saith he) that there have been merchants which were founders of great Cities, as he was that founded *Marseilles* in France. The wise *Thales Milesius* did also exercise Merchandise, likewise *Hippocrates*, and *Plato* defrayed the charges of a voyage which he made in *Egypt* with the money which he got there by selling of oil. So that it appeareth that not only a Prince may use this kind of men (I mean merchants) to the great benefit and good of his state, either for foreign intelligence or exploration, or for the opening of an entry and passage unto unknown and far distant parts, or for the furnishing of money, and other provisions in time of war and dearth, or lastly, for the service and honor of the Prince and Country abroad at all times requisite and expedient, but also this kind of life may be exercised and used with commendation, and without loss of one jot of honor in those who are honorable, or of eminent degree, as aforesaid.

Whereunto I add this further, that without merchandise, no ease or commodious living continueth long in any State, or Commonwealth, no not loyalty, or equity itself, or upright dealing. Therefore herein also, as in the former point, good order and rule is to be set, where it is wanting, or where it is already established, there it ought to be preserved: for the maintenance of so necessary and beneficial an estate in the Commonwealth, by constituting meet and well proportioned ordinances over the same, and over those things which are thereupon depending, between the merchants, and those things, which are merchandized, or handled likewise with convenable[17] and well appropriated magistrates and overseers for the maintenance and execution of the said ordinances. For it is very certain and true, that *sine imperio nec domus*

[15] Authority. [16] Visit frequently.
[17] Suitable.

ulla, nec Civitas, nec Gens, nec Societas, nec hominum universum genus stare, nec rerum natura omnis, nec Mundus ipse potest, &c.[18]

The peaceable, politic, and rich Prince, King *Henry* the Seventh, well marking the truth hereof, and perceiving that as in former times, so in his, many disturbances, grievances and damages had befallen to and among the English merchants his subjects, trading into the Low Countries, *ob defectum boni Regiminis,*[19] took order for the same, as well by confirming the ancient charters of his predecessors, Kings of England, unto the Society of M. M. Adventurers, as also by adding thereunto new, whereby he so strengthened and enlarged the authority and privileges of the said Fellowship, that ever since the same hath flourished in great prosperity and wealth, and out of it (as out of a plentiful nursery) have sprung and proceeded almost all the principal merchants of this Realm; at least such companies as have arisen since, have for the most part, fetched their light, pattern, and form of policy and trade from the said Society to the inestimable good and commodity of this Realm, our native Country: so that to change this course were to return to the old confusion, and disorder, and withal to bereave the land of so necessary and serviceable an estate, as *Merchandise is.*

Whatsoever is commendable, or is said of the best-founded companies, or merchants in general, maketh also for the Company of Merchants Adventurers specially: howbeit these things are particularly for our purpose to be considered in this Company: *The first Institution: The ancient estimation it hath had: The State and government of it, and such benefits, as grow to the Realm by the maintenance of it.*[20]

[18] *Without government, neither home nor city nor people nor Society nor the whole race of mankind can endure; nay, nor the whole world nor the universe itself.*

[19] *Because of the lack of good government.*

[20] This passage is a paraphrase of a summary in the anonymous defense of London that was appended to Stow's *Survey of London* (see *supra* page 66). The original reads as follows:

"Whatsoever is said of cities generally maketh also for London specially: howbeit, these things are particularly for our purpose to be considered in it. The situation; the former estimation that it hath had; the service that it hath done; the present estates and government of it, and such benefits as do grow to the realm by the maintenance thereof."

In the succeeding pages Wheeler borrows other ideas and even phraseology from the same source. The Latin quotations from Polydore and Cato both appear in the defense of London.

Of the first Institution of the Fellowship or Company of MERCHANTS ADVENTURERS, and the causes thereof

MARCUS *Cato*, a prudent Counsellor, and a good husband[1] indeed, saith: *Quod oportet Patremfamilias vendacem esse non emacem:*[2] And who knoweth not, that we have no small need of many things, whereof foreign Countries have great store, and that we may well spare many things, whereof the said Countries have also need. Now to vent[3] the superfluities of our Country, and bring in the commodities of others, there is no readier or better means than by merchandise. And seeing we have no way to increase our treasure by mines of gold and silver at home, and can have nothing from abroad without money or ware, it followeth necessarily that the abovesaid good counsel of *Cato* to be sellers and not buyers, is to be followed, yet so that we carry not out more in value over the seas, than we bring home from thence, or transport things hurtful to the State, for this were no good husbandry, but tendeth to the subversion of the land, and diminishing of the treasure thereof, whereas by the other we shall greatly increase it, the trade being carried, and managed under a convenient government and orders, and not in a dispersed, loose, and straggling manner. The practice whereof we may see in this Realm almost these 400 years together; first in the Staple, and Wool trade, and next in that of the M. M. Adventurers, and Cloth trade. And King *Edward* the Third thought it not enough to bring the working and making of Cloth into the Realm, except when the same was indraped, he withal provided for the vent thereof in foreign parts, to the most benefit and advancement of that new begun Art, and therefore whereas the abovesaid Company

[1] Manager.

[2] *The master of the household should be fond of selling, not fond of buying.* Cato, *De Re Rustica*, 2, *fin.*

[3] Sell.

(though then otherwise termed* than now) in the year *1248* had obtained Privileges of *John*, Duke of *Brabant*, the said King confirmed the same for the substantial Government of the said Company in their trade.

In the year 1399, the art of making of Cloth being grown to good perfection within this Realm, King *Henry* the Fourth first prohibited the invection[4] of foreign made Cloth, and gave unto the said Company a very beneficial and ample Charter of privileges, confirmed by Act of Parliament for the same purpose and intent as his predecessor King *Edward* the Third had done before him: whose example the succeeding Kings *Henry* the Fifth, and Sixth, *Edward* the Fourth, and *Richard* the Third followed, ratifying and confirming their Predecessors' doings on this behalf. The next in order following, King *Henry* the Seventh, like a wise and provident Prince, well marking and considering how necessary and serviceable the estate of *Merchandise* was unto this Realm, not only liked[5] and confirmed that which the above-rehearsed Kings had done before him, but also greatly enlarged and augmented the same by three several Charters, and by other his gracious and Royal favours from time to time, not only toward the said Company in general, but withal to divers Merchants in particular: *Mercatores ille saepenumero pecunia multa data gratuito iuvabat, ut Mercatura* (*Ars una omnium cunctis atquè mortalibus tum commoda, tum necessaria*) *in suo Regno copiosior esset.*[6]† And when upon variance fallen out between him and the Archduke *Philip*, he had drawn as well the said Company as that of the Staple out of the Low Countries, and placed them at *Calais*, he gave unto them within the said Town as large and beneficial privileges as they before had enjoyed in the said Low Countries, which were very large and favourable, entitling them by the name of *MERCHANTS ADVENTURERS*.

* The Brotherhood of Saint Thomas Becket of Canterbury.—[Wheeler's side-head note.]

[4] Bringing in; importation. [5] Approved.

† Polidorus in vita Henrici septimi.—[Wheeler's side-head reference.]

[6] *He frequently helped the merchants with outright gifts of money, so that trade (the one art that to all mankind is not only convenient but necessary) should flourish more abundantly in his realm.*

And albeit in this King's days, as also in the reign of King *Henry* the Fourth, the like complaint, as of late, was made by the clothiers, wool-growers, dyers, etc., against the Company of M. M. Adventurers, yet after due examination of the said complaint, the issue procured great favour to the said Company, and gave occasion of the enlarging of their former Charters, with an express restraint of all stragglers and intermedlers, that might disturb or impeach their trade. And whereas also the *Easterlings* at this time had entered into the said trade, the foresaid prudent Prince King *Henry* the Seventh, did not only straightly inhibit them so to do, but also took recognizance of twenty thousand marks of the Alderman of the Steelyard at London, that the said Easterlings should not carry any English Cloth to the place of residence of the M. M. Adventurers in the Low Countries, or open their fardels[7] of Cloth in the said Countries, to the prejudice of the said Company, by putting the same to vent there,[8] which they were not wont to do.[9]

In the time of the reign of King *Edward* the Sixth, *John Tulle*, *John Dimock*, and others, brethren of the said Company, informed the Bishop of *Ely*, at that time Lord Chancellor, of matter against the Company, but their bill being brought to the Council-board and examined, it was finally ordered that the said complainants should submit themselves unto the obedience of the Company's orders, and pay certain fines, which the Lords then laid upon them, besides that two of the principallest found to be the ringleaders of the rest, were committed to the Fleet, there to remain till such time as the Company of M. M. Adventurers should sue for their release.[10] And albeit the said persons renewed their complaints,

[7] Bundles. [8] Offering them for sale there.

[9] This recognizance, or bond, was required Oct. 31, 1493, but its later history is obscure. According to Schanz the money was declared forfeit on July 8, 1508, but other German historians are doubtful about this. (See Ian Colvin, *The Germans in England*, p. 145.) Certainly the later reference to it in Wheeler's *Treatise*, p. 133(see *infra*, p. 419) suggests that the terms of the bond were observed in the reign of Henry VII, but violated with impunity in the time of Henry VIII. The figures of cloth exports give no certain answer to the question, for they do not indicate how much of the cloth, if any, the Hanseatics sold in Antwerp.

[10] Tulle and Dimock were members who had joined under the terms provided by the Parliament Act of 1496 and hence were classified as of the "New Hanse." These members did not enjoy the same privileges as members of the "Old Hanse." The Privy Council upheld the

in the first year of Queen *Mary's* reign, and did put up a bill to the Parliament house against the Company, yet the same being answered by the said Company, was rejected and cast out of the Parliament house.

Since the time of King *Henry* the Seventh, the succeeding Princes, King *Henry* the Eighth, of famous memory, King *Edward* the Sixth, and Queen Mary, have continued, confirmed, and enlarged the abovesaid charters and privileges, but above all other, our most gracious Sovereign that now reigneth, Queen *ELIZABETH*, hath showed her gracious and favourable affection towards the said Company, in not only confirming the letters patents and charters of her most noble grandfather, and of other her Highness' Predecessors abovementioned, but also in adding thereunto other more large and beneficial Privileges of her own. For whereas the M. M. Adventurers, about the beginning of her Majesty's reign, by divers restraints, edicts, and proclamations made and set forth by the governors and commanders of the Low Countries, were impeached, and prohibited to trade into the said Countries, contrary to the ancient intercourses and the privileges to the said Company granted of old time, and consequently were occasioned to seek and erect a trade in the parts of Germany, which they did with their great charges and travail[11] for the vent of the commodities of the Realm, her Highness calling to remembrance this and other faithful and acceptable service at sundry times done by the said M. M. Adventurers in divers the great and weighty affairs of her Majesty and Realm,[12] and minding the increase and advancement of the said mer-

discipline of the Governor and assistants, against which the New Hanse members rebelled. In this policy they were influenced by Gresham, who consistently advocated a narrowing rather than a widening of the membership, and would have liked to end the practice of admitting members of the New Hanse. "The Fleet," mentioned here, was the famous debtors' prison.

[11] The "great charges and travail" of the Company in establishing marts in Germany doubtless included certain gifts to the city authorities. The Merchants Adventurers probably followed Hanseatic policy in this respect as in others.

[12] Their "faithful and acceptable service" to Queen Elizabeth included substantial loans, as has been shown in the Introduction (p. 4), but Wheeler is too discreet to specify such matters. It is more surprising that he omits mention of the fact that they furnished ships in time of peril; for example, they had over a hundred ships in readiness for the coming of the Spanish Armada. Possibly these facts were so well known to his readers that they did not need repetition here.

chants, as much as any her progenitors, (as her Highness professeth in the said charter) it pleased her said Majesty in the sixth year of her Reign, to give and grant unto them those gracious and ample privileges which the said Company now enjoyeth. And afterwards upon new occasion the trade of the said Company being much impeached by the wrongful intermedling of unfree persons in the same, it pleased her Majesty by a new charter, and letters patents under the great seal of England, in the eight-and-twentieth year of her Reign, to provide against such injurious, and unorderly intrusion, acknowledging the services done to her Highness by the said M. M. Adventurers, and pronouncing them to have been, and to be very beneficial members to the general state of the Realm, and Commonwealth of England. Which notable testimony of so incomparable a Princess after so many years experience and trial may alone, if there were none other, serve for a full and sufficient *Apology* of the abovesaid Company of M. M. Adventurers, against all the privy and open, foreign and domestic gainsayers, slanderers, and oppugners of the same, and withal for a certain and infallible argument that for the vent of Wool and woollen wares (the principal commodities of the Realm) it is most profitable both for the Prince and Country to use a governed Company, and not to permit a promiscuous, straggling, and dispersed trade,[13] whereof I shall have occasion to say more, when I come to show the benefits, which do arise unto the Commonwealth of England, by the maintenance of the abovesaid Company and the Government therein used.

[13] Wheeler implies that Queen Elizabeth consistently protected the company against competition by independent merchants ("interlopers") although, only a few months before, she had sanctioned their trade on the Elbe and Weser rivers. However, he may have been justified in not admitting this as an exception, for the company was excluded from that territory at this time.

Of the ancient estimation which the Company of MERCHANTS ADVENTURERS hath had

BY that which hath been abovesaid of the institution of the Fellowship or Company of M. M. Adventurers, is partly showed in what estimation the said Company hath been hitherto, with the Kings and Queens of this Realm, from the reign of King *Edward* the Third, a sufficient motive and reason, as may be well thought, for the present and future ages to have the said Company in no less estimation and liking. But this is not all, for if we would but look out of England to our neighbors in *Germany* and the Low Countries, we should see the M. M. Adventurers many ages together sought for, welcomed, embraced, cherished, and used in as good, yea oftentimes in better terms, than the Naturals[1] of the said Countries themselves, as appeareth by the ancient charters, large and beneficial privileges, and exemptions granted to the said Company by sundry Princes, States, Cities, and Commonwealths of high and low Dutchland, since the year of our Lord 1296[2] to this our time, which are yet extant to be showed to the great honour and benefit of this our native Country, and the Princes thereof from time to time. For thereby we have not only opened a passage and entry into foreign States and Countries, but also by our gainful and beneficial trade, have made them the faster friends to the State of the Realm of England, and the English Nation, besides the great wealth and commodity which hath arisen thereby to the Commonwealth.

COMPANY OF M. M. ADVENTURERS AT BRUGES

After the taking of *Calais* by King *Edward* the Third, the Earls and people of Flanders, for the better assurance and

[1] Natives.

[2] Wheeler mentioned 1248 as the year in which the Company (in its earlier form) received privileges in Brabrant. His mention of 1296 here suggests that even in his time the charter of 1296 was the earliest extant.

safety of their State, procured a league and Intercourse with the Kings of England and their merchants, whereby the said Earls and people found in short time such profit and commodity that *Lewis*[3], Earl of Flanders, in the year 1358 gave and granted to the English merchants so large and ample privileges and freedoms, that no Nation in Europe had the like in that Country at that time. By reason whereof, and that the adventure by sea and by land into Flanders was very short and easy, and almost without danger, the Company settled themselves in the Town of *Bruges* and stapled their commodities there. Which once known and blown[4] abroad, Merchants out of all parts of Europe, resorted thither, and made their habitation there, which appeareth by the houses at this day standing, which bear the names of the Cities and Countries whence the said Strangers were. So that in few years all the Towns in Flanders, especially *Bruges*, were grown to such wealth and prosperity, that the fame thereof went almost thorough[5] the whole earth, and at this day, although their great opulency, and concourse of Merchants be altogether failed, yet in many countries of Christendom, and out of Christendom, all the Netherlanders carry the name of Flemings, and the Low Countries of Flanders.[6]

COMPANY OF M. M. ADVENTURERS LEAVE BRUGES AND REPAIR TO MIDDELBURGH

After this, when the Flemings, through wealth and fullness of bread, did forget their bounden duty to their Prince, and withal grew to a proud disdain and contempt of all merchants strangers, and in particular of the English, by whom they had received their chiefest good and welfare, the Company removed from Bruges to a Town in Zeeland called Middelburgh, where they are now at this present residing, whither

[3] *Lewis* was a common English spelling of *Louis* in Wheeler's time.

[4] Published.

[5] Through. (Elsewhere Wheeler uses *through* for *thorough*.)

[6] Wheeler's implication that the Merchants Adventurers were largely responsible for the prosperity of Bruges is obviously absurd. It was the great market metropolis of the North before the English came there. As early as 1262, it was one of the four great markets of the Hanseatic League. (See Fox Bourne, *Romance of Trade*, p. 106.) Its decline was due primarily to the silting up of the Zwyn river, making it less accessible from the sea.

all other Nations followed them straight.[7] Since which those of Bruges, feeling the smart of their folly, have many times made suit and means to draw the English thither again, and in man's memory, they proffered a great sum of money unto the said merchants, with offer of more ample privileges, and immunities, than ever they had before in Bruges, or anywhere else; yea in a manner they proffered a blank to tie them to what the English thought good, to have the traffic again in their Town, which very fondly,[8] when they had it, they could not keep.

This Town of Middelburgh stood so near the sea, that the ditches and low places round about it, being continually full of salt and filthy ooze, for want of a fresh river or current to cleanse the same, bred such stench and noisome savours, that the English, used to a wholesome and sweet air in their own Country, were troubled with grievous agues and other sore diseases, and for their health's sake, were forced to leave the said Town, about the year of our Lord 1444, at which time *Antwerp*, being but a poor and simple Town[9] standing in *Brabant*, made great suit to the Company to repair thither, which they finally upon offer of very large and beneficial privileges, obtained. In which Town of *Antwerp*, and the Town of *Bergen op Zoom*, likewise in *Brabant*, the Company ever since hath for the most part continued, save that (as aforesaid) in the time of King *Henry* the Seventh, they were upon occasion removed to Calais for a time, till that by the earnest intercession of the Lady *Margaret*, Duchess of *Savoy*, they repaired again into the Low Countries, first to Middelburgh, then afterwards to *Antwerp*, where they were joyfully and honorably received, and entertained by the Magistrate and chiefest citizens of the Town, coming forth in solemn procession to

[7] Wheeler also exaggerated the influence of the English at Middelburg. The other nations did not follow the English there to the extent of making it their chief market. It is probable that its inferiority as a market, rather than its unhealthful situation, was responsible for the removal to Antwerp. In modern times Middelburg, and the Isle of Walcheren as a whole, are regarded as highly salubrious.

[8] Foolishly.

[9] According to Van Meteren's notes, "Antwerp in 1446 was not so poor and simple a town as the author would make it, for by the privileges obtained of the Duke of Brabant in 1315 and Edward II it doth appear that it was a good merchant town, let the privileges be read and judged." He adds further evidence from 1338 and later years.

meet and welcome the said merchants, as by the records of those times[10] sufficiently appeareth.

ESTATE OF ANTWERP AT THE COMPANY'S FIRST COMING THITHER

And here by the way it is not much from our purpose to insert somewhat of the state of *Antwerp*, at the first coming thither of the Company, wherein a man shall see that which almost is incredible. *Philip* surnamed the *Good*, Duke of *Burgundy*, and of *Brabant*, etc., gave privileges to the Company under the name of the English Nation, by which name the said Company ever since hath been most commonly known in the Low Countries, which happened in the year 1446. Which privileges the Town of *Antwerp* confirmed the sixth of August in the abovesaid year, giving to them besides a large house, which is now called the old *Burse*, and afterwards by exchange, another more goodly, spacious, and sumptuous house, called the Court of *Lier*, which the Company enjoyed till the said Town was yielded up to the Duke of *Parma*, in the year 1585.[11] At the abovesaid first Concordate and Conclusion of Privileges with the Town of *Antwerp*, or not long before, there were not in all the Town above four Merchants, and those also no adventurers to the sea; the rest of the inhabitants or townsmen were but mean[12] people, and neither able nor skillful to use the feat or trade of Merchandise, but did let out the best of their houses to Englishmen and other strangers[13] for chambers and pack-houses, contenting themselves with some corner for their profit's sake. But within few years the concourse and resort of foreign Merchants to that Town was so great, that houseroom waxed scant, rents were raised, tolls, excises, and all other duties to the Prince and Town wonderfully in-

[10] "No such records . . . foolish myths" (Van Meteren's marginal comment). However, Bacon's *History of the Reign of Henry VII* also says that the English merchants were received back at Antwerp "with procession and great joy." (Edition of 1790, p. 87.)

[11] Wheeler here mentions 1585 as the close of the residence of the Merchants Adventurers in Antwerp. In this year the Spaniards again sacked the city. The Adventurers, however, were comparatively inactive for several years after the "Spanish Fury" in 1576. Van Meteren in his marginal comments refutes Wheeler's assertion that in 1446 or thereabouts there were not above four merchants in Antwerp.

[12] Humble. [13] Foreigners.

creased, and the *Antwerp*-men themselves, who in few years before were but mean artificers, or lived by husbandry[14] and keeping of cattle (whereof one *Gate* of that City to this day beareth the name*) and had but six ships belonging to their Town, and those for the river only, that never went to sea, began to grow exceeding rich, so that some fell to the trade of merchandise, and others employed their substance in building; then their old rotten houses covered with thatch were pulled down, their waste ground, whereof there was store[15] within the Town, was turned into goodly buildings, and fair streets, and their shipping increased accordingly. Thus prospered not only those of *Antwerp*, but all other towns and places thereabouts, so that in our memory that now live, the said Town was grown to such wealth, strength, and beauty, as never none the like in so short a time. And no marvel, for within the compass of fifty years, an house that was worth but forty Dallers† a year, grew to be worth three hundred Dallers a year, and an house that was let out for sixty Dallers, came afterwards to be let for four hundred Dallers, yea some houses in *Antwerp* were let for 600, some 800 Dallers a year rent.[16] Besides their Havens for ships to come and lade and discharge within the Town; their public stately buildings, and edifices erected partly for ornament, and partly for the ease and accommodating of the merchant, were so costly and sumptuous as he that hath not seen, and marked them well, would not believe it: to say nothing of the fortification of the Town, which is such that the charges thereof would trouble the richest Prince in Europe: but as the Poet *Lucan* said,

Invida Fatorum series summisque negatum stare diu.[17]

[14] Farming. [15] Abundance.

* De Cot Poort.—[Wheeler's side-head note.]

† A Daller is three shillings sterling.—[Wheeler's side-head note.]

[16] Wheeler estimates a dallar as the equivalent of three shillings. It is difficult to translate the money values of the period into modern values. However, a day's wages for a skilled craftsman was about 8 or 9 pence, and professors at Oxford and Cambridge Universities received 40 pounds a year, so that we may figure that a dallar then was the equivalent of about 30 American dollars to-day. A rent of 800 dallars a year probably suggested a more considerable sum than $25,000 would suggest today.

[17] *The envious course of the Fates and the denial of long endurance to what is supreme.* Lucan, *Pharsalia*, I, 70.

So it fareth at this day with *Antwerp*, for it hath within these few years suffered very great change and alteration, and more is like to do, if it long continue shut up, and without trade and traffic under the yoke of the Spaniard, and the fear of an impregnable Castle stuffed with soldiers, a scourge and plague to that and to all free Cities. Thus much by the way of *Antwerp*, the late Pack-house of Europe, and of the state thereof, when the English merchants first repaired unto it, and of the great wealth it grew unto in a very short time, whereof the said English merchants with their gainful and beneficial trade were a great cause and means, which principally made them to be so much regarded and esteemed in the said Town, and by the Princes and Governors thereof from time to time, as well appeareth, among other proofs, by this one recorded by *Sleidan*,* and remembered by some that yet live.

INQUISITION IN ANTWERP LEFT OFF[18] FOR THE M. M. ADVENTURERS' SAKE

The Emperor *Charles* the Fifth would have brought the *Inquisition* into the Town of *Antwerp* in the year 1550, whereabouts there was much ado and great question and neither by the suit of the Town, nor by any intercession or request of their friends, could the said Emperor be diverted from his purpose; at the last it was showed him, that if the *Inquisition* were brought in, he would drive the English merchants out of that City, and out of the whole Low Countries also, the consequence whereof when he had well considered, he changed his mind, and so the City of *Antwerp* was saved from the *Inquisition*[19] which they so much feared, and by no suit, or means

* Sleidanus 22 libro Commentariorum.—[Wheeler's side-head reference.]

18 Withheld.

19 "And to attribute the city's prosperity solely to the Adventurers is a great fault and vain boast for that Antwerp was saved from Inquisition in 1550 by Englishmen as is alleged is frivolous and not so . . . " (Van Meteren's marginal comments.) Sleidan, who is cited by Wheeler, does not give the English the sole credit. He says: "When the Edict was proclaimed, all men generally were excessively startled at it, especially the *German* and *English* Merchants, who in great numbers traded in the Emperor's Towns and Provinces, but chiefly at Antwerp. So that they were of the opinion, that either the Edict must be moderated, or, that they must remove to some other place; nay, many shut up their shops, and thought of

besides were able to put from them. Of such estimation and account were the Merchants Adventurers with that mighty and prudent Emperor, and of such credit and reckoning have they been from time to time at home with eleven Kings and Queens of this Realm of England, and abroad with the Cities of *Bruges* in Flanders, *Antwerp* and *Berghen op den Zoom* in *Brabant*, *Middelburgh* and *Ziericzee* in *Zeeland*, *Amsterdam* and *Dort* in *Holland*, *Utrecht* the chief City of a Province of that name, and with the Dukes, Earls, Lords, and Rulers of the abovesaid Cities and Provinces lying within the Low Countries, ancient friends and confederates with the Crown of England. And in *Germany* with the Towns of *Hamburg* and *Stade*, and the Earls of *Eastfriesland* since the year 1564 till this day, at which time they obtained privileges of the Lady *Anne*, Countess of *Oldenburgh* and her sons *Egdard* and *John*, wherein they call the Company of Merchants Adventurers, *Inclitam illam et celebratam passim Anglicorum Mercatorum Societatem.*[20]

In all which places and Countries the foresaid[21] Company have so demeaned themselves that thereby they have reaped great love, credit, fame, and commendation, and have left behind them a longing for them again in those places where they once resided, or held their Marts, and procured a desire of them in many places where they never were: which appeareth by the honorable Testimony given of the Company by the abovesaid Towns[22] and foreign Princes abroad, and is otherwise well known to those who know any thing of the doings

nothing but flying from the danger. The Common Counsel and private citizens also of Antwerp, who saw what an incredible loss that would prove to them, were in great streights, so that when the Inquisitors came thither, they vigorously opposed them, and making their application to Queen Mary, their Governess, represented to her, how much it concerned not only them, but the whole Country also, that the Edict should not be put in execution. Wherefore, by reason of the many people of various Nations that then resided in Antwerp, the execution of the Proclamation was for that time superseded in the very same City, for which it was chiefly made." (Bohun's Translation, 1689, Book xxii, p. 498.)

[20] *That illustrious and everywhere celebrated society of English Merchants.*

[21] Aforesaid.

[22] Testimonials have been used in propaganda from very early times, as Wheeler shows. The fact that his testimonials are in Latin and mainly from foreign sources makes them more impressive for his purposes. Although this form of evidence was not extensively used in later pamphlets of the 17th century, it was very popular in handbills and other forms of advertising and has continued to be effective (if not approved) up to the present time.

of our neighbours. And lately when through the malicious and injurious working of a few of the *Hanse Towns*, instigated and holpen[23] forward by the King of Spain's ministers, a part of the said Company was put from the Town of *Stade* in the year 1597 and were forced to retire out of the Empire, the Towns of the united Low Countries, eleven or twelve in number, of the best scituate[24] each striving to be preferred, like so many rivals or competitors, offered themselves in most friendly and hearty sort, and invited the said Company to reside with them upon promises of such favour and privilege as ought never to be forgotten: but hereof possibly enough. Let us now look into the estate, policy, and government of the said Company, whereby we shall plainly see the causes and reasons of the love, estimation, and credit which it hath purchased abroad, and so the sooner believe that which hath above been set down and affirmed.

[23] Helped.

[24] Situated.

Of the State *and* Government *of the Company of MERCHANTS ADVENTURERS, and of such benefits as grow to the* Realm *by the maintenance thereof*

THE Company of Merchants Adventurers consisteth of a great number of wealthy, and well experimented[1] merchants, dwelling in divers great Cities, Maritime Towns, and other parts of the Realm, to wit, in *London*, *York*, *Norwich*, *Exeter*, *Ipswich*, *Newcastle*, *Hull*,[2] *etc.* These men of old time linked and bound themselves together in Company, for the exercise of merchandise and sea-fare, trading in Cloth, kersey, and all other, as well English as foreign commodities vendible abroad, by the which they brought unto the places where they traded, much wealth, benefit, and commodity, and for that cause have obtained many very excellent and singular privileges, rights, jurisdictions, exemptions, and immunities, all which those of the aforesaid Fellowship equally enjoy after a well-ordered manner and form, and according to the ordinances, laws, and customs devised and agreed upon by common consent of all the merchants, free of the said Fellowship, dwelling in the above mentioned Towns and places of the Land. The parts and places which they trade unto are the Towns and Ports lying between the Rivers of *Somme* in *France*, and the *Scawe* in the *German* Sea: not into all at once, or at each man's pleasure, but into one or two Towns at the most within the abovesaid bounds, which they commonly call the Mart Town, or Towns: for that there only they stapled the commodities which they brought out of England, and put the same to sale, and bought such foreign commodities as the land wanted, and were brought from far by merchants of divers Nations and Countries flocking thither, as to a fair or market to buy and sell.[3]

[1] Experienced.

[2] This list is far from complete. Possibly it includes only towns with a sufficient number of members to form a local fellowship.

[3] The foregoing passage is perhaps the best brief description of the Company. It has been frequently quoted and cited.

THE COMPANY OF M. ADVENTURERS IS ABLE TO MAKE AND DIVERT A TRADE[4]

And albeit through the troubles and alteration of times, the M. M. Adventurers have been forced to change and leave their old mart Towns and seek new (as hath been partly touched before) yet wheresoever they seated themselves, thither presently repaired other Strangers, leaving likewise the places whence the English merchants were departed, and planting themselves where they resided: so that as long as the Company continued their Mart, or Staple in a place, so long grew and prospered that place; but when they forsook it, the welfare and good estate thereof seemed withal to depart and forsake it, as in old time hath been seen in *Bruges*, and in our time in some others, and no marvel. For diligent inquiry being made in the year 1550 by the commandment of the Emperor *Charles* the Fifth, what benefit or commodity came to his State of the Low Countries by the haunt and commerce of the English merchants, it was found that in the City of *Antwerp* alone, where the Company of M. M. Adventurers was at that time residing, were at least twenty thousand persons fed and maintained for the most part by the trade of the M. M. Adventurers: besides thirty thousand others in other places of the Low Countries likewise maintained and fed partly by the said trade, partly by endraping of Cloth, and working in wool and other commodities brought out of England. In confirmation whereof, I have heard ancient merchants say that at the time when the abovesaid Company was entirely resident at *Antwerp*, a little before the troubles which fell out in the years 63 and 64[5] there were fed, and maintained in the Low Countries sixty thousand souls (and some have said a great many more) by the English trade,[6] and by the wares bought in the Low Countries to be carried into England,

[4] This boast was extremely offensive to opponents of the Company such as Milles.

[5] 1563 and 1564.

[6] Wheeler's successors (and perhaps he himself) may have regretted later that he emphasized so strongly the stimulus that the Merchants Adventurers gave to the industries of the mart-towns. He laid them open to the charge of providing employment to foreigners instead of English workmen, and thus unwittingly helped to pave the way for the adoption of Cockayne's fatal cloth-project.

which no doubt was the cause that the Princes of the Low Countries have been so favourable to the abovesaid Company and so loath to forgo or lose them, as knowing that therewithal they should lose a very fair flower of their garland, yea a sure root and foundation of their wealth.

THE PROFITS ARISING BY THE M. M. ADVENTURERS' TRADE AND RESIDENCE BEYOND THE SEAS

For on the one side, such is the value, profit, and goodness of the English commodities, that all Nations of these parts of Europe, and elsewhere, desire them, and on the other side, the English Merchants buy up and carry into England so great a quantity of foreign wares, that for the sale thereof all strange merchants do and will repair unto them. Now what these English commodities are, and how they be so profitable, may appear by the particulars following:

First, there is shipped out yearly by the abovesaid Company, at least sixty thousand white Cloths, besides coloured cloths of all sorts, kersies short and long, bays,[7] cottons, Northern dozens,[8] and divers other kinds of coarse cloths: the just value of these sixty thousand white Cloths can not well be calculated or set down, but they are not less worth (in mine opinion) than six hundred thousand pounds sterling, or English money.

The coloured cloths of all sorts, bays, kersies, Northern dozens, and other coarse cloths, I reckon to arise to the number of forty thousand cloths, at least, and they be worth one with another four hundred thousand pounds sterling, or English money.

There goeth also out of England, besides these woolen Cloths, into the Low Countries, wool, fel, lead, tin, saffron, coneyskins, leather, tallow, alabaster stones, corn, beer, and divers other things, amounting unto great sums of money. By all which commodities, a number of labouring men are set on work, and gain much money, besides that which the merchant gaineth, which is no small matter. Hereunto add the money

[7] Baize. [8] *Dozen* was also a kind of cloth.

which shippers, and men that live upon the water, get by freight, and portage of the foresaid commodities from place to place, which would amount to a great sum, if the particulars thereof were, or could be exactly gathered. Hereby in short may be seen how great and profitable the Company of M. M. Adventurers' trade hath been and is in the places where they hold their residence,[9] besides the profit raised upon the chambers, sellers,[10] and packhouses, which they must have for four or five hundred merchants,[11] whereby rents are maintained and kept up, and the great expenses otherwise, which the said merchants are at for their diet, apparel, etc., to say nothing of the Prince's, or Generality's profit, and revenues by their tolls, convoys, imposts, excises, and other duties, whereof there can be no certain notice had, but to show the greatness thereof, let this one sign so long ago, serve for all. That *Philip* the *Good*, Duke of *Burgundy*, and first founder of the order of the *Golden Fleece*,* gave the foresaid Fleece for a livery, or badge of the said Order,[12] for that he had his chiefest tolls, revenues, and incomes, by wool, and woollen cloth. Thus you have seen what profit is raised by strangers, upon the English trade, it followeth to show, what the M. M. Adventurers buy for return, of strange Nations, and people frequenting their Mart Towns, and bringing their Country commodities thither.

[9] Van Meteren cites the Netherlanders as saying that the English cloth-workers had destroyed the cloth-working for the territory about Bruges and caused dire want at Ypres and other towns. This fact is well known and it would seem that Wheeler must have been aware of it.

[10] *Sellers* here probably means cellars.

[11] Wheeler indicates elsewhere that the membership of the Merchants Adventurers was between three and four thousand. Here he speaks of accomodations for four or five hundred merchants. This supports the assertion of opponents (also the indication of custom-figures) that only a small proportion of the merchants were active in the cloth trade. Just how the others profited by their membership has not been satisfactorily explained. They may have received compensation for not using the "stints" or quotas to which they were entitled. Some may have confined themselves to the sale of imported commodities. Some may have speculated in foreign exchange. Doubtless all profited from the guild principle that a member was entitled to share in the bargains of his brethren.

* Carion. 5. Libro.—[Wheeler's marginal reference.]

[12] This explanation of the origin of the Order of the Golden Fleece bears all the earmarks of a merchant's legend. Carion, or Peucer (*supra*, page 69) could not have been a reliable source for it. Even if it had some basis in fact, there would have been a vast difference in Philip's attitude toward raw wool and toward woollen cloth.

GERMAN WARES

Of the Dutch and German merchants, they buy Rhenish wine, fustians, copper, steel, hemp, onion-seed, copper and iron wire, latten,[13] kettles, and pans, linen cloth, harness, saltpeter, gunpowder, all things made at *Norenbergh*, and in sum, there is no kind of ware that Germany yieldeth, but generally the M. M. Adventurers buy as much, or more thereof, than any other Nation.

ITALIAN WARES

Of the Italians, they buy all kind of silk wares, velvets, wrought and unwrought, taffetas, satins, damasks, sarsenets, Milan fustians, cloth of gold and silver, grosgrains, chamlets, satin and sewing silk, organzine, orsoy,[14] and all other kind of wares either made or to be had in Italy.

ESTERLING WARES

Of the Esterlings[15] they buy flax, hemp, wax, pitch, tar, wainscot, deal-boards, oars, corn, furs, cables and cable yarn, tallow, ropes, masts for ships, soap-ashes, Estrigd[16] wool, and almost whatsoever is made or groweth in the East Countries.

PORTINGAL WARES

Of the *Portingals*, they buy all kinds of spices and drugs: with the Spanish and French, they had not much to do, by reason that other English merchants have had a great trade into France and Spain, and so serve England directly from thence with the commodities of those Countries.

NETHERLANDISH WARES

Of the Low Country merchants, or Netherlanders, they buy all kind of manufacture, or handwork not made in England,

[13] Thin sheets of brass or other alloy.

[14] Evidently a rare material. I have not been able to identify it. Organzine was a kind of silk thread; possibly orsoy was also. It may have derived its name from the town of Orsoy.

[15] Here a distinction is made between the Easterlings and the Germans. Elsewhere Wheeler mentions the fact that all the Hanseatic merchants were sometimes called Easterlings, and he himself occasionally uses the word in this more comprehensive sense. Properly speaking, the Easterlings were the people of the Eastland, along the Baltic, with Danzig as their most important port.

[16] Estriche (Eastland) wool.

tapestry, buckrams, white thread, inkle,[17] linen cloth of all sorts, cambrics, lawns, mather,[18] and an infinite number of other things, too long to rehearse in particular, but hereby I hope it sufficiently appeareth, that it is of an exceeding value, which the M. M. Adventurers buy, and carry into England, insomuch that I have heard it credibly reported that all the commodities that come out of all other Countries, besides England, were not wont to set so many people on work in the Low Countries, as the commodities which came out of England only did, neither that any other two of the greatest Nations that frequented the said Low Countries for trade, did buy or carry out so much goods in value as the Merchants Adventurers. The knowledge and consideration whereof hath made them thought worthy to be made of,[19] cherished, and desired by Princes, States, and Commonwealths, and it would not hurt the state of the Empire a whit, to hold friendship, and entertain so profitable a Company and trade as this, whereby great multitudes of their poor people might be set on work, and get their living, and in process of time grow rich thereby, as the men of *Antwerp* and others of the Low Countries have done, which by the practices of the Pope and King of Spain and the unreasonable dealing of the *Hanses*, is in a manner kept from them.

The root and spring of all this almost incredible trade and traffic hath had its increase and proceeding from the politic Government, Laws, and Orders devised and observed of old time in the said Company, as aforesaid: especially since the reign of King *Henry* the Seventh, by the special order, commandment, and encouragement of the said Noble Prince, one day still being a schoolmaster unto the other, and men by experience, use, and knowledge of foreign people and their fashions,[20] orders, and kind of dealing, growing daily and from time to time to an exacter course and greater perfection of matters, and understanding of their own estate, and what is fittest for the upholding and maintenance thereof. These said ordinances contain in them all kind of good discipline, instruc-

[17] Linen tape or thread. [18] Madder. [19] Made much of; encouraged.
[20] Customs.

tion, and rules to bring up youth in and to keep them in order; so that the Merchants Adventurers dwelling in the above mentioned Cities and Towns of the Realm of England, send their young men, sons, and servants, or apprentices, who for the most part are gentlemen's sons,[21] or men's children of good means or quality, to the Mart Towns beyond the Seas, there to learn good fashions,[22] and to gain experience and knowledge in trade, and the manners of strange Nations, thereby the better to know the world betimes, and to be able to go through with the same, to the honour and service of their Prince and Country and their own welfare and advancement in the Commonwealth, whereof a very great number have showed themselves, and at this day many are, very notable and beneficial members. Besides, the said Company hath a Governor, or in his absence a Deputy,[23] and four and twenty Assistants in the Mart Town, who have jurisdiction and full authority as well from her Majesty, as from the Princes, States, and Rulers of the Low Countries, and beyond the seas, without appeal, provocation, or declination, to end and determine all Civil causes, questions, and controversies arising between or among the brethren, members, and supposts[24] of the said Company, or between them and others, either English or Strangers, who either may or will prorogate the jurisdiction of the said Company, and their Court, or are subject to the same by the privileges and charters thereunto granted.[25]

By the said Governor and Assistants are also appointed and chosen a Deputy, and certain discreet persons to be Associates to the said Deputy in all other places convenient, as well

[21] How large a proportion of the Merchants Adventurers were of gentle birth is difficult to estimate. The Sandys Committee in 1604 urged as one reason for freedom of trade that it would provide occupation for younger sons, but the suggestion may have been slightly ironical.

[22] Methods.

[23] Apparently it was unnecessary for the Governor of the Company to have continuous residence in the chief mart-town. A deputy might take his place there. Other deputies were assigned to the lesser mart-towns.

[24] Supporters.

[25] The right of holding courts and deciding cases affecting members was a great bulwark for the power of the Merchants Adventurers. The loss of it in Germany, by reason of the official exclusion of their Company from this territory, was seriously worrying them at this time (1601), as is shown by the alternative forms of discipline that they were compelled to adopt. (See *supra*, p. 52.)

within as without the Realm of England, who all hold correspondence with the Governor of the Company and chief Court in the Mart Town on the other side the Seas, and have subaltern[26] power to exercise Merchants' law, to rule, and look to the good ordering of the brethren of the Company everywhere as far as may be, and their charters will bear them out.

BENEFITS AND COMMODITIES ARISING BY THE COMPANY OF MERCHANTS ADVENTURERS

Further, the said Company entertaineth godly and learned Preachers with liberal stipends and other benefits; hath also Treasurers, Secretaries, and other needful Officers, the end of all which is: *The seemly and orderly Government and rule of all the members, parts, and brethren of the said Company wheresoever in their trade and feat of Merchandise. Secondly, the Preservation of Amity, and the Intercourse between the Realm of England and their Neighbours and Allies, and the Preventing of Innovations, griefs, wrongs, and exactions contrary to the same. Thirdly, the great Vent, Advancement, and keeping in Estimation of English Commodities, and the bringing in of foreign Commodities good cheap. Fourthly, the Maintenance of the Navigation. Fifthly, the Increase of the Queen's Incomes and Customs. Sixthly, and lastly, the Honor and Service of the Prince and of our State and Country, at home and abroad.*[27]

Now that all these benefits and commodities arise by the Company of Merchants Adventurers, I hope by and by plainly to show, and withal to prove that by the said Company, all the above-written points are better performed and brought to pass, than if all were set at liberty, as some have desired, and consequently that without the said Company, few or none of the foresaid benefits or commodities will be so well raised or redound to the State and Commonwealth.

[26] Subordinate.

[27] This summary is an early illustration of what is sometimes known as "the service viewpoint"; that is, dealing with a commodity or institution in such a way as to show its benefits to the readers.

Of Rule *and* Government, *the first point and commodity arising by the united Company of MERCHANTS ADVENTURERS*

I SHALL not need to say much in commendation of good Government and Policy, as having before touched the same in part, and showed how needful and requisite it is also in matter of commerce, trade, and the feat of Merchandise. Now that the Company of Merchants Adventurers hath for this point been anciently famous and highly praised and esteemed of Strangers, as well as of those of their own Country, and so continueth to this day (although much disturbed and disquieted by new Tulles and Dimocks) I think no man doubteth; so that I take it as granted that the State and Commonwealth hereby reapeth more profit than if men were suffered to run a loose and irregular course without order, command, or oversight of any: whereby many griefs, hurts, dissensions, and inconveniences, besides no small dishonour to the Prince and State would in short time arise, as heretofore they have done for want of sage and discreet Government, of which remedy seeing the foresaid Company is sufficiently provided, and that it hath been by the experience of so many Ages, and the allowance of eleven Princes of the Realm approved, methinks, it were an offence and wrong unto the State offered to go about to alter or hinder the same: *atque ita Cornicum oculos configere.*[1]

[1] *And thus to transfix the eyes of crows.* This is a proverbial expression used by Cicero (Cicero, *pro Murena*, 11) and by others. "Catch a weasel asleep" and "deceive the most wary" are commonly accepted English equivalents. Wheeler may be using the phrase in some such sense as "blind the most watchful," but from the context it seems more likely that he is influenced by its use in Cicero and has the highly figurative meaning, "to deprive the most expert of their means of subsistence." It is possible that this Latin phrase (picking crows' eyes) was commonly used by the guilds in referring to outsiders who tried to interfere with the monopoly of the qualified craftsmen.

That the Amity *and* Intercourse *between the* Realm *of* England *and their Neighbors and Allies are cherished, and all innovations, griefs, wrongs, and exactions contrary to the same are prevented, by the maintenance of the Company of the MERCHANTS ADVENTURERS*

THERE hath been of old time, very straight alliance and amity between the Kings of *England* and the Princes of the Low Countries, especially since the government of the said Countries came to the hands of the Dukes of *Burgundy*, and among the said Dukes, between King *Henry* the Fifth, and *Philip*, surnamed the *Good*, Father to *Charles* surnamed the *Warrior*, which *Charles* was slain before the Town of Nantes. This Duke *Philip* had almost from a child been brought up in the Court of England,[1] so that between the said King and him, and their subjects, was a very firm league, friendship, and intercourse, the causes whereof, and of the former amity, and league between the Kings of England from King *Edward* the Third, and the said Princes of the Low Countries, are reckoned to be three principally. First the aid of the said Kings in the pursuit of their just title to the Crown of France. Secondly, The safer keeping of *Calais* and the territory thereabouts in the possession of the said Kings. And thirdly, the nearness of *Flanders*, *Brabant*, *Holland* and *Zeeland* unto the Realm, and the commodious situation thereof for the vent of English commodities, in which Provinces the English merchants were at the time settled. This neighbourly league grounded upon the abovesaid causes hath constantly continued ever since, but more nearly was confirmed between King *Henry* the Fifth, and the abovesaid Duke of *Burgundy*, who lived in the year of our Lord 1420, so that

[1] Van Meteren notes that this Duke Philip was never in England. He comments that the Court of England was inferior in those days and that the Duke's antiquity was as great as that of the Kings of England.

since that time it hath never been broken, but at the death or change of any Prince, on each part hath been renewed, confirmed, and sometimes augmented, and namely between King *Henry* the Seventh, and King *Philip*, son to the Emperor *Maximilian*, and father to *Charles* the Fifth, Emperor, and for the maintenance and cherishing of the said league and intercourse.

AIDS GIVEN BY THE KINGS OF ENGLAND TO THE HOUSE OF BURGUNDY

It is well known to those which are conversant in history of things past, that since the winning of *Calais*, by King *Edward* the Third, in the year 1347, the Kings of England have with great Armies by land, and fleets of ships by sea, invaded the Realm of France, in the quarrel and for the aid of the house of *Burgundy*, as well as for their own particular claims and right, and especially King *Henry* the Fifth, as appeareth by divers writers of those times and since.

But to let pass so old matters, and only to rehearse somewhat of that which hath been done in the memory of men yet living, or not long before, I will in brief recount some special proofs of that abovesaid, giving this note by the way, that as the Kings of England and the Dukes of *Burgundy* were joined in league and friendship, so were the French and Scots, that whensoever England had war with France, Scotland had the like with England, so that the Kings of England have had always double wars with the French and Scots together, and have been forced from time to time to keep two armies, sometimes three at once in the field.

In the year 1492, King *Henry* the Seventh, in favour and aid of *Maximilian*, Archduke of *Austrich*, and son to the Emperor *Frederick* the Fourth, who had married the Lady *Marie*, daughter and sole heir to *Charles* the Warrior, slain before Nantes, as aforesaid, and against whom almost all the Towns in Flanders rebelled and took arms, and with the aid of the French, besieged the Town of *Dixmude*, the said King sent over the Lord *Dawbenye*,[2] and the Lord *Morley*, with an army

[2] Daubigny.

upon his own charges into *Flanders*, who raised the foresaid siege, and slew eight thousand Frenchmen and Flemings in the place, taking all their provision and ordnance. And in the year following, when *Nieuport*, a town lying upon the sea-coast of Flanders, was besieged by Monsieur de *Cordes*, a Frenchman, with twenty thousand French and Flemings, and that one of the principallest towers or bulwarks of the said Town was entered, and held by the enemy, yet by the valiant resistance of such Englishmen as were within it, and fresh supply sent by the foresaid King, the foresaid *Cordes* was forced to leave the said Town with shame and loss of many of his men and much provision. In the same year also, the said King *Henry* the Seventh sent an army by sea under the conduct of the Lord *Pominges*, to the aid of the said Archduke *Maximilian*, against the Lord of *Ravenstein*, General of the rebellious Flemings, who had taken the castle and Town of *Sluys* (the only haven and port to the seas of that old and famous Town of *Bruges*) but the Lord *Pominges* recovered the said castle by force,[3] and delivered it to *Albert*, Duke of *Saxony*, general for the foresaid Archduke. By the saving of which castle, and the abovesaid Town of *Nieuport*, the whole Earldom of Flanders was saved out of the hands of the French King, who otherwise, without the aid of King *Henry* of England, had joined the same to the Crown of France. In the year following, the said King *Henry*, in revenge of the great scorn and injury done to the abovesaid Archduke by the French King, partly in returning home the Lady *Margaret*, daughter to the said Archduke, who was affianced, and after the manner of great Princes, by Deputies married to the said French King, and partly by getting in crafty sort the Lady *Anne*, the only heir of the Duchy of *Brittany* from the said Archduke, to whom she was married, entered France with a great army, where the said Archduke promised to meet him with another army on his part. And although the said promise was not kept, yet the said King proceeded on his purpose, besieged *Bullen*,[4] and finally constrained the French King to

[3] Van Meteren declares that this account is incorrect and hints that Wheeler is altogether ignorant of history.

[4] *Bullen* was a common Elizabethan spelling of *Boulogne*, and also of *Boleyn*.

seek peace of him, and to give him a great sum of money, with the which (and great spoil got by his people) he returned into England, to his high honour and praise, without once seeing or having any help at all of the said *Maximilian.*

In the year 1512, at which time the French King made wars with *Ferdinand*, King of Spain, and invaded his Countries by land, King *Henry* the Eighth (of famous memory) sent an aid of ten thousand men by sea into Spain, under the leading of the noble Lord, the Lord *Thomas Grey*, Marquis *Dorset*, at the request of the above-mentioned *Maximilian*, then Emperor, whose only son and heir, *Philip*, had married *Joan*, the daughter and heir of the abovesaid *Ferdinand*. Two years after this, the said King *Henry* in favour and defence of the young Prince or Infant of Spain, *Charles*, grandchild to the abovesaid *Maximilian*, and afterwards Emperor himself, went over in person with a mighty army into France, and besieged the strong Town of *Terwin*[5] which finally was yielded unto him, maugre[6] the whole power of France, after he had discomfited and overthrown in battle the French army, slaying eight or ten thousand in the place, and taking prisoners the Duke *de Longueville*, the Marquise *Retelois* and besides 240 Lords, Knights, and Gentlemen of name and honour. In which battle the abovesaid Emperor with at least forty or fifty of the Nobility of the Low Countries, served under the King's Standard, receiving wages of him, and wearing the red cross, or cognizance[7] of England. After the rendering over of *Terwin*, the said King brought his army before the City of *Tournay* or *Dornick*,[8] at that time termed the Maiden City, (for that it never had been won by Prince) but King *Henry* got it, and having taken order for the sure keeping thereof, returned the way that he came, being a long march of 63 miles, with great glory and honour into England. And in the meanwhile the Duke of *Norfolk*, and his son the Earl of *Surrey*, had discomfited an army of fifty thousand Scots,[9] under the leading of their King *James* the Fourth, who was slain in

[5] Therouanne. [6] Despite.

[7] Badge or emblem worn by a knight and his followers.

[8] Doornik (the Belgian name of Tournai).

[9] The battle of Flodden Field.

the field with fourteen thousand of his people, whereof many were of the Nobility, besides 12 Earls, 20 Lords, 40 or 50 Knights, and many Gentlemen, taken prisoners.

In the year 1514 the said King *Henry* the Eighth did send a band of 1500 choice soldiers, under the leading of the Lord *Clinton*, unto the aid of the Lady *Margaret*, Regent of the Low Countries, against the Duke of Gelderland.

In the year 1530 a perpetual peace was agreed upon and sworn at *Paris* in France, betwixt the Emperor *Charles* the Fifth, the King of England, and the French King, during their three lives: and which of the three should first violate, or break this peace, the other two were bound to set upon him, as their open and joint enemy. This peace was first broken on the French King's part, by reason of a quarrel between the Emperor and the said King, whereupon the King of England, for his oath and promise sake, sent over into France a great army under the leading of the Duke of *Suffolk*, and prepared a great fleet of ships by sea, to annoy the said Country, and by this means drew the Scots against him. For the Duke of *Albany* in aid of the French, entered England, and began to spoil the borders thereof, against whom the Earl of *Surrey* was sent, who forced the Scots to retire, to their loss and dishonour, and entered Scotland at their heels, burning and spoiling the Country afore[10] him, and returning with great prey, and booty.

In the year 1543, the said King *Henry* the Eighth sent over Sir *John Wallop*, and other Gentlemen with a band of six thousand men to the aid of the foresaid Emperor *Charles*, when he went to *Landersey*. And in the year 1545, the said King in person with two Armies went over into France, in aid of the said Emperor *Charles*, at which time he besieged and took *Bullen*: but how ill the said Emperor kept promise with the said King, and afterwards without his knowledge or privity[11] made peace with the French King, I shall not need to say much, as being partly fresh in man's memory, and partly commended[12] to writing by such as lived in those days.[13] *

[10] Before. [11] Private knowledge, (implying concurrence.) [12] Committed.

* Sleidanus Libro Sexto.—[Wheeler's side-head reference.]

In the year 1557, Queen *Mary* in favour of her husband King *Philip*, and by his procurement and means, made wars upon France, sending over an army by sea, under the Lord *Clinton*, High Admiral of England, into *Brittany*, where they landed, spoiled, and burnt a great way into the Country, and another army of ten thousand men by land, under the Earls of *Penbrooke*, *Bedford*, and *Rutland*, by whose help King *Philip* got the strong Town of *St. Quintins*, and had his will of the French King. But the English by these wars, and breaking peace with France for King *Philip's* sake, lost the Town of *Calais*, which the predecessors of the said Queen had kept in spite of all France 210 years before that time. What other privy[14] helps Queen *Mary* gave unto her said husband, few or none can tell, but it is thought he had many an hundred thousand pounds from her that all the world knew not of.[15] These wars have the Kings of England taken in hand, and these aids from time to time have they given to the house of *Burgundy*, besides great and unknown sums of money sent, insomuch, that in the opinion of men of knowledge and experience, it cost the Realm of England threescore times an hundred thousand pounds at least, in the quarrel and defence of the Princes of the said house, within the compass of 76 years after that *Maximilian* married with the Lady *Mary*, daughter to *Charles* the *Warrior*, and heir to the said house: to say nothing of that which happened before, and now of late hath fallen out since the troubles in the Low Countries. In all which the Kings, and Queens of England have showed themselves faithful and friendly Princes, and good neighbours and allies to the said Low Countries, and truly and readily have holpen and stood by the Princes thereof in their greatest need and extremity: whereas we can not read that those of the house of *Burgundy* ever made wars against Scotland or France in help of the Kings of England directly.

[13] Sleiden's account does not seem to imply that the Emperor had been guilty of a breach of faith with the King of England.

[14] Secret.

[15] At this period it was a sore point with Englishmen that Spain had presumably profited from English taxes.

EMBASSAGE TO THE EMPEROR CHARLES THE FIFTH FROM KING EDWARD THE SIXTH

Neither were they, or any of them ever required thereunto but once, and that was in the days of King *Edward* the Sixth, being then but eight or nine years of age, and at such time as he had both war with Scotland and France at once, and besides was troubled with a great rebellion of his subjects at home. For which cause a solemn Embassage was sent to the Emperor *Charles* the Fifth, who laid before the said Emperor the feeble estate of the said King *Edward's* infancy and tender years, and the commotion of his subjects, even upon the neck of the wars and troubles with France and Scotland, putting the said Emperor in mind of the great armies, which at sundry times had been sent out of England in aid of his father and grandfather, and also of the dangerous and chargeable[16] wars begun, and taken in hand by King *Henry* the Eighth, the said King's father, for the quarrel of the said Emperor alone, as then but an infant also, and under years. They did not let[17] further to tell him of the great pains and travel[18] taken by the said King *Henry*, with his friends the Princes Electors and others of Germany, at the request of the said Emperor, to prefer him to the Imperial Crown and Dignity, which he now possessed and perhaps might else have missed. Lastly, they prayed the said Emperor to remember the ancient and faithfully continued amity between the Emperor and his Predecessors, Dukes of Burgundy, and the Predecessors of the said King *Edward*, and that the wars, which he now had with Scotland and France, was for none other cause moved, than in maintenance of the said amity, and in defence of the quarrel of the house of *Burgundy*, and at the request of the Princes thereof only. But, as the said Emperor had dealt before with Duke *Frederick* of *Saxony*, by whose means especially he attained to the Imperial Dignity, so he did the like with King *Edward*, for clean forgetting all old and new friendships, he gave the Ambassadors uncourteous words for

[16] Costly. [17] Hesitate.

[18] Travail; labor. Here, as elsewhere in the *Treatise*, it may connote an expenditure of money.

the alteration of the Religion by their King, and would do nothing except the same were changed again to the old. Whereupon they besought the said Emperor that he would at least be pleased to take into his hands and keeping the Town of *Bullen*, not long before got from France by King *Henry* the Eighth and that but for a time, till the said King *Edward* had quieted the troubles with his subjects at home. But this he would not yield unto neither, except the King would change his religion; which the King and his Council (having the fear of God before their eyes) utterly refused, choosing rather to lose earthly things, than heavenly. And therefore, seeing the Emperor would neither give aid himself, nor suffer any munition or soldiers to go out of his land into England, no not so much as an armour (as I have heard) that one of the Ambassadors had bought for himself at *Brussels*, a peace in the year 1549 was concluded with France and Scotland, with the restoring of *Bullen*, and upon other conditions according to the time. This peace fell out but little to the profit of the Emperor, for in the year 1551 began the great wars between him and *Henry* the French King, wherein the *Burgundians* felt the want of their old trusty friends, and allies, the King of England and his people.

And undoubtedly, if the Kings of England had not continually aided and assisted the house of *Burgundy*, and the Low Countries, they had both been French before this day, or if the French King might have been sure of England, and without fear thereof bent his whole forces by sea and by land against the house of *Burgundy* and *Spain*, neither should the Emperor have got so much advantage as he did against the French King, neither have been able to have troubled Germany, and the German Princes, nor other Princes, States, and Countries, as he did, neither should he have gotten so much possession and dominion in *Italy* and other places, as he got, neither lastly should his subjects have obtained so great wealth and riches, nor so much knowledge by land and by sea, as they have done. For surely, he and his people may thank the Kings of England for all these things: for the aid of the said Kings, and the traffic and resort of the English merchants have been the principal causes thereof, and therefore great reason had the Dukes of *Burgundy* to seek the friendship and amity of the Kings of England, and to cherish and augment the same by treaties and intercourse from time to time, which are yet continued in force. And whereof the foresaid Company of M. M. Adventurers have so good notice, record, and understanding, that upon any occasion whatsoever, they have them ready, thereby to defend the Right of the Realm and subjects thereof, against such as would either willfully or unawares break and violate the same, which ought to remain as sacred and untouched, for the preservation of mutual friendship and amity between both Nations, which oftentimes for want of due care and provision on this behalf in time, might turn into open enmity and alienation of good will, not without danger of war in the end, if some men might have their wills.

DON GIRALDO DESPES

As in the year 1564, *Don Giraldo Despes* Ambassador for the King of Spain in England, at the instance of the Cardinal *Granvelle*, dealt with a stranger,[19] yet living in England and well known there, to draw out a summary of all the doleances[20] of the Low Country merchants, promising redress therein, or tó bring the matter to an open war. Which whether the said stranger did or not, I can not justly say, but it is like enough his busy head considered,[21] and he hath conceived no small discontentment of old, that things go not as he would fain have them in England for his own particular fancy's sake and employment, without regarding the alteration of times, or breach of amity, which might fall out between her Majesty, and the States of the United Low Countries for that cause, so he might come to his purpose. For immediately

[19] At this point in the Van Meteren copy appears the signature "Emanuel Demetrius" in the same handwriting as that on the fly-leaf. Along with it in another hand is an obscure notation which seems to read as follows: "That stranger woulde answeare for him self iff to now rolled letter that the author Idgo Spinola." Possibly this means that the author of the letter of grievances was Spinola and not Van Meteren.

[20] Grievances.

[21] "It is lyke he boasts himself as smart [?] as this author any'd wayds." (Van Meteren's marginal notes.)

upon this followed that violent proceeding of the Duchess of *Parma*, in banishing of English cloth and commodities out of the Low Countries, by means whereof the commerce and trade for a time surceased, not without peril of war between the Princes and their people.

The Company therefore of the M. M. Adventurers are a great obstacle to the raising and bringing in of new and unwonted tolls, imposts, exactions, and grievances, which otherwise the subjects of the Realm of England, their ships and goods, would be charged with and oppressed, contrary to the treaties of amity and intercourses, to the impoverishing of the said subjects, and the hindrance of the navigation: which cometh to pass by means, and help of their common purse, and by officers maintained to keep register of all things needful, and to defend these common causes from time to time, when any innovation or strange exaction is brought in, tending to the hurt and hindrance of the merchants, mariners, and seafaring men, and consequently to the damage and prejudice of the whole state. And this a particular[22] man is not able to do, for either his purse or means will not reach unto it, or else being loath to spend his money and time, or to hinder his affairs and trade hereabouts, will rather yield unto a wrong, whereby it cometh to pass by little and little, that the ancient rights of the Realm are either lessened or infringed, and that which ought not to be suffered, unwonted tallages, taxes, and impositions, are levied upon the subject, to his great grievance and impoverishing, and to the bringing of the trade into strangers' hands only: a thing of long time practiced and laboured for by them, and chiefly prevented and withstood by the Company of M. M. Adventurers, which hath stirred up the Easterlings and some Merchants of *Antwerp* of late days against them.

THE ANTWERPENERS EAT THE MERCHANTS OF OTHER NATIONS OUT OF THEIR TRADE

The Easterlings continue still in their pride of heart and indurate[23] malice. The *Antwerpians*, and their new-born col-

[22] Separate; individual. [23] Deep-rooted.

lege[24] (the troubles growing upon them) were forced to be quiet, though within these three years, their first and last (perhaps) Consul and Secretary[25] have solicited the States General of the United Provinces with their complaints and accusations, to embrace and renew their old quarrels and pretences, and to set up on foot again their decayed Consulate, in recompense of the good services heretofore done, (which I could wish examined for that they vaunt themselves thereof) and for the great benefit that may hereafter redound to the said united lands by the same, as they would have the said States believe. The true purpose and drift whereof is nothing else (as I said) but to eat the Adventurers out of their trade, as they of *Antwerp* heretofore did the Merchants of other Nations, *Portingals*, *Italians*, *Dutches*, or *Germans*, and others, whereby they greatly enriched themselves, their Prince, and Country, which finally turned to the hurt, danger, and disquieting of all other Princes and States, as hath appeared by the doings and practices of the late King *Philip* of Spain and his Confederates. And to show that this which I have said is true, I will by the way more particularly rip up this matter.

First for the *Portingal*, we know that like a good simple man he sailed every year full hungerly (God wot) about three parts of the Earth almost for spices, and when he had brought them home, the great rich purses of the *Antwerpians*, subjects of the King of Spain, engrossed them all into their own hands, yea oftentimes gave money for them beforehand,[26] making thereof of a plain *Monopoly*; whereby they only gained and all other Nations lost. For that the spices, being in few men's hands, were sold at such rate as they listed, to their own private lucre and gain, and to the hurt and damage of all others.

The *Italians*, English, and German merchants, were wont to have a very profitable and good trade into Italy with kersies, and other English and foreign commodities serving that Country, but a little before the troubles of the Low Coun-

[24] Society.

[25] Van Meteren. (The signature "Emanuel Demetrius" is again inserted in the margin of his copy.)

[26] The practice of buying crops or cargoes before they were brought into the market was considered unethical. Forestalling of all kinds was generally prohibited in English markets.

tries, the *Antwerpians* were grown into that trade, and were become the greatest dealers that way, and further, to *Alexandria*, *Cyprus*, *Tripoli* in *Syria*, and other remote places, serving the same more than any other,[27] with linen cloth, worsteds, sayes, tapestry, and other Netherlandish wares, by means whereof the said Italians, English and Germans were forced to leave that trade or to do very little.

The *Dutch* or *German* merchants had the whole trade in their own hands, of all commodities brought to *Antwerp* from other places, that served Germany, buying up all themselves, and carrying them to the Towns, and Marts in their own Country. But in a few years the *Antwerpians* had also wholly got that trade, and the Germans in a manner did nothing, for the other in all Marts and Fairs in Dutchland, bare the chiefest swindge,[28] and served the same with commodities of all Lands and of all sorts, so that look what the German used to get, that they got, eating as it were, the bread out of his mouth.

As for the *Easterlings*, they had begun a Staple of their commodities at *Antwerp*, but in the opinion of wise men, if it had long continued, it would have eaten out clean and consumed their merchants and mariners from the seas as they began not a little to be diminished by those of *Amsterdam*, and other, but new upstart Towns in *Holland*, with their great number of hulks and other ships. Of the Spanish trade and merchants of Spain, because they were King Philip's subjects, there is not much to be said, but yet the *Antwerpians* had means to get a good fleece from them too: for the merchants of *Antwerp* being of great wealth, were able to sell these commodities which best served Spain and the *Indies*, at long days of payment, and by means thereof did set them at such high and dear prices, that when the days of payment came, and the Spaniard lacked his returns to keep credit with, he was forced to run upon the exchange or interest, till his provision came in, by which time his gains was consumed by usury, and

[27] "Doth not the English merchants the like? If they do not . . . [illegible]." (Van Meteren's notes.)

[28] Held the whip-hand. *Swindge* had several meanings, but here seems to be used to mean sway or influence.

many times some of the principal.[29] Besides, they sold the Spaniard their worst wares, and carried the choicest themselves into Spain, whither they traded more than all the Spaniards in the land did.

For the trade of the merchants of France: there hath been often war between that Country and the Dukes of *Burgundy*, as hath been above partly touched, by means whereof, there hath been much colouring of goods[30] between the one Prince's people, and the other, and that so ordinarily and cunningly, that the *Antwerpians* above all the merchants besides, were as privy, expert, and skillful in all the French tricks[31] and indirect trades and conveyances, as the Frenchmen themselves, by reason whereof, in time of peace, the French merchants were much endamaged and hindered: for the *Antwerpians* served *Germany*, *Spain*, *Portingal*, *Eastland*, and their neighbours of the Low Countries, with such things as the Frenchmen themselves used to sell and vent in those places.

Now let us look a while into England, and take a view what the *Antwerpians* and other Netherlanders, principally those of *Antwerp*, have done there, and you shall find that not past 80 years ago, there were not in all *London* about twelve or sixteen Low Country merchants,[32] and amongst them, not past four of any credit or estimation. For the merchandise which they then brought into England most, were stone pots, brushes, puppets[33] and toys for children, bristles for shoemakers, and such other pedlery ware of small value, and sometimes a little fish, and three or four pieces of linen cloth. But in less than the compass of forty years following, there were in *London* at least one hundred Netherlandish mer-

[29] Wheeler alleges that the Antwerpians sold goods to Spain on long credit terms and thus were able to get high prices as well as excessive interest and also to deliver inferior goods. Other writers have pointed out that Spain did not profit greatly by her imports of bullion from America.

[30] Colouring of goods—that is, selling the goods of others as one's own—was an offence commonly alleged against trade rivals. Probably it really was a frequent practice of those who enjoyed special trade-privileges in a market.

[31] Even at this period the English business man considered trickiness a French national characteristic.

[32] Van Meteren declares that this is not so, for in 1485 more than 20 merchants of Antwerp alone were listed among those who complained of English piracy.

[33] Dolls.

chants,[34] the most part whereof were of *Antwerp*, and thither they brought all kind of wares which the merchants of *Italy*, *Germany*, *Spain*, *France*, and *Eastland* (of all which Nations there were before that time divers famous and notable rich merchants and companies) used to bring into England out of their own Countries directly, to the great damage of the said strangers, and of the natural-born English merchants. Which English Merchants and their trade also the said Netherlanders (but especially those of *Antwerp*) as much as in them lay, even then sought and practiced to destroy and overthrow, and since have been many years about it, which in good time was discovered, and by the diligence and travail of the Merchants Adventurers principally, not without their great cost and charge, hath been hitherto withstood and prevented, and so will be still so long as that Company continueth on foot, let the other repine and mutter at it as much as they list, and seek to cross and hinder the Adventurers, wheresoever they can procure audience with their unseasonable remonstrances, spiteful declarations, and harsh complaints, to the raising up, as much as in them lieth, of the like stir[35] and disagreement between her Majesty and the States of the United Netherlands at this time, as happened in the year 1563 under the government of the Duchess of *Parma*, Regent for the late King *Philip* of Spain at that time in the Low Countries. When as through the complaint of the merchants of *Antwerp* principally, and of others of the said Low Countries, against the raising of the Custom of Cloth, and of foreign wares brought into England, and specially against an Act of Parliament made for the setting of her Majesty's people on work, by virtue whereof foreign wares, as pins, knives, hats, girdles, ribbon, and such like, were forbidden to be brought in ready wrought, to the intent that her Highness' subjects might be employed in making thereof, the said Duchess of *Parma* by proclamation forbade the carrying into England of any kind

[34] Wheeler's statements regarding the Netherland merchants may not be grossly inaccurate if limited to the contrast between their position about 1520 and about 1560, but are misleading as an index of their general progress.

[35] Public disturbance; strife.

of matter or thing, wherewith the said wares might be made[36] and banished out of the Low Countries all *Manufacture*, or handiwork, as bayes, etc., made in England, cloth and kersey only excepted, which also she afterwards forbade to be brought in upon pain of confiscation, under show or pretence of infection, (for that the plague had reigned very sore in *London* and other places of the Realm that summer) but in very truth the right cause was, for that she could not have her will in the above-mentioned points, and took that time of mortality, and want of trade in England, to be the readiest and fittest opportunity to attain thereunto. So that finally the M. M. Adventurers, after they had kept their cloths and other goods aboard their ships in the River of *Thames* and *Scheld* five months together, and might not be permitted to land them at *Antwerp*, were at length forced to depart with the same unto the Town of *Embden* in Eastfriesland, where they obtained privileges and contracted for a free commerce with the two young Earls, *Egdard* and *John*, and the Lady *Anne*, Countess of *Oldenburgh*, their Mother, Anno 1564, who neither feared, nor found any contagion in the English and their commodities, and by this means broke the violence of the foresaid Duchess's intention, erecting their trade in the abovesaid Town, and leaving *Antwerp* and the Low Countries.

PROHIBITION OF ALL TRADE WITH THE ENGLISH BY K. PHILIP.

Whereupon King *Philip* and his Ministers, grieving for that they could not have their will of her Majesty and her Highness' subjects, and that they must forgo so profitable a milchcow as the English trade was unto the Low Countries, an Edict or Proclamation was set forth in the month of May of the abovesaid year, that no person in the said Low Countries should have or use any trade with the English at *Embden*, buy any cloth or English woollen commodity of them, or carry them any wares upon pain of confiscation of the same; than the which dealing what could be more injurious or enemy-

[36] In those days also, embargoes on imports and discriminatory tariffs led to retaliatory legislation that hindered the export trade.

like in time of open wars? But herein the said King not only shot at the state of England, but withal he endamaged other Nations, and particularly those of the Empire, as though no Country merchants ought to trade anywhere but in his Countries, and when, and where, and with whom it pleased him, thereby to hold all the whole trade of Merchandise in his Netherlands alone, forbidding upon pain of loss of goods the Imperial merchants, as well as others, from occupying, buying, or selling within the limits of the Empire, as though he had been Emperor himself, and more than Emperor. In which point he touched very near the top and height of the Imperial Crown and Dignity, in that being but Duke of *Burgundy*, and in that respect but a subject of the Empire, he took upon him peremptorily to command, restrain, forbid, and injuriously to break the old and ancient freedoms and liberties of the Empire freely yielded, and so long religiously maintained and kept, as well towards all the subjects as towards all the friends and allies of the same, amongst which friends the English have been continually not the least, or last, as fetching their original out of the said holy Empire. At length when the King of Spain, for all the instigation of his Netherlanders and popish Ministers, saw that he could not prevail, and were at a stand,[37] he and they were glad and fain to come to a provisional agreement, and to accept of such privileges and liberties as the said Netherlanders enjoyed in England in the last year of Queen *Mary's* reign, which was the year of our Lord 1558, and to call in all those foresaid placates,[38] edicts, and prohibitions made against the English and bringing in of English wares.

THE DUKE OF ALVA ARRESTETH THE PERSONS AND GOODS OF THE ENGLISH IN ANTWERP AND ELSEWHERE IN THE LOW COUNTRIES

And although in the year following, and the year 1566, a diet was held at *Bruges*, for the taking up and compounding of all variances, difficulties, grievances, by certain Ambassadors sent from both Princes, yet nothing was concluded. The

[37] At a standstill. [38] Placards; official proclamations.

Customs, about the which the first and most question grew, were for all the Netherlandish merchants wrangling and importunity continued, as having been erected in Queen *Mary's* days (King *Philip* their natural Prince being married to her) and the former agreement made in the year 1564 between the Queen's Counsel and Don *Gusman de Silva*, Ambassador for the abovesaid King, stood, and so remained in force till the year 1568, when as the Duke of *Alva* in the Low Countries, and King Philip throughout Spain caused the persons and goods of the English merchants to be arrested and stayed, upon this occasion. It happened in the abovesaid year 1568, that a great ship of *Biscay*, and four pinnaces which the Spaniards call *Assabres*, were chased by certain men of war belonging to the Prince of *Condé* into the haven of *Plymouth*: in which great ship were the value of two hundred thousand pistolettes, which money the Spanish Ambassador at that time in England, *Don Giraldo Despes*, required to have delivered unto him, as belonging to the King his Master, with consent to convey the same to *Antwerp* unto the Duke of *Alva*, which was granted him. But while he attended order from the said Duke about the safe sending of the said money, her Majesty came to the knowledge that it did not belong to the King of Spain, but unto certain merchants of *Genoa*, and that the Duke of *Alva*, needing money, meant to seize upon the same, and turn it to the King's use. Which the owners fearing, chose rather that it should remain in the Queen's hands: whereupon her Majesty caused all the money to be landed, saying that she would borrow it of the Italians, with their good will and liking, and so preserve it from the French, who threatened to fetch it by force out of the haven where it lay.[39] The Duke as soon as he had knowledge hereof, suddenly commanded all the Merchants Adventurers to be arrested at *Antwerp*, and caused them to be kept safe in the English house, with a company of Dutch soldiers: he commanded also the ships and goods of all the English merchants, as well at *Antwerp* as elsewhere, to be attached and inventa-

[39] This high-handed act of the Queen caused the Merchants Adventurers considerable loss and inconvenience, but Wheeler does not hint the slighest criticism of her.

rised,[40] which he afterwards sold to *Fernando Frias*, a Spaniard, and others, to the use of the King of Spain.[41] When her Majesty understood of this hasty and unadvised dealing of the Duke of *Alva*, she gave leave unto her subjects for their indemnity, to arrest the Netherlanders and their goods in England. By means of these general arrests on both sides, the trade of the M. M. Adventurers ceased at *Antwerp*, but for the sale of the commodity of the land they presently contracted with the Town of *Hamborough*,[42] and there held their marts only for a time.

The Duke of *Alva* on the other side, to hinder the trade, and consequently to hurt the state of England, the last day of March 1569 by straight proclamation forbade all dealing with the English, either in carrying them any wares, or buying of them English commodity to be brought into the Low Countries, appointing for the more severe execution hereof certain spies, or promoters, among the which, as principal, was Doctor *Story*, of whose shameful and well deserved punishment and end, there is yet fresh memory. But these differences and troubles were afterwards in the year 1574 at a diet held at *Bristol* taken up, and agreed, and the Intercourse was renewed and confirmed in such manner, as was concluded at *Bruges* in the year '66 to the high honour and commendation of her Majesty, who meddled not with one penny of the arrests' goods, but gave the same wholly over unto her subjects, in recompense of their losses in the Low Countries, and honorably contented the owners of the money (about the which the question and trouble first rose) for the same: whereas to the contrary the King of Spain never recompensed his

[40] Inventoried.

[41] Such reprisals were not uncommon even after medieval times. Many an innocent merchant had his goods seized for some offence or alleged offence by a fellow-countryman, or by his Sovereign. A graphic picture of this particular seizure is given by T. Churchyard. "In 1569 our English merchants and mariners (amongst whom myself a poor clerk travailing towards Antwerp for my preferment) they some in one place, some in another, I at Flushing (upon Christmas Eve) were taken out of our beds and (our ships and goods by the Kings commandment imbargued) so carried to the Geuarghen huise as they called it." *A True Discourse Historicall of the succeeding governance in the Netherlands . . . etc.* By T. C. [T. Churchyard] and R. R. [R. Robinson]. (Based mainly on Van Meteren's *Historia Belgica* . . . London 1602.)

[42] Hamburg (also spelled Hambrough and Hambourgh).

subjects for their damages, but as is said, converted all the English merchants' goods which he found in the Low Countries or in Spain, to his own use, without having the least consideration of the loss of any man.

By the above-written discourse we may perceive the sleights, practices, and industry of the *Antwerpians* and Netherlanders, to draw the trade of all Nations into their own hands; the proud, unneighbourly, yea enemy-like edicts and proscriptions of the Duchess of *Parma*, upon the unreasonable complaints and demands of her merchants, no doubt egged on by the Cardinal *Granville* in hatred of the Religion professed in England; the rash and unadvised arrests, and detaining of the persons and goods of the M. M. Adventurers and others in the Low Countries and Spain by the King and the Duke of *Alva;* the *Heroic* courage, wisdom, and equity of our gracious Queen in defence and relief of her subjects wronged and spoiled in barbarous sort, contrary to reason, and against the intercourse and treaties sworn and established between both the Nations and the Princes thereof.[43] And lastly, the great care and travail of the M. M. Adventurers in midst of all these troubles, and their exceeding great losses and hindrances to seek and procure a place, first at *Embden*, then at *Hamborough*, for vent of the commodity of the Realm, and maintenance of the trade whereby so many live, the overthrow and destruction whereof hath been the principal mark and purpose of all the above-mentioned complaints, edicts, proscriptions, and arrests, and is now at this day of all the violent machinations and workings of the King of Spain and his Ministers and favourers (to which party the *Hanses* adjoin themselves with might and main) thinking thereby to stir up some notable commotion, trouble, or disorder in the State of England, and so the sooner to bring to pass their long purposed bloody and treacherous practices against the precious life of her Majesty, (whom the Lord long preserve amongst us) and against the true Religion and Church

[43] The chief purpose of all this historical material is to show that the complaints against the Merchants Adventurers, which he discusses later, are complaints against England, originated by her enemies and fostered by Spain in the hope of overthrowing the English Government and the English Church.

of the M. M. Adventurers in particular, but also to the great satisfaction, contentment, and good liking of all the abovesaid foreign States and people, insomuch that some great personages, drawn with the very report of the seemly dealing, carriage, and orders of the Company of M. M. Adventurers, have repaired to the Mart Town, to behold and see the same.

This course derived from common reason, and approved by *Experience*, (the surest Doctor in the school of Man's life) many years together hath been observed and continued in the abovesaid Company as a principal point, and one of the main posts and pillars of the same. For first, it cannot be denied, that to advance anything, and to make it of price and estimation, is to bring it in request: secondly, to bring it in request is to draw a concourse and multitude to desire it: and lastly, the best means to draw a concourse and multitude is to appoint a certain place, whither men may commodiously resort, where also if they may find not only that which they desire and have need of, but withal may vent that which their Country bringeth forth and hath plenty of, it is a double cause and allurement to invite them to such concourse and flocking together.[2]

From this reason is the order and institution of the Mart-Town so long and so seriously practiced and maintained by the M. M. Adventurers, which to be soundly and well grounded, I think no man will gainsay. Next late experience, as well at home as abroad, hath taught us that when another course was liked of by some, and that divers of the Company had disbanded themselves, and held not the foresaid commendable and merchantlike course, but erected unto themselves a private, irregular, and straggling trade, the commodity of the Realm lay unvented, or grew to be embased,[3] and sold at lower prices than before.

[2] The medieval philosophy of marketing was that the only sound way to sell was in stated markets at appointed times. As shown in the Introduction (p. 24), the origin of the market was for entirely different reasons.

[3] Depreciated.

A TREATISE OF COMMERCE

COMPLAINT OF THE WOOL GROWERS AND CLOTHIERS FOR WANT OF TRADE

For when as about fourteen years past, in the 29th year of her Majesty's Reign, the wool-growers, clothiers, weavers, and others living upon cloth-making, wanting their accustomed commodity, gains, and work, made a grievous complaint thereof, it was thought to be the only expedient to remedy this sore, to give liberty to all her Highness' subjects and others, to buy and transport cloth according to the limitation of the laws, any grants or privileges by her Majesty's prerogative heretofore to the M. M. Adventurers granted notwithstanding. Yet we saw that the malady was never a whit the better, but rather grew worse and worse, insomuch that the poor people in *Wiltshire* and *Gloucestershire* living wholly upon cloth making, in great numbers were ready to grow into a mutiny for this cause, to the singular rejoicing of the enemies of her Majesty, and in particular of the *Hanses*, who desire nothing more than the overthrow of the M. M. Adventurers and their trade; thereby finally intending to disturb the peace of the whole Realm.[4] At length when all men expected nothing else but an abolishment and dissolving of the abovesaid Company, as the sole and only cause of all this grief, the setting up of the Steelyard again, and the equalling of all the subjects and others in the Realm in transporting and carrying out of cloth, none of all these things fell out, but to the contrary, those of the said Company were sent for, and after they had been heard and had made known the true cause of the abovesaid sore indeed, they were willed to proceed in their trade, with promise of assistance and countenance from my Lords and others of the Council. Which assuredly their Honors would not have done, if that they had seen that the late innovation or liberty had brought forth, or was likely to bring forth the promised effect, or that without the said Company of M. M. Adventurers so great a quantity

[4] Wheeler's account of the brief experiment with liberty of trade in 1587 is truthful so far as it goes. The experiment was tried, however, in a period of depression when it had least chance of success. Unwin believed that the remedy was the right one but was tried too late. See Unwin, *Studies in Economic History*, p. 202.

of the woollen commodities of the Realm could be vented as in former times, when the said M. M. Adventurers were maintained and backed in their full privileges and rights.

The Merchants Adventurers were at this time encumbered with no small difficulties, for that neither of their Mart-Towns (*Embden* and *Middelburgh*) were very safe or fit for the utterance of their commodities, neither knew they where to find a place convenient for that purpose. For at *Middelburgh*, partly through the continual loans of great sums of money, upon the neck one of another required at their hands, without warrant or authority from her Majesty, and partly through the fear of danger they were put in by the Earl of *Leicester*, then Governor of the United Provinces, the trade was in a manner wholly damped, and divers of the principallest of the Company in that place, almost in flying manner, withdrew themselves and their goods into Holland. At *Embden* on the other side, things were in no very good terms, by reason of the Duke of *Parma's* prevailing in the Provinces next adjoining, and that the States sent their men-of-war into the River of *Embs*, whereby the trade by land grew exceeding perilous, and by water troublesome and chargeable. Some also to mend the matter, sticked not to put into men's minds a suspicion of the Count *Egdard* of *Eastfriesland*, as a secret pensioner and favourer of the King of Spain, and sure it is that his chief Officer *Ocko Freez*, then Drossart of *Embden*, showed himself by many signs and actions, very much inclined to the Spanish part. The *Hanses* also in the year 1582 at an Assembly of the Empire at *Ausburgh*,[5] by favour and assistance of the Spanish ministers and of the Princes and Prelates of the Romish Religion (the most part whereof were at the devotion of the house of *Austrich*[6]) had upon their complaints and injurious informations obtained a Decree for the expelling of the trade and residence of the M. M. Adventurers out of the Empire,[7] and otherwise by new occasions of losses sustained at sea by English men-of-war (though nothing were done to them contrary to the law of Nations) were

[5] Augsburg. [6] Austria.
[7] The Holy Roman Empire, at this time a somewhat loosely federated group of states.

sore incensed, not only against the said M. M. Adventurers, but also against the whole English name, so that there was little or no hope or likelihood to find any friendship or good entertainment at their hands.

COMMISSIONERS SENT TO TREAT WITH THE HAMBURGERS OF NEW PRIVILEGES

The Company all these difficulties notwithstanding, taking new courage, and moved in duty towards her Majesty and their Native Country, in the year 1587 sent their Commissioners Sir *Richard Saltonstall*, Knight, at that time their Governor, and Doctor *Giles Fletcher*, a Civilian, unto *Hamborough* with four ships laden with cloth, to try the minds of that people, and whether they could procure a residence in that Town again (whither they were invited by letters of the 19 of August, 1586, from the Senate). The *Hamburgers* notwithstanding their said letters, by the instigation of the Duke of *Parma*, who at this time was wholly intentive[8] in a manner to the matters of England, and had inkling of a commotion doubted[9] among the commons there, for want of work (the appeasing or increase whereof much depended upon the M. M. Adventurers' trade, and therefore sought by all means to disturb it) held themselves very nice and coy, and having daily in their counsel Doctor *Westendorp* of *Groeninghe*, sent thither by *Verdugo*, Governor of *Westfriesland* for the King of Spain, delayed and dallied with the foresaid Commissioners. So that after much labour spent, nothing in the end was concluded; for the *Hamburgers* being certified by the abovesaid Doctor *Westendorp* of the great preparation in hand, and the invasion intended by the King of Spain against England,[10] of the happy success whereof he promised and presumed much, and of the which the *Hamburgers* (it should seem) conceived no small hope, upon every day's news either confirmed or recalled that which beforehand with much ado had been passed and agreed upon between them and the M. M. Adventurers' Commissioners, excusing this their light dealing sometime by the unwillingness of their Commons, (whose

[8] Attentive. [9] Feared, suspected. [10] The threatened invasion by the Armada.

consents as they said they could not obtain) otherwhiles by want of authority from the rest of the Hanses, without whose privity and liking they might not conclude any such thing, and yet they had written the contrary in the abovesaid letter, in these words: *Neque tamen ad has nostras privatas Consultationes reliquarum Civitatum Confœderatarum consensum requirendum arbitramur.*[11]

SITUATION OF THE TOWN OF STADE

So that in fine[12] the Commissioners being wearied with these delays, and finding that at *Stade*, a town not far distant from *Hamburgh*, the trade might be well seated, thither they repaired, and procured a residence and privileges there in the month of September 1587.

This Town of *Stade* is an ancient free town of the Empire, in the territory of the Archbishop of *Bremen*, who as Protector of the Town hath a Toll[13] there, but no other command. It is situate from the river of *Elbe* about two English miles, out of the which is a creek called the *Swinge*, which ebbeth and floweth up to the Town, and is able to carry a ship of fourscore or an hundred tons, and maketh a safe and quiet harbour for ships in all weathers. The Town standeth upon the mainland of *Germany*, on the hither side of the Elbe, a day's journey from *Bremen*, three day's journey from *Embden*, as many from *Cassell* in *Hessen-land*, two day's journey from *Lunenburgh*, and from *Hamburgh* six hours: very near, and convenient for *Westfalia*, *Friesland* and the parts thereabouts: in the winter season and always far better and commodiouser than *Hamburgh* for transporting and sending of goods to and fro the abovesaid towns, and parts of Dutchland.

PRIVILEGES OBTAINED AT STADE

In this Town therefore lying so commodious and fit for trade, though old and unfrequented, the Company at their own great costs and charges, by their abovesaid Commis-

[11] *Nor do we consider that the consent of the Confederated Cities is required for these private negotiations of ours.*
[12] In the end. [13] The right to certain taxes.

sioners, obtained privileges with the allowance and good liking of the Archbishop and Chapter of *Bremen:* and there they found great and quick utterance of their commodities at good rates and prices, merchants resorting thither from all parts, for in the whole Town of *Stade* was not one merchant before the Company of M. M. Adventurers coming thither, but they lived generally all the inhabitants thereof upon tillage, feeding of cattle, swine, and other husbandry. The Town also with the houses and buildings thereof was almost utterly decayed and grown ruinous, but in the ten years that the Company resided in that Town, there was a strange alteration, so that it grew indeed to be another Town in regard of that it was before,[14] and as the estate of *Stade* mended daily, so the trade increased, till the publication of the Emperor's *Mandate* in the year 1597. The end of which *Mandate* a blind man may see to be none other than through the sides of the M. M. Adventurers to hurt and wound the State of England, that is, by the subversion[15] of that Company to stop the vent of English cloth, by the which so many thousands are fed and sustained in the land, and must want if the trade fail, to repossess the *Hanses* with their old antiquated and obsolete privileges, no way sufferable by the Prince or State, and to gratify the capital enemies[16] of this Realm. And therefore I could wish all the well-willers and lovers of the Commonwealth and State of England and all the good subjects of her Majesty, that through envy or misconceit they seek not or procure the decay or hindrance of the abovesaid Company, lest unawares they join hands with the common enemy, who seeketh not only the subversion of the said Company, but also of this whole Realm, from the which the Lord in mercy preserve us.

By that which hath been above set down, I doubt not but it already in part appeareth how true it is by late experience at home that the commodity of the Realm can neither so well

[14] Compare this passage with that describing the effect of the Merchants Adventurers upon Antwerp, pp. 328 ff.. Wheeler had seen the transformation at Stade, and possibly on this account was led to believe that a similar transformation had occurred at Antwerp nearly a century and a half earlier.

[15] Overthrow. [16] The Spaniards.

nor in so great quantity be vented by any other course as by maintaining the M. M. Adventurers in their trade and privileges: for further proof whereof, and that foreign wares are by this means brought into the land at the more reasonable rates, let us see what hath happened abroad, and consider the particular doings of some fellows[17] and brethren of the said Company.

NORENBERGH TRADERS, AND TRADERS OUT OF THE MART TOWNS

In the year 1584 and a few years before, some of the Company had found out and used a trade to the Town of *Norenbergh*,[18] and other parts of Germany, contrary to the old good orders of the Company, especially that which forbiddeth trade out of the Mart Towns, ordained for the keeping in credit and better vent of English commodity, and bringing in of foreign wares good cheap and at reasonable prices. So that where the trade was before times in the Mart Towns between English and foreign merchants, it was now grown (especially in the Town of *Embden*) to be between English, and English merchants. Those which used this trade, to excuse their doings, alleged that they did transport and carry from the Mart Towns as great a quantity of cloths, kerseys, and other woollen commodities, and at as good prices, as the merchant stranger did or would do, and that they brought to the Mart Towns as much foreign ware, and that as good and as good cheap, as the stranger merchants could do, and therefore, if the M. M. Adventurers were not of an envious disposition, they could be content that their own Countrymen and brethren should rather gain, than strangers.[19] Hereunto it was ans-

[17] The coupling of "fellows and brethren" probably does not indicate any distinctions among the membership, although such distinctions existed. Wheeler uses the term "fellowship" often, but "fellows" rarely. Very likely, however, the members who violated "the old good orders of the company" were not Londoners, but from one of the provincial fellowships.

[18] Nuremberg.

[19] Unwin, quoting this passage (*Studies in Economic History*, p.200), comments that Wheeler seems to put a powerful case against his client, the Company. He adds that the answer Wheeler give may show excellent principles for conducting a transaction where the amounts of supply and demand are both fixed and the seller has a monopoly, but not so desirable as a method of opening up a new market for an expanding manufacture in the force of competition. Wheeler's views, however, were undoubtedly acceptable to most business men of

wered: that although all this were true and granted, (as it was not, for that much might be excepted there-against) yet all men of sound reason and understanding might easily see and perceive that a commodity sought for at the Mart Towns is more esteemed by the seeker thereof there, than if it were brought home and offered to him to sell at his own doors, and the merchant's proverb is *That there is twenty in the hundred difference between*, *Will you buy*? *and Will you sell*? And therefore, admit that these traders to *Norenbergh* did transport from the Mart Towns as many Cloths, kerseys, etc., as the strange merchants did or would do, yet could not the said Cloths, kerseys, etc., bear such price and estimation in *Norenbergh* and other parts of Germany, being there offered to sell by English, as they would do, if they were to be sold by strangers, or the naturals of the place, for the above-written reason. The like might be said and understood of foreign wares, that the same would be bought as good cheap at the least in the Mart Towns, as they are to be bought at the strangers' own doors. Besides it was found that, as some sorts of silk wares were in a greater quantity than heretofore brought by the said *Norenbergh* traders into England, so were the same wares much falsified and impaired in respect of their former goodness and substance, since the beginning of the said new and disordered trade and dealing. Over and above all this, who knoweth not that the merchants strangers are either ignorant for the most part, or have not so perfect advice from time to time as the English traders had, how English and foreign commodities rise and fall in England? By reason whereof, there is more advantage in selling to the said strangers and in buying of them, than in dealing with the English Norenberg traders: for that they or their friends are weekly in the Cloth-market at London, and so may and no doubt do take knowledge, what price every sort and kind of Cloth and kersey beareth, and then, being throughly acquainted with

his day, for they were the traditional views of the guilds and livery companies. Indeed, they have survived, in a measure, in English commercial practice down to recent times. In this respect America and Germany have been less fettered by tradition, and less disposed to take the attitude that the superiority of their wares was such that buyers would seek them out.

the Exchange, do calculate the reckoning of the orderly Merchant Adventurer and share him such gain as liketh them.[20]

And when they bring their foreign commodities to the Mart Towns, knowing beforehand what is in request in England, they either sell the same at excessive prices, or as they list themselves, or ship them into England, and often reserving the best wares to themselves, do barter and sell the refuse in the Mart Towns. To conclude, they buy foreign wares at *Norenbergh* and elsewhere upon credit, for the current answering whereof, (as is well to be proved) they sell their English Cloths and kerseys at vile and base prices, so raising their gains upon foreign wares, and casting away the commodities of the Realm: and thus the strange merchants are put from their accustomed trade with the M. M. Adventurers in the Mart-Towns for English commodity, and the Merchants Adventurers from buying of foreign wares at the strangers' hands, as much as lieth in the said *Norenbergh* traders. Lastly whereas it was said by them that if the Merchants Adventurers were not of an envious disposition they would be content, and wish that their Countrymen and brethren should rather gain than strangers, the M. M. Adventurers are herein wrongfully charged, for they can be very well content to see their Countrymen (much more their brethren) to thrive and gain, but when as such gain (reaching also but to a few) is much more hurtful to the common weal of England and to the general body of the Company of M. M. Adventurers, than beneficial to the said few persons, traders to *Norenbergh* and other places out of the Mart Towns, there is no reason but that it ought to be forbidden and cut off. For such private and unwonted trade between English and English in the Mart Towns and such straggling by free and unfree English used in Germany and the Towns of the Low Countries out of the Mart Towns, is so unseemly, unmerchantlike, and far differing

[20] It may seem a little amusing, or perhaps shocking, that Wheeler openly avows that it is better to sell to strangers than to English merchants living abroad, because the former are not so well acquainted with the rise and fall of prices in England and hence may be persuaded to pay higher prices. But his audience felt that their interests were served by selling home products dearly and buying foreign products cheaply, and Wheeler argues convincingly that the practice of the straggling English merchants tended in the opposite direction.

from the ancient, laudable, and right English manner of the M. M. Adventurers our predecessors in former times,[21] and is so offensive to all foreign States and people, as nothing can be more: and hath been well seen and perceived in the *Hamburghers* and Earl *Egdard* of *Embden*, who were much displeased with the disordered trade at *Norenbergh* and elsewhere[22]: saying, that they had given the Adventurers leave to trade with all kind of foreigners in their Cities, but had no meaning that their Cities should be used as through Fairs[23] by trading from thence into other parts of the Empire, thereby to hinder the repair of foreign merchants to the said Cities. The said Earl went further and compelled such Englishmen as traded to *Norenbergh* to pay toll, not only for such Cloths, kerseys, and English wares as they should transport and carry from *Embden*, but also for such foreign wares as they brought from other parts unto *Embden*, to the great prejudice of the State and of the M. M. Adventurers, who by privilege were before free of all tolls and exactions whatsoever, either inwards or outwards. And surely it may be presumed that the

[21] Not only in foreign but also in domestic markets it was considered unmerchantlike to be too aggressive in the pursuit of trade. An aloof attitude was regarded as more seemly. Note the contempt that is heaped on the pedlarlike stragglers at Narva a few pages later. The regulations of the Merchants Adventurers repressed anything that savored of vigorous salesmanship and they nowhere suggest anything like the modern motto that "the customer is always right." This policy, however, appears for humorous effect in a contemporary play by Dekker. The patient linen-draper, Candido, is made the butt of some gallants who insist on his cutting a pennyworth of lawn from the middle of a piece worth eighteen shillings a yard. Candido remains patient, nevertheless, and expresses his philosophy thus:

> "We are set here to please all customers,
> Their humours and their fancies;—offend none:
> We get by many, if we lose by one.
> May be his mind stood to no more than that,
> A penn'orth serves him, and 'mongst trades 'tis found,
> Deny a penn'orth, it may cross a pound.
> Oh, he that means to thrive, with patient eye
> Must please the devil if he come to buy!"
>
> —Thomas Dekker, *The Honest Whore*, Part I, Act I, Sc. V.

[22] The attitude of the Earl of Emden is easily understandable. It was to the interest of Emden that the cloth trade be strictly confined to that city, thus bringing in the merchants from the other cities and contributing to the commercial importance of this center. Conversely, the other cities were aggrieved, and accused the Merchants Adventurers of maintaining a monopoly—as was, in fact, their intention.

[23] The meaning of "as through Fairs" is somewhat obscure. Perhaps Wheeler has heard the term "through-fare" (or "thorough-fare") used to designate a town through which there is much passing of goods and travellers, and has taken it to mean a variety of fair. The usual procedure at the periodic fairs does not seem to be akin to that of these Nuremberg traders.

Hanses derived that their false slander of the Company of M. M. Adventurers, in charging them with *Monopoly*, from none other head or ground than from this disordered trade used between a few unbridled and private English and English within the Mart Towns, and without the Mart Towns into the parts of Germany, whereby they show an exorbitant and unsatiable desire and greediness of gain, as not content with a reasonable trade in the Mart Town, but encroaching, as it were, upon the whole trade of those parts, and of other men, which can not choose but be a great eyesore and offence to all foreign and strange merchants.

Now although I hope by this time it sufficiently appeareth that the governed and well ordered trade of the M. M. Adventurers Company is far to be preferred before a dispersed, straggling, and promiscuous trade, so that it needeth no further proof or demonstration, yet because some men hold this to be against the liberty of the subject,[24] and think that the Adventurers by their orders restrain or limit the Cloth Market at home, it shall be necessary for these men's satisfaction also, to say something further of this matter. First, it is true that *Bonum quo communius, eo maius*[25]: and it were to be wished that there were enough for every man, but that will never be: furthermore, he loseth a piece of his liberty well that being restrained of a little, fareth better in that estate, than if he were left to his own greedy appetite: for we have seen by experience that many men in our time leaping from their shops and retailing, wherein they were brought up and gathered great wealth,[26] and taking upon them to be merchants and dealers beyond the seas, have in few years grown poor, or so decayed in estate that they might well have wished that they had never left their former trade and vocation, but

[24] It is significant that even so early as this the liberty of the subject had become a topic of popular theorizing. Wheeler's discussion is not very satisfactory. Parker, a half century later, developed at considerable length the idea that the good of the whole commonwealth is more important than the rights of the individual. Wheeler puts his emphasis on the idea that it is no service to give privileges to men who do not know how to use them and only hurt themselves.

[25] *The more wide-spread a good, the greater it is.*

[26] Retailers in London were not permitted to become members of the Merchants Adventurers.

suffered others quietly to enjoy their privilege, and disgested[27] the loss of a little scrap of liberty, hurtful to themselves, and rightly bestowed upon others for such services, deserts, and considerations, as no other subject need to envy them for the same, or to be aggrieved thereat, except they will challenge[28] the Prince of partiality, or not to have a due care of the subject, or say that the preferment or exemption which one man hath more and before another in the Commonwealth, is against the liberty of the subject, and so bring in an ill-favoured confusion, or intolerable equality, by usurping upon other men's rights and patrimony[29] so dearly obtained and with their great and excessive charges and travail maintained certain hundred years together, as the freedom which the Company of M. M. Adventurers enjoyeth hath been.

But (I pray you) let us see what would follow, if these men had that which they so much desire and contend for; surely nothing else than that which hitherto we have seen to have fallen out: neither can there any better end come thereof than heretofore of the like.

THE PEDLAR-LIKE DEALING OF THE ENGLISH STRAGGLERS AT THE NARVE

For example: the English had at the *Narve* in *Liefland*[30] a profitable trade and good sales for their Country commodity a good while together, till at length in the year 1565 a number of straggling merchants resorting thither out of this Realm, the trade was utterly spoiled, insomuch that many of them went about the Town with cloth upon their arms and measures in their hands, and sold the same by the *Arsine*, a measure of that Country, to the great embasing of that excellent Commodity, the discredit of our Nation, and the final en-

[27] Digested; bore patiently.

[28] Accuse.

[29] Parker naturally lays less stress upon the rights acquired by birth.

[30] Wheeler was evidently familiar with conditions at Narva (in Livonia) and probably traded there. The will of John Wheeler of Great Yarmouth shows that in 1610 he had a ship out on a voyage to this port. The history of English trading with Narva is confused. Logically it belonged in the territory of the Muscovy Company, to whom it was assigned after 1565, but at various times they allowed others to trade there "by connivance." At this period they were comparatively inactive themselves.

poverishing and undoing of many of the said stragglers, which being made known to her Majesty, and her Highness' right Honourable Privy Council, order was taken at the next Parliament that the Town of *Narve* should be comprised within the Charter of the *Muscovy* Company, to prevent the like pedlar-like kind of dealing ever after, and the making vile of the principallest commodity of the Realm.

Which one example, among other, may serve for verification of that which hitherto hath been said against the straggling and single merchants' trade in woollen commodity, wherein further may be noted that which by experience is found true, that in the ungoverned single trade, the first comer marreth the market for him that cometh after, and at his return making haste (as his manner is) to prevent those which follow, he setteth up his wares at an high price, which afterwards are hardly pulled down to a lower rate. The which is otherwise in the governed trade of the Merchants Adventurers:[31] for coming together, and at one instant to one market, at their Mart Town, where they are privileged with conditions and exemptions to their own liking, and for the furtherance of the commerce, sufficient order is taken for the preventing one of another, and keeping in estimation of the commodity of the land without using any such indirect dealing for this purpose as the *Hanses* have falsely imagined and as impudently published. Whereas the single and straggling trader, wanting all the abovesaid helps and means, lieth open to sundry wrongs, inconveniences, and grievances, which to strangers are incident and common in strange places, and thereby are made subject to many exactions, new tolls, and excessive payments and charges for one cause or another, and consequently are soon impoverished and driven from their trade by the foreign merchant, or after they have made the foreign merchants acquainted with the trade, are eaten out by them: which also would happen to the M. M. Adventurers, if they were not so united and held together by their

[31] Wheeler's explanation of the method of maintaining prices is neither clear nor satisfactory. Naturally, the Merchants Adventurers were accused of price agreements, and he cannot admit that they were guilty of this; but at the same time he must show that their "good orders" prevent price-cutting and unfair competition.

good government and by their politic and merchantlike orders.

Here it may be objected that the more buyers there are, the quicker sales, and higher prices, and therefore if all others, as well as the Merchants Adventurers, might transport Cloth, the more would be sold, and the prices would be the higher. To this I have sufficiently answered before, and proved the contrary by experience, fetched from the 29th year of her Majesty's Reign, when as all, both English and strangers, that would, were by letters patents directed from her Highness to the Lord Treasurer, enabled to buy and transport English Cloth, and for that the Charter of the City of London should not be in the way, or an hindrance thereunto (by reason that unfree men are thereby restrained from buying and selling within the said City,[32] and that the ordinary market-place at that time for Cloth was in Blackwell hall) the sign of the *George* at *Westminster* in the Kings' Street was appointed a market-place, for such clothiers to resort unto as would take the liberty of the aforesaid letters patents, but what followed thereof? I could never yet learn that one wain[33] load of Cloth was unladen at the said place, neither that the Steelyard merchants, nor any of her Majesty's subjects so enabled, as aforesaid, did ever take benefit by the same for forty Cloths, one man yet living only excepted, who since (as I have heard) hath often protested that in buying 200 Cloths, he lost a good sum of his principal, and no marvel, seeing those who had served and had been brought up in the trade of a Merchant Adventurer many years together, could hardly make one of one,[34] such was the longsomeness of return,[35] and the badness of the time at that instant, through the conjunction of many difficulties not here inserted, besides those

[32] Wheeler furnishes an interesting side-light on the trade restrictions of the day when he mentions the fact that only freemen of the city of London were permitted to buy in the cloth market at Blackwell Hall. This meant, practically speaking, only members of the Livery Companies, and there would be few members of other companies daring enough to interfere with the business of those who had been in the habit of buying cloth. The Steelyard men, at another time, might have been glad to avail themselves of the opportunity, but times were too uncertain, and the issue of the threatened naval conflict between England and Spain was then very doubtful.

[33] Wagon. [34] "Break even" is the modern slang equivalent.

[35] Excessive length of time before receiving returns on the investment.

which have been above touched. So that, not the want of buyers was the cause of the complaint of want of work and trade at that time, but rather the abovesaid causes. For it is very well known that the Company of M. M. Adventurers is sufficient and able enough, and over many to buy up and vent all that Cloth and those sorts of woollen commodity made and endraped within the Realm wherewith they usually deal, and which are vendible in the Countries whither they trade beyond the seas.

3500 FREEMEN OF THE COMPANY OF M. M. ADVENTURERS

For they are not so few as 3500 persons[36] in number inhabiting London and sundry Cities and parts of the Realm, especially the towns that lie conveniently for the sea, of which a very great many use not the trade, for that it sufficeth not[37] for all, but are constrained to get their living by some other means. And to the end that those which are traders may be equally and indifferently[38] cared and soried for,[39] and that the wealthy and richer sort with their great purses may not engross[40] the whole commodity into their own hands and so some have all, and some never a whit, there is a stint[41] and reasonable proportion allotted and set by an ancient order

[36] This statement of the number of Merchants Adventurers was quoted by several contemporary writers, including Stow and the unfriendly Van Meteren. Apparently it was regarded as an important fact that was not generally known.

[37] *Not* is erroneously omitted from the London edition.

[38] Without discrimination; impartially.

[39] A peculiar usage. *Sorie* and *sorry* were often used as a verb meaning, *grieve, mourn.* Of the illustrative passages cited by the *O.E.D.*, this is the only one that might have the meaning "to provide for."

[40] "Engrossing" (obtaining control of the bulk of the supply) was regarded as a cardinal offense in the English markets and others of the period.

[41] Quota limit. The quotas allowed to members doubtless varied from time to time. Their general character may be inferred from the schedule adopted in 1609. This shows them to be as follows:

Final (8th) year of apprenticeship.. 100 cloths
(with some restrictions)
1st, 2nd, 3d years of membership.. 400 cloths
4th to 14th years, an annual increase of 50 cloths per year
15th year and thereafter..1000 cloths

There was also a progressive increase in the proportion of cloths that might be shipped under the free license belonging to the Company. Thus it will be seen how great an advantage was reaped by seniority, for at this time all cloths not shipped under the free license had to be shipped under Cumberland's license, paying 2s. 2d. each.

At the time the *Treatise of Commerce* was written, this distinction had not been made. However, it is obvious that some members did not find it profitable to use their stints.

and manner, what quantity either at once or by the year every man may ship out or transport, which he is not to go beyond, or exceed. Which whole stint and proportion, if it were shipped or transported out of the land, would amount unto yearly the double quantity of all the Cloth of those sorts made in the Realm which the M. M. Adventurers deal in, whereby it is evident, that this stinting is not a restraint or limitation of the cloth-market (as some of late have misconceived) but rather an economical and discreet partition, or approportioning[42] among the members and brethren of the Company, of the commodities and benefits of the same: so that the wealthier sort are not forgotten, but withal are kept from engrossing the whole trade, contrary to the use and manner of a well ordered commonwealth or family, wherein all are provided for, and not some starved for want whilst others are swollen up to the eyes with fat and plenty. *For it is merry in Hall, where beards wag all,*[43] according to that old right English proverb of our ancestors, who full well understood what belonged to good housekeeping, and practiced the same better than in these our days is used, the more the pity.[44]

[42] Apportioning.

[43] This proverb apparently goes far back into English folk-lore. Wheeler's direct source may have been Thomas Tusser's "*Five hundred pointes of good Husbandrie,*" edition of 1580. In the section of this poem entitled *August's abstract* appear the following stanzas:

Let gleaners gleane,
(the poore I meane).
Which ever ye sowe
that first eate lowe.
The other forebare,
for rowen to spare.

Come home lord singing
com home corne bringing.

Tis merie in hall,
when beards wag all.

Once had thy desire,
pay workman his hire.
Let none be beguilde,
man, woman, nor childe.

Thanke God ye shall,
and adue for all.

(From *English Dialect Society* publications, Vol. 21, p. 126.)

The passage seems not to occur in Tusser's shorter original version of 1557, but the proverb exists in earlier forms, notably the following:

Swith mury hit is in halle,
When burdes waiven alle.
—Adam Davie, *Dreams.*

Merry swithe it is in halle
When the beards waveth alle.
—*Life of Alexander*, (formerly incorrectly ascribed to Adam Davie).

[44] Wheeler is not above contrasting the present with the past, and lamenting the decline, but he does it less than most other writers of his and later periods.

That the Navigation *of the* Realm *is maintained and advanced by the Company of the MERCHANTS ADVENTURERS*

SINCE the erection of the Company of Merchants Adventurers, and of other Companies trading *Russia*, *Eastland*, *Spain*, *Turkey*, *etc.*, the Navigation of the Realm is marvellously increased in number of good shipping, and of able and skilful masters and mariners, insomuch that whereas within these threescore years, there were not above four ships, besides those of her Majesty's Navy Royal, above the burden of one hundred and twenty tons, within the River of *Thames*[1] there are now at this day to be found pertaining to London and other places lying upon the said River, a great number of very large and serviceable merchant ships, fit as well for the defence of the Realm (if need were) as for traffic, whereof a good part are set on work by the said Company of M. M. Adventurers. The reason whereof is, that this and other Companies transporting at once, or at one instant, a great quantity of goods and wares, and being to make return of the same in foreign commodities, do go in fleets, or with great and warlike vessels, well furnished,[2] and this manner of going in fleet to the Mart Town tendeth to the safety and preservation of the shipping and goods of the subjects of the Realm, which amount to a great value, and would help the enemy and hurt our state very much if it should come into his hands, being thereby able to defend themselves from spoil and violence, so that since the troubles began with Spain, not one ship set out by the Company of M. M. Adventurers hath been taken by the enemy.[3] Whereas the single merchant going where

[1] "We find by divers records that 2 and 300 years ago there was more shipping in England before the Merchant Ventrs were . . ." (Van Meteren's notes.) Wheeler was perhaps accurate in his statement about London, but some of the other ports had declined in shipping, though hardly to the degree that Van Meteren suggests.

[2] Well equipped.

[3] Wheeler makes a very strong point by showing that not a ship of the Company was captured by Spain, for it is unlikely that independent merchantmen, sailing singly or in small fleets, would have been so fortunate.

and when he listeth, and not able to set a good ship on work, casteth how to come of good cheap, and either shippeth in strangers, or provideth himself of small vessels and pinks[4] to serve his turn for small quantities of wares, and fit to fly or run away, if he should chance to meet with the enemy, and yet he is many times snapped up, and made a prey to the Dunkirkers and other sea rovers, both to his own and the public hurt, as we have oftentimes known of late years. Whereby it appeareth that the Navigation of the Realm is maintained, advanced, and increased by the upholding of the Company of M. M. Adventurers, and of other later Companies also.[5]

[4] Light coasting vessels.

[5] The Corporation of Trinity House testified before Parliament in 1604 that the Merchants Adventurers were of great service in the maintenance of English Shipping.

That the QUEEN'S CUSTOMS *and* INCOMES *are augmented by the maintaining of the Company of MERCHANTS ADVENTURERS*

THE like reason is for the increasing of her Majesty's customs and incomes as is for the Navigation: for if the good and serviceable shipping of this Realm be maintained, bettered, and increased by the great trade and traffic of the said Company, and if that greater quantities of cloth are transported and uttered by them in foreign parts, than if all were free and set at large, as hath been above plainly and throughly[1] proved, it followeth necessarily that their said united trade is more advantageable and yieldeth more ample and certain profit and increase to her Highness' customs than a single, straggling, or loose trade by any means can do. The custom also, which the said Company payeth, cometh in yearly and at certain times in round sums and payments, whereby the turn of the Prince and State is the better served upon any occasion of need of money: whereas the payments of the single merchants come in by driblets and small parcels. And hereunto the good orders of the said Company are no small help, especially in transportation or shipping outwards, for that the most part of the commodities which the Merchants Adventurers carry out of the Realm, being shipped in appointed ships at *London*, the said Company have there certain overseers, by whose order and appointment they ship that which they ship, and when the goods arrive on the other side of the seas, there are also officers who attend and take view of the packs, fardels, and other parcels of commodity landed, presenting and informing of such which they find to have shipped in other manner than was appointed them to ship, or not to have entered and paid their custom and duties rightly to her Majesty, who are subject to great penalties and forfeitures for the same. This course devised for the better

[1] Thoroughly (see *supra*, p. 326).

collection of an imposition levied by the Company upon Cloth and other things for the maintenance and upholding of the said Company, doth not only the better make known unto them, but also unto her Highness' officers of the Customhouse, what every man shippeth away, so that by this means the custom is the trulier and fuller paid.[2] Whereas the straggler shipping his Cloth and other commodity in covert manner, hugger mugger[3] and at obscure ports, hath more advantage and means to defraud her Majesty of her duties and rights than those which ship at *London* and other great Port Towns, either by false entries, colouring of strangers' goods, and corrupting the Customers and other officers, who, for the most part, being needy persons in those small and remote Ports of the Realm, are more ready to take rewards, and closelier may do it, than the officers of the Customs at the Port of London: to say nothing of the great quantity of foreign wares brought into the Realm by the M. M. Adventurers, the custom whereof is better and trulier paid than if the straggler or stranger had the importation or payment thereof, or of the like quantity, and if the Records were searched, no doubt but it would so be found.

CUSTOMERS OF THE OUT-PORTS BACK-BITE THE M. M. ADVENTURERS

For it was not without some cause that heretofore we have seen so great fraternity, familiarity, kindness, and inward friendship between the Officers for her Majesty's Customs and strangers, and that the said Officers, above all others, now wish them again so heartily and call so loud for them, as though now the State were dangerously divided and unkindly at jar with her ancient allies and best foreign friends,[4] and

[2] Smuggling has been a favorite occupation of Englishmen and their cousins, the American colonists. Possibly the chief reason for the royal favor shown to the trading companies was that they insured full payment of customs duties. Whether smuggling was more prevalent in the outports than in London is uncertain, but at least there was more suspicion of it.

[3] Secretly; clandestinely.

[4] Milles' pamphlet attacking the Merchants Adventurers (see *supra*, p. 62) unwittingly helped to support Wheeler's contention that smuggling by interlopers and foreigners was more prevalent in the out-ports. Wheeler hints that the graft which the custom-officers obtained from this source explains their readiness to speak against the Merchants Adventurers. Note the quotation of Milles' statement that the trading companies had caused

therefore time to provide against a desolation which the land is ready to fall into (for want of these dear allies and kind friends, forsooth) whilst no man is found that layeth it to heart and bringeth them in again. Surely this is well preached for stockfish and Rhenish wine, etc. The Alderman of the Steelyard and *EMANUEL van Meteren*[5] have great cause to give them thanks, but not her Majesty or the State: the reasons I have sufficiently laid open and showed in this Discourse, whereunto I refer the indifferent[6] and discreet Reader. As for those strangers who have termed the Company of M. M. Adventurers *A Private, Particular, and Preventing Company*,[7] or have written or forespoken in that sort of the said Company, if it be so, as these Customers say, they have thereby well showed their skill in *P P.*[8] and that they are not only strangers to our State and Commonwealth, but withal privy underminers, and maligners of the good thereof. And let these Customers, while they warn other men, be wise, and warned themselves also, lest by their too too much leaning unto and favouring of such strangers, they prove not in the end bad Customers to her Majesty, and consequently corrupt and unnatural members of their Country and State. And withal let them understand and be well assured that the M. M. Adventurers both know and regard the essential parts, grounds, and pillars of Traffic, and of old time have put them in practice, and yet at this day do quietlier, better, and certainlier observe and maintain them, than the Customers of the out-Ports (I fear me) do their office.[9] Lastly, where they say that the M. M. Adventurers by a bare and idle pretence of the word *Order*, and orderly transporting of the credit and cream of the Land (*Cloth*) have brought the trade thereof to a kind

England to be "unkindly at iarre with their ancient allies." ("At jar" apparently meant "at odds" rather than "at war.") Note also the sneer that this is "well preached for stockfish and Rhenish wine"—the lesser gifts of the Hanseatic merchants.

[5] For Van Meteren, see *supra*, pp. 77 ff.

[6] Impartial. [7] Another quotation from Milles.

[8] This abbreviation is obscure. Perhaps it stands for "per procurationem," implying that they were paid agents of the foreign governments. Or possibly it was a jeering reference to their use of alliteration.

[9] "It is thought these customers may answer for themselves." (Van Meteren's marginal comment.) This suggests that he may really have had some connection with Milles, as Wheeler implies.

of confusion, and themselves into such a labyrinth, that besides the distress of the clothiers with all their dependants, and general complaints at home (to their Honourable Lordships endless offence and trouble at the Council table) the commodity itself is impaired, abased, and in a sort despised, etc.[10] Surely either their intelligence hath deceived them, or they show themselves to be carried with[11] a malicious spirit: for who knoweth not that the trade of the M. M. Adventurers is not in a bare or idle pretence and show, but in very deed the most orderly and best framed trade that may be? True it is, that some strangers and others (possibly of these Customers' familiars[12] and friends) have by open and covert means at home and abroad endeavoured and done their best to bring the said trade to some notable confusion, and those of the Company into a labyrinth to the impairing and embasing indeed of the commodity of the land, but thanks be to God and our always gracious Lady and Queen, they have not yet had their wills; neither shall they (I hope) though these odd[13] Customers took part with them never so much. And therefore they may well hold their clack,[14] and be content like subjects with that which those in highest authority have so long found good, and decreed shall be so in their wisdoms, and not take upon them like controllers, to check the doings which either of ignorance they understand not the ground and reason of, or through malice or unnatural affection towards strangers more than their own Countrymen, do misconcern and misreport of. But because I have often made mention of the *Hanses* in this discourse, it shall not by the way be amiss to show what these *Hanses* are, and what hath passed between this State and them in man's memory.

ORIGINAL[15] OF THE HANSES AND THEIR DOINGS IN ENGLAND

The *Hanses*, or Easterlings as they are commonly called, are people of certain free towns in Dutchland, either lying upon the Sea or some navigable Rivers, and were in old time

[10] The preceding passage is quoted from Milles almost verbatim.
[11] Moved by. [12] Intimates.
[13] "Odd" here may mean merely *singular*, *unusual*, or it may have the connotation of *inconsiderable*, *petty*.
[14] Hold their tongues. [15] Origin.

two and seventy in number, as they say: whereof *Lubeck* of the Wendish, *Brunswick* of the Saxon, *Dantzick*[16] of the Prusse, and *Cullen*[17] since it was of late years received into this confederacy of the Westfalish towns (for into these four parts or names they are divided) were and are the chiefest. These towns, by reason of their situation, and to put a distinction between them and other free towns of the Empire, were in old time called in Dutch *Aen zee steden*, or Towns on the seaside, or for brevity's sake *Ansesche*, or *Hansesche steden*, and in our language *Hanse stedes*, or *Hanse-towns*.[18] These Towns having united themselves for the sea trade and commerce, were full of good and great shipping and had an exceeding great trade and traffic in all the East Country wares and commodities, to wit, corn, stockfish, wax, hemp, steel, masts, firpoles, deal boards, pitch, tar, soap-ashes, etc., serving divers lands and places therewithal, and with their shipping in time of need, by means whereof they got unto themselves large privileges and immunities, to their great benefit, advantage, and enriching, and in our time they had their houses or places of residence in this Realm at *London*, in *Norway* at *Bergen*, in *Russia* at *Novogrod*, and in the Low Countries at *Antwerp*, whither they removed from *Bruges*. Each of these Houses had their Chief, or Alderman, and Assistants with a Secretary, Treasurer, Steward, and other necessary officers, but all of them held correspondence with the Town of *Lubeck*, as head of all the *Hanse* Towns. These Alderman and assistants had power to exercise Merchants' law among themselves in their house, at *London* called the *Steelyard*, so named by reason of the steel, which they in great quantity brought thither to sell,[19] and is a very large and spacious house, lying upon the Thames side, for that they were enjoined to dwell all in one house.

[16] Danzig. [17] Cologne.

[18] As noted elsewhere (see p. 15) this plausible derivation is rejected by modern scholars. But from the fact that it was generally believed long before Wheeler's time and long afterwards, it seems possible that it had a substantial basis.

[19] This derivation of Steelyard is also rejected (see *supra*, p. 16). However, Nash devotes considerable space to a discussion of the word (see E. Gee Nash, *The Hansa*, pp. 164–166), and seems to lean to this old and popular explanation. The Hanseatic merchants themselves, being well aware of advertising values, doubtless were perfectly willing to have this explanation accepted.

Among other their privileges in England, one was, that they might carry out and bring in their wares and merchandise for an old custom of one and a quarter upon the hundred, and thereby were exempt from all personal, or real charge or contribution, which all other merchants are subject unto, save that in time of need, they were enjoined to repair and help to keep one of the gates of London, called *Bishopsgate*. Now in King *Edward* the Third's time, wool was the best merchandise of this Land, and the custom thereof the chiefest income which the Prince received, as amounting yearly to the sum of 65 or 70 thousand pounds, which was much in those days. And we read that in the year 1355 there was granted by a Parliament to King *Edward* the Third, fifty shillings upon each sack of wool to be carried out of the Realm in six years, so that the said King might dispend[20] every day one hundred marks, which in six years time, amounted to fifteen hundred thousand pounds, reckoning for an hundred thousand sacks of wool a year transported, 50 shillings upon each sack. This wool was for the most part vented in the Low Countries, and there wrought and endraped into Cloth, but in process of time the drapery and art of making of Cloth was brought into this Realm, and the *Hanses*, who before time bought all their Cloth in the Low Countries, and so carried them upwards, did now buy much Cloth in England, and transported the same continually upon the old small custom, which at the first was set so low for the furtherance of the new begun drapery and art of making of Cloth. But at length it being grown very great and the wool trade almost wholly decayed,[21] it was found that the Prince and State lost exceedingly by the passing out of cloth upon the said small custom, and therefore in Queen *Mary's* days, after her marriage with King *Philip*, in the year 1557, and by his means the custom of Cloth, kersey, and other woollen commodity, besides foreign wares, was raised from 14 pence to 6 shillings 8 pence the cloth, to be paid by Englishmen, and 13 shillings and 4 pence by strangers transporting the same: by means whereof the Custom of Cloth endraped within the Land, was brought to

[20] Spend.

be equal with the Custom of Wool, when it was most, and when the said wool was carried out unwrought, and was draped in the Low Countries. Against this the *Hanses* opposed themselves, pretending their privileges so long ago granted, and by many Kings confirmed unto them, as they said, but for that in the year 1550 under King *Edward* the Sixth, upon due examination of their pretended privileges, there were many defects and faults found therein, and for that the *Hanses* for divers abuses and falsehoods in colouring and freeing of foreign goods, or such which ought not to enjoy the liberty of the *Hanses*, being none of their union or confederacy, and for other causes had been by a Decree of the Council adjudged to be fallen from their said privileges, part whereof were presently resumed and called in, especially that which concerned the carrying out of woollen cloth. They obtained no remedy all that King's days, but since they have been offered great favour, as by that which followeth shall appear.

SOME OF THE HANSES CALUMNIATION AGAINST THE M. M. ADVENTURERS

But not content herewithal, they made their often complaints to the Emperor's Majesty, of the wrong done them in seizing of their privileges in England. First in the year 1564, at which time the English Cloth was banished out of the Low Countries by the Duchess of *Parma*, for the causes heretofore expressed in this Treatise, and that the M. M. Adventurers held their Marts at *Embden*, and afterwards in the year 1582 at an Assembly of the Empire at *Ausburg*, charging the said M. M. Adventurers, that they had taken away the said *Hanses*' privileges in England, to the end that they might have the whole Cloth trade in their own hands, and so by their *Monopolish*[22] dealings, make Cloth dear in the Empire: setting also price before hand of that which they sell and of that which they will buy, and so committing open *Monopoly*.

[21] Wheeler hints that the high duty on wool and the low duty on cloth had much to do with the transfer of the cloth industry from Flanders to England. It is surprising that historians have paid so little attention to this aspect of the question. Although these were export duties, not import duties, they operated in much the same manner as a protective tariff in fostering an infant industry.

[22] Monopolistic.

Whereupon the Emperor wrote unto the Earl of *Embden*,[23] commanding him to banish the M. M. Adventurers out of his Country, as monopolish persons and hurtful to the Empire. The Earl discreetly considering that her Majesty might and could easily answer the slanderous complaints of the *Hanses* charging her Highness with wrong done unto them, as she did by her Letters sent to the Emperor in April 1581, by Master *George Gilpin*, at that time Secretary to the Company, and that the said M. M. Adventurers were now in his Town of *Embden* no more to be accounted *Monopolians*,[24] than they were heretofore in *Antwerp* and of late at *Hamburgh*, during their residence there ten years together and upwards, did not only not put the said Decree or Commandment of the Emperor in execution, but took upon him by his Orator[25] at *Spieres* to defend the trade of the M. M. Adventurers in the Empire, and to justify the entertainment of them into his Country, wherein Doctor *William Muller*, at that time Chancellor to the said Earl, and since *Sindicus*[26] of *Hamburgh*, was a chief Councillor or Actor. So that the Emperor, for that time, was well satisfied with the Earl's doings and answer, and the said M. M. Adventurers continued their trade at *Embden* till that by the Duke of *Parma's* too near and bad neighbourhood and other urgent causes they were forced of necessity and for the better vent of the commodity of the Realm, to seek a new place, and finally to agree with the *Staders*, as is above at large rehearsed. Howbeit the *Hanses* here ceased not, but persisted in their former pursuits and complaints, till the year 1597, at which time the said *Hanses* were much endamaged at sea by English men-of-war, who by virtue of a proclamation set forth by her Majesty, took many ships of the Easterlings going into Spain with corn, ammunition, and furniture for shipping, all which was made good booty and prize,[27] which

[23] Emden was not in the Hanseatic League; hence the League was unable to bring pressure directly to bear upon this city, but had to enlist the aid of the Emperor and of the Assembly of States of the Empire. The weakness of the nominal sovereign is clearly seen in the way the Earl of Emden disregarded his command.

[24] Monopolists. [25] Representative. [26] Syndic.

[27] The immediate cause of the publication of the Edict in 1597 was probably the seizure by Drake's men-of-war of about sixty Hanseatic merchantmen bound for Spain with food and ammunition. The Merchants Adventurers, of course, had no part in this seizure, but they

doing caused the *Hanses* to have the better audience in their complaints, the year before by *Don Francesco de Mendoza*, Admiral of *Aragon*, in the name of the King of Spain, and the Archduke *Albert* highly recommended to the Emperor, and earnestly solicited under pretext of withstanding and chastising of pirates and sea robbers. To the forwarding of this business holp[28] not a little, that in May and June 1597, *Florence*, Earl of *Barlamont*, Doctor *George Westendorp*, and *John van Niekercken*, Counsellors, were sent unto the King of *Denmark* and to the *Hanse* Towns, and namely to the Town of *Lubeck*, on the behalf of the King of Spain, and the Archduke *Albert*.

These Ambassadors, coming to the said Town of *Lubeck*, did in writing declare the ancient friendship between the house of *Burgundy* and the *Hanse* Towns and how much the said King had advanced and recommended their cause unto the Emperor, touching their privileges in England, by the means of his Ambassador *Don Guillame de St. Clement*, resident at *Praghe*.[29] They also complained that the *Hanse* Towns used so ample trade with the King's rebels (as they termed them) in the Low Countries, by means whereof they and the Queen of England were the more emboldened and strengthened against the said King, wherefore they required that the *Hanse* Towns would for a time forbear all trade whatsoever with the said rebels, that thereby they might the sooner be reduced under their King's obedience. But if they feared to do this, by reason of the league between *England*, *France*, and the *States* of the United Provinces, then they required that they would also deal and traffic with the King's true and loyal subjects in the Havens of *Calais*, *Gravelingh*,[30] *Dunkirk*, *Nieuport*, *Sluys*, and *Antwerp*, as well as they did with the *Hollanders*, otherwise their trade might be well accounted for Partiality, rather than Neutrality, promising further, that the said *Hanses* should

had to receive the punishment. Wheeler could not afford to criticize the English naval policy, whether he agreed with it or not. He had to defend all the acts of the Crown, since his argument depended on close identification of the interests of the Company with those of the Nation. Nevertheless, it is quite possible that the Mandate of 1597 would not have been issued if England had respected the rights of the Hanseatic merchants, as neutrals, to continue their trade with Spain unmolested.

[28] Helped.

[29] Prague (at this time the capital of the Empire). [30] Gravelines.

discharge their goods, buy, sell, and make return in the foresaid Havens, without any payment at all of toll, impost, license, or other charge whatsoever, and further should be assured and warranted by the Archduke *Albert* from all damage, or loss. These Ambassadors also seemed to be much grieved for the injury, which they said the Queen of England did unto the *Hanses*, in taking from them their so ancient privileges, for the recovery whereof they offered all possible assistance, and to receive them under the King's protection: moreover, to furnish them with ships, munition, money, and soldiers at all times, as need should require, offering them besides free trade and traffic in Spain and Portingal, so that[31] they separated and distinguished their ships from those of the King's rebellious subjects by some mark or token, as they should think best. Lastly, they showed that the King had given order to the Archduke *Albert* to send a notable Embassage to the Emperor, to procure the setting forth of the *Mandate* or Decree agreed upon at *Ausburgh* Anno 1582 against the monopolish English trade (as they pleased to call it) thereby to effect the restitution of the *Hanses*' privileges, and that his disobedient subjects, the Queen of England, and the King of Navarre, as disturbers of the peace of Christendom, and stirrers up of the Turk, might once be suppressed, destroyed, and rewarded according to their deserts. And albeit since the troubles of the Low Countries, the *Hanses* have been showed but small favour, the said Ambassadors requested notwithstanding that they would help to further the Embassage which the King of *Denmark* had promised to send unto the Queen of England, King of Navarre, and the rebellious States, and to compel them to right and reason, which the King of Spain and the Archduke should at all times acknowledge for a singular pleasure. About this time also the Kings of *Denmark*, and *Polone*,[32] the Emperor and the Princes of the Empire sent their Ambassadors into England, and unto the States of the United Low Countries, all which was procured and brought to pass by the King of Spain and his Ministers, to none other end, but to make the English as[33] pirates and

[31] Provided that. [32] Poland. [33] Make the English appear as.

robbers at sea, and the Netherlanders as rebels against their Prince, hated and odious unto all the world, taking upon them also the cause of the said *Hanses'* lost privileges, which they pretend to have in England; as by intercepted letters was sufficiently made known and manifested to the Queen's Majesty, and the States of the United Low Countries.

The King of *Polone's* Ambassador, *Paul D'Ialine*, had audience of her Majesty the fourth of August 1597, who in strange and unlooked for manner and terms declared unto her Highness that the subjects of the King his Master *Sigismonde* the Third, were not only not gratified with any new benefit or favour at her Majesty's hands, but to the contrary were deprived of commodities and freedoms which her predecessors had given and confirmed unto them, and consequently were debarred of all trade and traffic in her Kingdom. That likewise her Majesty had set forth certain edicts or proclamations by the which, contrary to the Law of Nations, the Navigation and trade into Spain was forbidden, and under colour thereof divers ships of the subjects of the said King had been taken at sea, and the goods therein made prize and confiscated, whereof he required reparation and restitution, and that the trade westwards might remain free and open to those of *Polone;* otherwise his Master the King should be forced to use such means, as thereby neighbourly freedom and restitution might be obtained. This was in brief the effect of the said Ambassador's speech, which with a very loud voice he delivered in the Latin tongue. Whereunto it pleased her Majesty to make him a short answer, and quick for that time,[34] referring him for further answer to certain of her Highness' Honourable Privy Council, to wit, the Lord *Burghley*, late High Treasurer deceased, the Lord High Admiral, Sir *John Fortescue*, and Sir *Robert Cecil* Secretary: to whom after the said Polish Ambassador had delivered his speech, which he made before the Queen, in writing, and excused his rough kind of speaking, showing that by his Commission signed and sealed by his King in the assembly of the States of *Polone*, he was thereunto en-

[34] An alleged transcript of the Queen's extemporaneous Latin speech is given by Stow. See Stow's *Annales*, continued by Howes, 1615 edition, p. 814.

joined, he received the answer following in the name of her Majesty, which properly pertaining to the matter of the *Hanses*, and answering fully and very pertinently the question made by them about their old privileges, I have thought meet to insert in this place.[35]

ANSWER MADE ON HER MAJESTY'S BEHALF UNTO THE AFORESAID EMBASSAGE

The said Honorable Personages therefore told him that her Majesty, understanding of his coming into England, was right glad thereof, as sent from the King her brother, for whom not long since she had by her intercession obtained, first a truce, and afterwards a peace of the great Turk, when the said King and his State were oppressed with sore war, which peace he yet enjoyeth, to the great good and benefit of his Kingdom, and therefore now expected not only a remembrance of the said good turn, but also due thanks for the same, for that never since she had received any from him. Her Highness had given him gracious audience, and read the King his Master's Letters willingly, wherein she saw nothing but that which ought to proceed *A Rege fratre, ad Reginam sororem charissimam.*

"But," said they, "you changing, as it should seem, the person of an ambassador, began a long speech, and turned the same almost into a sermon, the which notwithstanding, her Majesty heard with patience, signifying unto you only in a few words, beseeming the Majesty of a Prince, how unworthily you in your Oration had laid the fault of many things upon her Highness and with how great equity in deed she hoped that her actions would be well liked of all men, and so dismissed you, to receive further answer, according to your negotiation of us her Councillors, who are best witnesses of all her doings almost these forty years, as well with the Kings her friends as with her enemies, although we known no Prince in Christendom for enemy, but the King of Spain only, whose cause you very seriously handled in your speech. First therefore we required to see your Oration in writing, to the end

[35] Stow refers his readers to the *Treatise* for this reply. (1615 edition, p. 783.)

that we might give such answer thereunto, as were convenient, and for that you have showed unto us your commission sealed and signed by the King of *Polone* (as appeared unto us) in the assembly of that kingdom, whereby we have plainly perceived that you have uttered nothing in your oration which you had not order to declare, therefore we can in no wise blame you for anything by you said, although her Majesty looked not for any such matter.

"Concerning the points of your complaints, we observe them to be these. First you say that your King perceiveth, that his subjects have not only not received any new benefit from her Majesty, but are partly deprived of those which proceeded from her highness' progenitors and were confirmed unto them, and partly are in a manner excluded from all navigation or trade in this Realm. The second point containeth a grievous complaint of your King's subjects against the proclamations sent unto them, by the which all traffic into Spain is forbidden them, and consequently that their ships have been in hostile manner taken by the Queen's men-of-war, and the goods therein made prize and confiscated, and finally you required in the King's name restitution of the said goods or reparation of the damages and injuries (as they term them) received, and that they be not hereafter hindered in the foresaid traffic which by the common law ought to be free to all men, otherwise such means of necessity must be used, whereby they may get satisfaction by the aid and help of the said King. These being the chief heads or points of your Embassage, and of that which your K. requireth, her Majesty hath thought good to answer thereunto sincerely, and according to the truth of the matter in this manner.

"First, that your King is not rightly informed concerning the first point, in that it is said that his subjects are partly deprived of their privileges, and partly shut out from all trade almost in this Realm: for where there is mention made of his subjects, as subjects of the King of Polone, this doubt may arise, what kind of people the subjects are, because they must be understood either to be subjects of the Dukedom of *Prussia*, or else to be comprised under the name of the *Hanses*, who have no certain seat, or place whence they are:[36] for other than the subjects of the Dukedom of *Prussia*, and the *Hanses*, as merchants of Germany residing at *London*, the Queen's Majesty never understood that there were any that pretended any privilege of commerce above or before other merchants of all Europe. And whereas they complain as subjects of the King of Polone that they are deprived of their privileges, and almost excluded from all trade in this Kingdom: First concerning the right of their privileges, question was made almost fifty years ago in the time of King *Edward* the Sixth of the validity of their former privileges, and then the said privileges were rightly judged void, and forfeited for the manifest breach of the conditions thereof, and since the said *Hanses* could never prove that they had injury done them in the said revocation. Notwithstanding all this they had granted unto them in their trade into this Realm, and in the payment of their customs, more liberty than any merchants of whatsoever nation through all Europe; yea by especial grace and favour they were made equal and had as much freedom given in their trade and in the payment of the customs of their merchandises, as the natural-born subjects of this Realm, according to the true meaning and intent of their privileges from the beginning. And if they have not accepted of this, which by great favour was offered unto them, and so have forborne their trade in this Realm, the fault is in themselves, neither can it be rightly said that they are excluded (as it should seem by the King's writing that he is informed) but rather admitted and retained with the same favour as the very mere subjects and naturals of the Crown of England are, than the which benefit what can be greater? Unless, contrary to all human law, the Queen should have more care of them than of her proper subjects and how absurd, yea how detestable this should be, will be made manifest, if it be but considered what the office of a good Prince is in the rule and administration of his kingdom. For if in regard of his kingly office a king be compared to

[36] This reference to the Hanseatic policy of secrecy regarding their membership may seem to be legalistic quibbling, but some commentators (notably Anderson) think it was a very strong point.

the husband of an house, or to the pastor of the people, or (as he is said to be in the divine scriptures) to a foster father of the people committed unto him, who except he were stark mad, would call that Prince a good father or husband of the house, which should have more care of another man's family than of his own? Or a good pastor or shepherd, which neglecting his own flock, should look better to another man's than his own? Or worthy of the name of a nursing or foster King, which should neglect his own children and nourish other men's children with his milk? And so these things may be well applied to the present cause and question in hand, for if the *Hanses* should have better conditions than the proper subjects of the Kingdom, it would plainly follow that the Prince of this Realm should do his own natural subjects very great injury, contrary to the law of Nature and man's law; for by this means his subjects should become poor, or rather destitute of all honest and profitable traffic and navigation, and the *Hanses* should grow opulent and possess the whole trade of the Realm, as monopolists of the whole kingdom. And by these reasons, well weighed, it manifestly appeareth that those whom the King calleth his subjects, do most falsely complain that they are excluded from lawful trade in this Land, when as freely they may trade and with the same conditions as her Majesty's mere English subjects may do, and with far better than all other merchants, insomuch as that they are preferred before all the neighbour people of this Realm, *French*, *Scots*, *Flemings*, *Hollanders*, and the rest of the Low Country merchants, and before all the people of Dutchland, the said *Hanses* only excepted.

"Wherefore her Majesty is persuaded, that when the King of *Polone* shall understand these reasons, he will change his opinion; the like she expecteth at the hands of the Senators of that Kingdom, if these things be aright imparted unto them. For the complaints of the *Hanses* are so unjust and unreasonable, that it may be doubted whether the accustomed form of judgment in matters of doubt were observed by the abovesaid Assembly in this cause, or that credit was given to the complainants, the matter but slightly examined, or that place was given to their importunate prayers and requests. For her Majesty hath that opinion of the supreme authortiy, and dexterity of the Senators of *Polone* in their proceedings in the Assemblies of the said Kingdom (which cometh not to the King by inheritance, but by election and consent of the said Senators) that it seemeth absurd and not likely to be true that they in their public assembly would decree anything against the Majesty of such a Queen, whose like Christendom hath not had in this age, nor any other happier in noble acts, or in length of reign, or superior in Princely virtues, and yet that the same her Majesty should be unjustly accused, and without being heard, blamed, is a thing not to be taken in good part: for this among private men, was always accounted unreasonable, much more being done against a Queen of so great Majesty, which hath so well deserved of the King and his Kingdom. For it is apparent, that certain years past, the war which the Turk had prepared against the said King and kingdom, by her Highness' intercession ceased, and peace was granted to the King and his Realm, by the benefit whereof they to this day enjoy quietness and peace in that kingdom. The like good turn the Queen did in the year 1553[37] to the King's Father *John* King of *Sweden*, when as he, as well by his Ambassadors the Lord *Enicke* of *Wissenbrough* his Cousin, *Andrew Kithe* Councillor and *Raschias* his Secretary, as also by letters sent unto her Majesty, earnestly entreated her Highness to send an Embassage into *Muscovy*, to make intercession for a peace between the said King and the *Muscovite*, which she without delay willingly performed, and by her persuasion drew the *Muscovite* to make peace with the said King upon indifferent, and reasonable conditions. Which two excellent benefits done by her Majesty, the one to the Father, the other to the son, and to their kingdoms, are therefore rehearsed, because that in remembrance thereof, a better and more courteous course of proceeding might justly have been expected from the King and from the Senators of his

[37] Either this date is an error, or the Queen's ministers showed remarkable effrontery in claiming for her the benefits that were conferred during the reigns of her predecessors. 1553 was the year of Mary's accession to the throne. The embassage referred to was probably one that was sent out in the reign of Edward VI, but that fulfilled its mission after his death.

Kingdom than by your Oration (it appeareth) was by them determined. Insomuch, that if at the beginning of your instructions it had not been set down that your commission was decreed upon in the Assembly of the Realm, it might have been suspected that some points of your said Commission, not to be liked, were composed by some Spaniards and slanderous Jesuits, of which Jesuits it is said there is a great number spread through many parts of the Kingdom of *Polone*, whose malicious railings are often cast out in public places against her Majesty and this Kingdom, without condign punishment or any reprehension at all: and therefore it may be the more likely to be true that they as sworn men to the King of Spain, together with the Spaniards of late entertained by the King and heard in the public Assembly of the Realm, have procured this Embassage with these kind of Commissions in favour of the King of Spain.

"The second point of your Embassage containeth a request for free navigation or trade into Spain, which we deem to be such as the King of Spain himself hath lately in serious manner recommended for himself: for this prohibition was not set forth by the Queen's Majesty before she was of necessity compelled thereunto: lest the King of Spain, open enemy to this Realm, should be furnished with arms, ships, and ammunition with such facility and in such great abundance as he was from the maritime parts of Germany, by means whereof he might maintain long war against this Realm, so that if he could not get these aids and helps, it is manifest that he should be forced to leave off war, and offer peace not only to this Realm, but also to others against whom he most unjustly maketh war. Whereas therefore it is plain that this King of Spain, being an enemy to this Realm; is furnished, armed, and strengthened to continue unjust war with ships, victual, and other warlike provisions out of certain Cities under *Polone*, and other maritime Cities of Germany, in what sort can her Majesty (being oppressed by the Spaniard with unjust war) tolerate or suffer that such orders and helps so openly and so copiously should be carried to the said King her enemy for the continuance of the war against her? And although you many times repeated it, that the said her Highness' prohibitions were contrary to the Law of Nations, it is strange that you would allege this against the Law of Nature, when as by Nature itself it is ordained that every man may defend himself against force, which law not written, but born with us we have not learned, but received and drawn from Nature itself. Besides it is provided by the ancient laws that it may be lawful to forbid, yea to let and hinder, that no man minister arms, victual, or anything else whereby the enemy may be holpen to make war, as by this one, wherewith many other agree, you may perceive: *Cotem ferro subigendo necessariam, Hostibus quoque venundari ut ferrum et frumentum et Sales non sine periculo capitis licet.*[38] Neither may it here be omitted that this prohibition is plainly contained in divers Articles of the Charters given to the *Hanses* by the Kings of England, and first in the Charter of King *Edward* the First, King of England, in these words following: *Licebit prædictis Mercatoribus quo voluerint tam infra regnum, et potestatem nostram, quam extra mercantias suas ducere, seuportari facere, praeterquam ad terras manifestorum, et notoriorum Hostium Regni nostri.*[39] The very same clause and promise is in express words contained in the Charters of *Edward* the Second, and *Henry* the Sixth, Kings of England, which exceptions so oftentimes repeated, by so many Kings, ought to admit no reason to the contrary, especially on those men's behalf, who challenge their right by virtue of the said Charters only.[40] But we should have had no need to propound these our reasons unto you, but that we supposed you were ignorant how this question of prohibiting aid to be given to the King of Spain, for making war against us, was handled about two years ago before your King in his Council, when as certain merchants or mariners

[38] *As the whetstone is needed for sharpening iron, so also such things as iron and corn and salt may not be sold to enemies without risk of life.* Paul, *dig.* 39, 4, 11. Wheeler's reference in a side-head is H. lib. 39. tit. 4. de Publicanis. "H" is the symbol by which this Digest of Paulus diaconus was known in the Middle Ages.

[39] *It shall be lawful for the aforesaid Merchants to bring their merchandise or cause to be carried freely into our realm and dominion as well as to foreign parts, except to the countries of the open and notorious enemies of our realm.*

[40] It seems rather unfair to quote the charters of the Hanses as limiting their right to trade with enemies of England, when these charters had already been nullified by England.

of *Danzick* complained of the like prohibition, and had obtained an Edict against her Majesty's people, which Edict being oppugned with many reasons by our Ambassador Doctor *Parkins* here present, was abrogated and made void, so that there followed no execution upon the same, but the *Danzickers* were dismissed: which happened in the year 1595, so that to treat further of this matter, we should seem to do that which is already done.

"Yet we do not deny that which is alleged by some on your behalf, that these prohibitions are hurtful to your people, for that while the same are in force they cannot with their profit sell their corn and many other things growing in their country: but for this is an easy remedy. If your people would bring a great part of the goods by her Majesty prohibited into this Realm of England, where it should be lawful for them to sell the same with all favour, and with their great gain, and carry another part thereof into the Low Countries and France, or into Italy, so it be done without fraud and that the same come not into the Spaniards' Country; and by this means they may carry out and transport all their goods safe, to the greater benefit of the subjects of *Polone* than otherwise. Which might be proved manifestly by divers examples, and presently by this, that by carrying their commodities into the other Countries besides Spain, they should avoid the arresting of their ships, which happeneth every year in that Country; so that many times, to their great charge, they are compelled to rig their ships and fit them for warlike use, and so with eminent[41] danger to hazard the loss of ships and men in fight at sea, as too often the *Danzickers* and others have proved: and even this present summer it is known that the Commanders of the Spanish Navy have hung up and drowned in the Haven of *Ferole* many mariners, masters, and pilots of ships pertaining to the maritime Cities of the *Hanses*, for that they went about to deliver themselves and their ships from violent and constrained bondage. For the avoiding of the like loss and damage, her Majesty this last year by public writing set forth in Dutch, French, and Latin tongue, declared and

[41] *Imminent* is probably intended here.

gave warning that if there were any ships of foreign Nations by any means, either with or against their wills, detained in the Spanish army by Sea, at that time ready to invade England, it should be lawful for them, for their safety, to withdraw themselves out of the said army to ours, or to depart home quietly to their own Ports, without any damage to be done unto them by her Majesty's people: and it is certain that many ships, as well of *Danzick* as of *Hamborough*, were found detained by the Spaniards amongst their ships, which the English men-of-war did their best to save from burning when they did set fire on the Spanish Navy. And if the King of *Polone's* Councillors had known of this writing, it had not been congruent[42] that without mention of such a benefit done to the King's subjects, they should prosecute these matters in the worser part. Neither can we here pass over in silence that before her Majesty did put the foresaid prohibitions in execution, she many ways made it known, as well by public letters as also by admonition of the East country merchants, that she now was of necessity compelled for the defence of her Realm against the King of Spain, her open enemy, to forbid the transporting of arms, victual, and other things into Spain, wherewith the said King might set forth and furnish his navies and armies, and without the which he could not possibly continue the war against this Realm.

"Besides all this for the justifying and defence of the said her Majesty's prohibitions, it manifestly appeareth that the very like have been often made by other Kings, and namely by the King of *Polone's* Father, *John* King of *Sweden*, and by *Sigismond* King of *Polone*, grandfather to the King that now is, who by force took much merchandise from her Majesty's subjects, for that they were to be carried into *Muscovy*, which many honest English merchants, hereby brought into poverty, have cause to remember. The like was also oftentimes done by the Kings of *Sweden* to the subjects of *Denmark*, who would have traded into *Muscovy*. And for confirmation hereof we can show the authentic commissions of the said King *Sigismond*, given to his Admiral *Otto Mannickes* the 25th of May

[42] Congruous; suitable.

1566, and others of the 12th of March 1569 to *Asmo Genrick* and the like to *Hans Necker*, Captains of his, to whom authority was given under the said King's hand and seal to intercept, take, spoil, and make havoc of all those which by way of merchandise, or otherwise, should carry into *Muscovy* powder, ordnance, saltpeter, victual, or any other kind of ware tending to warlike provision. There be also letters extant, written in very earnest manner by the said King *Sigismond* unto her Majesty, dated in March 1568, wherein by many arguments he showed that the traffic or navigation into *Sweden* and the *Narve*, forbidden to all men in general, was most just and lawful, and by that means had provided that his enemies the *Muscovites* should not be furnished and armed not only with arms, weapons, and ammunition, but with other greater matters which might help his enemy, and to that end he writeth that he had set a watch in the sea of men-of-war, with commandment that if any man against their will would trade into *Muscovy*, they should take and seize upon him and all his goods. Of this prohibition the Councillors of *Polone* can not be ignorant, neither was that wise and provident King herein to be reprehended."

And after that these reasons were delivered unto the said Ambassador, he was asked whether anything could be justly opposed against them, whereunto he answered that he had none authority to dispute of these matters, but only to lay forth that which he had in commission, and to require an answer thereunto. The said Councillors therefore thought it not fit to use any longer speech on that behalf; but to conclude avouched for a full answer of all that hath been by the said Ambassador propounded, that seeing it is manifest that this deed of her Majesty is allowable, not only by the law of Nature to defend herself, but also by the express Civil law, and examples of the Kings of *Sweden* and *Polone*, especially by divers charters of the Kings of England, therefore her said Majesty could not be rightly accused either of injustice, or justice denied in any her doings, for as (said they) she hath always professed (taking the omnipotent GOD the searcher of hearts to her witness) it was never in her mind to commit anything against the sacred rule of Justice, so she will be ready to give ear to any complainant, either her own subject or stranger, and by her officers to do justice to the said plaintiff, according to equity and reason; the which she will also perform towards you, if you shall recommend any express cause of any subject of the kingdom of *Polone*. For her Majesty is so ready to give answer to *Pisman* of *Danzick*, who (as it is said) followed you from thence for the prosecuting of certain his suits for justice, that if you did not in such haste urge your departure, we her Majesty's Councillors, before your departure, should have authority to hear and determine his said suits, according to reason and equity. And to make an end of this long yet necessary answer of ours to your objections, for that many of the things published in your Embassage may by imputation be taken in ill part against the honour and dignity of her Majesty, all which by our said answer are plainly proved to have proceeded from your King ill-informed, her Majesty with good reason doth expect that when her answers shall before the King and the Senate of his Realm be compared with the complaints of the complainers, the said Senate will provide that the truth of her Majesty's actions be no less publicly by some means repaired and restored, than the contrary hath been attempted by false accusations and the King's public Embassage, that so it may appear that the King hath that regard of the preservation of mutual friendship as her Majesty doth expect from a Prince that is her confederate and brother.This answer was made by their Honors abovesaid on the 13th day of August 1597, at *Greenwich*, with the which the said Polish Ambassador departed, and herein the question between the English and the *Hanses* is fully laid open and answered, and their malice against the State of the land plainly discovered: so that it were more than time that they were restored and satisfied in their unreasonable pretences, as some without due consideration unadvisedly desire.

About this time, to wit, the first of August, 1597, the Emperor, continually called upon by *Don Guillelmo S. Clement*, ordinary Ledger[43] for the King of Spain at *Prage*, and stirred

[43] Ledger; resident ambassador or agent.

up as well by the abovesaid Embassages as by the importunate and clamorous solicitations of the *Hanses*, permitted a Mandate or Edict to be published and set up in the Empire, the tenor whereof ensueth, taken out of a translation of the said Mandate into the Netherlandish tongue and printed *cum Privilegio* at *Brussels*,[44] to the greater and more enormous injury and reproach of her Majesty and her Highness' actions and of the Company of M. M. Adventurers, as no doubt their meaning was, that were the authors and doers thereof, and consequently to make the whole English nation and name the more odious and condemned of all men, thereby also openly justifying and making lawful all the unjust and unlawful attempts and practices of the King of Spain and his Ministers against her said Majesty, Realm, and people.

THE EMPEROR'S MANDATE AGAINST THE M. M. ADVENTURERS

"We, *Rudolph* the Second, by the grace of God Elect Roman Emperor, etc. to all and singular Princes Electors, Princes Spiritual and temporal, Prelates, Earls, Barons, etc. send friendship, favour, and all good. Heretofore in the time of our right well-beloved Grandfather and Father, the Emperors *Ferdinand* and *Maximilian* (of famous memory) as also in the time of our Reign over the Empire, the Confederate Dutch *Hanse* Towns and some others thereby interessed,[45] many years together, and at sundry times and tides, not only at our Court but also at former meetings of the Empire, especially at *Ausburgh* in the year 1582 and at *Regensburgh* in the year 1594 last past, have in complaining wise declared and showed:* That they three hundred years ago and above had obtained and gotten notable privileges, immunities, free-

[44] Wheeler was probably correct in believing that the chief purpose of the publication of the Mandate in Brussels was to stir up ill-feeling against the English merchants and the English nation. *Cum Privilegio* (by Allowance) means that it was officially sanctioned. In England at this time new books were not to be printed and published until they had been seen and allowed by the proper officials, usually the Archbishop of Canterbury and Bishop of London. See E. Arber, *A Transcript of the Registers of the Company of Stationers of London*, vol. II., p. 810.

[45] Affected (adversely); interested, in a legal sense.

* Falsis narratis tacita et suppressa veritate.—[Wheeler's marginal note.]

doms, and exemptions within the Realm of England, partly by the especial grace and favour of the Kings of that Land, and partly with great sums of money, for the good and commodity of the Holy Empire, and the members of the same, and for the advancement of the general trade and commerce, which privileges, etc., they have held and enjoyed till now, not without their great and notable charge,[46] as having been granted, approved, and confirmed by fourteen Kings of England successively, and in the year 1470, by foreknowledge and consent of the States of the Land, both spiritual and temporal, made of the force and nature of a perpetual and irrevocable contract. Whereupon they held their residence and Officers within the city of *London* in an house or counter[47] called the Dutch Guildhall where they used to buy Cloth of the subjects of the Crown of England and carried the same from thence into Dutchland, by means whereof English Cloth was to be bought *good cheap** throughout all the said Country of Dutchland, from whence also on the other side a trade was driven with all kind of wares serving England, to the no small profit and gain, as well of us as of the subjects of the Empire and of the Crown of England. Which notwithstanding certain covetous Companies of Merchants, whereof some call themselves Merchants Adventurers, seeking their own private gain and lucre, are sprung up in the said Realm, who by bad means have wrought and practiced to the great and notorious hurt and damage of the foresaid *Hanses*, and have taken upon them to bring in many intolerable innovations, contrary to the abovesaid old customs, privileges, and perpetual contract obtained and purchased with the great costs

[46] The Hanses frankly admitted that they had purchased their privileges of the English Kings. Wheeler is less outspoken regarding the method by which the Merchants Adventurers obtained their privileges on the continent. In certain instances, at least, he would have his readers believe that no payments were necessary, because the English merchants were so eagerly desired.

[47] This appears to be merely an English spelling of the German word *Kontor*, which was commonly used by the Hanses to designate their home in a foreign city. The English "counter" (counting-house) is hardly inclusive enough to be an exact equivalent.

* Notwithstanding this good cheap the Landgraves of Hessen had at one time out of England 600 Cloths for their liveries: which they would not have bought there if the Hanses had sold Cloth so good cheap as here is said.—[Wheeler's marginal note.]

and charges of the said *Hanses*. So that it is come to pass that the Queen of England now reigning, will not any longer endure or confirm the said *Hanses'* privileges and perpetual contract, and now finally the last year to the further and more intolerable grievance of the foresaid *Hanse* Towns (specially for that they found it not reasonable nor fit to yield unto the said M. M. Adventurers a Residence according to their desire at *Hamborough*) hath wholly forbidden and cut off all privileged trade, both within and without the said Realm of England, thereby the better to strengthen the trade of the foresaid Adventurers Company, and to bring their Monopolish traffic into a full course and train with English Cloth and commodity in such form and manner as the Staplers Company have drawn the trade of English Wool into their own hands only. Which now is apparent in that the *Hanses* cannot enjoy their privileges and well-purchased traffic, whereas on the other side, the English Adventurers Company increaseth in number, to wit in Dutchland, first at *Embden*, where they were received by the Earl of *Eastfriesland* that then was, and afterwards in other places more, and now presently[48] at *Stade*, within the Archbishopric of *Bremen*, where they have settled the Cloth trade, and have drawn unto themselves only other commerces and commodities which the Dutch merchants in former times used to enjoy, and farther to the prejudice of the *Hanse* Towns, have erected an especial Society, Staple, College, Confederacy, and Alliance, by means whereof they have not only made divers and sundry Monopolish prohibitions, treaties, and accords hurtful to the commonwealth of the Holy Empire, against us and against the right and ordinance of the said Empire, and against all use of merchants, but also have raised Cloth and other wares according to their own wills to such a dearness,[49]* that

[48] At the present time.

[49] At this point and others later the Middelburg edition used the quotation mark (") to indicate a footnote. The London edition used asterisks.

* How came it to pass then that divers Factors and Servants of sundry the Princes Electors and Lords of the Empire bought their livery clothes of Merchants Adventurers at such time as the Hanses might ship cloth out of England as good cheap as the Merchants Adventurers? [Wheeler's marginal note.]

the price thereof is almost as high again as it was wont to be when the *Hanses* might use their privileges. Besides the said English Adventurers do not sell their Cloths after they have been wet and put in the water without retching[50] or stretching, as it ought to be by the policy, constitutions, and penal statutes of the Holy Empire; and for that the same hath been left* unpunished a long time, other merchants, which buy Cloth of the said Adventurers do take occasion of the like bad examples. Finally, through the drift[51] and dealing of these Adventurers, the Dutch Merchant hath the best of his trade taken from him, omitting here how that the Queen of England† with armed hand hath presumed or advanced herself to cause the Merchants Adventurers' ships to be convoyed from *London* to *Stade*, thorough the Dutch sea and within ours and the Holy Empire's jurisdiction and commandment: and besides, hath set up and published all kind of edicts tending to the hindrance and impeaching of the freedom of the sea and navigation, together with arrests which have followed upon the same, by means whereof the *Hanse* Towns, and other our subjects and the subjects of the Holy Empire, are forced to forsake and leave unfrequented the foresaid free navigation throughout the whole‡ Western sea, and in the *Ems* stream, and partly in the Eastern sea and elsewhere, for which cause the foresaid *Hanse* Towns and others thereby interessed, have called upon us and the Holy Empire, and in most humble manner have prayed and besought us to have

[50] Straining.

* There are none who desire a reformation in this point more than the M. M. Adventurers.—[Wheeler's marginal note.]

[51] Scheme; device. "Drift and dealing" may be interpreted as "plots and conniving."

† Unto this the Hamburgers gave occasion by exacting a toll by forcible hand laying their men of war before the Swinge for that purpose: Defensio autem non tantum omni iure est permissa, sed etiam pro defensione rerum & bonorum alium non modo vulnerare sed & occidere licet, & is qui illicitè exactam gabellam soluere recusat, neque Deum neque homines offendit.[52] [Wheeler's marginal note.]

[52] *On the other hand, not only is self-defense permitted by all law, but it is also lawful to wound and even kill others in the defense of property and goods, and he who refuses to pay an illegally levied tax offends neither God nor man.*

‡ Unto this see her Majesty's answer made to the Polish Ambassador.—[Wheeler's marginal note.]

consideration of all these matters and to give them herein aid and assistance.

"Forasmuch then, as we found that these complaints and grievances were of very great weight and importance, and seeing that by our neighbourly and friendly writing to the Queen of England we have but smally[53] prevailed, and lastly, for that we have little profited with our Imperial Mandate and ordinances heretofore set forth against the retainers of the said M. M. Adventurers, but to the contrary, perceiving that for the defence and justifying of these matters all kind of disputations, excuses, questions and delays were moved and brought forth, it seemed to us very necessary, before all other things, for our more assurance of the truth on this behalf, to cause a diligent and perfect information to be taken,* whether the English Adventurers Company did use any trade or *Monopolies* contrary to our and the Holy Empire's ordinances. Which being done, it was found by the deposition of not a few credible persons at *Frankfort* upon *Main*, in the Lent[54] Mart 1581, and by other information on this behalf taken, that all that is above written clearly appeared, and that which is more, that the foresaid Adventurers Colleges were heretofore forebidden and banished out of *Danzick* in *Prussia*, as also out of some places of the low† Burgundish and other Countries. Whereupon having with ourselves weighed the whole matter, according to the importance thereof, and considered that these things concerned not only the *Hanse* Towns, but also all the subjects and merchants of the Holy Empire, the further proceeding therein was deferred to a general Assembly of the Empire, holden at *Ausburgh* in the year 1582; against which we caused the acts and propositions concerning the same, to be

[53] In small degree.

* It were reason the M. M. Adventurers were heard what they could appose to this deposition.—[Wheeler's marginal note.]

[54] The spring mart (one of the four seasonal marts). It was sometimes called the Pasche mart.

† How the M. M. Adventurers were banished out of the Burgundish Low Countries, appeareth before, and if they be not now banished out of the Empire by the practice of the same men, the Spanish Ministers, let the wise judge.—[Wheeler's marginal comment].

sent unto all the Princes Electors, to the end that they might the ripelier[55] and better consider upon the same. And afterwards we laid the matter in deliberation of all the States of the Holy Empire, who after mature counsel and bethinking, gave us their advice and opinions upon the same, praying us withal, that seeing there was no means to obtain at the foresaid Queen of England's hands the full restitution of the foresaid *Hanses'* privileges, hereditary agreement, and contract, and that in the meanwhile the English Adventurers Company used and went forward with an hurtful *Monopoly*, against all right and reason, that we would with public edicts forbid the foresaid Merchants Adventurers their trade by water and by land throughout the Holy Empire, and the jurisdiction and command of the same. And further, that we would straightly[56] charge and upon great penalties enjoin every State whom it might concern, not to permit the said M. M. Adventurers or their consorts, confederated Companies, factors, and servants, to have recourse, or any common traffic in any place within the Holy Empire, but rather to expel, defend, and forbid the same, upon pain of our indignation, and loss of all royalties, fiefs, rights, and jurisdictions, which to the disobedient on this behalf might appertain or belong, either under us or the Holy Empire. And if so be, that contrary to this our Imperial commandment, the English Merchants Adventurers, or their factors or servants, should be so bold as to use or drive any trade either in buying or selling of English Cloths, Wool, or other wares whatsoever, at any place within the Holy Empire, that then each Magistrate and Ruler within his command or jurisdiction should be holden[57] where the said bought or sold goods may be found, and where such trade is used, presently[58] to seize upon and confiscate the said forbidden goods, as by the contents of the advise and determination to us at that time delivered at *Ausburgh* on the behalf of the Electors, Princes, and States, of the holy Empire, more at large appeareth.

"Howbeit we proceeded not to the publication of the said

[55] More maturely.
[56] Straitly; strictly. [57] Legally bound. [58] Immediately.

Mandates, but notwithstanding that the Deputies of the Hanse Towns earnestly insisted to have a final conclusion of this matter, we first of all sought by all gentle means to induce and move the Queen of England, for the confirmation of good neighbourhood, to give us and the Empire, as also the *Hanse* Towns, contentment in the above-written complaints and grievances, without compelling us for that cause to use any sharper means or remedy. And to that end we gave her Ambassador, at that time being at *Ausburgh*, to understand through what urgent and necessary occasions the foresaid Mandate was concluded and resolved upon by us and the States of the holy Empire, and withal to offer that, whensoever it should like[59] the Queen of England to suffer the matter to be brought to a friendly treaty[60] and communication, and to that end should appoint her Ambassadors with full commission, that we then on the other side would be willing to depute also certain personages of quality and countenance,[61] before whom both parties should appear at some convenient place within the Empire, and lay forth their doleances and griefs, and so grow to a composition and determination in all reason, and with a true and faithful heart and meaning. We also admonished and finally moved the *Hanse* Towns, to their great cost and charges, to send a particular Legation into England unto the Queen, where after they had presented our letters of intercession, which we gave them with them, a friendly agreement and composition was required, but they could not effect or profit anything on this behalf, but received of the Queen a clean contrary answer. In the meanwhile the Adventurers, with their Monopolish trade and dealings increased more and more, and multiplied in the Empire, and over and above this, the English did unto the subjects of us and the Holy Empire in the open sea, great violence and damage; which discommodity[62] began, continued, and increased whole twelve years long, to wit, from the Assembly at *Ausburgh*, '82 to the Assembly last held at *Regensburgh* '94, to the prejudice and contempt not only of our Imperial

[59] Please. [60] Discussion. [61] Public standing and credit.
[62] Inconvenience; injury.

intercession, but also of the writing of the *Hanse* Towns, and of the many ways sought for friendly appointment, insomuch that the *Hanse* Towns, at the last holden assembly at *Regensburgh* again complained on this behalf, and we, considering the manifest necessity of the cause, laid the same afresh in deliberation and consultation with the Electors, Princes, and States which there appeared, and with the Councillors, Ambassadors, and Deputies of the Princes which appeared not personally at the said assembly. And forasmuch as it was found to be against all right and reason, that the Hanses should be spoiled in the Realm of England of all their just title, hereditary agreement, and privileges gotten, as aforesaid with their great cost and charges, and that on the other side the Merchants Adventurers with their conventicles,[63] Company, and train, without any* permission of us as presently reigning Roman Emperor and supreme head of the Holy Empire, yea that which is more, contrary to all former recesses and mandates, should *de facto* intrude themselves, and go through with their trade, to the notable loss and damage of all the States of this Empire, great and small, and to the bringing in of a dearth in Cloth and wool, and by their Monopolish practices (which according to the constitutions of us and the Holy Empire deserve great punishment) to go about to weaken and overthrow the ancient and honest trade of merchandise used among the laudable Dutch Nation: without making mention in this place of the outrage, force, and violence, which the foresaid English have committed, with manifold robberies and spoilings at sea, to the dangerous consequence and prejudice of the jurisdiction and superiority which pertaineth and belongeth unto us and the Holy Empire in the same. Therefore in the foresaid assembly of the Empire, it was with one voice and consent concluded and resolved, and of us by the Electors, Princes, and States required,

[63] Assemblies, usually presumed to be for secret or evil purposes.

* Contractus sunt de iure Gentium liberi & ut liberi sunt ita etiam ignorante Magistratu ex generali legum concessione cumquovis non hoste libere & licite exercentur.—[Wheeler's side-head note.] [64]

[64] This passage is very obscure. The syntax seems to be confused, perhaps because of misprints.

that if so be (notwithstanding all the great pains and charges hitherto in vain bestowed) at our new instance and requisition, with deduction of all the circumstances thereto necessary, the Queen of England would not let the *Hanse* Towns enjoy their privileges free, certain, and whole, as heretofore of old they had them, and would not also suffer the commerce and trade open and unmolested, that then we should indeed assist the *Hanse* Towns, as the faithful subjects of us and the Holy Empire, and should cause the above-mentioned Mandate agreed upon at *Ausburgh* 1582, to be published and put in execution against the hurtful Monopolish Company of the M. M. Adventurers, without any favour, dissimulation, or composition. Which consultation in such manner by the Electors, Princes, and States in general, with one consent propounded at former Assemblies, and now again renewed, were according to right and reason confirmed and ratified, and consequently the fifth of July 1595, wrote unto the foresaid Queen lovingly and neighbourly requiring her anew, and setting before her eyes the foresaid reasons with many other motives thereto serving, that she would cause the old and continual complaints, together with the oppressions and damages of the foresaid *Hanse* Towns to cease. But we received such an answer unto this our writing that thereby it may sufficiently be perceived that our hitherto long used patience is not only received with small thanks, but withal, the said Queen presumeth to ascribe unto herself some interest herein, and to draw the same into consequence, as though by our deferring of the publishing of the said Mandates, the intrusion of the foresaid M. M. Adventurers were allowed, or that as if it stood in the liking, choice, will, and power of the Queen to take from the foresaid *Hanse* Towns their dearly purchased liberties and hereditary accord[65] and so well not, that in any other place than in England (where she may be judge and party[66]) that any treaty be held on this behalf, and besides requiring that her subjects according to their own good liking and pleasure may haunt, live, and exercise their merchandise within the

[65] Agreement.

[66] Party in a law-suit (either plaintiff or defendant).

Empire of the Dutch Nation, which for us and the Empire it falleth altogether grievous, and very contumelious[67] to dissemble any longer. Therefore then, whereas we in regard to our Imperial office and place, cannot any longer delay to put in execution the foresaid consultations and decrees of the years '82 and '94 for the furtherance of the common welfare and for necessity's sake, especially seeing the Monopolies and prejudicial, dangerous, and unlawful forestalling[68] (which as is abovesaid, are used among the English Adventurers Company) by testimonies and other credible informations, are altogether open and manifest, and not only according to the common written laws, but also according to the published constitutions of the Empire are forbidden upon great penalty and punishment, to wit, loss of goods and chattel, and banishment out of the land.

"Therefore is it, that we prohibit, banish out, and proscribe all the forenamed English Merchants, to wit, the whole Company of the M. M. Adventurers, together with their hurtful dealings, traffics, and contractings, out of all the Holy Empire, so that such hurtful commerces and dealings of the English Adventurers, with the conventions, compacts, and alliances on this behalf made, from this time forward shall be forbidden and made void, without that any man by himself or any other shall, or may hereafter exercise or practice the same; ordaining therefore and commanding expressly by our Romish Imperial power and authority, according to the resolution of the Electors, Princes, and States of the Empire agreed upon, renewed, and approved, that upon pain of the ban[69] and proscription of us and the Holy Empire, all and every merchants and dealers in English Cloth (to the Companies of M. M. Adventurers any ways allied or associated) together with their factors, agents, attorneys, and servants, that within three months after the publishing and setting forth of these presents, they depart and remove without further delay or opposition out of the rule, command, and land of us and of the Holy Empire, as also of the Electors and common States, and

[67] Shameful.

[68] The same accusations that Wheeler made against the Antwerpians and Hanses.

[69] The Imperial ban took away political rights and privileges.

specially out of the town of Stade, situate in the Archbishopric of *Bremen*, and out of all other parts and places where they commonly have their residence and conventicles, or exercise their trade: and that from hence forward they wholly and entirely abstain and forbear from all recourse and commerces howsoever they may be called, by water and by land, openly or privily, throughout all the whole Empire. And further we give commandment to all Princes Electors, Princes, States, and subjects of us and the Holy Empire, upon the forfeiture of all their royalties, fiefs, and other rights and duties obtained of us and the Holy Empire (which everyone whosoever shall dare wilfully to do here against *ipso facto* shall forfeit) that they unto the said English, naming themselves Merchants Adventurers, their societies, companies, factors, and servants nowhere in the Holy Empire, by land or by water, do give, yield, or permit any open or secret conveyance, passage, help, or other favour, but the same do altogether let[70] and prohibit. And, if so be that the English Adventurers, their adherents, factors or servants boldly shall go forward or proceed, contrary to this our Imperial Mandate and Commandment, either in buying or selling of Cloths and wool, or with exercising any other commerces, howsoever they may be called, in any quarter or place of the Holy Empire, in such case, hereby authority and power is given and earnestly is enjoined and required, that all magistrates and rulers, under whose command or jurisdiction such place immediately doth lie, and where such kind of trade is used, or where such bought or sold goods may be found, to apprehend the persons without delay, and to arrest and confiscate the forbidden goods. And further it shall not be lawful for any magistrate or ruler in the Empire, to give convoy or safe conduct with whatsoever words, meaning, colour, or clauses, the said convoys or safe conducts may be conceived or set down, to the English Adventurers' companies, merchants, or dealers, neither shall they be conducted or convoyed by any magistrate or superior in the said Empire. And in case that the magistrate or superior shall be herein negligent or slack, and that we or our Procuror Fis-

[70] Forbid.

cal[71] shall be thereof advertised,[72] then our will is that the said Fiscal (according to our commandment to him in earnest manner already given) on this behalf, to advertise the magistrate or superior, where the said merchants and dealers dwell or reside, and admonish the same such English trade forthwith out of hand to forbid. And if so be the said magistrate or superior do not so within the prefixed time, we will on our Imperial Court's part, or otherwise our foresaid Fiscal shall have full power, right, and authority to proceed to the execution of this our Imperial Mandate, and by virtue of his office presently to call in question the disobedient, without all favour or dissimulation, as the necessity of the cause shall require, without that it shall be lawful for the aforesaid misdoers to allege or produce any exceptions, or declinatory delay in any manner whatsoever.[73] And for that it is lawful and permitted to every man to give information against the transgressors, therefore whosoever first shall inform the magistrate, where offence is made, of the said offence plainly and truly, or in case of negligence in the said magistrate, our Fiscal, he shall have the fourth part of the offender's goods,[74] wherein also he shall be assisted and holpen by the foresaid magistrate or superior, or in default thereof by us and our Imperial Chamber right and by all other States of the Holy Empire: according to this let every man take knowledge how to demean himself. Given in our Royal Castle at *Praghe* the first day of the month of August Anno 1597, of our Romish Kingdom the two and twentieth year, of *Hungary* the 25th and of *Bohemia* also the 22nd. Subscribed *Rudolph*, Paragraphed[75] *I. D. W. Freymondt, ad Mandatum Sacræ Cæsareæ Maiestatis proprium*, and signed *An. Hanniwalt:* and the privy seal of the Emperor's Majesty was printed upon the same in form of a *Placard* or *Edict.*"

These are the words of the Mandate, which I have fully and truly set down, to the end that it may be the better ap-

[71] Procurator Fiscal; the highest law-officer of the Empire. [72] Informed.

[73] The voluminous and detailed warnings to the subjects of the Empire may possibly suggest a fear that some of them would not willingly obey the Mandate.

[74] The reward of one-fourth of the goods of the offenders seems to have been a customary method of rewarding informers.

pear, what the causes were of the said Mandate, and what good friends the *Hanses* are to the state of England. Concerning the causes, I note them to be three in number. First, *The taking away of the Easterling's Privileges in England.* Secondly, *The doings of the English men-of-war at the Sea.* And thirdly *The Monopoly used by the Merchants Adventurers.* To the first two causes her Majesty at sundry times hath sufficiently answered, and namely by her Letters written to the Emperor in the years 1585[76] and lastly by the answer given to the Polish Ambassador, as above at large is set down. As for the Monopoly, wherewith the M. M. Adventurers are charged, it is but a mere slander and injurious imputation, maliciously devised by the *Hanses*, to blear the eyes of the States and Princes of the Empire withal, and to draw[77] them, under colour of complaining on the M. M. Adventurers as monopolish traders, to aid and assist the said *Hanses* to recover their privileges again, and to maintain them therein, contrary to all reason against the English Nation, as I doubt not anon most plainly and clearly to prove.

Her Majesty, being informed of the abovesaid Mandate, sent Master *John Wroth* and Master *Stephen Lesure* with letters to the Emperor and divers of the Electors and Princes of Germany, declaring her Highness' opinion of this proceeding as an unjust practice and doing of the *Hanses*, and therefore required to have the said Mandate revoked or suspended, but being uncertain what would follow hereupon, it seemed good unto her Majesty in the mean time, to direct a commission to the Mayor and Sheriffs of the City of London, in manner following.

COMMISSION DIRECTED TO THE MAYOR AND SHERIFFS OF LONDON AGAINST THE HANSES BY HER MAJESTY

"*ELIZABETH* by the grace of God, Queen of England, France, and Ireland, Defender of the faith, etc. To our right

[75] Paraphed; signed with a special flourish and initials as a protection against forgery.
[76] This must be a typographical error for 1595, or else Wheeler intended to add this date also (as implied by the plural "years"). The Queen's letter of 1595 is given in full at the end of the *Treatise* and is referred to several times in the text.
[77] Induce.

trusty and well-beloved the Mayor and Sheriffs of our City of London, greeting. Whereas there hath been directed a Commandment, by the name of a Mandate, from the Roman Emperor to all Electors, Prelates, Earls and all other Officers and subjects of the Empire, reciting sundry complaints made to him by the allied Towns of the Dutch *Hanses* in Germany, of divers injuries committed against them in our Realm, and likewise upon complaint made by them against the Company of M. M. Adventurers, without hearing any answer to be made to the said *Hanse* Towns in disproof of their complaints, the same being most notorious unjust and not to be maintained by any truth. And yet nevertheless by this Mandate the English merchants, namely the M. M. Adventurers, are forbidden to use any traffic of merchandise within the Empire, but are commanded to depart from thence upon great pains, and to forbear openly and secretly, from all havens and landing places, or to use any commerce by water or by land in the Empire, upon pain of apprehension of their persons and confiscation of their goods, with sundry other extreme sentences pronounced against our said subjects. Hereupon, although we have sent our letters expressly to the Emperor, and to the Electors and other Princes of the Empire, declaring our opinion of this proceeding to be unjustly prosecuted by the said *Hanse* Towns, and therefore have required to have the said Mandate either revoked or suspended, yet being uncertain what shall follow hereupon, we have thought it agreeable to our honour, in the meantime, to command all such as are here within our Realm, appertaining to the said *Hanse* Towns situated in the Empire, and especially all such as have any residence in our City of London, either in the house commonly called the Steelyard, or in any other place elsewhere, do forbear to use any manner of traffic of merchandise, or to make any contracts, and likewise to depart out of our Dominions in like sort as our subjects are commanded to depart out of the Empire, upon the like pains as are contained against our subjects in the said Mandate. And for the execution of this our Commandment, we will that you, the Mayor of our said City of London and the Sheriffs, shall forthwith repair to the house, called the Steelyard, and calling before you such as have charge thereof, or do reside there, to give them knowledge of this our determination and commandment. Charging them by the 24th of this month, (being the day that our merchants are to depart from *Stade*) they do depart out of this our Realm: charging them also that they give knowledge thereof to such as be of any of the *Hanse* Towns, belonging to the Empire, remaining within any part of our Realm, to depart likewise by the said day. And you the Mayor and the Sheriffs, calling unto you two of the Officers of our Custom-house, to take possession of the said house the said 24 day, to remain in our custody until we shall understand of any more favourable course taken by the Emperor, for the restitution of our subjects to their former lawful trade within the Empire, and this shall be your warrant for the execution of the premises.[78] In witness whereof we have caused these our letters to be made patent, witness ourself at *Westminster:* the thirteenth of January in the Fortieth year of our Reign."[79]

In this state the matters have hung ever since, the M. M. Adventurers still expecting a Diet, or general assembly of the Princes and States of the Empire, in hope that by her Majesty's gracious intervention for them, the abovesaid Mandate may be either abrogated or suspended, and they restored to their former trade and privileges in the Empire, for without such an assembly this can not be done, (as appeareth plainly by the answer of the Emperor and Princes unto those letters

[78] Foregoing (stipulations).

[79] Wheeler allows us to infer that this order of the Queen was carried out and the Hanseatic merchants banished in January, 1598, although it would obviously have been impossible for them to close up their affairs in the eleven days the order allowed. Actually, they were granted extensions; first, to the end of February, and then to the end of March, with further indefinite extensions, provided the English merchants were well treated at Stade. See *Acts of the Privy Council*, J. R. Dasent, ed., N.S. vol. 28, pp. 333, 375, 413, 447, 465, 509, 567, 613. Finally, on the twenty-fifth of July a second warrant was issued. The manuscript of this is in the British Museum (Br. Mus. Mss. Eg. 2603 f 53) and has been reproduced in facsimile in E. Gee Nash's *The Hansa*, opp. p. 236. Except for the dates, the wording of this is almost identical with that of the first warrant as quoted by Wheeler. The slight differences may be due to errors of copying or transcription. Thus where Wheeler's version mentions the day on which our merchants are "to depart from Stade," Nash's transcription reads, "to be anoyde from abroad." But the correct reading of the manuscript seems to be, "to avoyde from Stoade." Other documents relating to this same affair spell Stade *Stoade*, and use *departing* and *avoyding* synonymously. See Lappenberg, *Urkundliche Geschichte des Hansischen Stahlhofes zu London*, pp. 188, ff. A letter from one of the Hanseatic merchants, quoted by Lappenberg, indicates that the Steelyard was finally closed on August 4, 1598.

which it pleased her Highness to write by the abovesaid Master *Wroth* and *Mr. Lesure*) and on the other side the *Hanses* still labouring to have the abovesaid Mandate extended and retched[80] farther than the contents thereof will bear, to wit, that all Englishmen generally and all English wares should be banished and forbidden the Empire: for that otherwise they see that they lose their labour and cost, and the Merchants Adventurers find means to continue their trade and to vent the commodities of their Country in Germany, maugre[81] all that their adversaries and ill-willers can do, though not in that sort that were convenient. But because you shall see what cause the *Hanses* have to complain in such clamourous manner as they do of injuries done them in this Realm, I will give you the view of a Decree of the Right Honourable Privy Council, given at *Westminster*, the 24th day of February in the sixth year of the reign of King *Edward* the Sixth in these words following.

DECREE AGAINST THE HANSES IN THE REIGN OF KING EDWARD THE SIXTH

In the matter touching the Information exhibited against the Merchants of the *Hanse*, commonly called the Merchants of the Steelyard, upon good consideration, as well of the said Information, as also of the answer of the said Merchants of the Steelyard, and of such records, writings, charters, treaties, depositions of witnesses, and other records and proofs, as hath been exhibited on both parties, it was found apparent to the Kings Majesty's Privy Council as followeth.

"First, it is found that all liberties and privileges pretended to be granted to the said Merchants of the *Hanse*, be void by the Laws of the Realm, forasmuch as the same Merchants of the *Hanse* have no sufficient Corporation to receive the same. It appeareth also, that such grant and privileges as the said Merchants of the *Hanse* do claim to have, do not extend to any persons or towns certain, and therefore uncertain what persons or which towns should enjoy the said privileges; by reason of which uncertainty, they have, and do admit to be

[80] Strained. [81] Despite.

free with them whom and as many as they list, to the great prejudice and hurt of the King's Majesty's Customs, and yearly hindrance of twenty thousand pounds, or near thereabouts, besides the common hurt to the whole Realm. It appeareth also, that if the pretended grants were good by the Laws of the Realm, as indeed they be not, yet the same were made upon condition that they should not avow or colour any foreign goods, or merchandises, which condition the said Merchants of the *Hanse* have not observed, as may appear by office found remaining of record in the King's Majesty's exchequer, and by other sufficient proofs of the same. It appeareth also that one hundred years and more after the pretended privileges granted to them, the foresaid Merchants of the *Hanse* used to transport no merchandise out of this Realm but only into their own Countries, neither to bring into this Realm any wares or merchandise but only such as were commodities of their own Countries; where at this present they do not only convey the merchandise of this Realm into the base[82] countries of *Brabant*, *Flanders*, and other places near adjoining, and there sell the same to the great damage and subversion of the laudable order of the King's Majesty's subjects trading those parties[83] for merchandise, but also do bring into this Realm the merchandise and commodities of all foreign Countries, contrary to the true meaning of the grants of their privileges, declared by the ancient usage of the same: by means whereof the King's Majesty hath not only lost much in his Customs, but also it is contrary to the conditions of a Recognisance made in the time of King *Henry* the Seventh.[84] It appeared also, that like as the privileges heretofore granted to the said Merchants of the Steelyard, being at the beginning reasonably used, were commodious and much profitable unto them, without any notable, excessive, or enorm[85] prejudice to the Royal State of this Realm, so now of late years, by taking of such and so many as they list into their Society, and by

[82] Low. [83] Parts; regions.

[84] This bond or legal obligation was referred to on page 322. How long its terms were observed is uncertain, but we may be sure that their violation was not a new thing in the time of Edward the Sixth. On the other hand, this reference implies that they had never paid the forfeit.

[85] Abnormal; extraordinary.

bringing in the commodities of all other Countries, as carrying out of the commodities of the Realm into all other places, their said pretensed[86] privileges are grown so prejudicial to the King and his Crown, as without the great hurt thereof and of the whole estate of this Realm, the same may not be long endured.

"Item[87] in the time of King *Edward* the Fourth, the said Merchants of the *Hanse* forfeited their pretended privileges, by means of war betwixt this Realm and them, whereupon a treaty was made and agreed, that the subjects of this Realm should have like liberties in the land of *Prusse*, and other places of the *Hanse*, as they had and ought to have used there. And that no imposts, new exactions, or other prests[88] should be set upon their persons or goods otherwise, or by other mean, than before ten, twenty, thirty, forty, fifty, yea an hundred years ago and above had been, or were set, which hath been and is daily much broken, and specially in *Danzick*, not only by prohibiting Englishmen freely to buy and sell there, but also in levying upon them certain exactions and impositions, contrary to the said Treaty. And notwithstanding that divers requests have been made, as well by the King's Majesty's Father as by his Majesty, for the present redress of such wrongs as have been done to the English merchants, contrary to the said Treaty, yet no reformation hath hitherto ensued. In consideration of which the premises, and such other matters as hath appeared in the examination of this matter, the Lords of the King's Majesty's Privy Council, on his Highness' behalf decreed that the privileges, liberties, and franchises, claimed by the foresaid Merchants of the Steelyard, shall from henceforth be and remain seised, and resumed into the King's Majesty's hands, until the said Merchants of the Steelyard shall declare and prove better and more sufficient matter for their claim in the premises, saving and reserving unto the said Merchants of the Steelyard all such and like liberties of coming into this Realm, and other the King's Dominions, buying, selling all, and all manner of traffic and trade

86 Feigned. 87 Also, (introducing another point in the list of charges).
88 Duties.

of merchandise in as large and ample manner as any other Merchants strangers have, or of right ought to have within the same. This order aforesaid, or anything herein contained to the contrary notwithstanding." This decree was firmed[89] by *T. Ely, Chancellor: Winchester*[90]*: Northumberland: Bedford: Westmorland: Shrewsbury: E. Clinton: T. Darcie: N. Wutton:* and *W. Cecil.*[91] By the contents whereof, a man may plainly see that whatsoever happened to the *Hanses* in England, they themselves gave the occasion thereof, and therefore had no just or lawful cause to complain.

QUEEN MARY REVOKETH THE FORESAID DECREE

Notwithstanding Queen *Mary* by the way of recess,[92] the land being full of troubles, revoked this Decree and restored the *Hanses* to their former Privileges, in the month of April Anno 1553, at which time the *Hanses* had their Commissioners in England about a Treaty offered by King *Edward*, and accepted by the *Hanses* after the abovesaid resumption, whereunto she was induced for two reasons: the one was, for that the *Hanses*' Commissioners promised that their inordinate trade, forbidden by the laws of the land, and their too too much frequenting the Low Countries, should be left; the other was, for that by means of the dangerousness and hardness of the time, the abovesaid Decree of the resumption of the *Hanses*' privileges could not be dealt in.[93]

REVOCATION OF THE FORESAID REVOCATION

But this promise of the Commissioners not being performed, the said Queen in the year 1556 caused her foresaid Revocation to be altered, and by a Decree restrained the *Hanses*' trade into the Low Countries with Cloth, and their bringing in of any other foreign wares than those of their own lands only, suffering them notwithstanding in other points, to use their

[89] Signed.

[90] This and the four following names are (like the others) signatures. They represent the Bishop of Winchester, the Earl of Northumberland, etc.

[91] W. Cecil (later Lord Burghley) was probably the chief author of the decree, but the influence of Sir Thomas Gresham is plainly evident in it.

[92] Recession; retreat from this position.

[93] Acted upon; executed.

pretensed privileges, and afterwards, by mediation of King *Philip*, yielding to a further moderation, with condition that the *Hanses* within one year next ensuing, should send their Commissioners into England, to confer, treat, and conclude with her Highness' Councillors, in what sort their privileges ought to be taken and used. A whole year passed and five weeks besides without any news or tidings of any commissioners, and to requite the manifold favours they had received, they at an assembly of the *Hanses* at *Lubeck*, published an edict against all Englishmen, forbidding all trade or commerce with them, and staying the carrying out of corn, which was provided for the service and necessity of the Realm. Yet for all these indignities, the said Queen was contented that Commissaries[94] on both parts should meet in England, and agree upon and set down a certain and immutable manner of trade to be held and observed on both sides. But the *Hanses* were so far from accepting of this gracious offer that they wholly refused it, as by a petition of theirs exhibited to King *Philip*, the third of June 1557, appeareth, wherein they declare the cause of that their refusal to be for that they could not have in this Realm any other judges of their cause but such as were suspect,[95] not sparing or excepting the Queen herself, of whose good will and favour they had received so often experience and trial.

MATTER PASSED BETWEEN HER MAJESTY AND THE HANSES

In these terms the *Hanses'* privileges stood all Queen *Mary's* days, after whose decease her Majesty that now is, succeeding, and finding them as they were left without any other ground or foundation than the Prince's[96] favour and good pleasure, yet at the solicitation of *Suderman* and others, Commissioners from the *Hanses*, her Highness was contented that a meeting and communication should be held in the year 1560, whereas the *Hanses* stood and insisted upon their old treaties,

[94] Commissioners. [95] Suspicious; distrusted.
[96] Here, as elsewhere, the Prince is the Sovereign, whether male or female. Wheeler here makes plain the English view-point that the Hanseatic privileges had been legally declared void, and now rested wholly upon the favor of the Queen, whereas the Hanses insisted upon them as a legal right.

and those appointed by her Majesty propounded certain other Articles, intitled, *A moderation of the old privileges*, with this clause of singular favour, *Neque tamen excellentissima Regina propter hanc Moderationem ab ullo superiori legitimo iure ulla ex parte recedi vult, sed saluum ius, saluas actiones, saluam denique reliquam omnem in hac Commercii causa materiam, et sibi ex altera parte, et suis successoribus, et ex altera parte Confœderatis Civitatibus, et eorum posteritati reseruat*[97]. But the *Hanses*' Commissioners not liking thereof, the treaty broke up without any effect. In which terms the matter hung till the year 1572, at which time new Commissioners from the *Hanse* Towns, coming into England for other causes, they renewed their former suit and petition: whereunto they received this answer. That concerning the Custom of their goods there should nothing more be exacted of them than was propounded to the former Commissioners in the year 1560, all this while her Majesty's subjects were deprived of all privilege, and in divers of the *Hanse* Towns hardly and extremely used, as at *Danzick*, *Deventer*, *Campen*, and *Swoll*,[98] to the great hurt and hindrance of the trade,[99] and because the *Hanses* unmeasurably frequented the City of *Antwerp* with English commodity, the M. M. Adventurers were forced to draw themselves wholly to the said City, and leave *Bergen op Zoom*, where they used to keep two Marts in the year.[100] But finally the said Adventurers were constrained to leave *Antwerp* also and to seek another place, as hath been above rehearsed, so that in the year

[97] *Nevertheless the most excellent Queen, by means of this moderation, does not in any sense wish to abrogate any earlier legitimate right, but reserves unimpaired right, freedom of action, and in short every other matter in this question of trade, on the one hand, to herself and her successors, and, on the other, to the confederated cities and their posterity.*

[98] Danzig, Deventer, Kämpen and Zwolle.

[99] This passage is somewhat puzzling. If the Merchants Adventurers adhered to the policies Wheeler has described elsewhere, it is hard to see how they could have been hindered in their trade by ill-usage of English subjects in the places named. Danzig was not in their territory; the merchants there must have been members of the Eastland Company. The other relatively small towns were in the Netherlands, but they were not used as marts, and if the Merchants Adventurers confined their trade to the mart-towns, the attitude of Deventer, Kämpen and Zwolle should not have been particularly harmful to them.

[100] The withdrawal from Bergen op Zoom is a curious effect of Hanseatic competition in Antwerp. Obviously it was not dictated merely by the desire to have a larger number of English traders in Antwerp, but also by the hope that concentration in that town would placate the Antwerpians, who must have looked jealously at any diversion of trade from their town to the neighboring Bergen op Zoom.

1567 they obtained privileges for ten years of the town of *Hamburg*, with this condition thereunto added: *Quod elapsis supradictis annis concessio dictorum Privilegiorum renovaretur, et continuaretur in infinitum, si interim non cederet in civitatis suae damnum, vel dispendium*[101]: That the ten years' time being expired, the foresaid privileges should be renewed and continued forever, if in the meanwhile no hurt or damage happened to their City thereby. But for all this when the ten years were almost complete and run out, the *Hamburgers* signified to the M. M. Adventurers that the time of their privileges expired, and that by a decree of the *Hanse* Towns made at *Lubeck*, they were enjoined not to grant to the said Adventurers any longer privileges, pretending the cause to be for that in England the said *Hanses* were restrained of their ancient liberties, and that daily new exactions were imposed upon their goods, contrary to former treaties, which done the said *Hamburgers* passed a decree, the 20th of June 1578, whereby they abrogated all former liberties granted to the said Adventurers, and ordained that after a prefixed day set down in the said decree, they should not enjoy any other privilege or immunity, than any other strangers in the said City. Which as soon as her Majesty and her Honorable Council understood, they requited the *Hanses* with a like decree, which yet was suspended till the 25th of July 1579, at which time her Majesty, not receiving any satisfaction at the *Hanses*' hands, but to the contrary understanding that the said *Hanses*, at an Assembly at *Lunenburgh*, the second of November, 1579, had set forth an edict for the levying of 7¾ upon the hundred of all goods brought by Englishmen into their territories, or carried out of the same, her Highness upon this occasion commanded the like decree to be made, for the taking of the like sum upon the goods of the *Hanses*. And in this estate the matter stood on both parts, till that by a petition put up by the Alderman of the Steelyard, this last decree of 7¾ upon the hundred was suspended for four months, but the first, be-

[101] This passage is substantially translated into English by Wheeler in the passage immediately following. He may have done this merely for emphasis, but perhaps a few of his readers were unfamiliar with Latin. (Some of the Latin passages he fails to translate are unnecessary to an understanding of his arguments.) For "cederet" see *infra*, p. 432.

cause it depended upon the restraint of trade of her Majesty's subjects, the Lords of the Council thought not good to suspend or revoke the same, till the contents thereof were satisfied, and fulfilled.

THE HANSES THEMSELVES ARE THE CAUSE OF THE RESTRAINT OF THEIR PRIVILEGES IN ENGLAND

And thus I have briefly and truly set down what hath passed, and in what state at this day the whole controversy between her Majesty and the *Hanses* standeth; by the discourse whereof I doubt not but it plainly appeareth that (as aforesaid) the *Hanses* have no just or lawful cause to complain, for that they have themselves been the cause of all that happened. For first, the resuming[102] of their privileges in King *Edward's* days proceeded of this, that they freed and coloured men's goods,[103] that were none of their Society, and for the other causes above rehearsed. Secondly, when as Queen *Mary* had revoked that which had been done by her Brother, she herself at length revoked the said Revocation, for that the *Hanses* had broken promise with her, in continuing an unlawful trade in the Low Countries, whereby she lost in her Customs within the space of eleven months, more than 9360 pounds sterling, besides the damage sustained by her subjects in their trade, and when as she offered a meeting for the deciding of all controversies, the *Hanses* utterly refused the same and would none of it. Thirdly, her Majesty that now is, when she came first to the Crown, commanded that the *Hanses* should be used as well (yea in some points better) than her own subjects, but they in recompense of this favour, not provoked with any new occasion, commanded that the exercise and trade of merchandise granted to her Highness' subjects by the *Hamburgers*, *cum clausula*

[102] Withdrawing.

[103] In all markets where guilds or companies had privileges, it was a serious offense for a member to sell the goods of a non-member as his own. The offense, however, was difficult to detect and prove. The Hanseatic merchants seem to have been either very scrupulous or very careful, and although they were suspected of "colouring" goods of non-members, their accusers had little evidence. In the trial about 1552, the one fairly clear case was that of the sale of goods formerly belonging to a deceased member. His heir was not a member of the Hanse; yet the goods were sold in England instead of being shipped back to Germany. The Hanseatics declared that it was a mistake; but they had been guilty of a technical offense, and a technical offense was all that their accusers needed to prove.

perpetuitatis[104] should be broken off, and disannulled; and afterwards, when her Majesty required a reformation of this their decree, they instead thereof imposed that exaction of theirs of seven and three quarters upon the hundred. And so with their new impositions, their refusing of a meeting and conference in England, their abusing of their liberty in the Low Countries, by doing many things to the prejudice of her Majesty and subjects, by diminishing the revenues of the Crown, by colouring other men's goods under the pretence of their privileges, they were finally deprived of their liberties and immunities at the pleasure of her Highness, yet always were more friendly used than any other the subjects of the Princes in amity and league with her Majesty. For the which they never showed any spark of thankfulness but have from time to time unjustly accused her Highness to foreign Princes and States, her Majesty's loving friends and Confederates, and to this day with much clamorousness and importunacy leave not off to do the same, without respect to the person and quality of so excellent and gracious a Princess, and doing that which is far unbeseeming their state and condition. But if they think to get anything hereby in the end, they are much deceived in mine opinion; their way to speed is to proceed *cum precatione et supplicatione*,[105] and not by way of force and compulsion: *Magnorum siquidem Principum et Regum heroicis animis natura videtur insitum, quod flecti, et duci, non cogi velint.*[106]

DEFENCE OF THE M. M. ADVENTURERS AGAINST THE HANSES SLANDER OF MONOPOLIES

The third cause whereupon the foresaid Mandate of the Emperors is grounded, is, *The Monopoly used* (as is said) *by the Merchants Adventurers;* which to be a false and injurious

[104] It should be remembered that the Hanses claimed perpetual privileges in England, by virtue of a clause added in the time of Edward IV. Nevertheless the privileges were annulled.

[105] Wheeler's advice to the Hanses to approach Queen Elizabeth "with prayer and supplication" was unquestionably sound, but it was the sort of advice they were incapable of taking, even if it had not been too late. The Merchants Adventurers used the policy, and the *Treatise* itself contains many indirect appeals to the Queen's vanity.

[106] *Although it appears to be implanted by nature in the heroic minds of great Princes and Kings hat they are willing to be persuaded and led, but not to be constrained.*

slander and surmise[107] needeth none other demonstration than the true sense and definition of the word *Monopoly* itself: *Quum Monopolium sit quando unus solus aliquod genus mercaturæ universum emit, ut solus suo arbitrio vendat.*[108] *Monopoly* is, when one man alone buyeth up all that is to be got of one kind of merchandise, to the end that he alone may sell at his own lust and pleasure.[109] Which well considered, hath no communion or agreement with the trade and practice of the Company of M. M. Adventurers, and the towns where the said company have resided or are resident in at this day, do know and can witness that those of the said Company have used and do use an honest, upright, and lawful trade *Emptionis, Venditionis, et Permutationis*[110] which by all law is permitted, *vita enim nostra sine contractibus, et commerciis, subsistere nequit,*[111] not only with Cloth, but also with all kind of wares and merchandises. So that whatsoever is free and at liberty to buy and sell, the same by no reason or right construction can be accounted a *Monopoly*. Neither have the Adventurers the sole transport and trade inwards and outwards of English Cloth and other wares, but it is well known and notorious that all the members of the *Hanses*, and not only they but also all the subjects of Upper and Low Germany, and all other strangers in league and amity with the Crown of England, may and do at their liberty and pleasure, buy and carry out of the Realm all sorts of Cloth and English wares, and may and do bring in and sell their own country

[107] Suspicion, (based on scanty evidence).

[108] Here again Wheeler translates his Latin, either for emphasis or for clearness.

[109] Wheeler's definition of monopoly was acceptable to most people of his time, and apparently satisfied the Parliament of 1601, though not that of 1604. However, a somewhat different definition is given in "A Discourse of Corporations." (Harl. Mss. 4243 ff 60 seq., reprinted by Tawney and Power in *Tudor Economic Documents* vol. III, p. 265 ff.) This manuscript says: "Monopoly is an encroachment [engrossment?] of the commodities into the hands of one or few . . . which by the statute of regrating and forestalling is prohibited, otherwise it would be too easy for a small number to become rich and make a multitude poor." And again: "The mischief of monopolies can never be avoided as long as there be any corporations." The writer attacked the trading companies, especially the Merchants Adventurers, and accused them of acting in collusion on prices. The argument of this unknown author is far abler than that of Milles. Tawney and Power conjecture the date as 1587–89, but I believe it was later than 1598, and that the author had seen Wheeler's *Treatise*.

[110] *Of buying, selling, and exchanging.*

[111] *For our life cannot continue without agreements and commerce.*

commodities without impeachment or hindrance, paying such duties and customs as they ought to pay.[112] Besides there are divers other Companies of merchants who are privileged to transport Cloth, etc. out of the land into foreign parts and Countries, as well as the Company of M. M. Adventurers, which they do in great quantity. Moreover, the Company of M. M. Adventurers hath no bank nor common stock, nor common factor to buy or sell for the whole Company, but every man tradeth apart and particularly[113] with his own stock, and with his own factor or servant. Whereupon it necessarily followeth that forasmuch as the M. M. Adventurers have not (as aforesaid) the sole dealing and traffic alone in their own hands, either in England or on the other side the seas, and that *Monopoly definitio cum suo definito*[114] in the least part agreeth not, the said Company by no sound reason or argument can be charged to be any such Monopoliers, or private gain and lucre seekers, as the *Hanses* would make the world believe they are, neither is it to be thought that by the said M. M. Adventurers the said *Hanses* are brought to such apparent loss and hindrance as by their complaints they bear the Emperor and States of the Empire in hand.[115] Concerning that which they allege, that the said Company have their government and officers, keep courts and assemblies, make laws, impose mulcts and penalties, and ship at set times and with appointed fleets, out of which they would infer a Monopoly, it needeth none other answer than I have already made in this treatise, wherein is truly and plainly declared the practice and manner of the Company of Merchants Adventurers in all the abovesaid points, and withal showed the good that cometh to the State and Commonwealth thereby, and how far it is out of the compass of *Monopoly*, a fault not only forbidden, but also worthily to be punished in all well

[112] The fairness of the duties and customs imposed on the Hanses was one of the chief issues in the dispute. Wheeler calmly passes over this with the assumption that they were perfectly fair. The majority of his audience probably needed no argument on this point, for in all markets they were accustomed to discrimination against the "strangers," whether these were merely persons from outside the city or outside the country.

[113] Individually.

[114] *Monopoly definition with their definition;* i.e., the description of a monopoly does not in the least agree with the description of the Merchants Adventurers.

[115] Bear in hand; deceive.

governed commonwealths, *Imò honestorum Principum subditis indignum.*[116] Besides, it is more than strange that the *Hanses* have the face to condemn that in others, as unlawful and Monopolish, which themselves both in England, and everywhere else where they now have, or have had their residence or counters, continually practiced; for who knoweth not that they had their aldermen or consuls, treasurers, secretaries, assistants, and other officers, and kept their meetings, courts, and assemblies, and used Merchants' law among them selves?[117] And if it were lawful and free for them so to do, why may it not be as lawful and free for the M. M. Adventurers to do the like?

But (say the Hanses) the Merchants Adventurers in their courts do set the prices of their own wares and of other men's, ordaining not to sell or buy otherwise, or at other rates or prices, which is plain *Monopoly*. This how true it is, I appeal to the consciences of the very *Hanses* themselves, and of all other merchants with whom the said Company do deal, whether this be a truth, yea or no. Besides, I may boldly and with a good conscience affirm that neither I in all the time of my service[118] neither the oldest man living in the said Company, can say that ever it was known or heard that any such matter of setting price was once mentioned in any court or assembly of the said Company[119]; neither indeed was there ever any such matter, but every man rather studieth to keep his feat and trade as secret to himself as he can, for fear of his fellow, lest being espied, it might be taken out of his hands. And fur-

[116] *Nay more, unworthy of the subjects of honorable Princes.* In other words, to accuse the Merchants Adventurers of monopoly implies an insult to the Queen.

[117] Wheeler points out that the organization of the Merchants Adventurers in the mart-towns was similar to that of the Hanseatic Kontors in England and elsewhere. He might truthfully have said that in many respects they had merely imitated the Hanses, but doubtless he did not wish to admit to his audience that English merchants had copied the methods of foreigners.

[118] Probably about thirty-two years.

[119] Wheeler's assertion that price-fixing was never discussed in the courts or assemblies of the Company was probably true, but may have been slightly disingenuous. The modern business man will find it hard to believe that so limited and closely-knit an organization as the Merchants Adventurers conducted their trade without a satisfactory understanding on the vital matter of prices. Whether the members adopted "gentlemen's agreements" or whether the bulk of the brothers followed in the wake of the older and larger traders is immaterial. Similarly, it is unlikely that their courts punished a member for price-cutting; but a price-cutter could be severely punished for some other technical offenses instead.

ther, it is a thing abhorred and condemned by the laws of the Realm, and therefore, if the Company of M. M. Adventurers could ever have been justly accused of the said crime, they should not have escaped so long without deserved punishment. Lastly, the very state and policy of the said Company cannot abide or brook any Monopoly, as being directly and *ex diametro* contrary and an overthrow to that *Economy* so carefully provided for and preserved by the good laws and orders of the said Company, whereby there is a distribution of the benefits and commodities of the Company to all the members of the same, so much as is possible with great providence and equity ordained, so that every man that will or is able, may participate thereof, so far as they will extend. Whereas if it were otherwise, the meaner sort should not be able to live by[120] the richer, for these in short time would with their great purses and means draw all the trade inwards and outwards into their own hands[121] and (as upon the Bankers in some places) all men's credits should depend upon their sleeves,[122] as having power to give credit to whom they list, to sell or keep up their wares at their pleasure, and to rule the markets as they think good; whereby it would come to pass that a few shall gain and grow mighty and exceeding wealthy, and all the rest shall have nothing to do, and in short time be brought to extreme misery and poverty; but the governed trade of the said Company is here in the way.[123] So that you see how far it is from truth, or likelihood of truth, which is objected against the Company of M. M. Adventurers on this behalf, as being rather an utter enemy than a friend or liker of that greedy and inordinate course; as appeareth partly by that abovesaid, and more evidently as well by the testimony of strangers of divers Nations, as also by attestations under the seals of great and famous Cities (whereof some are of the *Hanses* themselves) which I have set down, not only for the

[120] Exist alongside.

[121] It would seem that unless prices were maintained by agreement, the rich members could indulge in price-cutting until the poorer ones were driven out, rather than that price-fixing would benefit the rich only.

[122] There may be some special significance attached to the word "sleeves" here, but I have not traced it.

[123] Is here an obstacle.

credit, commendation, and justifying of the said Company, but withal for the more manifestation of the truth of that which hath been abovesaid.[124]

TESTIMONY OF STRANGERS AND WHOLE CITIES ON THE COMPANY'S BEHALF AGAINST THE SLANDER OF MONOPOLY

And first, the Senate of *Hamburg*, at such time as they caused to be denounced to the Company the expiration of their privileges, did in their Insinuation the nineteenth of July, 1577, expressly put these words: *Quæ quidem Denunciatio non eo animo fit, quod Societas Mercatorum, quæ se honestè in hac Civitate gessit, et integritate sua bonorum virorum benevolentiam meretur, Senatui nostro molesta, et gravis sit, verum solummodo, ut pactis satisfiat:* And afterwards, *Etenim si inclita Societas Mercatorum florentissimi Regni Angliæ diutius in hac Civitate commorari, mercaturam exercere, et hoc nomine nova pacta posteaquam priora expirarunt cum spectabili Senatu inire in animo habeat, Senatus officio suo, et æquitati non deerit.*[125] Whereby it appeareth in what estimation the said Senate held the Company of Merchants Adventurers, in that they not only commended them for their honest carriage and integrity, but also offer them further favour and entertainment in their City after the ending of the former privileges, which were agreed upon but for ten years, yet with this addition, *Quod elapsis supradictis annis concessio dictorum Privilegiorum renovaretur, et continuaretur in infinitum, si interim non caderet in Civitatis*

[124] Seldom, if ever, has a more imposing array of testimonials been presented than that which is appended to Wheeler's *Treatise*. The names of some of the merchants represented there were probably well known in England at the time. Guicciardini, the Florentine who heads the list of foreign merchants in Antwerp, belonged to a famous family. Louis Guicciardi's *Description of the Trade of Antwerp*, written about 1560 was as highly colorful as a modern effusion by a town boaster. See Tawney and Power, *Tudor Economic Documents*, vol. III, p. 149 ff.

[125] *Which denunciation indeed is not made with the thought that the Society of Merchants, which has borne itself honorably in this city and by its integrity merits the good-will of honorable men, is injurious and offensive to our Senate, but merely that it shall keep its covenants.* And afterwards, *For if the renowned Society of Merchants of the most flourishing realm of England should desire to dwell longer in this city, and trade, and for this purpose enter into new agreements with the illustrious Senate after the former have expired, the Senate will not fail in courtesy and fairness.*

suæ damnum, vel dispendium[126]: Now that the said City received neither loss nor damage by the Company of Merchants Adventurers, the above-written words of honest carriage and integrity proceeding from the Magistrates themselves in the same City do sufficiently bear witness, and since that time also more particularly the said Senate of *Hamburg* doth touch that point of *Monopoly* in a letter written to the Governor and Generality of the said Company in August, 1586, wherein they say that although they cannot deny but that there were complaints made under that name of *Monopoly* to the Emperor and Princes Electors, *tamen nostra cum suffragatione, et approbatione easdem institutas esse constanter negamus: Ideoque quum hæ Actiones ex aliorum potius suffragiis, quam ex nostra voluntate, et arbitrio dependeant, non dubitamus, Magnificentias, et Dominationes vestras diversorum discrepantes intentiones, et sententias maturiore iudicio discussuros*[127]: so that in this point a man may see they agreed not with the rest of their fellows, whose doings they disclaim as having no voice or allowance of theirs. Likewise the late Lord *Egdard*, Earl of *Eastfriesland* in a letter by him written in answer of a Mandate from the Emperor, the 26th of July, 1580, concerning the abovesaid slander of *Monopoly* and Monopolish trade used in *Embden* by the English, hath these words: *Now whatsoever is free to all men and forbidden to none, and whenas this tendeth not to the private commodity of one, or of some few singular persons, nor goeth upon any one sort of wares* (as he had showed that the Trade of the M. M. Adventurers did not) *whether this be a Monopoly or Monopolish trade, that refer I most humbly to your Majesty's consideration, besides the Title of Monopolies in the law declareth, whether it be so, yea or no: it was therefore never my meaning or thought to grant unto the English or any other such Monopolish trade, but such as the law permitteth to all men. And in very deed there is no such Monopolish trade used at Embden, and I therein refer myself to any*

[126] See page 424 where this clause is quoted. Note that the verb here is *caderet;* the previous quotation reads *cederet,* which is presumably a misprint.

[127] *Nevertheless we steadfastly deny that the same were originated with our support and approval, and therefore, since these actions depend rather on votes of others than on our will and decision, we doubt not your Magnificence and rulers will discuss with more mature judgment the conflicting charges and opinions of various individuals.*

just proof, and all both strangers and others, which understand these doings, can herein witness the same with me.[128] This testimony of the Earl, the Senate of the town of *Embden* confirmed by an attestation under their common seal, bearing date the 28th of July, 1582, the true copy whereof and of other the like under the seals of the Cities of *Antwerp*, *Middelburgh*, and *Stade*, I have set down at the end of this Treatise, whereby I doubt not but all the world may perceive that the imputation of *Monopoly* to the Company of M. M. Adventurers is but a malicious, injurious, and altogether false slander, devised by the *Hanses* (as I said before) to draw the Emperor and Princes of Germany to assist them in the obtaining of their unjust pretences and unreasonable demands in England, to the dishonor of her Majesty and hurt of the whole State, as much as in them lieth, which God defend that they should have their wills in.

HER MAJESTY CLEARETH THE M. M. ADVENTURERS OF MONOPOLY

Lastly, to knit up[129] this point, I will add hereunto as a golden *Coronis*[130] of all that hath been said, the judgment of her Highness our most gracious Sovereign, and the true defence of the said Company in certain her Majesty's letters to the Emperor and divers of the Princes of Germany: and namely in one to the Emperor written in November, 1595, the eighth of the said Month, in these words: *Monopolium porro de quo Hanseatici subditos nostros criminantur, calumniæ potius, quam veræ accusationis rationem præ se ferre videtur, ab ipsis enim Imperii subditis, qui Londini resident, diligenter inquiri iussimus, si quid solidi de iniquis subditorum nostrorum negotiandi rationibus referre possent: illi vero ingenuè responderunt, se nihil ea de re in commissis habere, acturos tamen se quamprimum per literas cum suis Maioribus, quumque demum quid responsi acciperent, id totum fideliter relaturos: quæstionem præterea ea de re cum subditis nostris institui mandavimus,*

[128] Unlike the other testimony, the letter of Earl Egdard (or Edzart) is not quoted in the original. The translation seems to be Wheeler's own, judging by its characteristics of style.
[129] Secure. Compare the modern *sew up, tie up, clinch.*
[130] Crown.

Illi vero authenticis scriptis edocent, negotiandi ipsorum rationes a plurimis Civitibus in Belgio, Prussia, atque alibi uti honestissimas probari, atque quum duæ Imperii Civitates sint, quæ eum nostris maximè negotiantur, Lubeca, et Hamburgum, illarum altera publicis literis, ut nostri ostendunt, testata est, ipsorum Negotiationem ab omni Monopolii suspicione vacuam esse, seque illius objectæ criminationis participes nunquam fuisse: ubi vero Hanseaticorum institores plura ea de re ex Dominorum suorum expectata in scriptis commissione opposuerint, se quoque pluribus in scriptis responsuros humiliter obtulerant.[131] This whole letter, for that it containeth matter worthy the knowledge concerning the *Hanses*, I have added unto the end of this Treatise. Her said Majesty in another letter to the Emperor, dated the 20th of December, 1597, sent by Master *John Wroth*, after her Highness had complained of the unorderly setting forth and publishing of the Emperor's Mandate for the reasons in the said letter at large set down, hath these words following: *Quæ si paulo attentius Majestas vestra ratione animoque ponderasset, et ea quæ literis nostris anno 1595mo, menseque Novembri conscriptis sunt comprehensa collatione cum vestris literis mense Iulii facta, diligentius considerasset (de quibus literis vel factiosorum hominum machinationibus vos cælatos esse, vel a quibusdam ex iis qui vestræ Maiestati sunt a consiliis non optima fide vobiscum actum esse magnopere suspicamur) nobis certè persuasissimum est, vos hanc rationem tam iniquam Edicti contra nos, subditosque nostros vestro Imperio haudquaquam subiectos, promulgandi nunquam fuisse suscepturos, sed potius repudiaturos has commentitias Hanseaticorum querelas: quibus quidam præter eorum merita par, atque eadem libertas in Mercaturis apud nos faciendis, quæ nostris hominibus conceditur, oblata est: denique facturos fuisse, ut actiones nostræ remotis partium studiis, fictisque delationibus ad rationis normam et æquitatis, ac iustitiæ ponderibus examinaretur.*[132] And in letters at the same time written

[131] See. translation of letter, pp. 446 ff.

[132] *Which if your Majesty should weigh somewhat more carefully with your reason and mind, and more diligently consider what was written in our letter of November 1595 in comparison with your own of July (concerning which letter we very much suspect either that you were summoned to the Council by the devices of seditious men or that action was taken with your approval by*

to the Princes of Germany and sent by the said Master *Wroth*, and Mr. *Stephen Lesure*, to wit, to the Administrator of *Saxony*, to the *Palgrave* upon the Rhine, the Elector of *Mentz*,[133] and divers others, her Majesty writeth in these words: *Eodem porro Edicto nonnulla in priscam quandam subditorum nostrorum Societatem (quam Adventurariorum vocant) obiecta commemorantur, atque ex iisdem proscriptionis veluti sententia infertur, qua et ex Imperii finibus discedere, atque ab omni intra eosdem emendi ac vendendi usu abstinere iubentur: quæ quidem res admiratione digna videtur, maximè quum literis nostris ad Imperatorem mense Novembri, anno 1595, a Comitiis quæ Ratisbona nonagesimo quarto habebantur datis ad singula Edicto hoc repetita abundè responsum, ac firmissimis rerum momentis satisfactum fuerit, quo sanè credendum nobis erat Cæsaream Maiestatem biennium penè silentio interposito rationibus a nobis allatis acquievisse. Quod si quid adhuc dubii superesse visum fuisset, et Iustitia, et Regiæ nostræ dignitatis ratio, quam sub divino numine absolutam gerimus, pro amicitia saltem nostra quam sanctè hactenus cum Imperio coluimus, aut per literas, aut per internuncium aliquem nobis exponendum illud postulasset: Nunc vero hunc in modum sub silentio ex improviso, etiam Typis exposuisse quæ ad nostram iniuriam (ipsa quoque in subditos nostros Iustitia violata) faciunt, indecorum omnino fuisse arbitramur: omnium enim opinione iniquum merito habendum viros probos nunquam auditos, aut vocatos ex malevolorum obiectis calumniis, nec probatis, et ne quidem ritè examinatis proscriptionis sententia, etiam contra ipsam sacri Imperii libertatem mulctasse.*[134] Thus you see what the opinion of her

certain of them who are deliberately ill-disposed toward your Majesty) we are quite convinced that you would never have undertaken to promulgate an Edict so unjust as this against us and our subjects, at no time subject to your Empire, but rather would have repudiated these false complaints of the Hanseatics, to whom indeed beyond their merits is equally offered the same liberty of trading among us as is granted to our own people; and that you would then cause our actions, free from party bias and false accusations, to be examined by the rule of reason and equity and with the scales of justice.

[133] Mainz.

[134] *Moreover, in the same Edict several charges against a certain ancient Society of our subjects (which they call the Adventurers) are mentioned, and from the same a sentence of confiscation, as it were, is produced whereby also they are ordered to depart from the territories of the Empire and to abstain from all practice at buying and selling within the same, which indeed seems remarkable, especially since, in our letter to the Emperor of November 1595, ample reply was made to the particulars repeated in this Edict by the Council held at Ratisbon in '94, and assurance was*

Majesty and of others hath been of the Company of M. M. Adventurers touching *Monopoly*, whereof they are slandered by the *Hanses*, which I doubt not is sufficient, though not possible to stop the mouths of the said *Hanses*, yet to convince[135] them of untruth and malicious forgery[136] on that behalf.

given by the strongest proofs; wherefore we most certainly believed that your Imperial Majesty, after a silence of almost two years, acquiesced in the arguments put forward by us. And if anything further of a doubtful nature appeared to remain, both justice and a consideration for our royal authority, which we hold by the divine will, or at least for our friendship which we have hitherto cultivated religiously with the Empire, would demand that it should be explained to us either by letter or through some messenger. But now, that it has been even published in prin after this fashion, suddenly and without notice, which is insulting to us, (even justice itself is violated against our subjects), we consider to have been altogether unseemly; for in the opinion of all it is rightly deemed unjust that worthy men, through the calumnious and unproved accusations of ill-disposed persons, were never heard or summoned to court, and indeed that they were punished by sentence of banishment, not after due examination, but even in violation of the very liberty of the Holy Empire.

[135] Convict. [136] Invention.

That the Maintenance of the fellowship of MERCHANTS ADVENTURERS hath been and is for the Honour and Service of the PRINCE *and* STATE *at home and abroad*

ALL that which hath been afore at large set down tendeth in effect to the proof of this point, as if it would please the diligent reader to remember the same and lay it together, would be soon perceived. For whereas I have said and showed that the Merchants Adventurers, as subjects of this noble Realm, have procured at the hands of foreign Princes and States many ample and beneficial jurisdictions, privileges, liberties, exemptions, and immunities, by virtue whereof they have erected a good and convenient government for the rule and ordering of themselves and their trade, and exercise civil jurisdiction beyond the Seas, that the said M. M. Adventurers are a means of the preservation of the amity and league between this land and the said foreign Princes and States, that they advance the price[1] and vent of our country commodities, and bring in foreign wares good cheap, that they are a maintenance of the navigation, and increase of the Customs at home, who seeth not, and confesseth that all these things are to the high honour of the Prince and notable service of the State and Commonwealth? Besides all this, some of the Princes of this land have known so well how to use this Company, and to make their uttermost benefit of them, that besides that the said Company have at sundry times upon urgent occasions given their credits for the loans of great sums of money beyond the seas,[2] for the service of the State, divers of the Governors and others of the said Com-

[1] This seems slightly inconsistent with Wheeler's declaration that the company has no price-maintenance policy.

[2] Note that Wheeler mentions only foreign loans to the State upon the credit of the Company, not loans by the Company itself. His silence upon this point may possibly be an indication that they did not care to advertise themselves as able and willing to lend money, even to the State. In fact, many of their loans, if not all, were made unwillingly.

pany, have in particular not been wanting, according to their duty, to do their Prince good and commendable service many times in the affairs of the State.[3] Further at the change of Princes and receiving in of new, at triumphs for victories and coronations, the said Company have not forgot the honour of their Prince and Country, but have spent and laid out great sums of money this way, so that at some one Prince's receiving in, they have consumed above two thousand French crowns in shows[4] or triumphal arches, and namely of the late King *Philip* of *Spain*, at his entry into the City of *Antwerp* in September, 1549, at such time as his Father, the Emperor *Charles* the Fifth, transferred unto him all his Seignories and States in the Low Countries. Besides that Master *John Sturgeon*, at that time Governor of the Company, was at the receiving in of the said Prince, accompanied with thirty Merchants of the Company on horseback, all in a livery of purple velvet in grain[5] coats, and paned hose embroidered full of silver waves like the waves of the sea: their doublets and drawing out of their hose[6] purple satin, their hats of purple velvet with gold bands, fair[7] brooches, and white feathers: and each of them a chain of gold about his neck of great value: buskins of purple velvet, their rapiers, daggers, spurs, stirrups, and bridles all gilt: the furniture[8] of their horses was of purple velvet, saddles and trappings, etc., embroidered with gold and green silk, and white and green feathers on their horseheads. They were attended with three score lackeys, appareled in white velvet jerkins cut,[9] embroidered with silver twist,[10] green satin doublets, with hose and buskins of the same, purple velvet caps and green feathers. Behind them rode the abovesaid Governor upon a white English gelding, in a long purple velvet gown, lined with purple satin: a black velvet coat and cap with a fair brooch therein, and a chain of

[3] George Gilpin, the predecessor of Wheeler, was a diplomatic agent for the Queen for years before he resigned his position as Secretary of the Company.

[4] Pageants.

[5] Velvet dyed in grain; i.e. deeply dyed.

[6] Probably the lining visible through the slashes or "panes" of the hose.

[7] Handsome; elegant.

[8] Equipment; harness.

[9] With ornamental slashes. [10] Cord.

gold about his neck: his doublet and hose with the trappings of his horse were as the others of his Company wore. He was attended on by six lackeys on foot, and three pages on horseback appareled as aforesaid.[11] In which their doing they showed themselves for the honour of their Prince and Country nothing inferior to the merchants of other nations, namely the Germans, Easterlings, Italians, Spaniards and Portugals, and surmounting[12] some of them in costly apparel, furniture of themselves and their horses, and in other preparation to entertain the said Prince, whereby they won great honour and commendation to themselves and the whole English name.[13] To say nothing of the late Duke of *Alanson's* entertainment into the said city of *Antwerp* in the year 1581, at which time Master *Christopher Hoddesden*, then and now Governor, received the said Duke with four score merchants of the said Company, all on horseback in very seemly and decent sort,[14] appareled in black velvet, and most of them with chains of gold about their necks,[15] for the which the said Governor and Company received thanks and commendation from her Majesty and the Lords of the Council, whereof some were beholders of that abovesaid, and made honorable report thereof unto her Highness at their return home.

In deeds of piety and Charity they have not also been wanting, as well appeared by the founding of chapels in old time at *Bruges* and *Middelburgh*, and since in maintaining the exercise of religion amongst them in all the places of their residence hitherto, yea even among those who could not well away

[11] The English merchants, it will be noted, were not so vulgar as to advertise their own famous cloth by wearing it. Doubtless they preferred to show their status as buyers rather than as sellers.

[12] Surpassing.

[13] This method of honoring the Prince and State was ridiculed by opponents like Milles, but it performed a useful and appreciated function in its time. Wheeler may have obtained the information for his description from records of the Company or from a detailed account by Corn. Scribonius Grapheus, which is cited by Thuanus. See M. de Thou's *History of his own Time*, translated from the Geneva Edition of 1620 by B. Wilson, 1729, vol. I, p. 266.

[14] Suitable fashion.

[15] Wheeler had probably seen this pageant; yet his description of it occupies but a few lines, whereas he devoted more than a page to the pageant of 1549. Although the number of merchants was greater on this latter occasion, they were less gorgeously attired, and besides some of his readers had witnessed the spectacle themselves, or had heard it described.

with[16] the same: as also by their Christian-like care and provision for the poor, the comfort whereof many a distressed person, soldiers, and mariners, etc. of our Nation have found and daily find. Besides their liberality is known to a great many who heretofore have tasted the same, especially those who have and do receive yearly pensions from them,[17] partly in remembrance and gratification of past service, and partly for their better relief, maintenance, and sustentation[18] in their old days, as also in learning and otherwise. Hereunto may be added the great and continual charges which from time to time they have been at, and still are in these troublesome times, through the manifold disturbance, removing, and alteration of the trade about the procuring of new privileges and residence for the better vent and utterance of the commodities of the Realm, and maintenance of the commerce and traffic in foreign parts. And when for the defence of the Realm, ships have been to be made out,[19] it hath cost them notable sums of money, as by their accounts thereof doth appear. All which could not have been done but by men united into a Society or Company, as would be too too evident if once all were set at liberty, as some would have it; for then it would in few years come to pass that we should neither have privilege nor jurisdiction abroad, the friendship and kind[20] usage of our neighbours would wax[21] cold and faint, yea we should go to the walls, be wronged and exacted upon everywhere, our Country commodities would grow vile,[22] or come into the hands and managing of strangers, at whose courtesy also, or at least of a few cormorants[23] of our own Nation, we should stand for that we have need of from abroad: by means whereof, the incomes and customs of the Prince would be sore diminished, and the Navigation decayed: and lastly, if there were

[16] Could not well endure. See Isa. I. 13. Apparently the business men of that day were not all religiously inclined.

[17] Even the bitter opponents of the Merchants Adventurers admitted that they were considerate and charitable. Van Meteren in his marginal notes grudgingly comments that for this policy the company "is to be remembered and partly blessed." They must have been among the earliest corporations to adopt a pension system, if not the very first.

[18] Support. [19] Sent out.

[20] The London edition erroneously inserts the word "of" here, reading, "kind of usage."

[21] Grow. [22] Become cheap; be depreciated. [23] Profiteers.

occasion either at home of any thing of importance to be done on the sudden for the defence of the Realm, the extraordinary help of the M. M. Adventurers would be wanting, and in foreign parts, if there were need, either of money or other provision for the service of the Prince and State, no man would be found, and so neither credit nor means would be found or had to serve the turn withal, neither any man to do any thing for the honour of the Prince and Country, howsoever necessary or urgent the occasion may be, either general or particular. All which I doubt not will be well considered of and weighed by her Excellent Majesty and those which under her Highness have the ordering and government of the affairs and state of this noble Realm, that so the Commonwealth may prosper and increase in honour and flourishing estate, and that those which travail and take pains to this end, and have from time to time been found profitable members, may be cherished and maintained in their well doing, and encouraged to proceed, by vouchsafing them gracious countenance and favourable aid and assistance in their causes, and by upholding them in the full and quiet fruition and use of their privileges, charters, and rights[24] given heretofore with so good consideration, and hitherto continued, to the high Honour of her Majesty, and the general good of this Realm, as I hope in this treatise to have plainly and evidently proved, to the reasonable satisfaction of all that love not novelties, or have no outlandish appetites[25]: especially of those in honorable and eminent place, for whose information principally I undertook this labour, humbly praying that it may be well accepted, and bring forth such good as is thereby meant unto her Royal Majesty, and the whole land with all the members thereof, the continual happiness and prosperity whereof the Almighty grant, by whom Princes reign, and without whom nothing is happy, or perdurable.[26]

And you, true-hearted Merchants Adventurers, for whose sake I have written this treatise, faint not in your orderly and hitherto well-continued course, under the favour and protec-

[24] A very pertinent hint to the Privy Council, in view of the recent violation of these privileges, charters, and rights.

[25] Liking for foreign things (and persons?). [26] Lasting.

tion of so gracious and excellent a Princess, which you have oftentimes proved, and seen, and by the aid and direction of so Honourable and wise a Council as that of her Majesty, of whom you may be well assured to receive all necessary and reasonable assistance in your honest and commendable exercise and feat of merchandise. Maintain the credit and honour which you have gotten abroad, continue in well doing, keep you to your ancient orders and *Policy*. Preserve union and concord amongst you diligently and carefully, *et valeant qui dissiduum inter vos volunt*,[27] note them notwithstanding, and look unto them betimes, for there are dangerous persons, lovers of themselves, and enemies to your good and the welfare of your Society, wherein they and the *Hanses* jump together and agree: for neither the one nor the other would have you to be a Company, for that is in their way,[28] and restraineth the one's inordinate gourmandise,[29] and thirst after private lucre, only regarding the time present and nothing at all the posterity (which is a pestilent and pernicious humor[30] in all commonwealths) and keepeth the other from preying upon the commonwealth of this Realm and having their will of the State. As for the said *Hanses*' slanderous complaints and accusations of *Monopoly* forged without ground of truth, it shall be for your credit to answer, where they shall be ashamed of their doings, and at length blush, *vendere tam vanos circum Palatia fumos*[31]: which you may easily do, and without any great charge.[32] And for the *Hanses* themselves, neither they nor their means are so great that the State need greatly to fear them, for if we will but consider the causes that made them of estimation and account in old time; namely, the multitude of their shipping and sea trade whereby they stored all Countries with the Eastern commodities, and served Princes' turns in time of war and of use of shipping: we shall find that they have in a manner lost both the one and the other long ago in

[27] *Away with them who wish dissensions among you!* Terence, *Andria*, 4, 2, 13.
[28] An obstacle to them. [29] Gluttony. [30] Disposition; tendency.
[31] *To sell empty smoke around the palace.* Martial, *Epigrammata* (*ad Fabianum*), 4, 5, 7. Martial used it to mean making empty promises of influence with the Emperor. Wheeler may be using it in a different sense: that of circulating baseless slanders about the Queen.
[32] An anticlimactic (but doubtless necessary) appeal to the thrift of the merchants.

comparison of that it hath been and is now at this day with them. And if her Majesty should forbid all trade into Spain after the example of other Princes, they would in short time be quit of the rest[33]; for that trade is their chiefest support at this instant, and might be taken from them if it so were thought meet unto her Highness, and the Lords and others of her Honorable Council. Besides of the two and seventy confederate *Hanse* Towns, so much spoken and vaunted of, what remaineth almost but the report, and those which remain and appear by their Deputies when there is any assembly, are they of one mind? Or are they able, but with much ado, to bring up the charges and contributions necessary and incident for the defence and maintenance of their league, privileges, and trade in foreign parts, and at home? Surely no. So that it appeareth that they are not the men they have been, and therefore although their stomachs[34] and malice no doubt be big enough, yet we need not much to regard what they can do, for most of their teeth are out and the remainder are but loose and scattered.[35] Much better therefore were it for them to seek the recovery of her Majesty's favour and grace by some other more decent course and means, than they have of late practiced. *Precatio et supplicatio* were fitter for them, and would become them better, as I said before. Let them remember the difficulties which some of the *Hanse* towns are already brought into by their neighbor Princes, and what yet hangeth over some other of their heads, for the preventing or removing of the like whereof the very opinion of the good-will and friendship of her Highness would not be a little available, and may profit much hereafter. Wherefore like wise men, knowing their fault and error, let them shape another course, for this which they hitherto have run will not bring them there where they would fain be. And when all is done, and that they have spent their money, and wearied the world with their importunate

[33] Be deprived of the rest.

[34] Anger.

[35] It was true that the Hanseatic League was already disintegrating. After this period they never recovered their dominance of the Northern trade, and during the Thirty Years War their power was broken beyond repair. The cities that prospered most seem to have been those that earliest asserted their independence of the Confederation, notably Hamburg.

complaints and outcries, do they think that they shall recover their privileges in England by forcing her Majesty or the State? I suppose they are not so senseless. As for the trade in Cloth out of England, which they so much contend for, I am of opinion if the matter were well examined, that the riotousness and unfaithful dealing of their servants and factors, the adventure of the sea, and charges, when they shipped and held the Steelyard at London considered, they did more profit by buying of the M. M. Adventurers at *Embden*, and *Hamburgh*, especially the merchants of *Hamburgh*[36] than by fetching of Cloth themselves out of England. But let that be as it may be, I must confess that the ancient friendship and Commerce between the Realm of England and the *Hanses* (howsoever they be now decayed) ought not altogether to be forgotten, that so by some good and indifferent means and agreement the trade and amity between the two most noble Dutch and English Nations might be made firm and stable, and the ancient and friendly neighbourhood confirmed against all human changes and chances, which are uncertain and variable: yet so that strangers be not preferred before the natural-born subject, who at all times is and must be ready to serve his Prince and Country with his person and goods at home and abroad, when the strangers and strange help will be far off and to seek. And therefore the demand of the *Hanses* in this behalf is very absurd and unreasonable, *Nam sitientibus nostris agris alienos irrigare, stultum esse Leges ducunt, et ordinatam Charitatem incipere a seipso, etia Theologi admittunt.*[37] Wherewith I will conclude this *Treatise*, hoping that therein I have sufficiently declared and made known that which I took upon me at the beginning, namely, *The Commodities of a well ordered Trade*, such as I doubt not I have proved that of the Society or Company of M. M. Adventurers to be, and the *Necessariness of the said Society* in this flourishing State.

[36] Wheeler may have written this passage with the expectation that it would come to the attention of influential persons in Hamburg. Even as early as this, the Merchants Adventurers may have been secretly negotiating for a return to this city; certainly they were soon afterwards.

[37] *For the laws account it folly for strangers to water our parched fields, and even theologians admit that well-ordered charity begins at home.*

Quem Deus incolumem servet, faxitque perennem.[38]

That so the members and parts thereof may continually and daily more and more prosper, and grow up in the same, to the honour of God, their Prince, and Country.

[38] *Which may God keep safe, and make everlasting.*

Copy of a letter from HER MAJESTY *in answer of a letter received from the* EMPEROR *in High Dutch, whereof the* Mandate *maketh mention but much differing from the contents of this copy*

ELIZABETH,

by the grace of God, Queen of England, France and Ireland, Defender of the Faith, etc. To the most serene Prince and Lord, Lord RUDOLPH, ever august Elect Emperor of the Romans, King of Hungary, Bohemia, Dalmatia, and Slavonia, Archduke of Austria; Duke of Burgundy, Styria, Carinthia and Württemberg; Count of Tyrol, etc. To our very dear Brother and Cousin; Greeting, and most auspicious increase of things most desired.

Most serene Prince, most esteemed Brother and Cousin, the letter of your Serenity, dated the 15th of July (and that indeed written in German,[1] which truly at first sight, since that kind of idiom has not at all been customary among us hitherto, caused no slight doubt about its authenticity) was presented to us about the end of October; which, indeed, from the subject matter we perceive to have been written at the instance of the Hanseatics. Insofar, indeed, as they themselves had decided to make false claim to certain obsolete privileges in our Realm, in the 82nd year,[2] in the Imperial Diet held at Augsberg, they extorted an injunction (as appears by this letter of your Serenity) with intent to disturb the common trade of the Empire and our dominions; and now recently, in the 94th year,[3] in the Assembly of Deputies at Ratisbon, on account of their losses at sea sustained within our waters (as they complain), some rules of trade in the Empire on the part of our merchants (which they call by the odious name Mo-

[1] The letter ought to have been in Latin. To send a letter in his own language instead of the universal language of diplomacy, was not only undiplomatic but also discourteous.

[2] 1582.

[3] 1594.

nopoly) being alleged and brought forth, they have finally demanded the force and execution of that Augsberg decree. Whereupon Your Serenity, in consideration of our mutual friendship (which we gladly cherish with the affection of a well-beloved sister) has now written, and exhorts us to consider about remedies for such evils, by which, without ground for complaint, everything may be maintained in the most flourishing state of amity. In that mind, certainly, we have ever been toward your Serenity and your Empire, as we have resolved ever to uphold the laws of closest friendship and to practise them inviolately; which inclination of our mind, indeed, we have been studious more than usually to make most clear in the present case, so in turn we shall never fail in the obligations of our mutual affection. As for the complaints of the Hanseatics, it is necessary to examine the general grounds for them; as, forsooth, they are found to be the less rightly put forward, they fall to the ground of themselves. Nevertheless, answer has already often been made elsewhere concerning the privileges mentioned; that they themselves lapsed before our inauguration and, especially through allegations and proofs to the highest public court of our Realm (from which no Court of Appeal is recognized), were entirely overthrown and abolished. We indeed for some time granted to the Hanseatics certain others, as the interests of the times demanded; until they themselves by their own extraordinary decree rashly drove out our subjects then residing honorably in Hamburg, without consideration for our dignity or friendship, without cause, and entirely without warning to us. Some time after, since we had received from your Serenity a letter of recommendation in their favor, we repeatedly showed ourselves sufficiently disposed to grant the same terms for doing business with us as our own subjects enjoy; nevertheless they have so far sought nothing of this kind from us. Now therefore, your Serenity, to whom Almighty God has subjected peoples, and taught by experience how to govern, should weigh carefully whether to give ear to those who busy themselves to raise from the ashes ancient privileges once for all taken away by due process of law and now for a long time entirely abolished, privileges which the changed customs of the times and men do not take over from the ancients. For what were the state of governments if aught now for a long time annulled for just cause should be revived at anyone's request? Nor indeed is it anywhere customary, nor does it seem to stand with any reason, that foreigners should be preferred to natives in the enjoyment of those things which are peculiar to kingdoms; nay rather, it stands as a singular favor if they are made equal: which is what, on account of the singular zeal of our friendship, we had for a long time decided graciously to grant to the cities of the Empire if any sought it.

Meanwhile, in fact, we have never denied to any subjects whatever of the Empire the power to move freely in our dominions and to do business after the manner of foreigners. We have always out of friendship permitted them their own house in our Metropolis where they might live after their own fashion, so that indeed they cannot rightly complain that they have ever been regarded as threatened enemies among us. But as for what they advance about losses suffered, the matter stands thus. Since in these later years we began to be involved in the Spanish Wars, after the manner of princes we decreed the shutting-off of warlike assistance to our enemies as much as possible, and to that end advised our neighbor states; and if any should attempt to carry contraband in this time of war to Spain, we declared that the same should be regarded in some measure as aiders and abettors of the enemy and should be penalized by confiscation of the contraband; whereupon our naval forces attacked several ships of the Hanseatics laden with contraband. But ships and mariners having been released through indulgence, only the goods contraband by the law of war and the ordinances of our Realm were forfeited to the treasury. Which losses of theirs indeed (for about others nothing is known to us), lawfully imposed as a fine, cannot be restored with any colorable pretext of equity.

Further, the monopoly of which the Hanseatics accuse our subjects seems to betray a sense of calumny rather than of true accusation; for we gave orders for inquiry to be made of the subjects of the Empire themselves who reside in London, whether they could allege anything concrete concerning the unfair dealings of our subjects, but they answered frankly that they had no information on this point; nevertheless they would attend to it as soon as possible through letters to their superiors. Moreover we ordered inquiry to be made among our own subjects concerning the matter; they indeed by authentic documents inform us that their methods of conducting business are approved by most cities in Belgium, Prussia, and elsewhere as most honorable.[4] And besides, since there are two cities of the Empire, Lübeck and Hamburg, which trade largely with ours, the second of them has testified in a public letter (as our subjects show) that their business transactions are free from all suspicion of monopoly, and that they themselves were never privy to the accusations put forth. When indeed the agents of the Hanseatics pledged in writing more on the matter from the expected commission of their Governors, they also proffered humbly to reply in a further letter. As for the Augsberg mandate prohibiting trade, we do not sufficiently understand by what reason the Princes of the Empire, if rightly informed, could take cognizance of privileges and other matters pertaining to our Realm, always independent of the laws of the Empire; nor do we see by what documents they could be brought to think that the prohibition of trade would be profitable to the Empire, your Serenity, themselves, or to the cities of the Empire. Wherefore we regard with reason that decree, as one that was surreptitiously obtained, to have been suspended by the highest law and to be suspended from now on. Meanwhile, lest anything be lacking to our mutual friendship, after our wonted fashion we will mercifully shield with our gracious protection the subjects of the Empire who chance to dwell in our Realm; and if Lübeck, Hamburg, or any other city of your Serenity, should humbly beg our favor in their own name, saying what rules of business they desire to be made for their greater convenience, they will readily understand that the recommendation of your Serenity has great weight with us; we, on the other hand, lov-

[4] Among the documents referred to were probably the letters from Antwerp, Emden, and Stade, which follow.

ingly beseech that your Serenity will not refuse to bestow equally your gracious favor on our subjects in your Empire. Meanwhile we implore every felicity from Almighty God upon you. Given at our royal palace at Richmond, the eighth of November, in the year of our Lord 1595, and in the 37th year of our reign.

Your Serenity's Sister and Cousin,
ELIZABETH

Attestation of the City *of* Antwerp *on the Company of MERCHANTS ADVENTURERS' behalf*

To all and singular who shall see or hear our present testimonial letter, the Burgomaster and Echevins of the city of Antwerp in the Duchy of Brabant Greeting: Since it is dutiful and in accord with reason to bear testimony to the truth especially if we are required to safeguard the rights of another. Hence it is that we express the utmost confidence in the request of the eminent lords of the Governor, the assistants and the general merchants of the English nation who for many years have resided in our city of Antwerp, and still reside, have always conducted business which is honorable, lawful, and also beneficial to the State, and moreover still conduct it, buying, selling, and exchanging goods, and entering into lawful contracts, nor have they exercised any discrimination among the merchants with whom they have made contracts, of whatever nation they might be, so long as they were solvent and of approved credit, to whom at times for cash, at times on credit, they have always sold without distinction cloths, kerseys, and their other wares, and still sell. In belief whereof we have at this time caused this letter to be fortified with the seal of this city. Given the 19th day of April, Anno Domini 1582.[1]

[1] This and the two following testimonials were apparently secured for use by friends of the Merchants Adventurers in pleading their case in the Diet at Augsburg in 1582.

Attestation of 28 Merchants *in* Antwerp *of Sundry Nations, concerning the Company's orderly Trade and clearness from* Monopoly

To all and singular who shall inspect or hear this letter the Burgomaster, Echevins and Consuls of the City of Antwerp Greeting. We make known and earnestly bear witness as follows. That on the day below written, at the instance of the eminent lords of the Governor, the assistants and general merchants of the English nation, resident in this city, there appeared before us Masters Ludovico Guicciardini, Florentine, Carolo Lanfranchi, Giovanni Angelo Vergano, Gaspare Revelasco, Lamberto Lamberti, Simon Tassa, Bartolomeo Luquini, Bartolomeo Balbi, of the Italian nation; Masters Jacobo de Pardo, Pedro de la Pena, Spaniards; Masters Fernando Ximenes, Rodrigo de Vega, Luiz Fernandez, Simon Rodrigues, Portuguese or Lusitanians; Masters Johann Putz, Jakob Lange, Jeremias Gennis, Germans; Masters Theodorik de Moy, Louis de Becque, Jakob van Yewerven, Gwalter Schot, Hendrik Moons, Daniel de Lommel, Arnold Boudewijns, Nikolaas Rampart, Hendrik van Homssen, Jan van den Steene, and Jakob Schot,[1] citizens and inhabitants of this town, and all merchants frequenting the Bourse of this town, men worthy of trust and well known to us, Who by their oaths solemnly made have sworn and affirmed, after being first summoned judicially for that purpose, that the aforesaid merchants of the English nation, as well in the city of Antwerp as in other places where they trade, have conducted fair and lawful business, and still conduct it, nor could they ascertain to what extent the same merchants have made a business of lending or giving money at usury, or have used monopolies; but on the contrary, the same have always conducted and

[1] Van Meteren, in his marginal notes, sneers at this list of merchants, saying that they are vicious and jealous men, ignorant of international treaties.

from day to day conduct fair business, consisting in buying, selling and exchanging wares, and entering into other lawful contracts. And likewise the aforesaid English merchants sell the cloths, kerseys and other wares to all and sundry nations of the Christian world without distinction, just as indeed the said deponents could never ascertain that the said merchants among themselves had set up any ordinances and statutes whereby they advance the fixed price on their cloths, kerseys and other wares, at which they ought to be sold at retail. Indeed their business has always been and is unfettered. Moreover the English Merchants resident in this city of Antwerp, and Emden, or elsewhere for the great part have different servants and factors, and separate dwellings and warehouses, as far as possible doing business individually and separately, at their pleasure, some on credit, and again some at greater price, some at less, or even by exchange of goods, and in other ways, without deceit. In testimony whereof we have caused to be attached hereto the seal of this city of Antwerp, the nineteenth day of the month of April, in the year of our Lord, the one thousand five hundred and eighty-second.

Attestation of the Town *of* Emden *in* East-Friesland *on the behalf of the Company of MERCHANTS ADVENTURERS*

To all and singular, of whatever rank and dignity, who shall see or inspect this our letter, We the Consuls, Senators, and Magistrates of the city of Emden, situated in East-Friesland under the protection of his sacred Imperial Majesty, our most merciful Lord, and under the present jurisdiction of the Holy Roman Empire, after due and humble expression of greeting and our respect, make known publicly and testify: Since the most illustrious English nation, for some years resident in this city, conducts business of divers sorts, and through its Secretary, and learned Proctor, and the distinguished man Mr. John More, has sought from us in full Senate testimony concerning its method of business and trade, we have decided by no means to refuse them that service in so far as our knowledge extends; Wherefore we affirm for certain and testify publicly that the Merchants of the said English nation, and their servants and business managers (whom they call Adventurers), insofar as is known to us, so long as they have been among us have always conducted themselves honorably and lawfully in their contracts and business affairs, and still carry on, practise, and transact honorable, unrestricted and lawful trade, buying, selling, and exchanging cloths, kerseys, and other wares, and do not act otherwise than is meet for upright and worthy merchants and traders to act. Accordingly, since it is the duty of a magistrate, when asked for that purpose, to bear witness to the truth, we have decided also to declare publicly our mind concerning the matter. In confirmation whereof we have with full knowledge hereto attached our seal. In the year of our Lord the one thousand five hundred and eighty-second, the twenty-eighth day of July.

Attestation of fourteen Merchants in Stade *of sundry places on the behalf of the Company of MERCHANTS ADVENTURERS*

To all and singular who shall see or hear this present letter, of whatever degree of dignity, honor and eminence they may be, We, the Consuls and Senators of the Commonwealth of Stade, in the Archbishopric of Bremen, after due offering of our respects, and honorable greeting, make known and publicly attest that, at the instance of Mr. Thomas Ferrers, eminent among the notable and discreet, Agent of her Royal Majesty of England, and of the Governor and other assistants and English merchants of the Society of Adventurers, for some years past resident in our city, and now for some time expecting their departure when the sea permits,[1] there have appeared before us, duly and judicially summoned, eminent and honorable men, witnesses worthy of trust, and daily frequenting the Bourse and market place of our city: Masters Giovanni Calandrino, of Lucca, Italian; Bartholomew Pels, William Bartolotti, Jacques de Greve, Antoine Boots, Jerome Hester, Simon de Bock, Matthew de Kestelt, of Antwerp; Francis Boudewin, of Bois-le-Duc; Guillaume de Bari, of Tournai; Antony Engelbrecht, of Aix-la-Chapelle; Antony Geir, of Cologne; John Philip Stamler and George Mauritius, of Augsberg; well and sufficiently admonished about speaking the truth and, on the understanding that they promised by a pledge of given right hands, having the force and effect of a corporal oath, that if required they do not refuse to be answerable about the matter, have deposed and attested that it is very well known to them and they themselves have verified that the Merchants Adventurers of the English nation, hitherto residing in our city and now prepared to leave, are

[1] This explanation of the delay in departing from Stade was probably a diplomatic fiction.

accustomed to sell not only cloths, kerseys, baize, but also other varied and divers wares imported hither from England, to all and sundry inhabitants of the Christian world without any distinction of nation or religion and on the other hand to buy, or accept in payment from others, all manner of goods, acceptable to themselves, and to forward them hence to England; and moreover in like manner it is absolutely open to all merchants to have their wares shipped into England and there sold, and for other wares of all kinds to be bought in Germany and all other regions and carried after payment of the regular customs, and this lawful and fair business of buying and selling and entering into other lawful contracts the English Merchants Adventurers have hitherto transacted no less than all other merchants; nor is it known to them, nor have they ever heard, that the English merchants hitherto residing among us have made a business of lending or giving money at interest, much less have they made agreements or statutes among themselves by which they have obligated one another either to sell their own wares at a fixed price, which it is unlawful to alter short of a penalty, or similarly to buy another's wares, but on the contrary it is known to all that cloths, kerseys, baize and all other wares, can be found, of the same quality and mark, among most of the English merchants of the Adventurers' Society, living in different shops and separate dwellings, both lords and factors, whether servants or agents, at one and the same time, and they not at a single price but at the most varied prices, at two, three, four, five, yea even more pounds, and if at one time for greater, at another for less price, for cash or on credit, pledges being given or exchange made of goods, as the circumstances of each required, and equally other wares of various kinds could be sold to them. Nor has it ever come to their notice, nor could they ascertain that the English merchants of the Adventurers Society, so long as they have lived here in Stade, were lawfully and legitimately accused, much less ever convicted, of monopoly by anyone, without any guile, fraud or underhand device. In testimony whereof we have knowingly ordered the usual seal of our city to be attached hereto. Given on the twelfth day of February in the year of the salubrious nativity of our only Lord and Redeemer Jesus Christ, the one thousand five hundred and ninety-eighth.[1]

[1] This testimonial was obviously secured after the Emperor's Mandate had been published, but before the Merchants Adventurers had actually departed from Stade. See *supra*, p. 417. For what purpose it was originally intended is uncertain, since it was hardly possible that a revocation of the Mandate could be obtained.

Attestation of the Town *of* Middelburg *in* Zeeland *on the behalf of the Company of MERCHANTS ADVENTURERS*

To all and singular who shall see or hear our present testimonial letter, the Burgomasters, Echevins and Senators of the city of Middelburg in the Province of Zeeland Greeting: Since it is dutiful and in accord with reason to bear testimony to the truth especially if we are required to safeguard the rights of another, hence it is that we express the utmost confidence in the request of the eminent lords of the Governor, the assistants and the general merchants of the English nation who for many years have resided in our city of Middelburg, and still reside, have always conducted business which is honorable, lawful and also beneficial to the State, and moreover still conduct it, buying, selling, and exchanging goods, and entering into lawful contracts, nor have they exercised any discrimination among the merchants with whom they have made contracts, of whatsoever nation they might be, so long as they were solvent and of approved credit, to whom at times for cash, at times on credit, they have always sold without distinction cloths, kerseys and their other wares, and still sell. We testify that it was never known to us, nor have we ever heard, that the said English Merchants Adventurers hitherto residing among us have made a business of lending or giving money at interest, much less have they made agreements or statutes among themselves by which they have obligated one another either to sell their own wares at a fixed price, which it is unlawful to alter short of a penalty, or similarly to buy another's wares, but on the contrary it is known to all that cloths, kerseys, and all other wares, can be found, of the same quality and mark, among most of the English merchants of the aforesaid Society, living in different shops and separate dwellings, both lords and factors, whether servants or agents, at one and the same time, and that not at a single price but at the most varied prices, at two, three, four, five and more pounds, and thus at one time for greater, at another for less price, for cash or on credit, pledges being given or exchange made of goods, as circumstances of each required, and equally other wares of various kinds could be sold to them. Nor has it ever come to our notice, nor could we ascertain that the English merchants of the aforesaid Adventurers Society, so long as they have lived here in Middelburg, were lawfully and legitimately accused, much less convicted, of monopoly by anyone, without any guile, fraud and underhand device. In testimony whereof we have ordered one of our Secretaries to subscribe this instrument, and to attach the seal hereto, as is our custom in similar business: Done the seventh day of the month of July, in the year of our Lord the one thousand and six hundredth.[1]

Schotte.

[1] This testimonial seems to have been "manufactured" by copying and piecing together parts of letters from other cities. Evidently Wheeler showed his Middelburg friends exactly what sort of testimonial he wanted—or else composed it for them. The date is not a certain proof that the *Treatise* was contemplated as early as July, 1600; the testimonial may have been secured in order to make the representation of the mart-towns complete.

APPENDIX

BIBLIOGRAPHICAL NOTE ON THE MIDDELBURG EDITION

As the London edition of Wheeler's *Treatise* is to be made available in a reprint announced by the Facsimile Text Society, it is unnecessary here to comment in detail upon the differences between the two editions. At first glance, the variants appear extremely numerous, but close analysis reveals the fact that they are almost entirely variants in spelling, due to the practice of the two printers, Schilders and Harison. Neither printer was consistent in his practice. Spelling at that time was unstandardized, and in each edition the same word appears in a number of different forms, the choice being determined largely by the exigencies of spacing out a line.

The spelling in the London edition, however, is somewhat closer to modern practice than that in the Middelburg edition. Schilders had gained his experience in England some twenty years earlier (see p. 28) and possibly had not kept closely in touch with the developments in English printing and English orthography since that time. At any rate, he uses a much larger percentage of doubled letters and superfluous "e's" and "u's." He commonly uses *ie* at the end of such words as *manie* and *secretarie*, where Harison commonly uses a final *y*.

Harison undoubtedly shows a tendency toward simplification of spelling. He even carries this tendency so far as to undouble letters and drop final "e's" where modern usage has retained them in the form used by Schilders. Thus for *fall*, Harison sometimes uses *fal;* for *manner*, *maner;* and for *else*, *els*. But his tendency is not a consistent practice. Like Schilders, he uses *hee* as well as *he*, *bee* as well as *be*, and in some words an even greater variety of obsolete variants. On page 4, Schilders uses *be* in line 8 and *bee* in line 10; Harison uses *bee* in the former place and *be* in the latter.

Both use the tilde (~) to indicate the omission of an *m* or *n*, whenever it suits their convenience to do so. Thus on page 6 of the Middelburg edition, Schilders prints *ordinãces* in line 7, and *ordinances* in line 13; Harison uses *ordinances* in the former place and *ordinãces* in the latter in the London edition. Neither printer uses the letter *j* in English words, and both commonly use *u* where modern printing has *v* and vice versa. Harison rarely uses *v* except where we would use *u*.

A more concrete idea of the differences between the two editions may be obtained from the detailed comparison of a few typical pages which is given below.

Partial List of Variants

The following list contains the variants in the two editions up to the end of the first section (p. 7) of the *Treatise* proper. The form in the Middelburg edition is given first, followed by that of the London edition (L). Where both forms differ materially from present-day usage, the modern spelling is added in brackets.

Epistle

First page

l. 4 Secretarie—Secretary (L)
l. 16 Whiche—which (L)

Second page

l. 5 vouchesaufe—vouchsafe (L)
l. 7 auncientlie renoumpned—ancientlie renoumed (L) [*anciently renowned*]
l. 8 MERCHAVNTES—MERCHANTES (L)
l. 11 whome—whom (L)
l. 15 Places—places (L)
l. 16 Gouuernement—Gouernement (L)
l. 17 fitt—fit (L)
l. 18 callinge—calling (L)

Third page

l. 4 manner—maner (L)
l. 5 Writers—writers (L)
l. 6 Praefaces—Prefaces (L)
l. 19 singulare—singular (L)
l. 22 lett—let (L)
l. 23 Treatice—Treatise (L)

Fourth page

l. 1 humblie—humbly (L)
l. 2 beseeche—beseech (L)
l. 3 Honor—Honour (L)
l. 4 Middelbrough—Middleburgh (L)
l. 4 VIth—sixth (L)
l. 6 commandment—commandement (L)

Text

Page 1

l. 5 principallie (omitted from L)
l. 11 Vita Civilis—Vitacivilis (L)
l. 15 twoo—two (L)
l. 19 Gouuernement—gouernment (L)
l. 19 Persons—persons (L)
l. 20 Things—things (L)
20 cõvenient—conuenient (L)
l. 21 fitt—fit (L)
l. 22 Humane—humane (L)
l. 23 civile—ciuil (L) [*civil*]

BIBLIOGRAPHICAL NOTE

Page 2

l. 1 councell—counsell (L) [*counsel*]
l. 3 pointes—points (L)
l. 3 especiallie—specially (L)
l. 4 cõversant—conuersant (L)
l. 5 institutiõ—institution (L)
l. 6 Pietie—pietie (L)
l. 6 civile—ciuill (L) [*civil*]
l. 6 facion—fashion (L)
l. 7 finallie—finally (L)
l. 7 mutual—mutuall (L)
l. 7 dewtie—dutie (L) [*duty*]
l. 7 Equitie, and Charitie—equitie & charitie (L)
l. 8 towardes—towards (L)
l. 10 namely the gouvernement of Things, convenient, and fitt for the maintenance of Humane Societie—namely, the Gouernment of things conuenient and fit for the maintenance of Humane Societie (L)
l. 14 employe—employ (L)
14 onely—only (L)
l. 15 travaile—trauaile (L)
l. 21 rowe—row (L)
l. 25 and—& (L)
25 witt—wit (L)
25 withall—withal (L)
l. 29 trafficque—traffike (L) [*traffic*]
l. 30 converse—conuerse (L)

Page 3

l. 1 fall—fal (L)
l. 5 whẽ—when (L)
l. 7 chaunge, and rechaunge, buye—change, and rechange, buy (L)
l. 8 them: the Prince—them. The Prince (L)
l. 9 freend—friend (L)
l. 12 woord—word (L)
l. 13 chaungeth—changeth (L)
13 raveth—raueth (L)
l. 14 Martes—Marts (L)
14 Markettes—Markets (L)
14 Marchandising—Merchandising (L)
l. 15 things—thinges (L)
15 Trafficque—trafficque (L)
l. 17 Nature—nature (L)
17 foorth—forth (L)
18 fruites—fruits (L)

18 beastes—beasts (L)
18 living—liuing (L)
l. 19 metalles, mineralles—metals, minerals (L)
l. 23 woordes—words (L)
23 trafficque—traffike (L)
l. 24 blood—bloud (L)
24 foũd—found (L)
l. 27 solde—sold (L)
27 enowe—enow (L)
l. 28 manie—many (L)
28 marchandise—merchandise (L)
l. 29 soules: to—soules. To (L)
l. 30 else—els (L)

Page 4

l. 1 marchandise—merchandise (L)
1 Contractes—Contracts (L)
l. 2 Legistes—Legists (L)
l. 3 thẽ—then (L) [*than*]
l. 4 wordes—words (L)
l. 5 Negotiations, or Traffiques—negotiations or traffiques (L)
l. 6 meer—meere (L) [*mere*]
6 marchandise—merchandise (L)
l. 8 be—bee (L)
8 generallie—generally (L)
l. 10 bee—be (L)
l. 11 Marchantes—Merchants (L)
l. 11 in deede—indeed (L)
11 Marchandise—merchandise (L)
l. 12 vacatiõ—vacation (L) [*vocation*]
l. 13 accoumpted—accounted (L)
l. 15 manie—many (L)
15 prooved—proved (L)
l. 16 bee—be (L)
l. 17 tearme—terme (L)
l. 17 them—thẽ (L)
l. 19 profite—profit (L)
l. 19 anie—any (L)
l. 20 &—and (L)
l. 21 States—states (L)
l. 22 honor, & enriching—honour, and enriching (L)
22 Counreis—Countries (L)
l. 23 Florẽtines—Florentines (L)
l. 26 populousenes—populousnesse (L)
l. 27 Provinces—prouinces (L)
27 wondreth—wondereth (L)

l. 28 steppe—step (L)
28 Kinges—kings (L)
l. 29 Riches—riches (L)
l. 30 feat—feate (L)

Page 5

l. 1 in his time saith—in his time, saith (L)
l. 2 Authour—author (L)
2 none—no (L)
l. 3 occupation—occupatiõ (L)
l. 5 Merchandise—merchãdise (L)
l. 5 accompted—accouted (L) [*accounted*]
5 honourable—honorable (L)
l. 7 trafficque—traffique (L)
7 Barbarous Nations—barbarous nations (L)
l. 8 gaigne—gaine (L)
8 in—into (L)
l. 9 (sayeth hee)—(saith he) (L)
l. 11 Citties—Cities (L)
11 Marseilles—Merseilles (L)
l. 15 oyle—oile (L)
l. 16 onely—only (L)
l. 21 vnknowen—vnknowne (L)
l. 24 Coũtrie—(same in L) [*country*]
l. 29 living—liuing (L)

Page 6

l. 5 preserved—preserued (L)
l. 7 ordinãces—ordinances (L)
l. 9 Marchantes—Marchants (L)
l. 11 cõvenable—convenable (L)
l. 12 overseers—ouerseers (L)
12 and—& (L)
l. 13 ordinances—ordinãces (L)
l. 14 and—& (L)
l. 15 Societas—societas (L)
15 hominum—hominũ (L)
l. 16 rerum—rerũ (L)
16 Mundus—mũdus (L)
l. 17 Riche—rich (L)
l. 18 Henrie the seventh—Henrie 7 (L)
l. 21 Englishe Merchantes—English M.M. (L)
21 subiectes—subiects (L)
l. 22 lowe—low (L)
22 defectum—defectũ (L)
l. 24 confirming—cõfirming (L)

24 auncient—ancient
24 Predecessours—Predecessors (L)
l. 26 Adventurers—Aduenturers (L)
l. 27 he—hee (L)
l. 28 Priviledges—Priuiledges (L)
28 saide Fellowshippe—said Fellowship (L)

Page 7

l. 1 Nourcerie—Nurserie (L) [*nursery*]
1 sprong—sprung (L)
l. 2 Merchants—Marchants (L)
2 Realm—Realme (L)
2 at least—at the least (L)
l. 7 Countrie—Countrey (L)
l. 8 cõfusion—confusion (L)
l. 9 bereave—bereaue (L)
l. 12 Companies, or Merchauntes—Companie or Merchantes (L)
14 speciallie—specially (L)
14 perticularlie—particularly (L)

BIBLIOGRAPHY

Manuscripts

Br. Mus. Addit. Mss. 18913, f. 5: Laws and Ordinances of the Merchants Adventurers of England. (Compiled by John Wheeler, 1608; later additions by others.)

Stowe Mss., 303 f 99: The Rise of the Fellowship of Merchant Adventurers of England.

Last Will and Testament of John Wheeler the Elder, merchant of Great Yarmouth (1610).

Books and Pamphlets

Anderson, Adam: An historical and chronological deduction of the origin of commerce (1764). Revised edition, 1801.

Arber, Edward: A Transcript of the Registers of the Company of Stationers of London, 1554–1640 (1875).

Ashley, W. J.: Introduction to English Economic History and Theory.

Ashley, W. J.: Surveys Historic and Economic.

Bacon, Francis (Lord Verulam): The History of the Reign of King Henry the Seventh.

Bland, Brown and Tawney: English Economic History: Select Documents.

Bourne, H. R. F.: English Merchants.

Bourne, H. R. F.: Famous London Merchants.

Bourne, H. R. F.: The Romance of Trade.

Boyle, J. R. and Dendy, F. W., ed.: Extracts from the Records of the Merchant Adventurers of Newcastle-upon-Tyne (Surtees Society).

Brent, N.: Discourse of Free Trade (1645).

Brentano, L.: History of Gilds.

Bruce, John, ed.: Diary of John Manningham (1601–03).

Burgon, J. W.: Life and Times of Sir Thomas Gresham (1839).

Busch, W.: England under the Tudors (Trans. A. H. Johnson).

Carion, John: The thre bokes of cronicles, whyche John Carion . . .gathered . . . whereunto is added an appendix . . . gathered by John Funcke of Nurenborough. (Gwalter Lynne, London, 1550.)

Cawston, Geo. and Keane, A. H.: The Early English Chartered Companies.

Clapham, J. H.: The Woollen and Worsted Industries.

Cheyney, E. P.: Introduction to Industrial and Social History of England.

Churchyard, T. [and R. Robinson]: A True Discourse Historical of the Succeeding governance in the Netherlands . . . out of the reverend E. M. of Antwerp his fifteen bookes Historia Belgica. London, 1602.

Colvin, Ian D.: The Germans in England.

Coke, Roger: A Discourse of Trade.

Cunningham, Wm.: The Growth of English Industry and Commerce.

Dasent, J. R., ed.: The Acts of the Privy Council.

Day, Clive: A History of Commerce.

Denton, Wm.: England in the Fifteenth Century.

Durham, F. H.: Relations of the Crown to Trade under James I. *Trans. Royal Hist. Soc.* N. S., Vol. XIII, pp. 199–248.

Ehrenberg, R.: Hamburg und England im Zeitalter der Königin Elizabeth.

Friis, Astrid: Alderman Cockayne's Project and the Cloth Trade.

Gardiner, S. R.: History of England from the Accession of James I . . . 1603–1616.

Gidden, H. W., ed.: The Book of Remembrance of Southampton.

Gras, N. S. B.: The Early English Customs System.

Green, Alice S.: Town Life in the Fifteenth Century.

Greene, R.: A Quip for an Upstart Courtier.

Gross, Charles: The Gild Merchant.

Hakluyt, Richard: The Principal Voyages of the English Nation.

Hales, John [?]: The Commonwealth of the Realm of England (ed. Lamond).

Herbert, W.: The History of the Twelve Great Livery Companies of London (1837).

Hewins, W. A. S.: English Trade and Finance, chiefly in the Seventeenth Century.

Johnson, A. H.: History of the Worshipful Company of Drapers of London.

Journal of the House of Commons.

Kramer, Stella: The English Craft Gilds.

Lambert, T. Malet: Two Thousand Years of Gild Life.

Lamond, E., ed.: A Discourse of the Common Weal (*see* Hales).

Lappenberg, J. M.: Urkundliche Geschichte des Hansischen Stahlhofes zu London. Hamburg, 1851.

Lingelbach, W. E., ed.: The Merchant Adventurers of England, their Laws and Ordinances. (University of Pennsylvania, Dept. of History, Transactions and Reprints. Series II, vol. II.)

Lipson, E.: An Introduction to the Economic History of England.

Lipson, E.: The History of the Woollen and Worsted Industries.

Lucas, Sir C. P.: The Beginnings of English Overseas Enterprise.

MacCulloch, J. R., ed.: A Select Collection of Early English Tracts.

MacCulloch, J. R., ed.: A Select Collection of Scarce and Valuable Tracts.

MacPherson, David: Annals of Commerce (1805).

Maitland, F. W.: Domesday Book and Beyond.

Malynes, Gerard de: A Treatise of the Canker of England's Commonwealth (1601).

Malynes, Gerard de: The Maintenance of Free Trade (1622).

May, John: A Declaration of the Estate of Clothing (1613).

Meteranus, E.: (*see* Van Meteren).

Milles, Thomas: The Custumers Apology (1601).

Milles, Thomas: The Customers Apologie . . . here only abridged [1609?].

Milles, Thomas: An abridgement of the Customers Apology [1609?].

Milles, Thomas: An Abstract almost verbatim of the Customers Apologie [1617?].

Milles, Thomas: The Replie, or Second Apologie (1604).

Misselden, Edward: The Circle of Commerce (1623).

Misselden, Edward: Free Trade and the Means to make Trade Flourish.

Mun, Thomas: A Discourse of Trade from England [1621].

Nash, E. G.: The Hansa.

Norfolk and Norwich Arch. Soc.: A Calendar of the Freemen of Great Yarmouth.

Page, W. S.: The Russia Company from 1553 to 1660.

Palmer, C. J., ed.: Manship's History of Great Yarmouth.

Palmer, C. J.: The Perlustration of Great Yarmouth.

Parker, Henry: Of a Free Trade (1648).

Pauli, R., ed.: The Libell of Englishe Policye.

Pearson, C. H.: The Early and Middle Ages of England.

Preston, John: The Picture of Yarmouth.

Raleigh, Sir Walter: Sir Walter Raleigh's Observations touching Trade and Commerce (1653) [written for King James I about 1605].

Report of the Royal Commission on Market Rights and Tolls (1889).

Salter, F. R.: Sir Thomas Gresham.

Schanz, Georg von: Englische Handelspolitik gegen Ende des Mittelalters.

Scott, Wm. R.: The Constitution and Finance of English, Scottish and Irish Joint Stock Companies to 1720.

Sellers, Maud, ed.: The York Mercers and Merchant Adventurers 1356–1917 (Surtees Society).

Sellers, Maud, ed.: The Acts and Ordinances of the Eastland Company.

Sleidan, John (Philippson): The General History of the Reformation of the Church [from *De Statu Religionis & Reipublicae Carolo Quinto Caesare, Commentarii*] faithfully Englished by Edmund Bohun, Esq. [London, 1689].

Stow, John: A Survey of London (1598).

Stow, John (and Howes, E.): The Annales or Generall Chronicle of England . . . continued and augmented . . . unto . . . 1614 by Edmund Howes, gentleman (London, 1615).

Swinden, Henry: The History and Antiquities of . . . Great Yarmouth (1772).

Tawney, R. H. and Power, E., ed.: Tudor Economic Documents.

Tawney, R. H., ed.: A Discourse upon Usury by Thomas Wilson.

Thomas, P. J.: Mercantilism and the East India Trade.

Thuanus [de Thou, James A.]: History of his own Time, Translated from the Geneva Edition of 1620 by Bernard Wilson (1729).

Townshend, Heyward: Historical collections.

Traill, H. D. and Mann, J. S.: Social England.

Unwin, George: The Gilds and Companies of London.

Unwin, George: Industrial Organization in the 16th and 17th Centuries.

Unwin, George: Studies in Economic History.

Van Meteren, Emanuel: Historia Belgica by E. Meteranus (1598).

Van Meteren, Emanuel (De Meteren): Historie der Nederland (Dordrecht, 1614).

Williamson, J. A.: A Short History of British Expansion.

Wilson, Thomas: (*see* Tawney, R. H.).

Zimmern, Helen: The Hansa Towns.

Periodical Articles

Aldis, H. G.: "The Book Trade 1557–1625," *Cambridge Hist. Eng. Lit.*, vol. IV, p. 432 ff.

Crotch, W. J. B.: "Caxton on the Continent," *The Library*, 4th series, vol. VII, pp. 387–401.

Durham, F. H.: "Relations of the Crown to Trade under James I" (Trans. R.H.S. New Series, vol. XIII, p. 199 ff.).

Lingelbach, W. E.: "Internal Organization of English Merchant Adventurers" (Trans. R.H.S. New Series, vol. XVI).

Lingelbach, W. E.: "The Merchant Adventurers at Hamburg," *Am. Hist. Rev.*, vol. IX, p. 265 ff.

Miller, L. R.: "New Evidence on the Shipping and Imports of London, 1601–1603," *Quart. Jour. Econ.*, XVI, p. 740 ff.

Anonymous Tracts and Broadsides

The Advantages to the Kingdom of England . . . by managing woollen manufactures under the . . . Merchants Adventurers.

A discourse consisting of motives for the enlargement and freedom of trade . . . etc.

The Trades Increase.

British Museum Tracts on Wool.

Broadsides in the collection of the Society of Antiquaries, London.

INDEX

INDEX

(Page-numbers between 121 and 305 refer to the facsimile of the Middelburg edition.)

INDEX

INDEX

INDEX

INDEX